WITHDRAWN

D0955800

SURVIVING BATAAN AND BEYOND

SURVIVING BATAAN AND BEYOND

Colonel Irvin Alexander's Odyssey
as a Japanese Prisoner of War

Edited by Dominic J. Caraccilo

STACKPOLE
BOOKS

Copyright © 1999 by Stackpole Books

Published by
STACKPOLE BOOKS
5067 Ritter Road
Mechanicsburg, PA 17055
www.stackpolebooks.com

All rights reserved, including the right to reproduce this book or portions thereof in any form or by any means, electronic or mechanical, including photocopying, recording, or by any information storage and retrieval system, without permission in writing from the publisher. All inquiries should be addressed to Stackpole Books, 5067 Ritter Road, Mechanicsburg, Pennsylvania 17055.

Printed in the United States of America

10 9 8 7 6 5 4 3 2 1

FIRST EDITION

Library of Congress Cataloging-in-Publication Data

Alexander, Irvin, 1896–1963.
    Surviving Bataan and beyond : Colonel Irvin Alexander's odyssey as a Japanese Prisoner of War / edited by Dominic J. Caraccilo.—1st ed.
      p. cm.
    Includes bibliographical references and index.
    ISBN 0–8117–1596–5
    1. Alexander, Irvin, 1896–1963. 2. World War, 1939–1945—Prisoners and prisons, Japanese. 3. World War, 1939-1945—Personal narratives, American. 4. Prisoners of war—Philippines—Biography.
I. Caraccilo, Dominic J. (Dominic Joseph), 1962– . II. Title.
D805.P6A43 1999   98-47675
                                              CIP

CONTENTS

FOREWORD
BY KEN HECHLER

Ken Hechler studied American history with historians Henry Steele Commager and Allan Nevins at Columbia University, where he received his Ph.D. in 1940. Following thirteen weeks of basic training in the infantry, he was sent to the Armored Force Officer Candidate School at Fort Knox, Kentucky, where he received a second lieutenant's commission in 1943. Upon receipt of his commission he was sent to the European Theater of Operations in 1944 as a combat historian under the command of the distinguished Col. S. L. A. Marshall. After being honorably discharged with the rank of major, he taught at Princeton University and then joined the White House staff of President Harry S Truman as a researcher and speechwriter. He was elected to the U.S. House of Representatives in 1958 and served nine consecutive terms. Hechler is the author of six books, including Working With Truman: A Personal Memoir of the White House Years *and the best-seller* The Bridge at Remagen. *He is currently Secretary of State of West Virginia.*

This is one of the most significant chronicles of World War II.

Its enduring value is enhanced considerably by the careful, sympathetic, and imaginative editing of Dominic J. Caraccilo.

To begin with, the very personalized manuscript produced by Col. Irvin Alexander in 1949 is written with such graphic and passionate emotion that no reader can escape revulsion against the brutality he suffered and closely observed while a prisoner of war of the Japanese. His sensitivity and keen powers of perception are evident in his superb narration. The editor has preserved all of the original spirit of this excellent memoir; at the same time he has gently aided the reader with useful guidance on personalities and situations that might otherwise remain obscure. The annotations are excellent.

As a West Pointer with sufficient command and combat experience under his belt, Colonel Alexander had a unique opportunity during the

1941–45 period not only to participate but also to observe through a practiced eye the awesome events which he describes so vividly.

His account of the heroic delaying action that the thinly-held Filipino and American troops managed on the Bataan Peninsula in the early days of the war does not contribute much that is startlingly new. But it does correct the false contemporary view that our defensive forces were thought to be considerably larger than they actually were. This story comes starkly alive when it depicts what it was like to endure three and a half years of unbelievably inhumane treatment by sadistic captors.

This book ought to be required reading in every school in Japan.

It probably will be denounced by some of the older people who feel that it was immoral for President Truman to have ordered the use of two atom bombs to end the war. Had Japan perfected the atom bomb first, would these same people have viewed its use as immoral? A national amnesia has gripped many of those who have tried to explain away the documented incidents of man's inhumanity to man that took place in POW camps. To be sure, the United States is guilty of a sorry record in holding loyal Japanese-Americans under the so-called "War Relocation Authority." Yet none of that treatment comes close to being compared with the unspeakable torture, murders, and horrors carefully documented by Colonel Alexander.

It is very difficult to read this account without anger welling up within the reader. Yet I am certain that Colonel Alexander, with all his compassion and humane spirit, would never have condoned the retaliation of "an eye for an eye, and a tooth for a tooth."

The manuscript concludes with an eloquent plea for preparedness. I do not believe the writer gives himself enough credit for the kind of training, courage, and leadership that shines through his moving story. He was professionally trained to be a military leader, yet many of his troops and fellow prisoners were citizen soldiers, airmen, sailors, and marines. I am reminded of a conversation I had with Reichsmarschall Hermann Goering shortly after we captured him in 1945. I brought up the subject of the surprise seizure of the Ludendorff Bridge at Remagen on March 7, 1945, which materially shortened the war in Europe. He expressed genuine puzzlement as to how "a bunch of cooks, clerks, carpenters, and average men from all walks of life managed to defeat those Germans who had been drilled and trained since their early youth in military discipline."

One of the enduring lessons of this book is that leaders like Colonel Alexander seemed able to instill in their men their own determination, will to live, and courage to survive. Thousands perished, but it is evident that his example inspired many to draw on their almost superhuman willpower to overcome the pangs of hunger, the dysentery, the maggots and the lice, not to mention the outright physical brutality of their captors.

As a result, many more than anticipated were able to come home to freedom.

INTRODUCTION

The bulk of military memoirs and researched books, both past and present, covering the World War II struggle for the Bataan Peninsula in the Philippines, fall into three categories. In the first category are accounts written by junior officers and enlisted soldiers who, over many years, attempt to capture their recollections in an unbiased manner. While many of these memoirs are informative, they tend to be convoluted by information acquired both intentionally and unintentionally over a period of time before they are written.[1]

The second set of published works are those memoirs written immediately after the repatriation of the U.S. prisoners in the Philippines, such as *General Wainwright's Story* by Lt. Gen. Jonathan Wainwright.[2] These accounts tend to be quite accurate in the sense that they convey the opinions and emotions of the authors who actually experienced the brutality of their Japanese captors. In most cases, however, these firsthand accounts written soon after World War II were published in the literary format of the day and, more importantly, convey only what occurred at the highest level of command. There exist very few midlevel commander and staff officer memoirs about the war in the Philippines written immediately after the war. Consequently, when reading these memoirs the historian is left relying on the "big hand–little map" generalities of what might have occurred at the lower echelons.

The third set of published works covering the struggle in Bataan are not firsthand accounts. Rather, these books are written by those historians, academicians, and others who were not personally involved in the war in the Philippines, but chose to devote years of their lives studying it. These reports, though adequately researched and thoroughly documented, do not take into account the essential perspective of the human struggle for survival that each prisoner endured while in captivity. The Bataan Death March[3] was indeed an emotional and physical struggle and arguably can best be presented in words by those who survived its wrath.

The human perspective of a midlevel officer is what makes Col. Irvin Alexander's *Surviving Bataan and Beyond* unique. It is written with all the emotion of someone who endured the unconscionable terror of three and a half years of captivity with the Japanese. Furthermore, it brings to the reader a midlevel officer's view of the politics behind the surrender, the unit and individual actions at the battalion level, and the struggles encountered by a battalion-level officer desperately trying to maintain some sense of order and pride in himself and his men as they struggled to survive a horrific experience.

Alexander's memoir is unique in the sense that it was written in 1949 and, after lying dormant for nearly fifty years, has been transcribed for publication using a present-day format (including photographs, notes, maps, and index) while maintaining the integrity of the language and cultural acceptances of that era.

Finally, Colonel Alexander's manuscript is particularly different from other memoirs written about Bataan in that his account begins before the war, while he and his family were stationed at Fort Stotsenburg, and it brings us on a journey through a series of prison camps, including the trek to Camp O'Donnell and then to the infamous Cabanatuan and Bilibid Prisons. Moreover, Alexander's story does not end with the repatriation of prisoners from captivity on the Philippines as do so many other memoirs written by Bataan POWs.

Notable in Alexander's account is that his journey continues beyond Bataan. He ends his manuscript by portraying a vivid and horrific account aboard the hold of three different Japanese *Maru* prison ships.[4] Sailing to Japan, these ships were attacked numerous times by American dive bombers and U.S. Naval submarines. Many American POWs lost their lives in the dreadful holds of these ships and in the subsequent prison camps, if they were "lucky" enough to make it to Japan. From Japan, Alexander and his fellow survivors traveled to Korea and finally were repatriated after ending their infamous extended Death March at Camp Jinsen.[5]

Irvin Alexander's story is a fascinating odyssey: it is one man's struggle to survive a brutal and, more often than not, unfathomable captivity. Though the 1946 publication of *General Wainwright's Story* is a definitive account, it may have forestalled the publication by other commanders and staff officers of their own versions of the campaign.[6] Reluctant to engage in public controversy with their chiefs, midlevel commanders and staff officers remained silent, including Irvin Alexander. We may never know why

Colonel Alexander didn't have his manuscript published, for he died in 1963 without ever sending it to a single editor. Over the years the memoir has often been used as a reference for many other published accounts, but it has never been published in its entirety. *Surviving Bataan and Beyond* is presented here just as Irvin Alexander wrote it nearly a half a century ago.

IRVIN ALEXANDER'S LIFE

Irvin Alexander[7] was born on November 5, 1896, in Heltonville, Indiana. He was the firstborn to a local merchant named Virgil L. Alexander and his wife, the former Kemmie Cain.[8] After graduating from Heltonville High School in 1915, he entered the University of Indiana at nearby Bloomington, and there, like many fellow students, he enlisted in the Indiana National Guard. He served his time honorably with the Guard, being assigned to Company I and the Machine Gun Company of the 1st Indiana Infantry. During the March 1916 Pancho Villa attack on Columbus, New Mexico, President Woodrow Wilson deployed Alexander's unit to the border to protect Americans and to prevent repetitions of the outrage.[9] After rising to the rank of corporal, he was discharged on June 13, 1917, and was sworn into the U.S. Corps of Cadets at West Point the next day as a member of the Class of 1921.[10]

Cadet Alexander attended the U.S. Military Academy (USMA) for a year and five months before graduating early under wartime conditions on November 1, 1918. Official records obtained from the military records section in St. Louis, Missouri, list him as a graduate of the USMA Class of 1918; however, the *United States Military Academy's Register of Graduates* has Alexander listed as a member of the Class of 1919.[11] The confusion about which West Point class Alexander graduated from is due in part to the return of the early graduates to the Academy to finish their studies as "student officers" on December 3, 1918.[12] After completing his academic requirements as a student officer, Alexander graduated for a second time on June 11, 1919, officially becoming a member of the West Point Class of 1919 before being commissioned in the Regular Army as an infantry officer.[13]

A 1964 published obituary written after Alexander's death by his good friend and West Point roommate, Brig. Gen. Willie Palmer,[14] described Cadet Alexander in the following manner:

> Alex[15] was content and indeed proud to describe himself as "goaty" [a term used by cadets for those not very academically inclined]. Raised in a rural community and on active service for

most of the year preceding his admission, he felt greatly handicapped in the academic competition. Actually, he was never in difficulties with the professors. Standing 190 in a class of 284, he
impressed us as a shrewd, observant chap who quietly absorbed
everything he could about this unfamiliar world of West Point,
meanwhile showing himself to be friendly, generous, and ready for
a good time.[16]

Alexander's career as an infantry officer, with periodic breaks to serve
in the quartermaster corps, spanned thirty-one years. Immediately after
graduating from the Academy in 1919, he traveled to France from July 13
to 20 on a tour to observe the Belgian, French, and Italian battlefronts of
World War I. He then continued on this unique professional venture by
visiting with the Army of Occupation in Germany until September 17,
returning to the U.S. on September 26, 1919.[17]

Upon returning from his first overseas trip, Alexander attended the
Infantry Officer Basic Course at Fort Benning, Georgia, on October 1,
1919, and graduated successfully in June 1920. His first tour with troops
was in the Philippine Islands from September 1920 until June 1924, where
he served as a company officer with the 15th Infantry. The preponderance
of this tour was served temporarily in Tientsin and Tongshan, China, as a
company commander and battalion adjutant.

Despite his "goaty" traits as a West Point cadet, Alexander discovered
that he was actually quite studious. In fact, in July 1924, First Lieutenant
Alexander was reassigned to the U.S. Military Academy as an instructor in
the Law Department.[18] He taught at USMA for two years and then pur-
sued a course in aerial flight at Brooks Field, Texas.

After learning that flying fixed-wing aircraft would not be part of his
future, Alexander was reassigned in November 1926 as a company officer
with the 9th Infantry at Fort Sam Houston, Texas, with a subsequent
assignment as a personnel adjutant at Camp Bullis, Texas.

During his time in Texas, Alexander was detached to the assistant secretary for the National Board of Elections in Nicaragua from May 28 to
December 28, 1928. Toward the end of this duty he was asked by a young
company commander, Matthew B. Ridgway, to accompany him as he traveled back to the states overland. According to Ridgway's own memoir,
Soldier: The Memoirs of Matthew B. Ridgway, the trip was "memorable. . . .
We left about mid-December of 1928, and took a boat from Cortino, on
the west coast of Nicaragua, to Libertad on the Pacific coast of El Salvador.
We went overland from there . . . some of our travel was by jitney bus [and]

antique automobiles. . . . Much of the enduring affection and admiration I have always felt for our neighbors to the south stemmed from that trip."[19] Arriving back in Texas, Alexander ended that extraordinary trip and finished his tour in September 1930.

Prior to leaving Texas, Alexander courted and married Lucile Elizabeth Spindle of San Antonio on December 20, 1929. Alexander and his wife "Lu" departed Texas for Fort Monmouth, New Jersey, in September 1930, where he attended the Communications Officer Course until June 1931. After qualifying as a signal officer, Alexander set off with his bride for Vancouver Barracks in Washington state. Traveling by boat from the east coast, the Alexanders passed through the Panama Canal and arrived in Portland, then traveled to Washington that summer.[20]

In Washington, the couple's only child, Irvin Spindle Alexander, was born on June 14, 1932.[21] Alexander affectionately called the young Irvin "Sammy" because he reminded him so much of Lucile's father, a friendly and lively man who was "friendly to all and never [seemed] to meet a stranger."[22]

While at Vancouver Barracks, Alexander served as a communications officer and regimental adjutant with the 7th Infantry Regiment and then did a stint as the post signal officer. The majority of his tour, however, was spent working with President Franklin Roosevelt's Civilian Conservation Corps (CCC).[23] In 1935, after seventeen years of active duty, he was promoted to the rank of captain and became a general officer's aide-de-camp. In June 1936, after five years in the Pacific Northwest, the Alexander family returned to Texas.

For nearly three years at Fort Sam Houston, Texas, while serving as a company commander in the 9th Infantry, commander of the brigade headquarters of the 3rd Infantry Brigade, and post adjutant, Captain Alexander successfully thwarted attempts to retire him after twenty years of service because of high blood pressure. Forced to engage in evasive action to forestall an early retirement from service, Alexander volunteered for duty in the Philippines on a detail to the quartermaster corps.

Duty in the Philippines was viewed as choice picking in 1939, and the three Alexanders enjoyed their short stay at Fort Stotsenburg, a U.S. Army post located near Angeles, about fifty miles north of Manila. It is clear from his memoir that the Alexanders loved and greatly appreciated the country and its beauty.

After arriving in April 1940, Alexander was assigned as a company commander of Company I, 31st Infantry, and, after being promoted to the rank of major on July 1, 1940, he was reassigned as assistant post quarter-master, Detachment Quartermaster Corp, Post of Manila and Fort Stotsen-burg. It is here that his literary journey begins.

While the majority of what occurred on the Philippines during Colonel Alexander's tenure will be covered in the following pages, it is important to place in proper perspective his duties and the chronology of events leading up to the war.

Major Alexander, his wife, and their young son were living comfort-ably at Fort Stotsenburg when rumblings of war darkened the sky over the South Pacific in the spring of 1941. In May, seeing that war against the Imperial Japanese Army was inevitable, the U.S. government returned military dependents to the continental United States. Lucile and Sammy, unaware of the turmoil that was in store for Irvin, Sr., departed Fort Stot-senburg on May 14, 1941.[24]

Alone and facing the possibility of war, Alexander focused his energies on working hard and accomplishing his missions as the assistant post quartermaster. The post quartermaster, Lt. Col. W. E. Durst, known as "Poppy," rated Major Alexander as "very well informed; has necessary intelligence [and] judgment to make decisions with force to accomplish them." Brig. Gen. E. P. King,[25] the post commander, indicated that Major Alexander was in the "upper third; quiet, unassuming, capable, loyal, [and a] gentleman . . . especially desirable [for the] next grade . . . rated very satisfactory on physical endurance."[26] These qualities, recognized by his superiors, would become evident in the demanding months and years to come and, in the short term, earned him a promotion to lieutenant colonel on September 15, 1941.

The Japanese attack on Pearl Harbor on December 7, 1941, was a somber day for the American forces in the Philippines. With the destruction of Pearl Harbor, the Japanese had their sights on the Philippines, attacking the islands en masse the next day. The capture of the islands was crucial to Japan's effort to control the Southwest Pacific, seize the resource-rich Dutch East Indies, and protect its Southeast Asia flank. Its strategy called for nearly simultaneous attacks on Malaya, Thailand, Hong Kong, Singapore, the Philippines, and American-held Guam, Wake, and Hawaii.[27]

General MacArthur defined the Allied plan for the defense of the Philippines on December 3, 1941, four days prior to the Japanese attack on Pearl Harbor, by assigning the forces under the U.S. Army Forces Far East (USAFFE) command in the following manner.

He listed four major tactical commands defending the islands. The North Luzon Force, under the command of General Wainwright, had the responsibility to defend the most critical areas of the Luzon Island, including the Lingayen Gulf, the Zambales Coast, and the Bataan Peninsula. Wainwright and his four infantry divisions—the Philippine Army's 11th, 21st, 31st, and 71st Divisions, and one cavalry regiment, the 26th Philippine Scout (PS) Regiment—were instructed to protect airfields and prevent hostile landings in the area, particularly at those points opening into the central plains and the road network leading to Manila.[28]

The South Luzon Force was commanded by Brig. Gen. George M. Parker, Jr. Like the North Luzon Force, Parker's force, consisting of the 41st and 51st (PA) Divisions, was to protect the airfields in its sector and prevent hostile landings, and to hold the beaches at all costs.

The Visayan-Mindanao Force, consisting of the 61st, 81st, and 101st (PA) Divisions, was commanded by Brig. Gen. William F. Sharp and charged with the defense of the rest of the archipelago. Located between the North and South Luzon Forces was the reserve area. It included the city of Manila and the heavily concentrated area just to the north of the city. This area was directly under the control of General MacArthur's headquarters and contained the Philippine Divisions of the 91st (PA), the 86th Field Artillery (PS), the Far East Air Force, the Harbor Defenses, the Philippine Coast Artillery Command, and the headquarters of the Philippine Detachment and Philippine Army.[29]

The Japanese invaded the Philippine Islands on December 8, 1941. At the onset of hostilities in the Philippines the U.S. Air Corps fought valiantly but air superiority quickly sided with the Japanese. Describing the beginning of the war, Lieutenant Colonel Alexander writes in detail in his memoir about his good friend, Capt. Colin P. Kelly, Jr., one of America's first heroes in World War II. Captain Kelly became the first West Point graduate (Class of 1937) to be killed in action while piloting a B-17 during an attack on Japanese naval forces invading the Philippines.

Legend at the time had it that Kelly dropped bombs on the battleship *Haruna* and then intentionally crashed his disabled B-17 on the battleship, supposedly sinking it.[30] In fact, he achieved no such hits. Moreover, there were no battleships in Philippine waters at that time; the *Haruna* was hundreds of miles away supporting the Malayan invasion.[31]

Actually, Kelly was shot down on a return flight on December 10, 1941, by the Japanese ace Saburo Sakai. Despite significant damage to the plane, Kelly was able to maintain control long enough for his crew to bail out. Unable to parachute to safety himself, Captain Kelly died in the crash near Aparri, Luzon—the pilot of the first B-17 to be lost in air-to-air combat in the war. Alexander, having lived with Kelly at Fort Stotsenburg since Kelly's arrival on September 12, 1941, describes in fascinating detail in his memoir what he personally observed about this incident.[32]

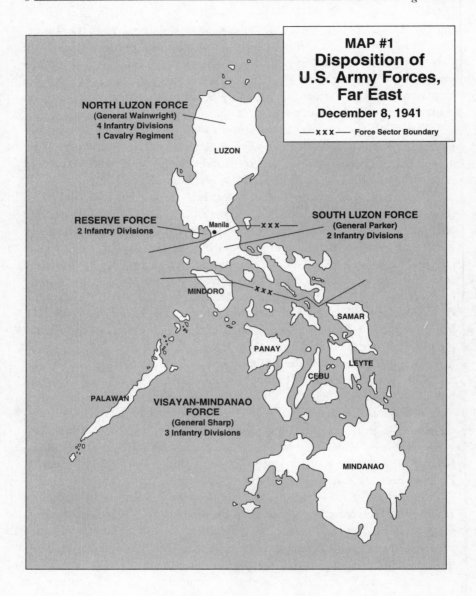

MAP #1
Disposition of U.S. Army Forces, Far East
December 8, 1941
— X X X — Force Sector Boundary

NORTH LUZON FORCE
(General Wainwright)
4 Infantry Divisions
1 Cavalry Regiment

LUZON

RESERVE FORCE
2 Infantry Divisions

Manila
— X X X —

SOUTH LUZON FORCE
(General Parker)
2 Infantry Divisions

MINDORO
X X X

SAMAR

PANAY

LEYTE

CEBU

PALAWAN

VISAYAN-MINDANAO FORCE
(General Sharp)
3 Infantry Divisions

MINDANAO

Japan's ambitious strategic plan and the continuing war in China sharply limited the size of the enemy force available to invade the Philippines. Nonetheless, Lt. Gen. Masaharu Homma,[33] commander of the 14th Army, and Lt. Gen. Hideyoshi Obata's 5th Air Group neutralized U.S. air and naval power in the Philippines in the first forty-eight hours of the war.

With the Janapese gaining a position never anticipated in the USAFFE plans, the defense of the Philippines now relied solely on its ground forces. Being poorly trained and equipped and having no lines of supply or escape, the ten Philippine Army (PA) reserve divisions, incorporating the meager U.S. defense forces, seemed destined to yield quickly to the invading Japanese. But the valiant and determined resistance of the Allied forces held the Bataan Peninsula for the next four months.[34]

Alexander remained on quartermaster duty during the initial phases of the invasion. As the assistant quartermaster for the Post of Manila and Fort Stotsenburg, Alexander, a true infantryman, requested a reassignment to combat troops and returned to the infantry in early January 1942, but not before winning the Silver Star for gallantry during the evacuation of Fort Stotsenburg.[35] While his memoir describes in detail the actions occurring at the onset of hostilities, the following citation briefly illustrates Lieutenant Colonel Alexander's heroics:

> Colonel IRVIN ALEXANDER, 012414, [then Lieutenant Colonel], Quartermaster Corps, United States. For gallantry in action in the Southwest Pacific Area, from 8 to 18 December 1941. During a period of repeated enemy bombing attacks on Fort Stotsenberg [*sic*], Luzon, Philippine Islands, Colonel Alexander, Assistant to the Quartermaster, displayed a courageous disregard for his own safety in prosecuting the accomplishment of the increasingly vital supply mission. On 13 December, although under continual hostile aerial bombardment, he personally directed the loading and dispatching of hospital patients and personnel on a hospital train, completed the task himself, and expedited the departure of the train. On 18 December, at the risk of his life, he removed an unexploded bomb from a quartermaster warehouse where it was endangering men of the command. Through his gallant deeds and unremitting concern for the welfare and safety of his troops, Colonel Alexander upheld the finest traditions of the military service.[36]

On the first day of January 1942, Alexander was reassigned back to an infantry unit. While serving as a combat infantry advisor for the 71st Infantry (PA),[37] he fought valiantly against a formidable Japanese enemy but eventually was ordered to surrender his forces to the Imperial Army on April 8, 1942.[38]

Before surrendering to the enemy, Alexander was seriously wounded on January 24, 1942, while on duty in close proximity to the 1st Infantry

Regiment (Philippine Constabulary) near Aglaloma Bay.[39] Realizing that a company commander had been wounded and would therefore be unable to lead his unit to repel an enemy landing party near the bay, Alexander immediately took charge and went forward to assume command.

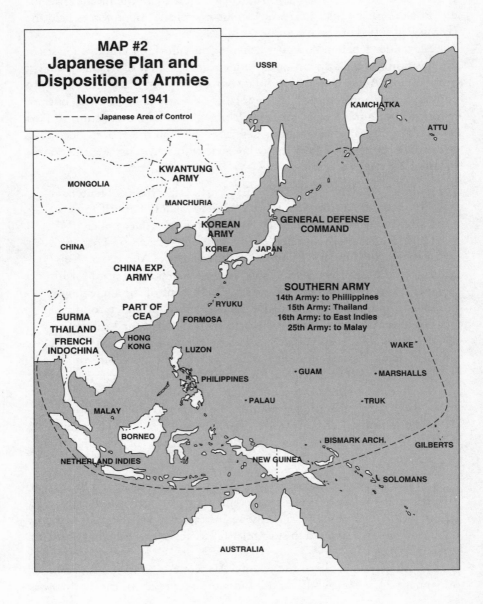

MAP #2
Japanese Plan and Disposition of Armies
November 1941
— — — — Japanese Area of Control

USSR

KAMCHATKA

ATTU

MONGOLIA

KWANTUNG ARMY

MANCHURIA

CHINA

KOREAN ARMY

GENERAL DEFENSE COMMAND

KOREA   JAPAN

CHINA EXP. ARMY

SOUTHERN ARMY
14th Army: to Phillipines
15th Army: Thailand
16th Army: to East Indies
25th Army: to Malay

PART OF CEA   RYUKU

BURMA THAILAND FRENCH INDOCHINA

HONG KONG

FORMOSA

LUZON

WAKE

·GUAM   ·MARSHALLS

PHILIPPINES

·PALAU   ·TRUK

MALAY

BORNEO

BISMARK ARCH.

GILBERTS

NETHERLAND INDIES

NEW GUINEA

SOLOMANS

AUSTRALIA

On arrival, he found the unit disorganized, with stragglers beginning to drift to the rear. He reorganized the unit and, by setting a personal example of courage in the face of heavy fire, pushed the company forward to within thirty-five yards of the enemy position.

Despite the heavy concentration of fire in his vicinity, Alexander continued to expose himself and steady his men. Severely wounded in the hand and chest, he continued to lead his troops forward until he collapsed from shock and fatigue. Along with two Purple Hearts for his wounds, Alexander earned the nation's second highest award for heroism that day, the Distinguished Service Cross.[40]

After evacuating, Lieutenant Colonel Alexander was hospitalized for sixteen days recovering from his wounds. He had lost his right first finger and his left fourth and fifth fingers in addition to enduring a severe chest wound after being hit by fragments. Released from the makeshift field hospital on February 9, 1942,[41] Alexander was promoted to the rank of colonel on April 8, 1942, just one day before the official surrender of the Philippines. Unfortunately, Alexander would not learn of this promotion for quite some time.

Spending three and a half years in captivity, none of the American prisoners of war suffered more than the group that included Irvin Alexander. In addition to the Death March, and the starvation and degradation that befell all Japanese POWs, three times Alexander and his group were placed on Japanese prison ships (including the infamous *Oryokuo Maru*), which were bombed by U.S. aircraft and torpedoed by U.S. Naval submarines, taking a tremendous toll of life among the helpless POWs. Only 425 out of the original 1,619 leaving the Philippines survived the voyage to Japan, reaching the port at Moji (now Kitakyushu) aboard the *Brazil Maru* on January 30, 1945.[42]

Switching ships on two separate occasions, the Japanese ordered all prisoners to strip naked each time and to discard all their belongings. With no clothing having been issued to the captives since they left the Philippines in mid-December 1944, the prisoners froze in the January weather. Alexander was down to 90 pounds from his normal 150 pounds when he arrived in Japan.[43] The select few to survive this ordeal were then transported to Camp Jinsen, Korea, but not before another 154 died from wounds received aboard the ships while camped in Japan.[44]

While the surviving prisoners were in Korea[45] the United States dropped the atomic bombs on Nagasaki and Hiroshima, bringing the war to an abrupt end on August 11, 1945. Repatriation, however, would take another two months and it wasn't until mid-October 1945 that Colonel Alexander was met by his wife and son in San Francisco, California.

The long and treacherous Death March had finally ended for Irvin Alexander.

The Alexanders led a fulfilling life after the war. While spending six months at Brooke General Hospital in San Antonio, Texas, to recuperate, Alexander had an opportunity to reacquaint himself with his family. After recuperating, he returned to active duty. His first assignment after returning to the States led him to the office of the inspector general in Washington, DC. He received high ratings in that position and was then reassigned, to his great pleasure, to the Indiana National Guard as a senior Regular Army instructor on August 18, 1947. "The wheel had come full circle. The rustic youth who had set out for Mexico with Company I had come back to the Indiana Guard as an experienced, battle-tested, combat veteran."[46]

Alexander's work with the Guard at Indianapolis was quite successful, and there was even talk about making him a general officer, when tragedy struck on April 16, 1949.

Preparing to return home from a long-distance meeting one evening, Colonel Alexander was offered a ride from another colonel who had purchased a new car. Although Alexander had already acquired a plane ticket, he accepted his friend's offer and together they set off for Indianapolis. Shortly after they left an elderly motorist collided head on with their vehicle. On impact, Colonel Alexander's head hit and passed through the windshield of the car.[47]

He was at the point of death for days and remained in the hospital for thirteen months, then transferring to two other hospitals over the next year. Struggling for his life and to maintain some sense of stability, Colonel Alexander wrote his 289-page memoir.

On June 30, 1950, after thirty-two years of service to the nation, Irvin Alexander retired with 90 percent physical disability.[48] Retirement was kind to the Alexanders. He bought land in Nashville, Indiana, about forty miles south of the University of Indiana. Soon after, Alexander, wanting to see if his "brains were addled"[49] by the accident, commuted to the university and in due course received B.A. and M.A. degrees in Spanish.

In 1956 the Alexanders moved to Europe for a year so Irvin could study at the University of Madrid. They fell in love with the Spanish language and culture and traveled to Mexico for several months every winter thereafter, invariably including visits with Lu's family in San Antonio and with Sammy and his family, also in San Antonio.[50]

During this time, Alexander found great joy in his three grandchildren, Julie Ann, Katherine Ann, and Bruce Alan. It was on one of these visits to San Antonio that he died unexpectedly, very early on Christmas Day 1963 at age sixty-seven.[51] His wife Lucile lived until December 11, 1992, passing away at age eighty-five. Their son, Irvin Spindle Alexander, after serving briefly as a corporal in the military during the Korean War, then pursuing a successful career as an aerospace engineer at NASA, and then as branch chief for Institutional Quality for the Space Administration, predeceased his mother on March 11, 1991, at the age of fifty-eight.[52]

General Palmer summed up Irvin Alexander's character best in the final chapters of his friend's obituary in the Summer 1964 issue of *Assembly:*

> Irvin Alexander was endowed with the strongest traits of his Scottish ancestors whose fighting qualities are legendary: tenacity, stubborness [*sic*], refusal to quit. He loved the Army and his part in it; he enjoyed authority and the making of decisions. Friendly, reliable, steady, he was a man people found they could depend upon in time of need. His health was already impaired when he went to the Philippines "one jump ahead of the retiring board," and nothing but the most indomitable spirit and a lot of luck could have brought him through those terrible years. It is even more amazing that he recovered from the horrible accident of 1949, and had 14 happy years with Lou [*sic*] after that. He always said it was borrowed time.
>
> Alex faced all his challenges and mastered them all, according to the choices open to him. He emerged unblemished, a son of West Point whose record as a man and as a soldier we all can envy. May she have sons like these from age to age.

ON EDITING THE MANUSCRIPT

Having written my own combat memoir, I assumed editing someone else's would be easier, but this was not the case. After spending more than two years researching to identify individuals mentioned in the original manuscript, locating sources for maps and photographs, and editing Colonel Alexander's written text, I came to realize that this project was a major undertaking. Maj. Ty Smith, an infantry officer in the U.S. Army, author of *Fort Inge* and editor of *A Dose of Frontier Soldiering: The Memoirs of Corporal E.A. Bode,* was my inspiration for beginning this work. He told me that if I wanted to pull this off I would have to become an expert on Bataan. After reading dozens of books and numerous documents, letters, and other literature, I have no doubt that Major Smith's advice was correct. Whether I have become an expert or not, I will leave up to the reader.

Specifically helpful in this endeavor were the Special Collections Section of the U.S. Military Academy Cadet Library, which initially located the manuscript for me; and Ms. Sara Spindle of San Antonio, Texas, Colonel

Alexander's sister-in-law, for her diligence in providing me even the most trivial bits of information that would make this book come to life. Her memory is impeccable and her cooperation in this effort has been invaluable.

I am also honored, as I know Colonel Alexander would be, to include The Hon. Dr. Ken Hechler, Secretary of State of the State of West Virginia, author of numerous books including *The Bridge at Remagen,* combat historian and professor, former congressman, and adviser to U.S. presidents, as the writer of the foreword for *Surviving Bataan and Beyond.*

Heartfelt thanks, as always, go to my beautiful and talented wife, Karen, and our three wonderful children, Robert, Jacob, and Jenna, who are understanding and good natured about having a husband and a dad who, when not off leading troops himself, is lost somewhere among the soldiers of the Second World War. And to my parents, Robert and Marie Caraccilo, whose love for history is what jump started my quest to learn.

All in all, Colonel Alexander himself is the one who has made editing this work relatively easy, for his love for language is apparent, as he had mastered the skill of writing the English word. His original manuscript was written well; nevertheless, there are many subtle points that need explanation and correction.

Alexander's use of the third-person voice, presented at the beginning of each original chapter, as if he were talking directly to his wife, is effective. He sets the stage for the topic he is about to present and then writes each chapter in the first-person narrative style. While the manuscript doesn't follow a strict chronological order, it is cleverly developed so that the reader is initially introduced to the action of the Bataan Death March and then drawn into Alexander's life on Bataan just prior to the Japanese invasion in early December 1941.

I have attempted to maintain the integrity of the original manuscript as much as possible. For instance, many of Alexander's statements in this book would be considered politically incorrect and obviously racist today. For instance, he calls his captors "Nips"—certainly a racist term by today's standards, but considering the times and the menacing attitude the captives had toward the Nippon government after the bombing of Pearl Harbor and the ensuing battle for Bataan, it was acceptable at the time of the original writing. Though some may not condone this sort of language, I chose to keep it as is to portray the true feelings of the POWs while in captivity.

The subtle changes I made include categorizing the manuscript by thirteen distinct chapters as opposed to the original seven. Additionally, I included many subchapter headings to help the reader identify specific sections of interest. I saw no value in retaining Alexander's tortured punctuation, abbreviations, and poor spelling; thus "Austraila" becomes Australia;

"grey," gray; "severly," severely; and "diahrrea," diarrhea, just to name a few. Alexander also had the habit of capitalizing everything, including "company," "engineers," and "headquarters." All of these words have been placed in the lower case unless they portray a *specific* element or title.

To avoid the endless and distracting use of brackets I have tried to limit their use to only those places where it was required to add a completely new word for clarification. For the most part, Alexander's sentence construction, while long and laborious at times, is acceptable as is.

Much research and cross-referencing was needed to fully identify who the individuals in the manuscript were; explain what the strategic, operational, and tactical strategy of the war or battle was at any given time; and clarify any other idea that left the reader begging for more information. This is why there are an abundance of notes at the end of the book. The reader is encouraged to study the notes while reading the book to attain a better understanding of what took place, when, and by whom.

The decision to embellish the original version of Alexander's manuscript in the ways discussed above was not an easy one. In the end I decided to follow the likely policy of any would-be 1949 editor by correcting and standardizing spelling, punctuation, and grammar. For the World War II researcher whose study requires the original Irvin Alexander manuscript, it can be found in one of two places: The U.S. Military Academy Special Collections Section, found on the fourth floor of the Cadet Library in West Point, New York, or at the Center for Military History, Carlisle Barracks, Pennsylvania.

Many of Alexander's conclusions about the war and the U.S. Army of that particular era are timeless. They could as easily be statements about the army during the post-Vietnam period as in the late 1940s.

> Discipline among the civilian personnel was almost as severe as in the military services. A worker who was suspected of contemplating a strike in [the] war industry would have been lucky to live twenty-four hours. There are men back home in our country today who were facing the enemy during the times strikes were in progress in essential industries of the United States and have seen their own men die when they might have been saved if there had not been a shortage of equipment. Those men are bitter in their denunciation of a political system that will permit the well paid workers, who stay safely at home, take any action for their own preferment which costs the lives of the poorly paid young men who are fighting in their defense.

Let us be grateful that men like Col. Irvin Alexander decided to step forward and take action during World War II. The 1940s were a precarious time, to say the least. Freedom in the world was a precious commodity during that era, and as the fiftieth anniversary of the war passes us by we should be thankful that there were men brave enough to fight for this nation. Be proud of the men like Colonel Alexander and the rest of the "Battling Bastards of Bataan," for it is undoubtedly because of their efforts and those of warriors like them that we as a nation live in freedom today.

> We're the battling bastards of Bataan;
> No mama, no papa, no Uncle Sam
> No aunts, no uncles, no cousins no nieces;
> No pills, no planes, no artillery pieces
> . . . And nobody gives a damn.[53]

COLONEL IRVIN
ALEXANDER'S PREFACE

One of the convalescents of the war undertook to tell his wife the story of the war as best his fevered mind recalled it.[1] His story is uncomplicated by reference to documents or research designed to correlate his story with accepted history. It is strictly limited to personal experiences of the writer and to stories told [to] him by others soon after events they related occurred and, of course, a few conclusions which are believed to be logical. It is admittedly small in perspective, in fact it might be called a mole's eye view of the war.

[Many] of the chapters are introduced by brief sketches of the country as seen from the Brown country house, where the manuscript was conceived, although much of the actual writing was done from a hospital bed.[2]

With exception of the leading sketches, no paragraphing has been done[3] as it is believed that much rewriting and many changes would be necessary before the manuscript could hope to reach a final form. The writer is admittedly an amateur and he has simply told his story without any attempt to dramatize himself or others.

PART 1

A Humbling Experience

Chapter 1

Reflecting Back

"Here we go starting the day early," he tried to say to himself, but the chattering of his teeth forced him to think it rather than say it. He pushed himself up to reach for the heavy wool blanket folded on the foot of the bed. The attempt failed, and he fell back on his pillow while the room seemed to continue revolving around him. This little exertion, added to the chattering of his teeth, left him so weak that he had to rest.[1]

After his heart had slowed down, he very carefully raised himself for another try at the blanket. Ignoring the whirling room to concentrate all his attention on the blanket, he finally succeeded in reaching it and pulling it over [himself] as he fell back on the pillow again.

He rested quietly, all but his chattering teeth. Gradually he became aware that his pillow was wet and [he was] becoming uncomfortable. While trying to turn the pillow [over] he recognized very dimly his wife coming in the door with the coffee percolator and heard her cheery voice greeting him.

"Lazy Bones, are you ready for your coffee?" she asked. Then she noted the chattering teeth and part of her cheerfulness vanished. She poured the coffee, lifted his head, and continued, "So you are starting early this time? Take this quinine and by the time you finish your coffee you will stop wearing out your teeth and feel better."[2]

He went to sleep almost immediately after she left, and gradually the noise of his teeth chattering ceased. When he awoke she was sitting quietly in an easy chair by the bed. Her smiling face was clear and the room was no longer going round and round.

"How do you feel now?" she asked.

"Pretty good," [he replied]. "Maybe I could eat something. If you will turn on the bath and help me into the bathroom, I'll soak in the hot water while you get us some breakfast."

Later he was sitting bundled in the easy chair gazing out the window. The breakfast tray lay on his lap, but it was forgotten as the scene outside absorbed him.

"You have eaten hardly enough to keep a bird alive, dear," she interrupted. "Please eat a little more before it gets cold."

Ignoring the subject of food, he slipped the tray on to a nearby chair and began talking about the colorful panorama outside.

"Just now this must be one of the most beautiful spots in the world. Jacob's coat of many colors could never have approached in brilliance these autumn scenes of nature.[3] One expects to see different hues in the various types of trees with their different shades among different species. For instance, I can identify three different kinds of oaks from here and notice the changing colors in that large maple. The leaves still look so healthy it does not seem possible that they will be gone all too soon. Only the lone poplar down by the draw shows signs of shedding. Now that the fog over Salt Creek has lifted, the mass color on the hill beyond the Nashville road sparkles its defiance to all of the artists.[4] It is [so] quiet and peaceful and lovely that I almost forget the dreams I had during my nap."

"Were they about the war?" she inquired.

"Oh yes," he answered, continuing to gaze out the window.

"I heard 'Photo Joe' coming over at daybreak as he used to every day.[5]

"Since he was not greeted by anti-aircraft fire, and as various scenes of the Death March began passing in review, I concluded that the war [in my dream] must be over on Bataan.[6]

"The first scene occurred off the highway near our camp just before we started the long trek to Camp O'Donnell.[7] A tall army colonel had been stopped by a Japanese soldier who was trying to appropriate [the colonel's] wristwatch. The colonel merely held his arm high, where the little soldier could not reach it.[8]

"A passing Nip officer seeing the difficulty ran over, unhooking his Samurai sword as he ran. He did not draw the sword, but using the heavy sword and scabbard as a club, he struck the colonel on the head knocking him down. Then kicking him in the ribs until he got up, he hit him on the other side of the head, knocking him down again. After the colonel was back on his feet the second time, he was forced to stand at attention with the blood streaming down his face. The Nip officer tore off [the colonel's] wristwatch and threw it in the road from where it was rescued by a surprised Nip [enlisted] soldier who was marching by.

"Shaking his sword in front of the colonel's face, the Nip shouted 'You are brave, but you must be humble,' and ran on, leaving the colonel standing at attention."

Chapter 2

Being Captured

On the following day, as he was admiring the world from his window, his wife reminded him that he had gone to sleep before he could tell about the Death March.

"I feel almost normal today," he said. "I'll tell you as much as I can remember. What was I talking about when I went to sleep?"

"You were telling about the colonel who was beaten by the Nip officer for not being humble."

That was a most valuable object lesson for me. I learned at the very beginning of imprisonment that even [if] I did not feel humble, I must not advertise the fact. We were advised by a Nip interpreter that we must proceed to an assembly point near Mariveles,[1] sixteen miles away, and that we could use our own transportation.

There were ten of us so we started out in two cars, the car I was in being in the rear. With me were Al, Griff, Hugh, and Sherry.[2] The narrow and winding graveled road was completely filled on one side with POWs heading toward Mariveles, and on the other with Japanese tanks, infantry, and supply columns going toward Bagac.[3]

We kept moving as fast as we could, the first ten miles of the trip being uneventful. Unfortunately, we came to a sharp curve where our side of the road was partly washed out. We had to stop, waiting for a break in the Japanese column which would let us go through. Before the break came, a Nip officer marching by rushed over to the car and in broken English shouted, "Out! Out! Out!"

One glimpse of his contorted face convinced us that we had no choice in the matter. Out we came, I being the last one because I had to follow the driver past the steering wheel. As I reached for my musette bag[4] the Nip shouted furiously, "No! No! No!"

When I saw the sword[5] raised in both his hands and heard the venomous words, "Enemy! Enemy! Enemy!" I ran on to join my companions.

That is how I lost all my possessions, except my canteen which, fortunately, I had on my belt.

We trudged on down the road keeping well to the right to avoid the clutches of the Nip soldiers going the other way. We ignored their gestures and their calls hoping that none of them would leave their columns. From the end of one of their columns, a Nip soldier ran across the road and, pulling Al out into the middle of it, he measured feet with him. A moment later, after Al had caught up with us he panted, "For the first time in my life I am happy that I have big feet. If my shoes had been nearer a fit for that bugger, he would have taken them right off of me."

As we came around the next curve, we saw the car with the other five of our group stuck in the ditch. They told us that a Nip tank had crowded them off the road. Helping them, we soon had the car on the road, after which we proceeded with six of us inside the car and four standing on the running boards until we arrived safely at Mariveles about sunset.

We could find no assembly area for Americans [at Mariveles], although there was a large area filled with the Filipinos. Since the Nips had carefully screened the Americans from the Filipinos before we left our camp, we knew that we were going to receive different treatment, either better or worse.

Still looking for an American area, I went into the Quarantine Station, passing several Nip sentries who paid me no attention. In front of a large building, which proved to be the headquarters of a Nip infantry regiment, I found a Nip soldier who spoke English. He stated that he knew of no assembly area, but he suggested that I wait until he inquired. In a few moments he returned and directed me to a cleared space under a tree to wait for the colonel who wanted to talk to me. About fifteen minutes later the others of our group that I had left on the gateway of the area rejoined me, and while we were talking the Nip colonel arrived.

Colonel Ito,[6] the Nip colonel, was the most impressive officer of his race I saw during the war. He was a man of about fifty, tall and slender, and even his GI uniform could not hide his gracefulness. As he approached in the growing darkness what caught our attention and held it was the most magnificent mustache any Nip ever wore. It was slender and dark, with its soft silky strands extending from tip to tip for more than a foot. The tips were pointed and, while they did not appear waxed, they were molded in graceful curves which were different from those of any mustache I had ever seen.

The colonel, accompanied by a young Nip soldier who acted as interpreter, sat down by a tree. The colonel, speaking softly, motioned for us to draw up close around him in a semicircle and sit down. The interpreter asked us if we were hungry and at our spontaneous affirmative answers the colonel clapped his hands without waiting for a translation.

A young soldier reported, standing rigidly at attention in front of the colonel until he had received his orders [and] then departed on the double. Through the interpreter the colonel asked the name and rank of each of us, then turning to me he asked what I thought of his soldiers. I told him, truthfully, that I had been greatly impressed by his soldiers and his camp, for it was obvious to me from my little observation of the way his men were performing their duties from their dress and physical appearance that his command was a crack regiment.

Obviously pleased, [the colonel] smiled, telling us that they had arrived from Japan less than a month before and that his regiment had spearheaded the attack that broke through our lines to bring about the surrender of Bataan.

He [then] broke into the translation with the words, "My orders, Forward! Forward! Forward!"

It did not take me long to realize that the colonel understood English as well as the interpreter and I suspected that he could talk it as well. He was clearly a well educated, intelligent and cultivated gentleman and, I thought, probably a "soldier of the old school."

Two Nip soldiers appeared with trays carrying a glass of sweetened milk for each of us and several packages of Japanese biscuits. We polished off all the food in no time, after which the colonel, with a beaming face, produced a bottle of very good wine that he handed to the interpreter, who poured a glass for each of us except himself.

When the wine was gone the colonel spoke in Japanese to the interpreter, who pondered how to translate it. Finally [the interpreter] said, "The colonel says—now that you have eaten—," but he stopped as if he did not know how to finish the sentence.

After the colonel asked [us] some pointed questions about Corregidor, which had not [yet] surrendered, it dawned upon me that he had a plan. He apparently was expecting to be a part of the force that was preparing to attack the island; therefore, he hoped to obtain some information from us. His questions were asked to the group in general so that any one of us might answer. After several somewhat innocuous questions, he asked one that seemed to be of considerable military importance. A young captain started to answer, but I sharply interrupted him, saying I would answer the question. The colonel eyed me coldly after I had made an evasive answer, then he got up and stalked off, telling the interpreter to put us in the bus by the side of the building.

"Weren't you frightened?" she asked.

I was uneasy until we got away from there the next day which, by the way, was the thirteenth of April [1942]. Another reason for uneasiness was that we were within easy range of the guns of Corregidor in the middle of a Japanese regimental area which certainly was a very fine target.[7] Fortunately we were not fired on, although I was awakened during the night by numerous heavy explosions, which I was relieved to note were a long way off. Sometime later I learned that our bombers had made a raid on Nip air installations near Manila.

The next morning we were given a few biscuits for breakfast, but the cordial atmosphere of the night before had vanished. The colonel was out in the area watching the activities of his troops. Hugh, becoming interested in the Nip drill formations, wandered away from the bus and was standing idly watching the troops when the lieutenant colonel of the regiment, rushing up to him, started kicking him on the shins. Hugh was so astonished he almost fell down getting back to us.

The colonel, who was standing nearby, was looking at Hugh when the incident occurred, but he did not bat an eye. He looked at me coldly as Hugh joined us, and my desire to part company with him was acute indeed. When the interpreter came to tell us we were to go immediately to an assembly point twenty miles away, I did not even feel badly that our car had been appropriated so that we had to walk. I pointed out to him that we could expect to meet up with many Japanese troops who might not know our status. He asked me to give him a list of our names, which I did, and in a few minutes he was back with a curiously painted list of Japanese characters for each of us. We did not know what the characters said but we felt it was safer to have them after we had cleared the well-disciplined camp.

When we were ordered to march, there was a hurried scurrying by the five of our party who had had the car to carry valuables that far. Some of [our] belongings were distributed among us, some were given to the Nips, and some had to be left behind. I had no problem for the Nip officer had parted me from my property the day before.

As we marched away one young cavalry officer had a fine pair of English riding boots slung over his shoulder. I asked him what in the hell he expected to do with them. He replied to the effect that they were his property and he intended to take them with him. I merely shrugged my shoulders for I saw that the youngster had not yet realized what was happening to him.

"Did he take his boots on into prison camp with him?" she interrupted.

He did not. Three days later, when the going got tough, he lost all affection for those boots and he threw them away in apparent relief.

Chapter 3

The Journey Begins

We had marched two or three miles when we came in sight of a Japanese supply camp alongside the road. As we approached it, a grinning Nip soldier came to the road waving us to come in. We did not want to leave the road, but he insisted in perfect English that he had some tea for us so we marched in.

He gave us a cup of tea apiece, telling us that he was born and grew up in Hawaii and that he had been on a visit to Japan when the war started and [was subsequently] forced to join the Japanese Army. He did not appear to be worried about the final outcome of the war for he seemed to think that the Nips had already won.

He would not let us go until an hour later when a Nip soldier drove into camp with an empty bus. Our Hawaiian friend arranged for us to ride in the bus, thereby saving us ten weary miles of marching up the mountain. We could not help a feeling of elation as we sat on the cushions of the bus creeping up the steep road. It did not take long for this feeling to dissipate, for passing the familiar places of the Zig Zag at Little Baguio, such as Hospital No. 1, the entrance to department headquarters, and Hospital No. 2, we saw no one except Japanese soldiers.[1]

Our feeling of sadness changed abruptly to one of apprehension when we became aware of artillery fire close by and identified a Japanese battery in position along the road firing on Corregidor. As we rode by, we anticipated that [the] retaliatory fire from the heavy guns of Corregidor might blow us off the road, but we passed the area without incident.

Later that day a group of American POWs were not so fortunate, for just as they were passing the battery shells from Corregidor blasted the area, destroying the Nip battery [and] at the same time killing one American and wounding several others.

27

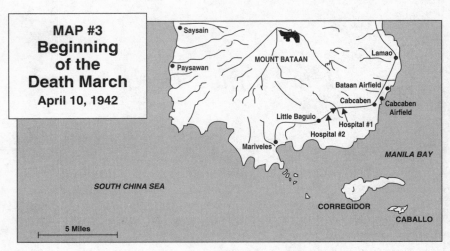

MAP #3
**Beginning
of the
Death March**
April 10, 1942

Saysain

Paysawan

MOUNT BATAAN

Lamao

Bataan Airfield

Cabcaben

Cabcaben
Airfield

Little Baguio

Hospital #1

Hospital #2

Mariveles

MANILA BAY

SOUTH CHINA SEA

CORREGIDOR

CABALLO

5 Miles

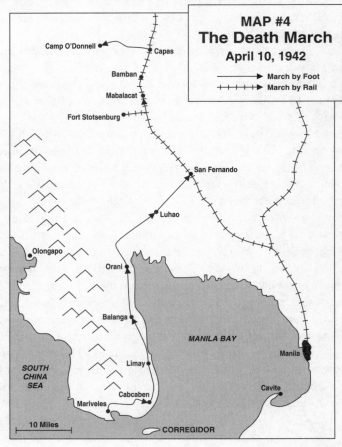

MAP #4
The Death March
April 10, 1942

→ March by Foot
+++++► March by Rail

Camp O'Donnell

Capas

Bamban

Mabalacat

Fort Stotsenburg

San Fernando

Luhao

Olongapo

Orani

Balanga

MANILA BAY

Manila

SOUTH
CHINA
SEA

Limay

Cabcaben

Cavite

Mariveles

10 Miles

CORREGIDOR

We had just left the artillery position behind when we came to a stream where Nip engineers where repairing a bridge which had been blown up by our troops several days earlier. As our bus inched across the bridge we could see a detail of Americans in the water up to their waists handling heavy timbers. One of the workers, a gray-haired man almost sixty years old, I recognized as an artillery colonel that I had talked to a few days before. When I saw him later, he told me that the Nips had worked them brutally for three days from dawn until dark, providing only one light meal a day.

A mile beyond the bridge we came to a large Nip motor pool into which our driver turned, it being his final destination. We then began marching again under the blazing sun. After we had marched about an hour we arrived at what had been our front line position of a few days before.[2] A trail led off into the jungle shade and, there being no Nips in sight to stop us, we went a quarter of a mile off the road where we could lie down in peaceful quiet and comparative freedom. We decided to spend the night there, knowing little [that] it was to be the last [night] for many, many long months that we could rest outside the ring of barbed wire and bayonet.

Griff built a small fire and, collecting the remaining cans of food from everyone, he mixed and heated the contents, dividing the resulting concoction equally among all of us. It was not very much, but it was our last meal for five days and, while we did not consider the mixture very tasty, it was the best meal we were to have until the following November.

After our light repast, I scouted around, finding a small dump of property which had been abandoned when the position had been evacuated. There was little of value there, but I did find a dirty musette bag, a battered messkit spoon, and a well worn toothbrush.

At a small stream I washed those articles as best I could in order to replace the ones I had lost. The spoon and toothbrush I put in the pocket of my shirt and I used them exclusively for almost a year because they were the only ones I had.

About sunset two American officers wandered into our little camp to stay all night with us. One of them was Colonel [Otto] Harwood,[3] the quartermaster officer, who with his wife and two pretty daughters went over on the boat with us.

His head was wrapped in a bandage, both his eyes were blackened and one side of his face was swollen terribly. We all asked him what in the world had happened, so he sat down wearily and told his story.

When the department quartermaster office moved from Manila to Bataan some of the native permanent clerical help had come along,

continuing to perform their duties on Bataan. One of them, a pretty mestiza whom everyone liked, had been especially faithful. That morning she
and other clerks were walking along the jungle trail to the highway when
they met a Japanese soldier doing guard duty at what was left of a dump.[4]

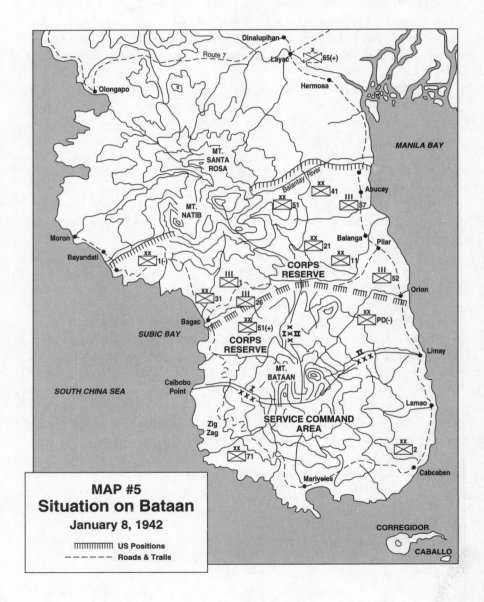

MAP #5
Situation on Bataan
January 8, 1942

� US Positions
– – – – – Roads & Trails

As the girl started by, the soldier grabbed her and started to drag her into the jungle. Colonel Harwood being in no doubt as to the soldier's intentions, interfered in an attempt to save the young lady. The Nip soldier turned on him furiously, knocking him down with the butt of his rifle. He was on the verge of bayoneting him when a Nip officer appeared, calling the soldier back to the dump.

Colonel Harwood and the clerks lost no time in leaving that place well behind them. When they were some distance away, one of the men produced a dirty pair of coveralls, which the girl put on. Then, mussing her hair and covering herself with dirt she went on her way masquerading as the wife of one of the Filipinos.

I do not know what happened to the girl, but "Lady Luck" was certainly with Colonel Harwood that day, for he survived the prison years and is now back home with his family.

I am sure you wonder why, when we were off the road away from the Nips for a day, we did not keep going into the hills instead of reporting to prison camp. I know you remember that I always insisted the hills were better than prison, but you cannot visualize the conditions which existed at the time of the surrender.[5]

If you will look at the map, you will see that we were on the east side of Bataan a few miles north of Cabcaben. We were unarmed, out of food, and in a jungle country where food was difficult to find. We did not know where the Nips were and we did not know whether any Filipino we might meet could be trusted.

To get to the coast it would have been necessary to travel a hundred or more miles of unknown mountain trails where we could not expect to avoid contracting malaria and dysentery.

After we reached the coast we were nowhere because the Nips controlled the sea. The rainy season [was] almost upon us, which would have added greatly to our difficulties. We were already weak and half starved; as a matter of fact, most of us were showing symptoms of beriberi.[6] Also, our commanding general had made a bona fide surrender of all of us.

Even with all of those difficulties, if we could have foreseen what the future held for us, we probably would have taken to the hills.

Chapter 4

The "Hike" Continues

ORION

The following morning, [April 14, 1942,] every man decided to resume the journey toward the prison camp because that way seemed to be the only one that offered a chance for survival. We arrived at Orion before noon, signed a huge prisoner of war book, and passed into a large barbed wire enclosure where we stayed without food until [the] afternoon of the second day.

Water was obtainable from two taps which were guarded by Nip sentries with fixed bayonets. Except for the middle of the night hours, there was always a long line of waiting men at both of the taps.

The camp was filthy, but so commodious that we had no trouble selecting a reasonably comfortable place in the shade. We found many friends there; some of them [already] showing the effects of mistreatment. I remember that one general had a bandage on his head and beating marks on his face.

Some of those friends I was never to see again and most of those that finally did arrive at Camp O'Donnell showed effects of severe hardship for the Death March began at their camps near Orani and ended at Camp O'Donnell.[1] The horrors of the Death March were aggravated by the vast differences between the Americans and Japanese in language, temperament, customs, manners, training and discipline, which, all combined, created a colossal misunderstanding.[2]

Those differences were hard to adjust to because the Nips, being on top of the heap, insisted that all adjustments had to be made by Americans, who had not been in the habit of accepting the dictates of others since Colonial days when they had adopted the premise that all men are created free and equal. Because of those differences, the half-starved American prisoners were clubbed, bayoneted, and subjected to countless indignities in an unsuccessful effort to fit them into what the Oriental mind conceived as the appropriate mold for captives of war.

About two o'clock on the second day, [April 15, 1942,] we were formed on the road in groups of one hundred and in columns of four. Three mean-looking Nip sentries, all privates who spoke no English, were assigned to each group. Each sentry carried a loaded rifle with fixed bayonet. We do not know what orders the senior sentry received, but we concluded the first day, and we never saw reason to change our conclusion, that he was ordered to deliver one hundred men, deducting from that number only those who were killed on the way.[3]

We had not been marching long before we learned to be wary of [the] trucks coming from the north. The road was narrow and the truck drivers were indifferent as to how many American casualties they might cause. I was on the inside of the column when we started and I had a shoulder almost dislocated by a speeding truck before the first hour had passed. Some of the trucks carried Nips who tried to tap us ungently on the heads with the butts of their rifles as they passed by.[4]

At the end of an hour we came to a halt near a roadside water spigot and the men at the head of our column rushed to fill their canteens. The sentry there ran to the water line yelling and swinging his rifle. He drove all the men back to the column, sticking the last man painfully in the seat of his pants with the bayonet. After a few moments the sentry relented so that we all were able to fill our canteens before we resumed the march. That day, having only eight miles to go, we arrived at the next enclosure before dark with ninety-nine men, one having lagged behind the column too far and too long, thereby getting himself shot for causing the Nips trouble.

The new camp was as large as the previous camp and covered with filth from previous campers. There was no food, the only luxury being a bath in the river which ran through the place. The next day, [April 16, 1942,] we did not start marching until the middle of the afternoon and [since] the next camp was about ten miles away, we arrived after dark.

I forgot to tell you that the Nips made no distinction between officers and enlisted men POWs. We were all just numbers to them. The Nips issued instructions that command authority had ceased to exist among the Americans and that no orders would be given by POWs of any rank.[5] That Nip order resulted in a complete breakdown of discipline and authority.

Perhaps I failed to tell you that we went on half rations January 5, 1942 and that rations were cut again soon afterwards.[6] Many men were very bitter about the food shortage for they believed that they had not received their proportionate share. Some blamed the quartermaster for inequitable distribution, others blamed each higher headquarters for stealing part of the food intended for lower units, and still others claimed that their own unit commander had lived well while his men starved.

I had no doubt that mistakes were made and I know there were a few instances of deliberate misappropriation of food, but, with few exceptions, everyone was starving. Many of the men were young recruits who had received little or no disciplinary training and that, coupled with some justifiable ill will and many foul rumors, made them welcome the Nip order absolving them from higher American authority.

If an officer spoke to a soldier the natural response was "Go to hell!" No officer could expect any assistance whatever except from another officer and I heard many men remark, "He got what was coming to him," at the death of an officer.[7]

On the first two or three days of the march the ditches along the road were filled with water. The scum-covered water stank and it was not unusual to see bodies of animals, Nips, Filipinos, and Americans bloated and rotting in the water. Many times I have seen heat-crazed young soldiers, who did not know how to conserve the water in their canteens, throw themselves down by the ditches and drink the filthy water. I never saw an old soldier or an officer make that mistake which, I think, is one reason why there was a much larger percentage of deaths among the younger men at Camp O'Donnell during the following six weeks.[8] It did you no good to try to stop any man from doing such an absurd thing, for he told you very positively that it was none of your business and did it anyway.

The new camp was very small and we, being the last arrivals, were marched to the last space which was merely a narrow strip along the fence. There was barely room to sit down and if we had not been able to extend our feet through the fence there would have been standing room only. Therefore, we sat through the long night with the unpleasantness of a poorly filled latrine between our seats and the fence. The only encouragement we had was that some rice had been distributed before dark and if we had arrived earlier there would have been food for us.

The next morning, [April 17, 1942,] we were up early standing in groups along the road trying to get the kinks out of our weary bodies, but we did not march until about 10:00 A.M. While we were standing so long on the road, we [noticed] a small area which had been crowded with about one hundred men who felt too sick to march. In spite of their afflictions they were cheerful, telling us they expected to be moved by truck later. What happened to those men is not positively known, but we never saw any of them again and it is my belief that they were all slaughtered in the camp where they were.

About 11:00 A.M. we started on what was to be the worst day of the march. The day was terrifically hot and there was no shade along the road; as a matter of fact, there had been little shade since we left the front line position. We had been in the cool shelter of the jungles since the first of January and we had been short of food and salt for some time. The lack of salt was felt more strongly than the lack of food, because a man, especially a white man, cannot be active for long under a tropical sun without plenty of salt in his system.

At the first halt we knew we were in for a terrible day. There was not a cloud in the sky and there was not a breath of wind. Our faces had already begun to cook because on the road we felt the effect of the rays of the sun reflected from the pavement as well as its direct rays. When we halted there was already a column ahead of us using the water spigot which, the guard considered, was sufficient reason [for] not allowing us to refill our canteens.

An officer who tried to get water got a bayonet wound in his arm instead, and his wound became so painful that he had to support his arm with a cushion during the remainder of the march. Three men who did not get up promptly to resume the march were shot.

While we were crossing a bridge an officer who could no longer stand the agony of the march ran to the rail and jumped off, breaking his neck. A man, [whom] I know, threw himself in the ditch, where he lay motionless with his face in the water. The guard, looking at him, concluded that he was already dead and marched on. After the column passed by, the man revived to crawl away from the road, only to be recaptured the next day. Why he was not shot then no one knows, but he rejoined us later.

An army chaplain of the Catholic faith, who had been suffering malaria, began to slow down. Starting at the head of the column he gradually fell back to the rear. Three priests had tried to hold him up and keep him going, but they simply could not do it. They were hurriedly doing their best to give him the last rites of the church when the sentry forced them at bayonet point to go back to the column. After he was released by the other priests the chaplain staggered, to fall half in and half out of the ditch. The sentry prodded him with his bayonet, but the chaplain being too far gone to move, the [sentry] concluded that it was useless to waste a bullet on a dying man. The chaplain, who recovered his senses after the column had gone, was carried by Filipinos until he was recaptured months later. After many other terrible experiences, he came home to preside over a small parish in Ohio.[9]

At the third halt, we refilled our canteens before we tried to rest lying in the hot sun. When we started marching again a couple of more men were killed because they were slow in getting up. I was beginning to have difficulty walking, but I made it to the next halt. I knew I was suffering from heat exhaustion because I could not cool off and my heart continued to beat at a good one hundred and fifty a minute. I suggested to my friends that they roll me over in the grass and leave me as I did not believe I could continue. They refused to consider the suggestion for they said, inasmuch as I had been looking after them during the war, [now] they were going to look after me. One friend produced a salt tablet, another a small lump of sugar candy which they gave me immediately before we started to march. I was holding on to the arms of the men on each side of me but I could not move my feet for I could not see and I had no sense of balance.

I heard several shots when we started moving and I almost fell over the body of one man on the road. I could not help shuddering at all the brutality. Griff, to whom I was holding on my right, thinking he had to cheer me up, told me to think of my wife and child and how much I wanted to get back to them. I snapped at him to forget the pep talk for as long as I could lift a foot I would keep going. He laughed, apparently convinced, for I heard no more of his encouragement.

About every hour new relays of my boys took over, Hugh, Griff, and Al doing most of the work, and we marched that way for the last six miles of that seventeen-mile march.[10] About eighty of the one hundred men who started that march finished it, the majority of those lost falling out because of heat stroke or heat exhaustion. If it had not been for the generosity of my friends I could not have made it either. That last period was a nightmare, because a conscious and painful effort was required to move each foot in front of the other at every step.

LUBAO

After we marched into the enclosure that night I fell where we halted, sleeping where I lay. The next morning, [April 18, 1942,] I discovered my feet had spent the night in a latrine. Sitting up and looking around, I recognized the large warehouse at Lubao,[11] which I had visited several times the year before when the army had rented it for a supply depot during maneuvers.

Immediately I thought of our young son, who, when [he was] eight years old, had accompanied me on my visit to Lubao the previous year. I recalled that when we arrived at Lubao he had asked me where we were.

Apparently I had not enunciated the Lubao very clearly, for he had looked at me scandalized and asked, "What, Loose Bowels!" I was greatly amused as I explained the name to him and so was he when I finished. For weeks after we returned to the post, he enjoyed confidentially explaining to our male friends about our visit to "Loose Bowels." The explanation was reserved exclusively for males as, insofar as I know, he was careful that no female ever heard the story. I wondered very sadly and doubtfully if ever I should see the kid again.

The facilities consisted of a modern sheet-iron building 150' x 75' located exactly in the middle of a hurricane fenced area 300' x 150'.

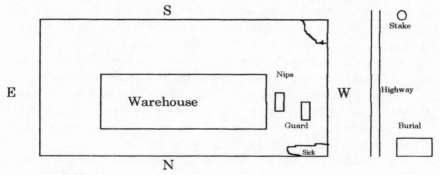

Lubao Camp: As drawn by Colonel Alexander in the original manuscript.

From my position in the corner about ten yards inside of each of the southhand west fences, I had a pretty good view of the part of the compound where most of the prisoners were crowded. I estimated that there were about a thousand POWs in the area. About twenty feet east of where I sat a water faucet was running wide open. A sentry was sitting by it giving orders in Japanese to a waiting line of at least one hundred POWs, some of them carrying three or four canteens. While the length of the line varied during the next two days, it was plenty long all during the daylight hours.

Once when I woke up in the middle of the night, I rushed to fill my canteen because there were only ten men in line. At the northwest corner of the fence in the shade of a large tree, where a small area had been set aside for them, were almost a hundred sick. Many of them had malaria, some of them had dysentery, but most of them were suffering from undiagnosed illnesses. There were three American doctors, but the only medicine available was the small amount carried in a field kit belonging to one of [the doctors]. All of the patients were lying on the bare ground, their only available comfort being water.

Between the sick area and the water faucet a large table had been placed for the convenience of the senior Nip. Sitting at the table, part of the time with his feet on it, was a short, sleek and well-pleased-with-himself Nip officer. He had drawn his samurai sword, placing it conveniently on the table beside him. Every now and then he looked over the blade carefully, testing its edge. He always appeared pleased with the condition of his prize weapon and anxious for an opportunity to use it. He reminded me of a butcher expertly examining his favorite knife.

Between the Nip officer and the front gate was a row of chairs facing the officer, and near it was a rifle rack for the use of the members of the guard who were not on post. Except when cleaning rifles or equipment, the guards sat at attention looking directly at the officer. The officer took no notice of his own men, apparently his main interests being his sword and the American prisoners. Frequently, he called for an American who spoke Japanese to whom he issued instructions for the conduct of the prisoners.

"They must be quiet, the water line must maintain discipline, all knives and articles that might be used as weapons must be turned in."

While issuing those instructions the officer assumed a regal attitude, but after he had dismissed the interpreter, he always laughed, as much pleased with himself as a child playing with toy soldiers. Several times the interpreter moved around among the prisoners announcing that the Nip officer wanted all watches and jewelry, that he was tired of [the] POWs' failure to carry out orders and that, in the future, the punishment for failure to comply [with] his orders would be death.

I had already pinned my ring to the inside of my drawers and the only other valuable I had was my wristwatch.[12] I decided to leave the ring where it was but to throw the watch away. So wandering back alongside the warehouse where no Nips could see me I tossed my watch over the fence into the tall grass.

I had hardly got back to my resting place before the Nip officer yelled, jumped up, and ran over to the water line. A young American soldier, perhaps not more than twenty years old, started to run but he returned when the Nip followed, motioning him to come back. Calling the American interpreter, the Nip took him and the kid to the officer's table. The Nip told the kid that he had seen him crash the water line contrary to orders, then summoning a Nip soldier he directed him to execute the American immediately. The kid broke down and begged for his life, but the officer ignored him, impatiently motioning the sentry to lead him away.

The Nip soldiers led the youngster out to the front gate, across the road, tying him to a stake about twenty-five yards from us. One of the soldiers knelt down in the road and fired two shots at the youngster, missing him both times. The soldier, who was in a rage by that time, walked over to the stake where the youngster was tied, fixing his bayonet on the way. I could not bear to look anymore, but I do know that after about five minutes the Nip returned with a bloody bayonet, which he carefully washed, and soon afterwards there was a call for a burial detail.

An old friend of mine, whom I had not seen since the start of the war, came down the water line. After he had filled his canteen he stopped to talk to me for more than an hour. His first remark was, "What happened to you?" I didn't know what he meant until he said, "Your face looks like a boiled lobster."

After one look in his pocket mirror, I had to admit he was right, for my face looked to me like a slightly underdone piece of meat. Even my lips were burned and cracked. By the time we reached Camp O'Donnell, five days later, my entire face, including my lips, had begun to peel. There being nothing to stop the process, it was only a few days more until I had a new face. I showed my friend my dilapidated overseas cap, which was the only head covering I had. He replied that it was no wonder the sun had almost cooked me.

Later that day Al appeared with a sun helmet which, he insisted, he had procured especially for me. We adjusted the hat to fit me very easily so, due to Al's thoughtfulness and energy, I acquired a head covering which helped make the remainder of the trip considerably less uncomfortable.

Looking out on the highway the morning after we arrived, [April 19, 1942,] we saw one lone American coming down the road, marching like he was just one in a column of a hundred. When he reached the gate he marched right in without the Nips saying a word to him. As he came closer we saw he was Matt, whom I had been too far gone to know was missing.[13] He sat down bubbling all over with his good fortune. Sherry filled his canteen for him and then he told us that when the heat got him the day before, he rolled over in the grass hoping the Nips would not miss him, which they didn't.

Waking up after sleeping all night, he just marched on in without anyone bothering about him. We still do not know why he was not shot. He rejoined us at the psychological moment for early that afternoon the interpreter announced that chow was being served at the east end of the warehouse. The instantaneous rush toward the long delayed food endangered the lives of the weaker men along the way, but luckily there were no fatalities.

My resting place being at the west end of the compound, my position in line was toward the tail end, so that it was an hour later before I was able to eat. The food consisted of a messkit nearly full of steamed rice and a heaping tablespoon of salt; nothing more. Ordinarily I would scorn such a meal, but it being my first one in five days I ate it without losing a single grain.

The next morning, [April 20, 1942,] after we had our rice and salt, four hundred Americans were marched away. I was still a bit under the weather so I stayed in the background, as did all of the other nine who started with me. Griff had a recurrence of his malaria which forced him to go to the sick area.

In the middle of the day the Nips called for a burial detail of ten men. The detail arrived at the burial area under guard to find they had to dig a group grave for ten men. As they started digging a party of Filipinos brought the almost naked bodies of ten Filipino soldiers, which they dumped by the grave, and marched away.

After the grave was finished and the burial detail started to carry the bodies to it, two of the bodies groaned, one of them rolling over trying to sit up. The Americans excitedly called the attention of the Nip guards to the two Filipinos who were still alive. The Nips were furious, one of them grabbing a spade knocked the moving Filipino on the head and then forced the detail to drop all ten bodies in the hole, which they covered. We wondered what would be the fate of our sick who could not walk out of Lubao. Those whom we left behind the next day we never saw again. Much later we learned that a detail of Filipinos buried a number of Americans in the burial ground across the road a few days after our departure.

That afternoon we were notified that four hundred men would march in the morning, which was good news for we all had concluded that we were in the need of a change of scenery. Even Griff, who had found some quinine, announced he would be with us on the morrow and sure enough he was. Not only did he make that march while running a temperature, but he survived almost forty more attacks of malaria before he got back home.

In the late afternoon about five hundred more Americans marched in and, for some reason unknown to us, the Nips ran us all inside the warehouse, closing the door. There was not enough room for everyone to lie down so most of us did not sleep too well. About 4:00 A.M. the doors were opened, giving me a chance to get out and fill my canteen. It was a luxury to lie on the bare ground where I could stretch my cramped muscles.

While I was lying there near the water tap watching the men in the short line filling their canteens, Sherry came through the line and after getting his water he came over to sit down beside me. I asked him why he came through the line in the normal way, at which he chuckled and answered that he just wanted a little variety.

The first morning after we arrived, Sherry noticed that there was always a large stream of water going to waste beneath the canteens which were being held under the tap. Such a waste of water appeared to him to be criminal and he resolved to do something about it; so taking a bath towel with him, gesturing and displaying all his magnetic personality, he talked the guard into letting him wet the towel in the wasting water. A few minutes later he was back with a canteen hidden in his towel which he filled while he was wetting the towel. During the two days we were there, he repeated this trick perhaps fifty times, many of them for the benefit of his friends, my canteen being one that he filled at least four times.

While Sherry's ruse did not operate to the disadvantage of anyone, he well knew that if he had been caught he probably would have been executed. I had watched him at the line many times, admiring his skill and courage tremendously. That first day I told him I was sure that he was predominately Scotch or Jewish and, furthermore, I had no doubts as to his success in life provided he escaped hanging. He escaped hanging by the Nips, and is now [1949] a judge in California.

When the call came for the four hundred to march that day, we rushed to the east end of the warehouse to be among them. We had no trouble getting in the group which, to our pleased surprise, received rice and salt before we started the march. Two days of rest, together with a few meals of rice and salt, had done wonders for my physical endurance. The day was just as hot as the day on which we had arrived at Lubao, but the food, rest and sun helmet, which was a big protection, all combined to help me march the twelve miles into San Fernando that day without difficulty.[14]

For eight or nine miles after we left Lubao, there was a canal paralleling the road on the west side, taking the place of the usual drainage ditch. As all traffic passed to the left in the Philippines, when we stopped for a rest we sat right on the edge of the canal. What a relief it was to dip our bath towels in the canal to cool our heads, necks and arms during the rest periods. Just before we started each time I soaked my towel again to carry it over my neck and shoulders, adding greatly to my comfort for the next ten minutes.

SAN FERNANDO

At the first halt, I noticed two grayhaired, graybearded officers whom I judged to be almost sixty years old. They were emaciated, their faces were haggard and it was obvious that they were having a hard time. They kept going, however, and finished the march making up their lack of energy with brains and will power. Four men much younger than the grayheads could not keep up with them. When we fell in to continue the march after the last halt just two miles out of San Fernando, which was our destination for the day, the four young men did not get up. We expected them to be shot, but the sentry called two calesas[15] which were standing nearby, ordering the Filipino drivers to load the four men and deliver them to the prison enclosure. To our surprise, they sped by us in style, arriving in camp long before us. That was the only instance I know of when a Nip guard gave a prisoner any consideration whatsoever.

The enclosure at San Fernando was built around a cockpit, but instead of sitting up in the seats we slept on the ground underneath them.[16] The camp was plenty large so we did not have to worry about cramped sleeping accommodations, all we had to do was to lie down in the dust and filth almost any place. The dust and the filth were nothing new for we had experienced the same conditions in all of the enclosures in which we had stopped. They had been used by large groups of prisoners, sometimes Filipinos, sometimes Americans, for the previous five days. Any sod that may have survived the hot season had been trampled into dust by the passing of many feet long before we arrived.

Numerous partially filled latrines were scattered over the area and, judging from the general accumulation of filth, there was no reason to believe that any effort had been made to police it. Everyone who has served with native troops is well aware of the aversion which they have for constructed latrines and how little they believe in the desirability of keeping their living areas clean. Those characteristics, added to the weakened physical condition of the prisoners and to the prevalence of dysentery, accounted for the indescribably unsanitary conditions in all the areas through which we passed.

It was indeed fortunate that the extreme weariness of mind and body partially dulled our perceptabilities [*sic*] to the horrible conditions under which we existed. Generally there was no water available for washing either our bodies or our eating utensils, which partially accounts for the huge death rate which overtook us after we arrived at Camp O'Donnell.[17]

A TRAIN RIDE TO CAMP O'DONNELL

On our second day, [April 21, 1942,] at San Fernando, after our morning meal of rice and salt, we had a call for five hundred men to leave at once. We moved out from San Fernando cockpit and marched to the station of the narrow gauge railroad where we were loaded into steel boxcars, eighty men to a car.[18] There was standing room only in the cars, which the sun soon made into sweat boxes. We had about thirty miles to go, but it took three hours to make that distance.

As we passed through Angeles and Dau, which are near Fort Stotsenburg, the stations were crowded with Filipinos, some of whom I recognized. Many of them had small packages of food which they tried to hand to us. The Nip guards drove them back from the train and the Filipinos had to content themselves with throwing their packages at the car doors. It had been the same story all along the route of march; whenever we had passed Filipinos they had tried to share their meager food with us and the Nip guards had always driven them away.

When we arrived at Capas, the railhead for Camp O'Donnell, we were formed into the usual columns to march the remaining eight miles. Upon coming over the top of the last hill, with the camp in sight about a mile away, the head of the column picked up speed, leaving the weaker men struggling in the rear. Before the column came to a halt for the normal rest period, those stragglers almost lost their lives merely because they were being left behind.

Finally we arrived at our new home, but we were not allowed to enter until we had been searched by the Nip guards. Several of our friends in the camp came as close as they dared to tell us to be sure we had no articles of Japanese equipment or money on us at the approaching search. Two American officers were found with Japanese money and were immediately marched to be summarily executed. The rest of us were held waiting for the Nip commandant who was to give us a Japanese welcome.[19]

When he arrived he mounted a platform and, assembling us closely around it, he addressed us through a poorly Trinidad Nip interpreter. The Nip commandant was [a] diminutive captain barely five feet tall. We estimated that he was over sixty years old, and we guessed that those years had not been kind to him. His uniform was about two sizes too large, which caused speculation as to whether that was because the uniform manufacturers in Japan did not make clothes small enough for him. Later, we learned that he had been retired for twenty years until he had been called back on active duty again only a few months before. Possibly he had been a more robust man in his younger days before old age had shrunk him.

When he started speaking, it was hard to believe that so small a creature could make so much noise. While we could not understand a word he said, we did not have to wait for the interpreter to know that we did not like him or what he said. Blood rushed into his contorted face as he spoke, and his eyes flashed more venom than a cobra. He told us that Japan had won the war already and she would never give back an inch of ground she had gained if she had to fight five hundred years. He told us we were captives, cowardly and dishonorable, and that we were not to be considered as prisoners of war. He told us that we must obey explicitly all his orders or suffer death, and that we must remember the United States could never do anything to help us because our army had been defeated and our navy sunk.

The commandant continued his shouting for twenty minutes, but long before he departed we knew positively that never could we expect consideration from a man who hated Americans as much as he. As the commandant strutted away we heard a stage whisper from our party saying, "Little Hitler himself, isn't he?" With that wonderful welcome we ended that Death March to become residents of Camp O'Donnell.

PART 2

Last Days of Freedom

Chapter 5

Building Up a Wall of Fear

One morning when he opened his eyes, the first thing he saw was the rising sun. The morning haze being almost a fog, it filtered out the bright rays so that the sun shining through it looked like a dull red ball which at that moment appeared to be resting on the distant line of the hills. Becoming aware that the ball was moving away, he got out of bed to go to the window where he could watch it better. He continued gazing at the sun, fascinated by its unusual appearance, until he heard his wife strike a match to light a cigarette.

After he turned away from the window, she said, "You must be getting well for you haven't been out of bed for a week until today."

"Maybe so," [he replied], "Did you plug the percolator in?"

"Oh, I forgot to bring it up last night," [she answered.]

"Do I have to go get it?"

"Don't be silly," [she said finally.] "You had better put this blanket around you and get back to bed."

When she came back he was sitting up in bed working a crossword puzzle, but he promptly put it down to reach for the coffee cup. After two cups of coffee, he sat up straight and stretched.

"Do you feel like talking today?" she asked.

"I feel fine," he said, "That big bloody rising sun reminded me acutely of Japan and the war. The Nips loved to call Japan the land of the rising sun; of course you remember that their national flag was a sun. The flag used exclusively by the 'Imperial Japanese Army' was nothing but a rectangle of white cotton cloth almost filled by a bright red ball. At the start of the war we insisted that it was a setting sun, instead of a rising one, and we never changed our opinion during the tough days of our long imprisonment.

"The Nip planes were marked with a red dot on each wing, which was what we habitually looked for on every plane that came over. One of our pilots, who had been in Australia at the time of Pearl Harbor, insisted that everyone down south called the plane markings bloody a—holes. Now that I seem to have the urge, I might as well tell what I can remember about the shooting war."

[Hearing this she replied,] "I have been waiting for you to tell me about that for a long time."

IN THE BEGINNING

You remember, of course, when we were at Fort Stotsenburg, before you had to come home, how often I pointed to rugged [Mount] Pinatubo and its jungle-covered foothills to tell you how much more friendly that Negrito land was than a Nip prison camp could ever be.[1] And I am sure you will never forget how we spent the Sundays of your last weeks visiting Lingayen,[2] Bataan, and Olongapo so that you would know the country that was soon to make headlines. You probably recall the tortuous Zig Zag road we had to go up and down again on our visit to Olongapo.[3] That was the Zig Zag where the American 38th Division had such a hard sledding in the spring of 1945.[4]

There never were any doubts about the intention of the Nips, the only question was when were they going to start [the attack on the Philippines]. I clung to a forlorn hope that I could finish my tour and get back home before they started, because I knew our pitifully weak military force[5] was nothing but a sacrifice force, which could expect to hold the Nips six months at best.[6]

To my misfortune, the Nips came too soon, for I had one month left on my tour at the time of Pearl Harbor. As I recall, it was on the first of December 1941 that [Major] General [Edward P.] King came back from Manila, where he had attended a commander's conference at General MacArthur's headquarters.[7]

Assembling us at his office, he informed us that General MacArthur was of the opinion we would be at war within two weeks and he had directed that appropriate protective measures be taken.[8] The next day all of our ground forces left [the] barracks, taking up concealed bivouacs in the nearby jungle.

At breakfast on the morning of 7 December [1941,] our radio told us that Pearl Harbor had been attacked with considerable naval damage. The announcement brought our breakfast to a mournful end, for we knew war was inevitable, and that we were on the hottest of the war's hot seats.[9]

As we went about our duties that morning we had little more information, but we heard a rumor that Baguio had been bombed.[10] At lunch that day I turned on the radio at 12:30 P.M. to hear the news from Don Bell, our favorite Manila announcer.[11] He reported that Baguio had been bombed that morning and there was an unconfirmed rumor that [the bombing of] Clark Field also had been initiated. Clark Field being less than a mile from where we were sitting, I laughed as I started to say, "Another example of the accuracy of the news."

In the middle of the sentence my face froze, for I became aware of the whistling approach of hundreds of bombs. This shrieking was followed by terrific explosions, which made our house shake and groan like it was in the midst of a violent earthquake. We rushed out to the parade ground to see columns of smoke and dust rising from the airfield. Searching the sky, I discovered the attackers, a V-shaped formation of fifty-four bombers, high up, at perhaps 20,000 feet heading for home. The war had begun for us.

Every day, and frequently several times a day, for the next two weeks we were under bombardment. We watched the disappearing bombers for several minutes before we went into the house to get our hats. [One particular time] we were out front in the car, heading for the scene of the bombing before the Nip Zeros[12] appeared, possibly twenty of them. As they started working Clark Field over, which they continued to do for what seemed like a half-hour, we lost no time in abandoning the car to take to the road-side ditches, from where we watched the performance. Apparently the purpose of the Zeros was to destroy everything the bombers had missed, for they dived repeatedly, strafing and bombing.

From what I saw later and from talking to our pilots, I am convinced that most of the damage done to our planes caught on the field was done by the Zeros. Apparently all our defenses were caught by surprise, although I heard some ground fire from automatic weapons and machine guns, and I did see two Zeros crash. After all but one of the Zeros had gone, we resumed our journey, watching the lone plane very carefully. Before we had gone a quarter of a mile we were most happy to see that last one disappear, trailing a long stream of black smoke.

At the edge of the flying field, we met a highly excited young fighter pilot who was somewhat the worse for wear. He told me that there had been eighteen P-40s on the field being serviced when the attack started, all of the pilots being in the BOQ [Bachelor Officers' Quarters] having lunch. He said one bomb made a direct hit on the BOQ killing several men, the others running for their planes. The first three fighters got off, but a Zero caught the next three just as they were about to leave the ground. Two of them burned, but one got away, he being the last one. Our friend was the pilot of the left plane of the third group which was starting to take off when they were hit. With his plane on fire, he swerved to the left off the field to escape with a scalp wound and a few cuts and bruises.

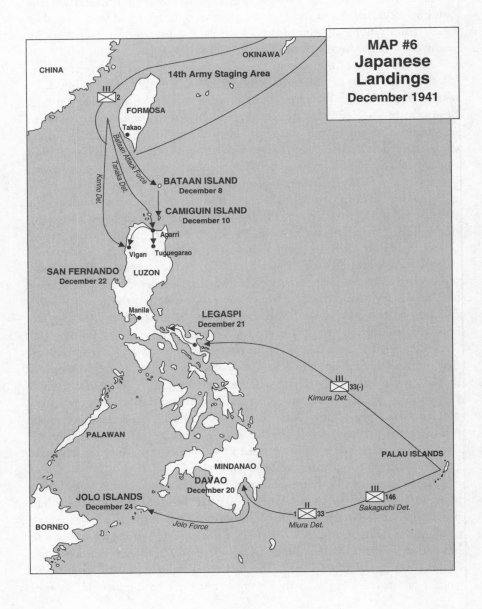

As we passed the commanding officer's quarters, he was standing on his front porch looking ruefully at the damaged field. I asked him if his personnel had suffered many casualties. He answered that he did not know exactly, but he was afraid that there were many. We helped get the wounded to the hospital before we rode around the field counting the wrecked planes. We saw more than fifty of all types, some burned, some burning, but many of them merely riddled by Zero bullets. We stopped by slit trenches, which were near the barracks and hangars, where we heard many stories of gallantry and many others of narrow escapes.

THE HEROES IN THE FACE OF THE UNKNOWN

The army chaplain, Blake,[13] I believe his name was, who went over on the boat with us, had distinguished himself by rescuing wounded all during the attack, for which action he received a high decoration two weeks later. The poor man died in 1944 while in the hands of the Nips without having seen his medal.

[A] sergeant, who was commissioned on Bataan in January 1942, explained how he happened to be living on borrowed time. He was standing by the V of a slit trench trying to induce two recruits to take cover. The recruits jumped in just as a bomb hit inside the tip of the V killing both of them, while the sergeant standing outside did not receive a scratch.

I also learned [during the attack] that all wire communication with Manila was out, which explained why the air warning system had failed. That same afternoon the Clark Field troops started moving to the jungle, completing the move by noon the next day [December 10, 1941]. From that day until they evacuated the field two weeks later they were commuters from their jungle camps.

The mention of the gallant Chaplain Blake reminds me of his penetrating voice and how fast he talked, and that I received my last airmail letter from you a few days before Pearl Harbor. You had written it from the army hospital in San Francisco where the kid was recovering from his operation.[14] I remember you told me about the obnoxious woman who came through the ward asking the soldiers very personal questions and offering to save their souls. When she came to the kid she exclaimed, "My young friend I know you go to Sunday school." You told me how embarrassed you were that, before you could open your mouth, the kid answered that at Stotsenburg he went every Sunday, but when Chaplain Blabbermouth Blake started to talk he sneaked out the window and ran away to play. The woman, with her mouth wide open, stared at him stunned, until the roars of the soldiers in the ward convinced her that she had business elsewhere.

And you [also] told me about Joe E. Brown coming through the ward with Dr. "Brick" Mueller, California's famous football All-American.[15] They stopped to talk to the kid with Joe E. Brown launching a monologue on football, but he did not get very far before the kid interrupted to tell him a football story. Joe, looking sadly at Brick, pointed to the kid saying, "There is the only man who knows more than I do." And I suppose you will deny following that story with, "Chip off the old Block."

The day after the beginning of the war, we were advised by Manila that for the time being we at Stotsenburg were to function as a general depot for Clark Field and all other troops within our reach. That was our job until, on the twenty-third of December, we received secret orders to evacuate the post and proceed to Bataan. We had two weeks of war at Stotsenburg before we received the order and, believe me, they were well-filled days and nights, too.

We obtained aviation gasoline, spare parts and food for Clark Field, gasoline for the tanks, and food, gasoline, and supplies for all nearby troops who were not supplied from other sources. We shipped parts salvaged from the damaged planes and trainloads of wounded to Manila. To do our work we had to take over all civilian trucks we could get our hands on and to utilize all teams and wagons we had.

There being a great need for labor, we hired all the Filipino civilians we could get to come to the post. The civilians we had employed regularly as laborers were called the "Bull Gang."[16] Most of them stayed with us, bringing in a few friends. Some of those laborers worked as faithfully as men could work, going on to Bataan with us when we left the post. Even with the addition of the new civilians we always had a labor shortage which our few soldiers, both American and Filipino, tried to make up for.

Our bakery personnel were divided into shifts so that the ovens were kept busy constantly day and night. While our work was interrupted many times by air attacks, we soon learned to get back to duty immediately after the raids were over so as to lose the least amount of time.

AMERICA'S FIRST HERO OF WORLD WAR II

The saddest duty we had to do at Stotsenburg was to bury our friend Colin Kelly.[17] Kelly came to live with our small group about three months after you left. He was a wonderful youngster who would certainly have been a top notch combat commander in the air corps if he had lived a little longer. Everyone who knew him had great faith in him and affection for him. As I recall, when I wrote you about my B-17 ride with Kelly down to Mindanao, you answered that regardless of how much confidence I had in Kelly, for me to keep my feet on the ground.

A few days after the war started, Kelly's squadron was loading bombs at Clark Field for an attack on a Japanese naval force reported to be moving south in the waters of Northern Luzon,[18] when the warning of an approaching air attack forced all planes to take off. According to report, Kelly was the only one of his squadron to go looking for trouble, although he had time to load only three five-hundred-pound bombs. North of the bay at Aparri, Kelly sighted a large ship, which later was identified as the old Nip battleship *Kongo*.[19] Before he started a practice bombing run, he saw three Zeros taking off from the Aparri airfield, but they disappeared.

He continued the practice run and, in spite of considerable anti-aircraft fire, he circled to make his business run over the big ship. The second run, including the release of the bombs, was nothing but routine target practice. The bombs hit in a perfect bracket; the first one a near miss on the port bow, the second one amidship and the third one a near miss on the starboard stern. Smoke streamed from the ship as all escort vessels, in order to get out of range of a possible explosion, moved away from it at full speed. Heading for home, the last sight they had of the *Kongo* [was that] she was still belching smoke, and moving slowly toward shore.

Manila's radios and newspapers reported the ship as sunk, but we heard later she stayed afloat to be towed to Japan for extensive repairs. Kelly was very proud of his crew as he left the scene of his success homeward bound. After an uneventful trip, he started to let down when Clark Field came in sight, and he called his bottom gunner to the radio to get authority to land. The gunner was still at the radio when the plane came out of an overcast to start its approach to the field. Without any warning whatever the instrument panel began to disintegrate, followed almost immediately by the explosion of the oxygen tank. Kelly was blown out of the escape hatch, followed by all of the crew except the copilot, who, try as he might, could not move. The plane was in a tight spin, the copilot being held fast by the centrifugal force until a sudden unexpected lurch released him to follow the others out of the hatch.

When [the copilot] told me this story later, he said that the Zeros, which they had seen taking off at Aparri, had followed them in under the clouds to make their attack without anyone suspecting they were there. The Zeros followed the crew down after they had bailed out, shooting at them all the way, but they hit only one member of the crew, and his wound was not serious. After the Zeros had gone, the crew found Kelly dead with his chute unopened, which led them to believe that he had been knocked unconscious as he went out the hatch. The rescue squad, which brought the crew to Clark Field, left Kelly's body at the Stotsenburg Hospital where we held the funeral services that night.

USING THE RAIL SYSTEM
At the start of the war a strict blackout was imposed on Stotsenburg and Clark Field which did not bother us at all when we had moonlight, but after the moon disappeared we were left in total darkness. What made our activities at night still more exciting was the establishment of a heavy guard. The guards were composed of old retired Philippine scouts, who reported for duty at the post as soon as they heard about the war. No more devoted and loyal soldiers lived than those old scouts, but most of them were decrepit, few of them had handled firearms since they had retired and none of them were very familiar with the post. They could do guard duty, but little else. After one of them accidentally shot himself in the leg with his pistol, we developed a considerable caution in passing sentry posts at night.

One dark night Hugh and I had to go to the hospital. Hugh doing the driving, I had my head out of the window listening intently for sentry challenges when we ran off the road at an intersection to bang into the curb. My head bounced off the door jamb, cutting a gash in my forehead, but Hugh promptly got us to the hospital where I acquired three stitches.

After the doctor was through, he gave me a mirror to see his handiwork. At that particular moment my head looked so bad to me that I could not help saying, "My God, what a face," to which he replied, "You should remember you were no lily to begin with." I had a laugh at his retort, and the only answer I could think of was that I was thankful one did not have to be a lily to have a good time.

Why we did not take over the railroad system in the islands I do not know, but actually we did continue to get a fairly good service in spite of the bombings.[20] I sent Sergeant Castro, a fine scout soldier, to the junction at Dau to represent our office with the main line officials of the railroad, and he never failed to fill our needs.

Beginning on the ninth of December, the railroad stations in Northern Luzon were required to report all planes heading south by the number, type and time of passing.[21] This information was valuable to us as it gave us advance warning of bombing raids; however, it was of more value to the station master for he, getting the message first, promptly took off to the jungle on the dead run leaving his assistant to handle his business. He always came sauntering slowly back after a safe interval, his dignified appearance being in sharp contrast to his earlier frantic sprint toward the jungle.

About the middle of December, we started shipping the sick and wounded to Manila by special train, once a day. It made no difference what time of day we scheduled the train, it seemed to me that the bombers always came over to cause us as much trouble as possible, but we were never hit.

Some of the Nip planes had a peculiar whine which was distinct from the sound of ours. A number of individuals, after a little exposure to bombings, became self acknowledged experts in identifying an approaching plane as Nip or American by the sound of the motor, but most of us continued to look for the wing markings.

One day a pompous officer came to the station to watch us load a train of wounded. While we were in the process of loading, a lone plane circled the area keeping so far away that we could not see its markings. Our pompous friend shouted for us to go on with our work because the plane was a P-40 as anyone could tell by its sound.[22] On its next trip around the plane dropped a stick of bombs which hit some distances away, but our friend departed as fast as he could go. To us, that officer was known thereafter as Colonel P-40.

We had a number of litter patients to go on each train, which usually meant we had to put the litters on the top of the seat backs because, as a rule, we were furnished day coaches. That arrangement was not too awkward, because we could put litter cases on one side with walking patients on the other side to watch them.

Each train was manned by a doctor and such nurses and soldiers as our surgeon thought were needed.[23] For equipment the doctor brought a medical chest, and we placed a large can of water in each car. One of my jobs was to go throughout the train after it was loaded to count the passengers so that I could give the station agent the transportation request for their fare.

One day after it was loaded, I was passing through the train counting just as the bombers arrived. By that time the bombers had ceased to worry us so much as they did at first. That day all I had left to count were two cars of litter cases, so I continued counting while doctors, nurses and walking patients all ran for the safety of the trenches.

About the middle of the last coach, I passed a good looking sergeant with one leg in a cast resting peacefully on a litter. After I had passed him I heard him say, "Stay with me baby." I whirled around to see that I was being followed by a charming young Filipino nurse. I could not blame the sergeant for being interested, for she was a petite mestiza who was really lovely despite the fact that she wore no makeup. Her trim figure was clad in [a] newly starched white uniform which, obviously, had been made for her. She moved gracefully, eluding the sergeant's outstretched hand to follow me out of the car. Once outside on the platform she became panicky and, with no one else in sight to turn to, she rushed up to me almost throwing her arms around me as she wailed, "Major, Major, where can I go?"[24] As soon as I pointed out the trenches to her she deserted me, running like a frightened deer to the trench into which I had seen the surgeon's gray head disappear and, leaping into the air, she also disappeared into the middle of it.

I have asked myself many times why I did not conduct her personally to a place of safety, but the only answer I have ever found was that I had work to do. After the raid was over, the surgeon had to be helped out of the trench for he was so fat that he had to be helped out on previous occasions.

After the girl left me, I ran down to the engine to find it unoccupied, but the engine men came back a few minutes after the raid was over so that they were ready to pull out by the time we were loaded. The last train with the remainder of the patients and nurses left on the twenty-fourth of December [1941]. That was our most troublesome train, for in addition to Nip annoyance we had to get a large number of litter patients and the nurses aboard in time to make train connections.

Almost immediately after the arrival of the busload of nurses, the bombers visited us, but [since] all of the patients had not arrived, we had to wait. We tried to make the nurses reasonably comfortable in the shade, not too far from our cold storage plant, so that they could take refuge inside it if they felt like it. One of the nurses told me that her nerves were shot, making her feel sick [to] her stomach. I could understand perfectly how badly her edgy nerves could make her feel, so I took her to the [building that used to be the] finance office where she [sat in] an easy chair near the concrete vault which had guarded our money until a few days before. All she had to do when the bombs started to fall was to step inside the concrete walls of the vault.

The last load of patients arriving at last, we proceeded with the loading. After the patients were aboard and the nurses were getting on, the bombers paid us a surprise visit, dropping a few bombs pretty near us which started a stampede for shelter by everyone who could walk. I looked in the big horse car in which we had loaded most of our litter cases to find everything in the greatest confusion because a number of men had tried to crawl toward the door when the bombing started. I called to a nurse who was standing in the doorway of the cold storage plant. She brought a doctor and the three of us untangled the litter patients to rearrange the car.

We had just finished that job when the bombers returned, but they dropped no bombs for a change. The nurse stayed with the patients who gave us no more concern, because her calm and confident presence gave them all of the encouragement they needed. In my opinion, the voluntary decision of the nurse to stay with the patients during a raid, instead of seeking shelter, was noteworthy. I do not believe she ever received recognition, although I made an official report of the incident in writing.

Leaving word to get the nurses aboard as soon as the raid was over, I went to the engine, only to find no trainmen again. Going on down the track a short distance, I found them in a ditch. After I had convinced them the immediate danger was over, they came back with me. Five minutes later the train departed and five minutes after that the bombers returned, but the train, speeding on its way, reached Manila safely.

EARNING THE SILVER STAR

The surgeon came by just before he left to tell me that the Christmas dinner including turkey had already been prepared at the hospital, but that they had been forced to leave it in the kitchen ready to eat when they had evacuated the hospital. He suggested that I go get it for my men, but I was so busy with more important matters that I forgot all about it. Many times during our long periods of semistarvation I thought of that big turkey which had been left to rot.

A couple of days after the war started my nerves were so much on edge that I felt sick as a dog. Making a special trip to the hospital, I found the surgeon coming out of his air raid shelter. After I had explained that I needed something to relax my inside so I could work, he gave me a pill and a small bottle of belladona with written instructions for using it. That medicine proved to be an effective cure for the few cases of nervous strain that I had during the war.

I had hardly got out of the hospital when its air alarm sounded. Looking toward Clark Field I saw nine bombers coming out of a very low overcast, heading directly my way.[25] Sticks of bombs started falling from the leading planes before my feet started acting, but when they did start they moved me in record time the fifty yards I had to go to the culvert which ran under the road between where the Granades and we used to live.[26] I dived in the entrance urged on by the explosions of the first bombs.

Before the bombing ended my eyes became sufficiently adjusted to the semidarkness for me to see two other men who had sought shelter there. They were two Filipinos, who at that moment were the whitest ones I had ever seen. Their faces were stricken with such terror and their bodies were shaking so violently that I could not help roaring with laughter. At first, they looked at me as if I was demented, then when they realized I was laughing at them they looked so unpleasant I was glad I had my gun. You may be sure that as soon as it was safe to go, I left.

When I got back to my office, it was reported that approximately twenty-five bombs had fallen in our area of which only five had exploded. My boss, [Lieutenant] Colonel "Pop" Durst, who came up at that time, looked like he had been playing with a wild cat, for his face and hands were cut and scratched and his clothes torn and dirty.[27] A big slug of whisky would have done him a bit of good, but we did not have it. He sat down weakly, almost whispering, "If I had been a fast man I wouldn't be here now."

He told me he had come out of the office to see a big stick of bombs heading his way. Almost without thinking, he was following the station agent, running the fastest race of his life, when one of the bombs overtook him, [exploding] directly in front of him not more than forty feet away. The noise of the explosion, with its accompanying burst of red light, helped him set his brakes and dive into a ditch alongside the road. He thought his time had come, but after the bombs had gone a little experimenting with his limbs convinced him that he could walk back, although he had lost his desire to run. There were numerous pieces of sand in his face and hands, but no bomb fragments. He called the ordnance officer, asking him to come and help us get rid of the duds in our area, which he did. The ordnance officer pointed out that in many cases the arming devices on the fuses had not been set because the low level attack had not given their wrappings time to come off.

We helped explode the bombs with TNT in order that our men could get back to work. One bomb we could not find, although from the hole in a warehouse roof and another hole in a high stack of canned goods we knew that it was buried somewhere in our food supply. Pop, Pat and I estimated where it was, but we were careful not to let the Bull Gang into the secret.[28]

Our supplies dwindled each day, gradually nearing the bomb. One morning we had a visit from the big Filipino boss of the gang, who informed us that they could not work in the warehouse anymore. Following him to the warehouse he pointed out a one-hundred-pound bomb, which had just been discovered on the floor underneath a small stack of food cases. The Filipinos would not go near it, so Pat and I had to uncover it. Then backing a wagon to the door, four of us carried it out and deposited it ever so gently in the wagon. Pat, driving the wagon, took the bomb a safe distance away where it could be exploded harmlessly. As soon as the bomb was out of sight our men went back to work.

The ordnance officer who came to help us said the bomb was probably safe, but I noticed that the entire time he was near it he was sweating far more than could be explained by his slight physical exertion. I am frank to admit that I also felt vastly better after the thing was gone.[29]

Upon receipt of orders for the evacuation of Stotsenburg we shipped the Clark Field personnel, less the ordnance officer and his work detail, to Manila. The ordnance officer had instructions to destroy whatever bombs were left and all air equipment of value which could not be moved. The property being somewhat scattered, the ordnance officer proceeded methodically to destroy it where it lay. He warned us to protect ourselves at 10:00 P.M. on the twenty-sixth [of December 1941] being the hour he had set for the explosion of the remaining two-thousand pound bombs.

Our job was to ship all useful property which could be moved by rail or truck. That meant working every night for the three remaining nights, using all the civilian and soldier labor we could get to load railroad cars with artillery pieces, ammunition, food and other valuables.

Those were the days of the most back-breaking work for all of us, but there were no complaints from anyone. It saddens me to recall that all our toil was love's labor lost, for the Nips bombed the train which picked up our cars two days later, completely destroying it. The only satisfaction we got out of it was that the Nips did not get to use the supplies either.

We were loading cars with ammunition about a mile from Clark Field on the night of the twenty-sixth of December. Although there had been a number of explosions, some of them of considerable proportion, I had not been concerned because I was convinced we were out of the danger area and that most of the bombs had already been exploded. I had not mentioned the warning the ordnance officer had given me about the danger of explosions as I did not want our work to stop unnecessarily.

A little after 10:00 P.M. six soldiers and I were on a large truck unloading armor piercing shells when an unbelievably terrific explosion occurred at Clark Field. All air seemed to have been forced from around us by the blast, leaving us in a partial vacuum so that it was difficult to breathe.

A guilty feeling that I had used bad judgment in not protecting my men rushed over me. Before I could think of anything to do the six men dived off the truck to crawl under it. Not stopping to consider the problem further I followed them, but by the time I hit the ground all space under the truck had been taken. It seemed to me that it was almost a minute after the explosion occurred before fragments and particles began to fall. After they did start we were treated to a generous serenade of them pattering on the metal roofs nearby. None of them quite reached us, which was a help to me in getting the men back to work. When I talked to the ordnance officer later he told me that the big explosion had been the destruction of six or eight two-thousand-pound bombs.

As soon as we knew we were headed for Bataan, we invited all organizations to come and see what we had.[30] Many supply officers did come, so that by the time we were ready to leave the post, all of the food and clothing were gone. We had given away every drum of gasoline our visitors could haul off, but even so Pop had to destroy part of our supply the morning we left. Of the supplies we had to start with, nothing of value had to be destroyed except gasoline, and nothing of value was left for the Nips. The last thing Pop and I did on Christmas morning before we left Stotsenburg a few days later for a new camp [was] to visit the post cemetery for a final farewell to Kelly, the one member of our household we were leaving behind.

BACK TO THE INFANTRY

Traveling by night, and staying in concealed bivouacs during the day, we reached the heavy jungle of Bataan on the thirty-first of December [1941] without losing a man or a food laden vehicle. My job on the journey was to conceal our camp, men, kitchens, and vehicles before dawn. All day long, every day, there were enemy aircraft overhead, but we escaped their notice for the entire trip.

While we were at breakfast on New Year's Day [1942], I told Pop that I had had enough supply experience and that I would like to get back to an infantry outfit. Immediately he took me to Headquarters Philippine Department to see the commanding general, who at the time was in charge of coast defenses of the southern tip of Bataan.[31] When Pop told him my story he replied, "You are just in time." Then he told us about the Philippine Army regiment on the west coast of Bataan between Mariveles and a point a few miles south of Bagac.[32] He said the regimental commander was a Filipino colonel who had been an aide-de-camp to Mr. [President] Quezon and, while he did not know him personally, he was convinced that he would need plenty of guidance.[33]

He directed an order be issued assigning me as "Senior Advisor" to the regiment and also assured me he was trying to find additional American officers to add to the two captains already assigned to it. I was highly elated as we returned to Pop's camp. After Pop had ordered the cooks to prepare an early lunch, he called Bob, a young recruit truck driver [who had] recently arrived from the Texas panhandle, telling him to collect his equipment and eat chow with me, for he was assigned to act as my driver from then on.

As soon as chow was over Pop helped us to load up the newest car in his pool, and bade us "God Speed." Before we moved off, I asked Pop if he could get Hugh, a young officer from Stotsenburg, pried loose from his cemetery assignment so he could join me as one of the much needed assistants, but he merely shook his head. You can imagine my surprise when, two days later, Hugh, with the happiest grin I had ever seen on his face, reported for duty.

"I am sure glad you got me out [of] that undertaking job," he announced as he produced a couple of cans of beans, which he proceeded to prepare for our supper. Hugh added to the two captains already assigned to the regiment [giving] me an American officer for each battalion.

WITH THE NEW REGIMENT

On my way to join the regiment I stopped to inquire the way from the occupants of a command car which we met at a road fork. It was my good fortune to find that the occupants were Sam and his driver. Sam, who was the senior of the two American captains on duty with the regiment, offered to guide us to the command post, briefing me as we went along.

I rode to regimental headquarters in the command car with Sam, listening to his report on conditions within the regiment as he knew them. The regimental commander greeted me most affably, introducing his staff and bringing me up to date on his problems. I found an understrength regiment of which only a few of the officers and enlisted men had had more than a year of service. The greatest part of their service had been spent in garrison performing administrative duties, not more than a handful of them having had any combat experience.

All except a few of the officers were newly appointed reserves, and except for some of the noncommissioned officers, the men were recruits. None of them had more than a passing acquaintance with the jungle area of our sector. There was an alarming shortage of equipment, what there was being obsolescent if not obsolete. The water distance from the south end of the sector to the north was nearly twenty miles, but the shore line distance, due to the innumerable indentations, was much longer.

The next morning I started a personal reconnaissance of the sector beginning in the north but, because of the few and difficult roads in the sector, which forced me to go on foot across mountain trails and sandy beaches, the going was slow. With the hard going, the many conferences and other duties which I could not avoid, it took me ten days to cover the area.

In the meantime, the defense of the sector was assigned to the 71st Division [(PA)] which came into the area with no infantry troops and only a little artillery.[34] As I was the senior American infantry officer in the sector, the division commander used me as the division infantry advisor, as well as regimental advisor. As soon as I had completed my reconnaissance, I pointed out what I considered the six most critical points along the coast where enemy landings might be made. I then recommended that American air corps squadrons, grounded due to lack of planes, be requested for assignment to the sector for use in the defense of at least three of the most dangerous points.

The general succeeded in obtaining a headquarters squadron and four letter squadrons, three of which were assigned defensive positions to protect the most critical areas, the others being held in divisional reserve.[35] A few of the officers and men of those squadrons, who had served with ground combat units, were of the greatest value because so many of the men were recruits. Most of the men were equipped with the Springfield rifle, although a few had nothing but shotguns. We had no machine guns for them, but they obtained guns salvaged from damaged airplanes, improvising mounts and sights. They were so anxious to learn their ground duties and improve their defensive positions that on every visit a marked improvement could be noted.

On the seventeenth of January [1942] the division commander directed that, with the assistance of his G3, I prepare a plan for the defense of the sector.[36] That afternoon I dictated my plan which his G3 OK'd, and placed on the division commander's desk. He approved and published it without making a change on the eighteenth, sending it out to the major combat units by messenger on the same day. In the meantime, our forces in Northern and Southern Luzon had been forced back to San Fernando, holding the Nips off long enough to permit our troops to make an orderly withdrawal into Bataan, where they occupied prepared positions. The I Corps [was] on the west side [of Bataan with] the II Corps on the east.

The Nips followed the withdrawal rapidly, hitting the II Corps hard, apparently expecting to go right on through, but after making some progress they were stopped cold. They then tried the I Corps on their right with the same result. After the Nips had remained quiet for a few days, except for their air, ground, and naval reconnaissances, we anticipated a new attack to hit us any day, but where [they] would hit we did not have the slightest idea.

Every sector continued to improve its defenses as much as possible. On the morning of the twenty-third of January we were no longer in doubt, for the division commander called me personally to, "Put Plan Four into effect."[37]

ON THE FRONT LINE

The Nips had hit our sector, but very few details were available as we moved out to take our planned counteroffensive action. I was informed that the Nips had attempted to land at Aglaloma Bay, but had been discouraged by the heavy machine-gun fire of our defenders. After they had been driven off they had moved out of sight around Quinauan Point, immediately to the north of Aglaloma Bay, where they probably were in the process of landing.

Aglaloma Bay was the most dangerous locality in our sector because of its deep water favorable for landing and the excellent roads leading from it to the critical West Coast Highway.

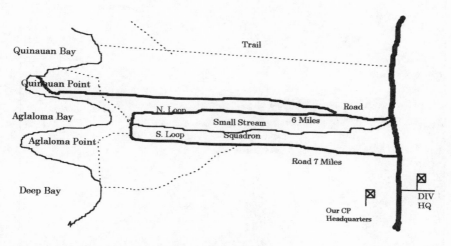

Sketch of Aglaloma Bay Area drawn from Alexander's memory without having seen a map for more than seven years.

It was my opinion that the Nips had not given up their attempt to capture Aglaloma Bay, their assigned mission, and that they would keep on
trying to carry out their mission until they were liquidated. Our mission as
received from higher authority was: first, to prevent an enemy landing
in our sector; and second, in the event a hostile landing was effected, to
isolate the force and destroy it.

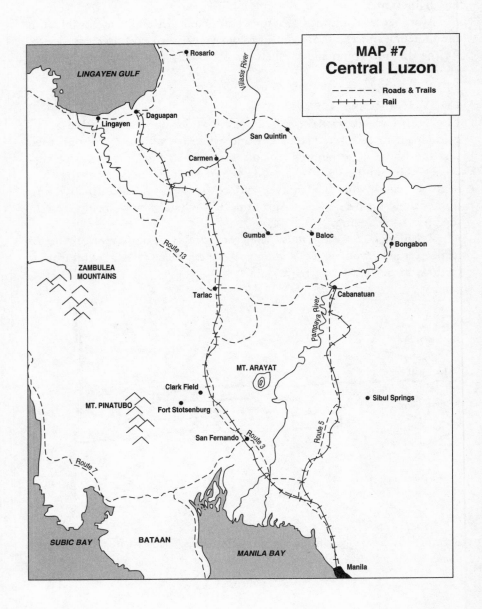

In accordance with these instructions, our Plan Four, which contemplated a hostile landing near Aglaloma Bay, in brief, called for us to hold tight on the sides of the landing force while we attacked it in front with our reserve. My instructions, as we moved out, were for the regimental commander to conduct his reserve battalion[38] via the North Loop Road to its junction with the unimproved road to Quinauan Point; thence, after assuming an appropriate protective formation, to proceed along the unimproved road until he reached the cross trail connecting Aglaloma Bay with Quinauan Bay where I would join him.

Sam was directed to take the trail immediately north of the one followed by the reserve battalion. Until he arrived at Quinauan Bay where, after satisfying himself that there were no Nips in the area, he was to collect the strongest patrol that could be spared and proceed up the trail to Quinauan Point. Matt was to go to the bay just north of Quinauan Bay, alerting and assisting our troops there and, after reconnoitering the area, he was to join me on Quinauan Point.

Hugh and I planned to proceed down the South Loop road to the junction of the road to Deep Bay, alert and assist our troops there, after which he was to reconnoiter Aglaloma Point and rejoin me at Aglaloma Bay. In the event he did not find me, he was to continue on to Quinauan Point. After Hugh left me, I planned to proceed another mile to the headquarters of the [34th Pursuit] Squadron defending Aglaloma Bay and, after taking whatever action might be necessary, I intended to move north up the trail to Quinauan Point.

We moved out without trouble and after starting Hugh on his way [to] the trail junction, we drove on to the headquarters of the squadron. There I directed Bob to load his rifle, but when he tried it he found the gun had a defective bore, which made it no good to him except to use as a club. From that time on he was known to us as "Boob McNutt."

When I located the squadron commander, [1st Lt. Sam Marett,] about 3:00 A.M., he informed me that the Nips had landed at Quinauan Point and driven in the two outposts he had located near the tip of the point. I suggested he send a small patrol to the stream just north of him, with orders to follow it to the bay so that he would be certain no Nips had infiltrated to his back door during the night. [He agreed to this plan and acted on it] immediately.

We then went on down to Aglaloma Bay where I obtained firsthand information of the attempted landing. I advised the squadron commander that it looked like we had the Nips isolated on Quinauan Point, in which case we would attack as soon as we could. For reasons of security, and as a source of information, I ordered him to keep patrols operating along the faint trails on the north and south rims of the little peninsula. Those trails had been patrolled by the squadron prior to the attack, so they were well known to many men of the organization. The patrols which were established helped influence the final result of our fight as I shall tell you later.

Just after daylight Hugh arrived all out of breath, having completed his long scout, mostly on the run. He reported that a Nip force had started to land at Deep Bay, but that our "Q" boats had driven them away in a fast engagement during which several Nip boats had been sunk, the others fleeing toward the south.[39] He had found no evidence of Nips ashore, which was good news indeed.

I telephoned the division commander, giving him the information I had obtained, assuring him that I was well aware of the danger to the highway[40] of a strong Nip force on Quinauan Point, and telling him my plans. He told me that he had just received a message reporting that the Nip boats, probably those running from the engagement at Deep Bay, had landed in a very rough area which our Navy Bluejackets were defending near Mariveles.[41]

He had heard of no report of any Nip landing in our area, except at Quinauan Point. So it was with considerable relief that I headed with a small patrol up the trail to Quinauan. At the junction of the trail with the road on top of the ridge, I contacted the regimental commander and his reserve battalion commander.[42]

The regimental commander reported that he had made contact with the Nips on the road about two hundred yards west of us, but that he did not know how many there were. He stated that he had just given the reserve battalion commander orders to prepare for an immediate attack. I concurred with his action and told him all I knew, including the fact that we had American patrols operating on his flanks. I requested a small patrol to accompany me on a reconnaissance, as I wanted to check the trail on the north side of Quinauan Point.

As soon as the four Filipino soldiers reported to me, we followed an American patrol along the north trail for about a mile, seeing nothing but big trees and matted jungle growth. I began to have some doubts about our impending attack, so I turned the patrol into the jungle to take the shortest route back to where I had left the regimental commander.

We had gone off the trail little more than two hundred yards when we heard a wild burst of small arms fire coming from the direction in which the American patrol had disappeared, then complete silence. I waited a little while but there being no more firing, I continued on my way with my patrol. It was not until late evening that I talked to the leader of the American patrol who told me how they had unexpectedly come face to face with a Nip patrol that was just as surprised as they were. Both patrols took to the jungle before opening fire, so there were no casualties; at least the Americans had none. Apparently both sides had a good scare for neither group continued its advance.

Very soon after the patrols met our attack started, the heavy fire of the action orienting me, so I was able to move the patrol to a position where it could protect our right flank. We had hardly halted when we heard a party of Nips about a hundred yards away. We could make nothing of the incessant chatter, but we could tell that they were carrying heavy loads, for about every minute when they rested we could hear the clatter of several objects hitting the ground.

I knew that the road down which we were attacking bent to the north about two hundred yards from where the attack had started, so from the noise I deduced that the Nip defenders were moving supplies up the road. There was no use in our opening fire because it would not have been effective. The jungle was so thick it would have been necessary to advance within twenty yards of the Nips to see them, which I was trying to decide [if] that was the proper thing to do. I heard a strange noise coming from close by, but it took me about thirty seconds to identify it as the snoring of one [of] my soldiers who was sleeping with his head on his rifle. Our being in the foremost denseness within hearing distance of the Nips had not prevented one good soldier from getting his rest.

The noise of the firing remaining stationary, it was clear that the attack was making no progress, so I decided to see what could be done about it. I gave the patrol leader hurried orders to stay where he was to protect the north flank before I ran through the jungle toward the sound of the firing. That I arrived safely at my destination was due to the good fortune that there were no Nips along the way.

Upon my arrival at the position of the battalion I was informed [that the attack] had been halted by heavy rifle and machine-gun fire from the Nip position astride the road. The size of the enemy force was undetermined, but it might have been as much as a battalion judging from the sound of the firing.[43] The battalion commander explained that he had attacked frontally without making any attempt to explore either flank. When I tried to get a company to make an envelopment of the right flank of the Nip position I got nowhere, because the Filipinos did not want to leave the vicinity of the road.

After I had moved over to the right of the line to try to start the envelopment myself, the Nips must have spotted me for they opened up with heavy machine-gun [fire] which snipped off many leaves uncomfortably close to my head. I lost no time hitting the dirt, but before my head got there a bullet struck the ground in the same spot where my head hit an instant later.

Wiping the dirt out of my eyes, I realized I was badly scared, so much so that my brain seemed to be paralyzed. My mind seemingly refused to tell me what I needed to do until a slow, dry voice from the other side of the road queried, "That guy was sort of shooting at you, wasn't he?" In spite of myself I had to laugh at the lugubrious voice which broke the tension that had gripped me. Across the road I spotted the owner of the voice. He was an engineer officer who had no business being there, but just couldn't stay away from the shooting.

I explained to the battalion commander the necessity for a flanking attack and assured him that I would go with it. A Filipino corporal, who saw the logic in my plan, jumped up shouting and kicking his men to get them moving. It was difficult to get the men started, but we had begun to get results when the Nip machine [gun] opened up again, killing the corporal and several men, thereby putting a stop to our flanking attack. That corporal was a gallant man who deserved recognition, but later, when I tried to find out his name, I was unable to locate anyone who even remembered the incident.

Before the attack had started, a platoon from the squadron at Aglaloma Bay arrived, and moving into position on the left of the battalion, they participated in the attack, advancing some distance before they were stopped by heavy fire. With the attack bogged down, I realized I had to get help to accomplish my mission.[44] Leaving instructions that no ground should be given up, I advised the regimental commander that I was going to a telephone to report our progress to the division commander. My engineer friend, who had remained to help rescue the wounded, promised that he would stay there until I got back. He was the only American present for Sam and Matt had not been seen since we left camp, and I had sent Hugh to [Quinauan] Bay to find out what was happening there, but I hoped they would all be back by the time I had returned from the telephone.

The nearest telephone was at Aglaloma Bay about two miles away by trail. The trail was winding and did not lead directly there, so hoping to save time I started on the run across country through heavy jungle. Again, luck was with me for I met no Nips, and the journey being largely down grade I did not lose any time.

As I approached the bay, the jungle became more dense and slowed me down [and] I had almost reached open country when I came to a steep decline which would have been called a cliff back home. In the tropics where vegetation grows everywhere, it was no surprise to me to find that the declivity was covered with vines, roots and shrubs. Half walking and half scooting on my behind, I made good progress on the way down until one foot slipped, at the same time the other caught in a root.

Without my being able to do a thing about it, my head changed places with my feet, in which position I began a headlong flight on my belly, coming to an end thirty feet down where the ground flattened out near the beach. I got back on my feet somewhat painfully, for on that slide of such a short distance my whole body had been in contact with numerous hard and sharp objects, but I was none the worse for wear except that both of my hands were full of very fine thorns which I did not have time to remove.

A few minutes after I picked myself up, I reached the telephone to report the tactical situation to the division commander, requesting both artillery and tank support. I also told him that I thought the Nips had landed a reinforced battalion of sufficient strength to require American or scout troops to dislodge him. He directed me to stay by the telephone until he called me again.[45]

While I was waiting for the return call, Hugh showed up, reporting that everything was quiet in the Quinauan Bay area, but that he could get no information [on] Sam or Matt. A detachment of one of the air squadrons in division reserve reported to me at the telephone where I was waiting for the general's call, so I sent it with Hugh to follow the trail up the ridge to its intersection with the road leading to Quinauan Point. He was to form a reserve, waiting for me there until I arrived to set up a command post.

When the division commander called he first told me that he was sending Doc Smith[46] and a medical section to meet me on the point, then he told me that there was no artillery available at the moment, that the use of tanks was not considered practicable, and that all of the two reserve squadrons were being sent to me.

I advised him of the location of my headquarters on Quinauan Point, and requested telephone communications. He said that he would see that I got a phone but that it would take time to install it, then he said that he was sending two British Bren gun carriers to report to me at Aglaloma where I was at the telephone, and that I should wait for them to conduct them to Quinauan Point.[47]

It was dark before the Bren carriers reached me, so we lost no time in starting up the hill [to] Quinauan Point. The carriers which had engines and track-like tanks made a great deal of noise advertising to the Nips that we were being reinforced by heavy equipment.

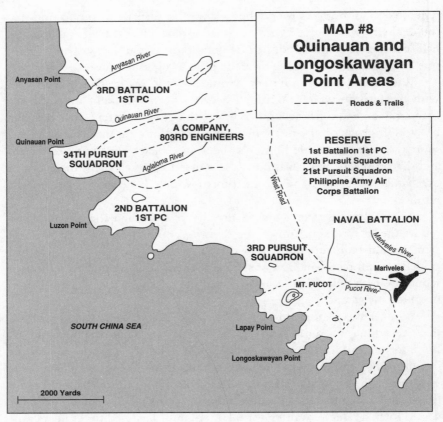

MAP #8
Quinauan and Longoskawayan Point Areas

- - - - - - Roads & Trails

Anyasan River

Anyasan Point

**3RD BATTALION
1ST PC**

Quinauan River

**A COMPANY,
803RD ENGINEERS**

Quinauan Point

**34TH PURSUIT
SQUADRON**

Aglaloma River

RESERVE
**1st Battalion 1st PC
20th Pursuit Squadron
21st Pursuit Squadron
Philippine Army Air
Corps Battalion**

West Road

**2ND BATTALION
1ST PC**

Luzon Point

NAVAL BATTALION

Mariveles River

**3RD PURSUIT
SQUADRON**

Mariveles

MT. PUCOT   Pucot River

SOUTH CHINA SEA

Lapay Point

Longoskawayan Point

2000 Yards

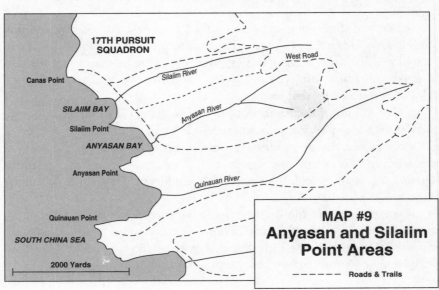

**17TH PURSUIT
SQUADRON**

West Road

Canas Point

Silaiim River

SILAIIM BAY

Silaiim Point

Anyasan River

ANYASAN BAY

Anyasan Point

Quinauan River

Quinauan Point

SOUTH CHINA SEA

MAP #9
Anyasan and Silaiim Point Areas

- - - - - - Roads & Trails

2000 Yards

At the east of Aglaloma Bay, before we turned east on the North Loop, we met a stretcher detail carrying a wounded officer to the dressing station at Aglaloma Bay. The wounded officer, on hearing my voice, stopped his party to talk to me. Turning on my flashlight, I recognized the commander of the air detachment that had been fighting alongside the reserve battalion all afternoon.[48] He had been hit rather painfully, late that afternoon, making it necessary for him to relinquish command. He insisted on bringing me up to date on the tactical situation before he went on to the dressing station. For his fine combat performance I helped to get him a Silver Star after the action was over.

Riding one of the carriers was a novelty for me, and although the ride was rough, I was glad of a chance to rest my "dogs." We continued east along the North Loop until we reached the road junction which led to Quinauan. We had gone down that road only a short distance when we overtook one of the reserve squadrons which was under orders to report to me.

Taking up a short advance guard, we proceeded on our way until we reached the road junction with the cross trail, where we joined our reserve. There Hugh, who had established a headquarters for me, reported that our troops in the attacking force were sleeping on their arms where I had left them, and that the location of the battalion command post was along the road only two hundred yards north and south of our reserve, adding to our regular patrols a half-hour patrol between the reserve battalion and our headquarters.

A small area was set aside as a bivouac area, where we went to sleep without unrolling our packs. Before I could get to sleep Matt reported in to tell me that everything was quiet to the north of us, but that he had heard nothing of Sam. Matt's report was all I needed to assure me that we had the Nips bottled up on a little peninsula and that from then on I could concentrate on my mission of keeping them where they were until they could be destroyed. To destroy them we had to continue attacking, although in the prolonged offensive action we could not avoid numerous casualties among our own troops. I realized that, very probably, I would be under fire again, but I did not worry too much about that.

Up until that day I had always worried a little bit as to how I might react under small arms fire when I came to grips with the enemy. I knew that I would be frightened, but I wanted to be assured I could control that fear. I wanted to be able to do my duty regardless of danger, and be sure that my family would never have cause to feel that I had disgraced them. The brief action of the first day had led me to believe that I could *wall in my fear* and continue to do my job even though the going was tough, a most comfortable thought on which I dropped off to sleep.

Chapter 6

Heroism and Convalescence

EARNING THE DISTINGUISHED SERVICE CROSS

Some of our men stirring around a little after 4:00 A.M. on the twenty-fourth of January [1942] woke me up. It was still dark, but there was a faint hint in the sky that day would soon break. Many of us were sitting up trying to rub the sleep out of our eyes when all hell broke loose. Apparently, the Nips opened up with all of their machine guns and automatic weapons at a given signal. Bullets were cracking in the air above us cutting many leaves from the trees around us. The sitting bodies of our reserve forces swayed and rolled to the ground like stalks of corn being blown over by a sudden violent wind.

As bullets were passing well overhead, everyone was sitting up again in a moment wondering what was happening. The firing lasted for two or three minutes then abruptly ceased, leaving us in painful silence. Immediately I started a new patrol down the road toward our front line to find out how our troops were behaving. Fifteen minutes later I had a report that all was quiet there, so I concluded that the enemy opened up just to discourage a daylight attack by our troops.

After daylight, a small headquarters battalion of Filipinos reported to me. The division commander having started them to me the afternoon before [obviously didn't know] the country, [for] the battalion had spent the night [only] a half mile away.[1]

While we had a bite of cold breakfast I started planning a new attack. The plan decided upon was to continue the attack frontally with the detachment [from] the [34th Pursuit] Squadron and the Filipino [3rd] Battalion already in line, enveloping the right flank with the newly arrived Filipino [2nd] battalion, while I held the air force detachments and the two Bren gun carriers with me in reserve. Hugh was assigned to the Filipino commander of the reserve [1st] Battalion with instructions to push as hard as he could. Matt was detailed to accompany the enveloping [2nd] Battal-

72

ion with instructions to push on to the end of the point and attack to the southeast. The attack was to start on my signal after all [the] troops were ready, but I insisted that everyone be in position by 9:00 A.M.

About 8:30 A.M. Hugh came back to report that the battalion commander and his staff had disappeared, but that the troops were still in position. While I was trying to figure out what had happened, the Filipino officers [of the PAAC] showed up, all out of breath, stating that the early Nip attack had forced them to run for their lives, but that, after running through the jungle to Quinauan Bay and by making a wide circle, they had escaped to rejoin us after covering perhaps five miles of trailless jungle, a part of which had been up and down hill.

I pointed out to the commander that the Nips had not attacked, they had merely fired their machine guns from defensive positions. He would not believe me until I pointed down the road toward the front line, telling him that he could go find his troops in the position they had been all night. His mouth stood open a long time, but he could find nothing more to say. I decided to delay the attack until 11:00 A.M., in order that the late arrivals could get ready.

Doc Smith arrived, setting up his medical station across the road from the command post where I became his first patient. The thorns in my hand were beginning to fester and cause me some pain, so I went to Doc for help. Using a sharp pointed blade of his pocket knife he relieved me of the thorns, although he had to listen to some choice language from me each time he probed for a deep one.

He had almost finished the job when our attack started. One of the Nip's defensive machine guns, which opened fire in our direction at the start of the attack, was shooting so high that it sprayed the lower branches of the tree under which we were sitting. Looking up I could see that we were in the clear by fifteen feet, but Doc, who was looking down at my hand, did not know that and, besides, it was his first time under fire. As I looked at him his neck appeared to be trying to contract in order to pull his head through his shoulders like a turtle going in his shell. His eyes were nearly closed and his face looked almost frozen in unhappy, but resigned, expectation. At my amused giggle, Doc made an immediate recovery to become a bit vicious in digging out the last thorn in my hand. During the fighting that followed Doc stayed near the firing, doing everything that a medical officer could do.

After the completion of the repair job on my hand, I went down the road to find out how Hugh was getting along. He pointed out to me the location of a machine gun near the road that was holding up the attack, so I sent a messenger to guide one of the Bren gun carriers up to me. The vehicle was a very light tractor operated by a crew of two and armored for protection against small arms fire only. When the carrier arrived, the crew dismounted to crawl up to a position where Hugh could show them the

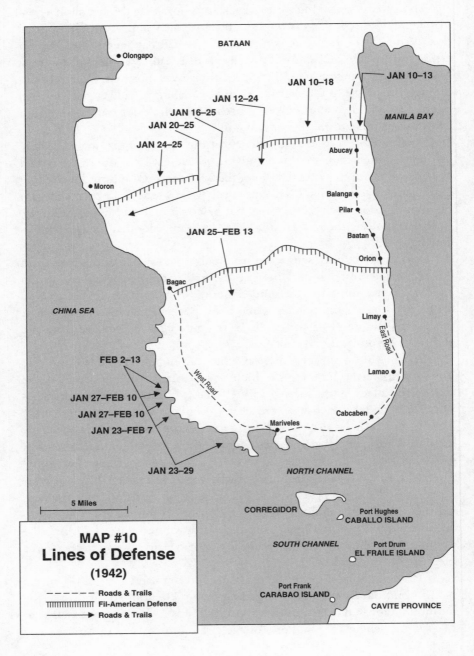

BATAAN

• Olongapo

JAN 10–13

JAN 10–18

MANILA BAY

JAN 12–24

JAN 16–25

JAN 20–25

JAN 24–25

Abucay •

• Moron

Balanga •

Pilar •

Baatan •

JAN 25–FEB 13

Orion •

Bagac •

CHINA SEA

Limay •

East Road

FEB 2–13

Lamao •

JAN 27–FEB 10

JAN 27–FEB 10

Cabcaben •

JAN 23–FEB 7

West Road

Mariveles •

JAN 23–29

NORTH CHANNEL

5 Miles

CORREGIDOR

Port Hughes
CABALLO ISLAND

MAP #10
Lines of Defense
(1942)

SOUTH CHANNEL

Port Drum
EL FRAILE ISLAND

- - - - - Roads & Trails
TTTTTTTTTTT Fil-American Defense
———▶ Roads & Trails

Port Frank
CARABAO ISLAND

CAVITE PROVINCE

machine gun position. The mission assigned to the carrier was to move [as] rapidly as possible toward the gun position, engaging it with fire from its 50 caliber machine gun.

The vehicle made its run as planned, turned around the curve in the road and opened fire, to be greeted immediately by fire from a small cannon. The first cannon shot hit the heavy steel bumping bar in front of the carrier, bouncing off harmlessly, but the second shot went through the light armor of the carrier, exploding near the machine gunner and wounding him severely. The driver, seeing he was outclassed in fire power, backed into the jungle far enough to turn around, then he came out at full speed. We waved him on to the first aid station where Doc Smith dressed the wounds of both men before he sent them to the hospital. The vehicle was not greatly damaged so, after getting a new crew, it was returned to its position in reserve.

I received two messages from Matt, one at jump off of the attack, and the other upon reaching a point about halfway through the jungle to the coast. I sent a message directing him to keep going, but I heard nothing more from him and I never found out how far he got. Hugh's attack kept creeping forward slowly, but heavy fire from the Nip position was causing heavy casualties.

Walking wounded coming back along the road attracted Filipino soldiers far in excess of the numbers required to help them. One man who had a leg wound, but who could still walk, had five riflemen friends half carrying him, his pack, and his rifle. I stopped them all and, calling a first aid man to take the wounded soldier, I took the others back to the firing line.

Several of the men kept repeating, "We have not had our chow, we are too weak to fight."

I had just turned the men over to an officer when Hugh appeared from the direction of the firing line with a soldier who was helping him hold his left hand in the air. He had been shot through the wrist, so I ordered him back to the aid station. Before going back he explained that the enemy fire was heavy, that the men had had nothing to eat that day, and that unless an American officer was there with them the soldiers would leave. As Hugh went away, I could see the look of relief on his face that he was leaving a hot spot for comparative safety with a wound that was not dangerous.

After talking to the battalion commander, directing him to hold the line where it was, I went back to report to the division commander who had come up to the command post. I told him that I was the only American officer left with the regiment, and that I had to go forward in order to keep our front line from evaporating. The division commander, hoping to give me all the encouragement he could, told me that it would be a feather in my cap if the attack proved successful. I assured him of my best efforts, but I started away with very grave doubts that I would acquire any feathers for my crown on that occasion.

Before I had gone, [Colonel] Willoughby, General MacArthur's intelligence officer, and Ted, another staff officer, came back by our headquarters from a reconnaissance along the north side of the road.[2] They walked along with me as I went forward to press the attack. They were as unhappy as I was when we met many stragglers that had to be sent back into the line. Finding a number of officers standing behind trees, we tried to get them to take some tactical action, but we had no success. I expressed a bit of uneasiness about our flanks during the attack which we were about to make.

The [colonel] directed Ted to look after the right flank of our line, telling us at the same time that he was going to take a company to the left flank for its protection. Ted and I moved a little ways off the road and continued forward, talking about the situation as we went along. Apparently the Nips heard us, for they dropped one of their mortar shells between us.

We were not more than thirty feet apart when the shell exploded with an ear-splitting roar, accompanied by a huge ball of scarlet fire. Neither of us got a scratch, and neither of us lost a step. I had so many problems on my mind that I was not having too much trouble keeping my natural fear walled in, but Ted, who really had no business there under fire, appeared to be enjoying himself. He laughed and, referring to the explosion of the mortar shell, he said, "You act like you can neither see nor hear anything."

I reached our firing line and tried unsuccessfully to push it forward. There were no Filipino officers present, and the men were not going to be pushed, so I saw I had to lead them. I crawled ahead of the line about ten feet, and by shouting and waving my arms, I managed to get the line to crawl up to me. One man, who fired his rifle before he came abreast to me, almost deafening me, received the worst tongue lashing he ever had in his life, although I doubt that he understood a word of what I said.

We moved a couple of times more, while Ted kept shouting a description of what he could see from his flank. He said we were very close to the Nip line which was made up of individual foxholes, except for a machine gun position on the flank which had two or three men with it. His voice came to me very clearly, although I could not see him. He announced that he could see a Nip sticking [out] his head, to which I answered, "Shoot the son of a bitch!" His voice suddenly sounded like he was very excited as he yelled, "Look out! They are turning in your direction!"

I could not see a thing as I raised up on a knee, holding my rifle in front of me with both hands. Something struck the rifle with a metallic sound, jarring my hands pretty severely. Feeling an additional jolt on my right thumb, I turned it up to see a phosphorous core of a tracer bullet burning into my flesh. Before I became aware of any pain in my right hand, I had started jerking it violently without any conscious effort on my part. At last the phosphorous came off, leaving the top half of the thumb almost as dark as a piece of charcoal. Not until the pain eased up did I notice that one finger of my left hand had been shot away, and another one had been considerably mangled.

After I recovered my wits I ran a little to the left rear of where I was hit, so that my location would not be the same when the Nips fired again, and then I was sick. For thirty-six hours, with the exception of four hours' sleep, I had been going at top speed. I had made countless decisions, some of which might have been of sufficient importance to influence the critical situation. I had one scanty meal during the action while I had been working so hard to get results with poorly trained and poorly equipped troops that did not even understand my language.

I was in doubt as to the results of the engagement, and I was suffering somewhat from the shock of my wounds. In a little while I felt better and, sitting up, I heard [Colonel] Willoughby call my name. I answered him, telling him that I had been hit and I did not feel too well. The [colonel], coming directly to me, had started to bandage my left hand when the Nips, presumably having located me again, opened fire with a light mortar.

The shells exploded high in the trees, the pieces falling through the leaves sounding something like rain on a metal roof. Neither of us were hit, but the [colonel] thought that we had better move, so we went through the jungle until we came out on the road. We met Ted there and discussed the military situation. I pointed out that, if I left the line, the soldiers would straggle away letting the Nips come through without opposition. Ted volunteered to stay there until a substitute could be sent up. I learned later that Matt came in and took over from Ted about dark.

The [colonel] took me to the first aid station where Doc Smith bandaged my hands. Looking me over further, Doc asked, "What is this blood doing on your shirt front?" I had to confess that I had not known the blood was there. Unbuttoning my shirt, he pulled out the shreds of a map and, after only a brief examination, he announced that I had a sliver on my breast bone which could be left right where it was until I got to the hospital.

After he was through dressing the injury, he unfolded the map, counting the folds. He scowled as he told me that the sliver had penetrated fifty-four folds of heavy paper to get to me, and that, if I had not carried the map in my shirt front, I would have saved him the trouble of dressing my wounds. I was fascinated at the lace like pattern of the cut map, which reminded me of a piece of woolen cloth that the moths had been into. I asked Doc to refold the map and put it in my musette bag, for I wanted to get it home to the kid. No, I did not bring it back, because I lost it on the Death March.

While Doc was working on me, Boob McNutt drove up in my car and reported that he was waiting to drive me to the hospital. Upon leaving the aid station, I had that same feeling of relief I had noticed and deplored in Hugh when he left us. That feeling was a mixture of thankfulness for being still practically in one piece and of pleasure at the opportunity to go to a place of comparative safety and comfort. On the other hand, I had a small guilty feeling that I was running away from the boys.

When [Colonel] Willoughby walked me over to my car and directed that I get on my way to the hospital, telling me that he would handle all problems in the absence of the division commander, I was convinced that he would take care of the situation. Vaguely, I wondered where the division commander had gone, but I did not find out until days later that he had gone on a personal reconnaissance which had involved him in a battle of his own with a Nip sniper. An hour after I had departed for the hospital, he came limping into the hospital with a Nip bullet in his heel.

AT HOSPITAL NO. 2

My ride to the hospital over a good road in a comfortable sedan was indeed a luxury, because it was not unusual for a wounded man to have a long rough trip before he could rest in bed. My hands were not painful, so after the first six miles of bumpy road were behind us, I enjoyed the ride.

After a little more than an hour, Boob drove me into the receiving station of Hospital No. 2.[3] At that office I met an old friend from Stotsenburg, who took my pistol and equipment to his tent so that I would not have to turn them in at the hospital.

After filling out a number of papers, the receiving clerk took me to the operating tent where there were already two wounded soldiers waiting. I had been sitting there a few minutes when Hugh appeared from the operating tent where his hand had been dressed. Naturally, he was surprised to see me, and he was so concerned that he held up an impatient orderly who was waiting to take him to his ward until he found out the nature of my wounds.

It was almost a half-hour before my turn came to climb on the operating table. When I entered the tent I found myself among friends, for a large part of the operating staff on duty at that time had been at Fort Stotsenburg prior to the war. At least five of the officers I saw in the operating room that night had been stationed with us [at Fort Stotsenburg].

They certainly did a fine repair job on me in the minimum of time and with no pain what[so]ever. I should qualify that statement slightly, for Jim came over to look at the piece of metal in my chest while my left hand was being sewed up.[4] Casually picking up a pair of tweezers, he got a good hold on the metal and pulled straight out until my skin was as tight as a drum head [and] then, before I had time to call him more than a few uncomplimentary words, he gave the tweezers a twist like turning a corkscrew and extracted the slug.

I being the last patient needing surgery at that moment, everyone left for supper after I came off the table. It was a distinct surprise to me to find that darkness had arrived already. Captain Lewis, one of the surgeons who had operated on me, told me to keep close to him so that I would not stumble and fall on the rough trail that led to his ward.[5] He said that, the officer's ward being already full, he would be glad to fix me up a bed at his place. He had one vacant bed under a tent fly where two other officers had been assigned earlier in the day.

One of the officers was "Chick," an artilleryman, whom I had known for years.[6] The other one was the swaggering, loud-talking young cavalryman who lived around the corner from us at Stotsenburg. We talked while I, learning how to use my bandaged hands, laboriously got undressed. After that they may have talked a long time, but the moment my head hit the pillow I started drifting into a long dreamless sleep.

The morning activity of the hospital woke me about 7:00 A.M. [January 25, 1942.] The noises and the snatches of conversation were familiar, but the sight before me when I opened my eyes was bewildering. Instead of confining clean white walls around me, I was still hemmed in by the jungle. There were the towering trees which appeared to reach the sky and almost concealed it except for occasional small patches. The underbrush had been cleared from the area occupied by the ward, and the beds, which had been placed in rows as neatly as the trunks of the trees would permit, extended as far as I could see. Two wall tents on one side for the offices of the doctors, nurses, and corps men, two water faucets for the water needs of the patients and, as I found out later, two latrines in the trees near the far corner, constituted all the facilities for that ward of more than two hundred patients.

Captain Lewis, accompanied by two nurses, one American and one Filipino, both dressed in olive-drab coveralls, came by on the daily ward round. As we needed no medical attention in our corner, the captain stopped just long enough to orient us a bit on our living conditions. He announced that we could expect to be fed twice a day unless the ration was further reduced.

We knew that all of us had gone on half rations on the fifth of January [1942,] but we had not heard that we had been cut again on the twelfth. [Captain Lewis] told us we would be expected to look after ourselves as much as possible because of the shortage of help. Then he pointed out the latrine, telling us that we could get a reasonable amount of exercise walking down there and back, but that he hoped we did not contract diarrhea for, in that case, there would be too much exercise for our scanty food intake.

My first visit to the latrine gave me no cause to recover from my astonishment at the primitive conditions existing in the ward. An unappreciated long walk brought me to a clump of dense underbrush around which, by following the path, I found the latrine. It was a ditch with furniture. Its furniture consisted of a flimsy wooden trestle-like contrivance which furnished a four by four for a seat, a two by four for a back rest and a one by four for a foot rest. There [was] so much space between those boards that I could not see how anyone but a healthy man could avoid falling in. The swarm of flies buzzing around gave me plenty a reason to think of Captain Lewis's reference to diarrhea.

My walk from my corner of the ward to the opposite corner and back had given me an opportunity to see that the patients were almost all wounded soldiers, about fifty of them being American and the rest Filipinos. I saw the two soldiers who had been wounded when they made the Bren gun carrier attack on the Nip machine gun. They were in good spirits and, apparently, were making an uneventful recovery. Actually, of the two hundred wounded cases, some serious, in that primitive ward there was only one death during my two weeks in the hospital. He was a man who had developed gangrene before he arrived because it had taken him such a long time to get to the hospital after he had been wounded.

Our 9:00 A.M. meal arriving at the ward office reminded me that I had not washed up that morning. I rushed back to my bunk and washed as best I could with my bandaged hands, but I need not have hurried for, after I was ready, I had to wait some time before the orderlies distributing the food reached us.

One look at the meal was enough to make me doubt that the anticipation had been worthwhile, for all we had was two heaping tablespoons of corn beef hash and one small slice of field bread. The two meals a day that followed for the next two weeks were exactly the same, except that once each week at the afternoon meal we were astounded to receive, in addition, a medium sized portion of delicious fruit pie.

After breakfast the nurses were changed and the new ones started the morning baths. The new Filipino nurse, starting her day's work in our corner, gave me a bath and an alcohol rubdown because with both hands in bandages I could not take care of myself. While she worked she talked and I listened. She was a Chinese-Spanish mestiza, twenty-six years old and from Cavite. She was a graduate nurse who had worked in Manila's finest hospital prior to the war. Her brother was a pilot in the Philippine Army and, at the time being without planes, his squadron had been sent to the beach defenses north of Quinauan Point.

She bathed me every day I was in the hospital, and I came to know her as an extremely competent, intelligent, and faithful woman who was devoting twelve hours every day to the patients of our ward. No one would have called her beautiful, but her personality and devotion were so outstanding that it was always a pleasure to all patients to see her trim little figure approaching.

The American nurse on duty with her was a tall blonde California girl, whose peaches and cream complexion stayed with her despite the primitive conditions in which she lived. I had not seen an American girl for a month, but I do not think that fact influenced my judgment as to her beauty, for I believe if I saw her now I would not change my mind.

The Filipino nurse finished my bath and, picking up her basin, she started to go across the aisle to bathe the Filipino soldier in the nearest bunk. Suddenly, she dropped her basin with a clatter and yelled to "California" down by the tent to send the doctor right away. When Captain Lewis arrived, they helped the soldier who had been squatting alongside the bunk back to bed. After giving the soldier a quick examination, Captain Lewis came over to tell us the story.

The soldier, a small but tough looking boy, was from a mountain tribe which spoke its own peculiar dialect. When he had been brought in two days before with a bomb splinter in his belly, it had taken some time to find a Filipino interpreter who could talk to him in his own dialect. Although an emergency operation had been necessary to save the man's life, he had been totally unconcerned about it.

What concerned the nurse was the sight of the man squatting on the ground beside his bed, just twenty-four hours after his operation. The poor soldier, who had never heard of a urinal, and being unable to ask anyone how to use it, had, by necessity, depended on his own ingenuity. The

Filipino, back in bed and none the worse for getting out of it, had to receive a lesson from the interpreter on the approved method of using a urinal while lying in bed.

The patients being predominately Filipino, soft voices speaking various dialects could be heard calling hospital corps men at all hours of the day and night. The two words heard most frequently were, *Tubig,* the Tagalog word for water, and "duck."[7] Duck is the American soldiers' name for urinal, the army type of which roughly takes the shape of a duck. It was natural for the Filipinos, who had no such word as urinal in their language, to adopt the word duck. It seemed to me that there was a continuous call for one or the other needs of the soldiers and I oftentimes mused which was cause and which effect. [However,] in the end I decided that like the argument of which came first, the chicken or the egg, you can take your choice.

At night when the wardmen were busiest and most tired, the voices calling *Tubig* and duck became more insistent, and I realized after a little while that the individual voices were distinguishable to the orderlies. The call of *Tubig* could be ignored, and the answer to the call of duck could be delayed, but there was a limit so that when the call of duck reached an anguished crescendo, even the most callous orderly had to grab the urinal and hurry to the suffering patient.

In the afternoon of my first full day in the hospital, several Nip planes came over on what appeared to be a reconnaissance mission. Our young cavalry officer stopped talking and, getting out of bed, he went over to stand in a small slit trench nearby. A few trenches had been prepared for the duty personnel of the hospital in the event of raids, but it was impracticable to prepare places for the patients, the majority of whom were bedfast.

Very few of the patients or hospital assistants paid any attention to the planes, so our cavalryman was alone in his trench. He must have been ashamed of his weakness, but back he went to the trench when another plane came over. Chick told me that the young man had had a couple of close calls in his own outfit and had developed pains in his abdomen as a result. He was what his own people called "windy" in describing an individual who could not take it.

Late that afternoon one of the surgeons came to see him with the report that they could find no condition in his abdomen that should cause pain. The young man's face had terror written all over it as the surgeon departed. When the next Sunday came the officer had a long talk with his priest and Sunday afternoon he informed Captain Lewis that he was ready for duty. He left us Monday morning to go back to his outfit, but he did not get there. On his way back to duty a bomber, working over the high-way he was traveling on, dropped a bomb almost on him, blowing off both of his legs. When the news of his death came back to us, I could not help pondering over the accuracy of his premonition of death. When we heard all of the details we had still more to think about.

According to an authentic report, he had seen the plane and halted the bus in which he was transporting a detail of troops. He hit the ditch just as the bombs fell, one of them hitting on his side of the road. The truck was not touched, nor were any of the soldiers hurt.

On my second morning in the hospital, [January 26, 1942,] Captain Lewis and the California nurse came along to change the bandage on my left hand. My normal male reaction of pleasure at having a beautiful girl wait on me came to an abrupt end for she, instead of handling the wound with care, ripped off the old bandage with such force that it felt like the sore fingers came off with the bandage. I rose right up in bed to tell her, bluntly, that I never wanted her to hold my hand again.

After my hand was dressed, Captain Lewis took the old dressing off of Chick's wound, revealing a neat bullet hole in his chest. There being no hole in his back, it was obvious that the bullet was still in his body, although the X-ray did not show its location. The X-ray indicated that it had passed through the lung to a rib in his back, to be deflected to an unknown position. Chick did not feel any pain that might have been caused by the missing bullet. His recovery being uneventful, he returned to duty, and eventually went through three years of imprisonment with it still in him. After the doctor went on, Chick told me how he got his wound, and about his adventures getting to the hospital afterwards. This is his story:

Several days prior to the attack on Quinauan Point, the Nips had been putting some pressure on [II] Corps, north of us, in what appeared to me to be a plan to keep our forces well occupied so they could be of no assis-tance to us when the landing was made at Aglaloma Bay.[8] Their operations were somewhat successful in that they were able to infiltrate a sizable force to a position on the flank of the unit furthest to the north.

One morning, Chick, who was commanding the artillery of our advanced forces on the west coast, had the unpleasant experience of having his headquarters unexpectedly brought under the fire of a Nip machine gun. Grabbing a light machine gun he ran out to a position from where he could return fire. Almost immediately after he opened fire he was hit in the chest, and the Nip fire ceased. It did not begin again, causing him to believe that he had shot the Nip at the same time he was hit.

Making his way back to his headquarters, where, after receiving first aid treatment, he lay down to wait for transportation to take him to the hospital. Sending for our old friend, Alva, who went to the Philippines on the boat with us, he turned over the artillery command to him.[9] He then broke out the last bottle of scotch he had been hoarding and tried to make himself comfortable. He did not remember much that happened the next day because he was running a considerable temperature, but the second day a Red Cross bus was loaded with wounded, Chick among them, and started to the rear.

Before they had gone a mile they were ambushed by the Nips, but Chick, being at the rear of the bus, jumped out at the first burst of fire, and running along the jungle edge he escaped to make his way back to his headquarters. His report was positive information to Alva and Colonel Berry, the force commander, that the Nips had closed the road to I Corps, and that their position was in grave danger.[10]

Colonel Berry immediately reported the situation to higher headquarters, which directed him to destroy the heavy equipment and withdraw. The guns and transportation which could not be removed were blown up, for the only remaining exit was a narrow trail. Alva, being thoroughly familiar with the area, was given command of the advance force as the withdrawal got under way.

Chick, who was lying on a litter, had eight Filipino soldiers detailed to carry him. The carrying party made good time, easily holding their place in the column for the first couple of miles, but when the trail began to climb steeply over a high ridge they began to fall behind.

Chick saw that they could not carry him much further, so he got on his feet and marched for nearly twenty miles up and down crude trails, across sandy beaches and across one stretch of a half-mile of knee deep water. Not until they had cut back on the road behind the Nip position did Chick become a patient again. There they met a doctor on the road who put Chick in a car and sent him directly to the hospital. For a man who had had a bullet through a lung for several days, I thought that march of Chick's was remarkable, deserving to be recorded in history. Alva, Colonel Berry and Chick were decorated for their conduct in that engagement.

About a week before I went to the hospital I had been inspecting the defenses of the sector occupied by one of the dismounted squadrons. Another visitor that day was Captain Woolery, a young pursuit pilot friend of the squadron commander.[11] It was a most interesting visit for me, because Captain Woolery told us all about what the few P-40 pilots we had left were doing. After Woolery had gone, the squadron commander told me that Woolery had been flying tough missions since the war started because he was one of the most dependable and experienced pilots left in the Philippines. I have forgotten which one of them told me that they were improvising bomb-racks for three P-40s in order to make a surprise attack on Nichols Field.

One afternoon after I had gone to the hospital, a pilot friend who dropped in to see me told me that Captain Woolery was going to lead an attack on Nichols Field that very night, taking off from the landing strip about one mile north of the hospital. That night, with great excitement, I heard the planes leave and nothing more for perhaps an hour. At last I heard them return, and noted that all three ships made a safe landing, but I had to wait until the next day for the news when another visitor came to see us.

According to his report, when Woolery approached Nichols [Airfield], the Nip base personnel thought his [plane] was one of their own and turned on the lights, permitting our three ships to make an unopposed lighted attack. They circled, coming around again to drop all their bombs, which were of 25 lb. fragmentation type, on grounded planes, repair facilities and living quarters.

We never knew definitely the results of that raid, but a Nip soldier told one of us months later that many men had been killed and many planes destroyed. I had no chance to congratulate Woolery, for a few days later he was missing in action.

After I had been in the hospital about one week, Ted came to see me bringing an envelope from USAFFE. He said he was in a hurry, but that he had to wait until I read my letter. Opening the letter, I found a General Order from General MacArthur's headquarters awarding me the decoration, which I wear sometimes, for the Aglaloma Bay fight.[12]

Ted held out his hand saying, "Congratulations, you have earned it," and ran away. It was a good thing he did go, for I could not control my emotions. The unexpected receipt of the decoration had pulled out the stops, and I could not help weeping shamelessly. After I had arrived at the hospital, I had had time to review my conduct prior to and while under fire. There were some mistakes that I could not escape knowing I had made, and there were other instances when I felt I might have done better. I had tried my best, but the results obtained fell short of what I had hoped for. I realized the difficulties in leading untrained and poorly armed troops, but I could not forget that I was resting comfortably in bed while many others were still fighting the battle I had started them on.

The General Order could not change my analysis of myself, nor could it convince me that I deserved it more than the unknown Filipino corporal who had been killed in action and many, many others whose gallant actions had gone unnoticed. Even so, it gave me a warm feeling to know that higher authority appreciated my efforts, and it was good to know my family would receive a copy of the General Order even though I failed to survive Bataan. I told myself that regardless of whether or not I got back home again, I could not legitimately complain of my fate.

That evening the Stotsenburg nurse for whom I had provided the finance officer's concrete vault as protection during a bombing raid came to pay a call. There being no chairs, she made herself comfortable on the foot of the bed. She told me how all the nurses lived along a little stream about a quarter of a mile away. Their camp was arranged like our ward in a clearing among the big trees. The one known path to their camp was guarded by a big "Off Limits" sign and a sentry. She said that their facilities consisted of an open latrine and cold water bathing in the running stream. I did not visit their camp as I was not invited. According to her, there was no proof of "Peeping Toms," but a few of the nurses had postponed their bathing until after the sun went down.

She told me she was going to marry a young air corps captain whom we had known at Stotsenburg as soon as he came back from the front. His squadron was then helping to push the Nips out of the jungles of Quinauan. She asked many questions about the dangers of the area, and she wanted to know my estimate of how much longer it would be before she could expect to see her "Intended" again. My indefinite, "Not long," was true enough, for two weeks later the captain came along with the chaplain and she became Mrs. Captain. They had five days' leave, and all of the jungles of Bataan for a honeymoon. She was transferred to Corregidor before the fall of Bataan, but he went to prison camp. She, being pregnant, was one of those added to the last group leaving Corregidor before its surrender, and it was her good fortune to get back so that the baby could be born at home. Her husband was not so fortunate, for he lost his life when the ship carrying him and other POWs to Japan was bombed a few years later.

On Ground Hog Day 1942, I had a surprise visit from two war correspondents representing *Life* magazine. Together they comprised one of the few, if not the only, man and wife team in the game. It will be hard for you to imagine how astonished I was to see the tall good looking man in slacks and a white shirt with the tall, slender, beautiful young woman, beautifully dressed in pink, and groomed as if she were going to tea in the "Waldorf," walk down our primitive hospital aisle and come up to my bed.

He introduced them[selves to me], and told me that USAFFE had given him a short list of officers who had had the most recent combat experiences with the Nips and had done well at it. Sitting up in bed, I bowed as best I could to the lady, and pointing with a bandaged hand to the foot of the bed, I asked her if she would not like to sit in the easy chair. [I then pointed] to the other side of the bed [and] asked the gentleman if he would not like to sit there. There was no other possible place to sit, and he played up to my mock courtesy by answering that he was sure they would be most comfortable in the easy chair.

After they sat down, he told me he would like to get my personal impressions of the Nips, the Filipino soldiers and how the war was going in general. I asked him if the press releases which they were sending out conformed to the "Voice of Freedom" radio broadcasts.[13] He grinned, and answered that they did, to which I had to reply that it did not appear to me to be the appropriate time to air my views. We talked about the war in general, and had an altogether pleasant off-the-record visit.

I recall that I asked him how the morale was on the "Rock," for I knew that they lived in the tunnels on Corregidor.[14] He answered, "Terrible, it is amazing how much better the morale is over here where you are in actual contact with the Nips. It seems that you all breathe a different air than they do over there." He stood up saying, "Annabelle, we have to catch the boat." During all that time she had not said a word, but the sadness in her eyes, if I read them correctly, told me that she had been overwhelmed by the sight of all the wounded crowded into the forest. As they left he told me he would be back another time, but he did not make it, for a few days later they flew to Australia where he was killed in an airplane accident.

OUR FILIPINO FRIENDS

I made several visits to the large officer's ward, for I knew many of the doctors and nurses there and nearly half the patients. Hugh and the air corps officer who had been wounded on Quinauan were there. [There was also] another officer [there] who had arrived at the point with a battalion of Philippine Scouts[15] the day after we had been hit, only to be wounded by a sniper within an hour after he got there.

He was able to tell us that our troops had concentrated artillery fire on the defensive position for a whole day before they had driven the Nips back to the tip of the point. He also told us that the remains of Sam's car had been found inside the Nip lines, but there was no information of Sam. Even after the Nips had been destroyed, we never did discover anything more about either Sam or his driver.

From the many officers I visited, I learned of the excellent fighting qualities of the scout soldiers, and how the Philippine Division of the

American Army had to be used every time where it was necessary to stop a determined Nip attack. As a matter of fact, the troops of the Philippine Division and the 26th Cavalry were the only ones that could be relied upon to take offensive action requiring discipline, training, and fine leadership on the part of officers and noncommissioned officers.[16]

In addition, my experiences in trying to lead troops whose language was unknown to me, and whose training and leadership were meager, were still freshly engraved in my mind. Our Philippine Division, or rather its main combat units, at the beginning of the war, consisted of the 31st Infantry, an American Regiment, the 45th Infantry, the 57th Infantry, and several battalions of field artillery grouped into a brigade; all Philippine Scouts.

The 31st Infantry had furnished a large part of its officers, and the best of its noncommissioned officers, [who] had been commissioned for the training and assistance in combat of the Philippine Army Divisions. Many of the soldiers left in the 31st were recruits. On the other hand, the scouts had a large percentage of their officers, all of their old well-trained noncommissioned officers and, with the exception of the 45th Infantry, there were few recruits among them. There had always been a waiting list for enlistments in each scout unit, permitting the selection of the best men whenever vacancies occurred.

The scout ration being much better than the average Filipino's diet, the scout soldiers had more energy and endurance than their fellows. The scout soldiers had considerable prestige in the islands. Their morale was high, their equipment and training were excellent, and they had an intense loyalty to their officers and to the United States.

In addition to the two scout regiments of infantry on Luzon, there was one additional scout combat regiment, the 26th Cavalry. It was a small organization of less than a thousand men, but under fine leadership it more than did its part in demonstrating the high quality of scout soldiers. Nor were the scout artillery batteries behind in that respect for, without exception, they did everything that could have been expected of them.

The contrast between the scouts and General MacArthur's Philippine Army was striking. With the exception of a few demonstration troops, [the Philippine] Army had been a paper organization until shortly before the war. Upon the insistence of President Quezon, the officers, except part of the general officers, of this army were Filipinos. Even if there had been an adequate method of selecting the best officers from the material available in the Philippine Islands, it would have been impossible to find more than a small fraction of the requirements of the Philippine Army, for experience, training and leadership qualities were hard to find in one man.

Very few Filipinos had been permitted to own firearms, [therefore] the average man had never seen a rifle. [Since] the soldiers of [the Filipino] Army [were] drafted, a large percentage of them came from small barrios of mountain and jungle regions. Many of them had never worn shoes or any type of army clothing. Because of an inadequate diet, all too many of the men were undersized, under-muscled and lacking in energy. The level of education was low, and there was little patriotic desire to defend the Commonwealth.

There was no common language which was understood by all Filipinos, the variety of dialects adding greatly to the difficulties of training and administration. Even what we considered to be the basic elements of sanitation and personal hygiene were generally unknown [to the Filipinos]. The importance, if not the necessity, of having American officers with all troops was that the Filipinos had almost a blind confidence in American officers and little in their own.

I am telling you these details to help you understand why Philippine Army troops might be depended on in defensive action only, and then only when well handled, while Philippine Scout troops were the equal of Nip troops under all combat conditions.

Battalions of scouts had to be called upon eventually to destroy the Nips at Quinauan Point, in the navy area where the Nips landed at the same time they landed at Quinauan, and at other points on at least two other occasions.

One officer told me of various engagements the 31st Infantry had fought. He told me of the heavy artillery bombardment which they had been subjected to, and how they had stood up well in all instances, except for two units which had been led to the rear by inexperienced officers in their first fight. He told me of the heavy Nip night attack which had been stopped after bitter fighting.

In that attack one of the regiment's guardhouse bums had distinguished himself. That soldier was in the guardhouse for his fifth time awaiting trial for drunkenness and AWOL and a probable discharge as an undesirable when the war started, but when the regiment went into bivouac at the start of the war, he was given his chance to return to duty, and he took it.

Under combat conditions he had been a good soldier, and on the evening of the Nip night attack he was assigned as a light-machine gunner. During the course of the action the Nips infiltrated around his company, resulting in its pulling back about three hundred yards. The soldier stayed where he was, keeping up a steady fire, and helped cover the retirement. The next morning the company came back to its old position to find the old soldier dead at his gun with dead Nips all around him. His heroism was just another example of the difficulty in knowing in peacetime how a man will act under fire.

One young officer of engineers[17] told me how he and a Filipino officer had been on a demolition detail, blowing bridges and blocking roads behind our troops retiring into Bataan, when their car broke down several miles south of San Fernando. The Nip tanks, following rapidly behind them, had cut them off in late afternoon so that they had to hide in a bamboo thicket awaiting darkness. There was a big ditch on their side of the town where a number of women were cowering, in comparative safety, because of the occasional shells the Nip tanks were firing into the town.

About sunset a number of Nip vehicles stopped at a small building about twenty-five yards from where they were hiding. A Nip officer or noncommissioned officer, they did not know which but he was wearing a sword and looked important, got out of a car and, strutting around, he noticed the women in the ditch. He went over right away and, after inspecting them, motioned for one to come out.

None of them wanted to move, but finally an old crone stood up and started out. The Nip almost had apoplexy as he shoved the old woman back into the ditch and grabbed the arm of a young, good looking girl. He pulled her out and took her with him into the building.

Some minutes later the girl came out running, putting her pants on as she ran toward the bamboo. Seeing the two officers she stopped and, with tears streaming down her cheeks, she sobbed, "See what he did to me." The Filipino officer, talking almost in a whisper, begged her to go for he could not help her. She went on and, as soon as darkness came, so did the two officers. Because of his knowledge of the country, the Filipino was able to lead them safely to Bataan, but they had two days of hard walking before they contacted an American scout car.

VISITING WITH FRIENDS AND SHARING STORIES

Charlie, who went over on our boat, and served in the artillery at Stotsenberg when we were there, came to see Chick and me one day.[18] Between the two of them telling of their experiences, I was kept well entertained. Chick related how, during the withdrawal into Bataan, the Nips had tried to run our rear guard down by mounting their advance guard in trucks. Each time that happened, our artillery had to go into action and discourage the truck column by dropping some shells along the road.

One day he said he had the opportunity to act as his own observer from the top of a high church steeple where he could see for ten miles down the road. The Nips in trucks came along as usual, and Chick let them come until they got to a stretch of road between rice paddies about four miles away. After they got well into that artificial defile, he opened up on the head of the column and worked it over thoroughly for a half hour. The column had to stop and the trucks, not being able to turn, [caused] the Nips to bail out of them like ants, but they had nothing to hide in but the marshy land of the paddies. He laughed till he almost cried at the recollection of the remnants of that advance guard resuming the march all covered with mud from head to foot.

Charlie told us of boxing in a truck column running parallel to our lines at sunset one day. Our guns had kept shooting for some time after dark, but the exact results were unknown. He also told us of one shoot which he had conducted from his forward observation point.

Charlie was an experienced artilleryman, and he had an opportunity to put his knowledge to good use when his observation post picked up the forward advance of part of the battalion across an open field of grass. [He] had his own and another battalion at his disposal [and] directed them to use shrapnel.

All our 75mm batteries had several hundred rounds of that type of ammunition, which is ideal against personnel if the officer conducting the fire knows how to use it. Charlie knew how and, boxing in the field, he combed it back and forth for a good two hours. He had observers watching the edges to see how many [enemy soldiers] ran out of the area. They watched until darkness set in without sighting a single Nip leaving the area.

I told them [of] Alva's story of how the Nips had brought a battery of mountain guns brazenly into the open to fire on his position. Alva merely changed his position to an alternate one about eight hundred yards to the rear where the Nips could not reach him, and methodically destroyed each gun in the battery, one after another.

[While in the hospital] I had noticed a gaunt American soldier, who had lost a leg halfway between his ankle and his knee, bobbing here and there through the ward on his crutches the first morning I was there, but I did not know him. One day he came up to my bunk and asked me if I had not been at Stotsenburg. When I told him yes, he said he had been a tank driver there with one of the tank battalions, and thought he had remembered seeing me talking to General Weaver.[19]

Then he told me some of his tank experiences in northern Luzon at the beginning of the war, one among them being how he lost his leg. He told [me] that one night when his tank was guarding a bridge, a Nip tank rolled right up to the bridge and stopped. Their first round was a direct hit on the Nip tank causing it to slip slowly into the ditch and turn over.

Apparently, the crew was killed outright, for there was no sound of activity the remainder of the night.

The American tank withdrew before dawn and hid in a little town where two other tanks were hiding. The Americans were expecting to make up for lost sleep, but a Filipino excitedly reported the approach of Nip tanks. Sure enough, there were five enemy tanks speeding toward the town. In short order, a tank dogfight started in the town, lasting for possibly half an hour, after which the Americans moved out, two of their tanks having been hit but not badly damaged. He could not be sure what the Nip damages were, but he had seen only one Nip tank get away.

During an attack which his platoon was making, he saw a bright red ball which looked as if it had been lobbed in a high arc like a tennis ball. He could not judge it accurately because of his limited vision through the tank aperture, and then he lost sight of it entirely. The next thing he knew the red ball went through the top of the tank as if it were paper and out through the bottom.

He did not have time to move as the ball hit his foot, cutting it off and cauterizing it all in one operation. The pain was intense, but he was able to keep the tank going until he arrived at his headquarters where he found a doctor. He had been rushed to the hospital where he was given a hypodermic of morphine to ease the pain.

Except for dressings on the stub during his first two weeks in the hospital, he had received no other treatment. He had been told that he would have to have the stub amputated when he got back home, but there was nothing more to be done while he was on Bataan.

Captain Lewis told me one morning that a young soldier of the engineers had been brought in the day before from Quinauan Point.[20] I found him the next day when the captain was dressing his wounds. Unquestionably, he was the most wounded man I have seen, yet his wounds were not serious. He had been shot in the shoulder in a spot where it would be the least damage, but it was his back that had taken the punishment.

From his heels to his neck, every six inches of his back had been marked by machine gun bullets. The creases were shallow at his heels, deeper along his buttocks, shallow again across the small of his back and deeper again across his shoulders. When the machine gun opened up on his flank, he had remained as flat as possible, inching his way along until a tiny rise in the ground gave him a little protection. His whole seat felt as if it were covered with blood, but an experimental sample gave him the explanation. He had had a can of beans in a hip pocket, but what was left of the can held no more beans.

The soldier was cheerful and happy to be alive, and enjoyed talking about his experiences. He was a member of a small American battalion of engineers, which had been sent to the Philippines about six months before for the purpose of constructing airfields. Most of the men were recruits with little military training when they came over, and their work after they arrived had not increased their combat knowledge. They had been sent to Quinauan Point, two days after I had been wounded, to assist in the destruction of the Nip landing force.

In their first attack, the soldier's company had worked around the right flank and opened fire on the Nip position. Almost immediately they had been pinned down by heavy Nip machine-gun fire. One of the guns, which had a clear line of fire through the jungle, was visible less than fifty yards away. The soldier slowly crawled toward that position to get within grenade range. It took him a long time, but at last he reached a point that was close enough and the jungle clear enough for him to chance a throw. He armed his grenade, and raising himself quickly on his left he threw it, receiving a Nip bullet through his shoulder before he could hit the dirt again. The explosion of the grenade silenced the machine gun, but one [enemy machine gun] on his flank, that he had not known about, opened up to make all the marks and ridges from his heels to his shoulders.

After he eased himself out of range of that gun, he crawled back to the firing line of his company to find it gone. After a little more crawling he was able to walk the hundred yards to where his company had fallen back. He was sent immediately to an aid station where his wounds were dressed. Before he was sent on to the hospital, he talked a buddy out of a pair of trousers for, as he said, his old ones were a mess.

I saw the soldier's battalion commander a month later, to find that the action the soldier described had not been reported to him. He promised he would investigate and, if the man deserved it, he would be recommended for a decoration. I heard after I arrived in prison camp that the soldier had been awarded a Silver Star for his conduct in the Quinauan fight.

I went to see Hugh again before I returned to duty to learn that the so called "One Man Army" was a wounded patient in the next tent. I went to see him to get such information as might be of value in fighting snipers. I pried a little information from him, but the subject of his nurse friend was of much more interest to him than snipers.

Pop and Charles came to the hospital to see me twice during the two weeks I was there. At the last visit Pop told me that I was now a celebrity among our old Filipino soldiers, and that Sergeant Castro[20] wanted to pay me a visit the next afternoon, if I had no objection. Of course, I was always glad to see Castro, but I was not prepared to receive him properly when he arrived the next day, for he did not come alone. I saw him a long ways off as he headed a column of Filipino women which seemed to fill the ward.

They came right up to my bed, forming a semi-circle, and stood there grinning for fully fifteen minutes while the sergeant did the talking. Castro introduced them as wives, daughters, sisters, and daughters-in-law of our Stotsenburg soldiers. Never have I felt so important, for never have I known soldiers who were so devoted, nor soldiers who wanted above all to show that devotion [by having their wives come see me]. In spite of this show of esteem, I was glad to see them leave, and I thanked my lucky stars that I had not been in the officer's ward to provide my officer friends with so much ammunition to make me the butt of their rough wit.

Part of a nearby ward was occupied by badly wounded Nip prisoners. Some of them had been captured while they were unconscious, and others too weak to resist. Surrender being a terrible disgrace to the whole family, according to Nip teaching, many of them did not want to live, and two did commit suicide while I was there. When the wounded recovered sufficiently, they were transferred to a well guarded stockade near Hospital No. 1. Because of the stigma of disgrace, I would estimate that not more than one hundred Nip prisoners were captured in the Bataan fighting.

One day, shortly before I left for duty, our ward was visited by Vice President Osmena.[21] Our Filipino nurse was all excited because he was coming, for he being a Chinese mestizo, their families were quite friendly. When the visiting party entered the ward, the nurse ran up to the vice president introducing herself. He knew who she was right away and was very cordial. She brought him up to my bed and introduced him, and they talked there for at least five minutes. He was extremely courteous to me and, indeed, he impressed me far more than any other Filipino I ever knew.

Chapter 7

Overtures to the End of Battle

BACK INTO THE FRAY

Boob McNutt picked me up at the hospital just two weeks after I entered it. Both of my hands still had bandages on them, but they were healed enough for me to go back to duty.

Some distance from the hospital, who should I see standing at the road junction but Eddie.[1] He insisted that I come up the side road to his head-quarters which was a mere few hundred yards away. A Filipino dressed in worn coveralls appeared from the bamboo and joined us, practicing her English and her best smile. She said she had come from the women's refugee camp to find her husband who was a scout soldier.[2]

Even though we could not give her any information, she did not seem to be in any hurry to leave. A lone Nip bomber coming low over the area drew anti-aircraft fire, so Eddie ordered the girl to get into the slit trench. He and I were standing near the trench when an anti-aircraft shell fell with a shriek and exploded quite near us. The shell explosion seemed to explode Eddie for, without stopping to think, he landed in the trench on top of the girl. He crawled out with a very red face, almost shouting, "Look at me jumping on top of that girl." The departure of the plane allowed the girl [to] go her way, and me to resume my journey.

The next day a bomber dropped his load on Eddie's headquarters, leaving a bomb fragment in his side which he carried until he died three years later. Boob told me that the Nips had been cleaned out of Quinauan Point, but that there were more Nips farther north; however, he could not tell me the details.

My first few hours back at my headquarters were devoted to familiarizing myself with the tactical situation. A week before, the Nips had sent another force by water to join the Quinauan Nips for the purpose of carrying out their original plans.[3] The new landing had been made several miles to the north, where they were encircled in the same manner as we had encircled the previous landing force. All the Nip troops on Quinauan, and those in the sector defended by the navy further to the south, had been liquidated, while the newest expedition to the north was in the process of being destroyed.

That afternoon, [Captain Sloan], the commander of our most northern squadron, who had been active in patrol work, met the Nips on a jungle trail while leading a patrol.[4] The Nips retired, but not before one of them had badly wounded the [captain] with a grenade. That gallant officer was rushed to the hospital, but he died on the operating table.

I lost no time in visiting Quinauan Point, not because of any morbid curiosity, but because I wanted to know what kind of a position the Nips had taken, and all other facts that might prove of value in future operations.

Our arrival on the ground was greeted by a most disturbing incident. The remains of ten Filipino soldiers were being removed from a small crater, which was unquestionably a new one. An officer, who was supervising the work, told me that a Filipino picked up a dud mortar shell and threw it carelessly toward a group of his companions and, of course, it exploded. This object lesson caused me to exercise considerable caution during my walk through the battle area.

The area all around the Nip position had received such a terrific bombardment that I had some difficulty finding where I had been wounded as all of the trees and jungle growth had been blown away. Going back up the road and pacing the distance, I picked a spot in the cleared area which I thought was very near where I had been when I was wounded a little more than two weeks before.

Twenty-five yards farther into the shell craters, I found the front of the Nip position. Walking all over the foxhole position, I found it was about two hundred and fifty yards wide. On each end were sizable flanking positions of foxholes. After looking at that position, I saw why our attacks had failed, and why artillery had been necessary, because any infantry advance overrunning the first line of foxholes could be mowed down easily by fire from foxholes farther in the rear.

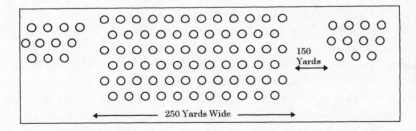

Alexander's Sketch of Enemy Area at Quinauan Point.

There were a few Nip bodies, many detached limbs and [many] impediments in and among the foxholes. Walking along the road, I almost stepped on two closely cropped brown heads which were lying in the road with no bodies in sight. I could not tell whether the heads had been severed by Samurai swords or had been blown off by shells.

Along the beach near the end of the point where the Nips had made their last stand were several hundred bodies swollen so that they looked like overinflated rubber figures. The peculiar sickening smell of decaying human flesh kept me well away.

A few days after I returned to duty, Sherry, who had taken my place while I was in the hospital, returned with a part of the regiment which had been fighting against the most recent landing farther to the north. He reported that they had finally destroyed the force, bringing the Nip loss in the three landings to approximately two thousand killed and forty captured. He also introduced five new American officers who had reported for duty during my absence which, counting Boob and myself, gave us a total of ten.

The division commander sent for me the next day to tell me that many of the Filipino troops sent into the sector as a result of the Nip landing would remain, permitting him to reduce the amount of coastline assigned to each organization for defensive purposes. He informed me of the new sector assigned to the regiment, which was about one-third as great as its sector had been when I joined it.

It was heartbreaking to know that no longer was there a divided opinion as to the possibility of a Nip landing on the west coast of Bataan, nor as to the danger of a successful landing cutting the highway joining our east and west commands. There were a few people who doubted that, had the Nip landing force on the twenty-third of January [1942] been successful, followed by an advance to the highway and that position been maintained, the I Corps on the west coast would have been cut off from supplies and been subjected to attack on two sides. Moreover, the Nips would have been in a much better position to have closed Manila Bay completely, and to have attacked Corregidor at once.

I had wondered many times why the [Japanese] landing force on Quinauan Point had assumed the defensive, instead of brushing us aside and pushing on to the highway, for it was stronger than anything we had opposing it for several days. We did not find out until the fall of Bataan that the Nip commander on Quinauan had far overestimated our strength, and decided that [the] defense was absolutely necessary until he could be reinforced. The Nip reported to his superior that he was opposed by an American division which had forced him to dig in.

After the fall of Bataan, when the Nips came into our area, they took the [Filipino] division commander over all of it and kept asking him where the American division had gone. It took him a good part of a day to convince them that no American division existed. It is my belief that the active patrolling of the pursuit squadron on Quinauan Point, the loud noise of the movement of Bren gun carriers into our area, American voices present during the attacks, and later, the attack of the American battalion of engineers, all helped influence the Nip commander in his estimate.

At division headquarters I saw my first Nip prisoner being questioned. A Filipino, in halting Japanese, was doing the interrogating. After everyone was through, I asked the prisoner which of the American weapons he feared most; bombs, artillery, machine guns, grenades, or bayonet? The question was translated, and the answer, after some delay, came back [from the interrogator that], "He say he no like any of those things."

I went back to the regiment to tell Sherry that he would remain as my executive, and to give him details of the shortening of our lines, which was to begin the next day. It was a pleasure to find that Hugh had returned to duty with us. The reduction in the size of our sector did not reduce my expenditure of energy, as there seemed to be never-ending days of inspection of defensive positions, location of machine guns, location of reserve units and checks on the system of night outposts and night patrols.

The regimental commander, who had been content to stay behind and let me run the whole show, became insistent that he make the tactical decisions when there was no enemy in front of us. One tactical decision which I considered important, and over which we could not agree, I took to the division commander, who backed me up. Thereafter, when we disagreed, I had only to ask him if he wanted to take the problem to division headquarters to win the argument.

Authority to make a number of promotions in the regiment was received in March. I made up a list of recommendations, relying upon the observations of the American officers and upon what I knew of the combat efficiency of the various Filipino officers. A list prepared by the regimental commander agreed with my list in about ten percent of the cases. At least fifty percent of his recommendations obviously were not merited, but were based on friendship, politics, seniority and standing in civil life.

I discussed the promotion problem with the regimental commander, calling his attention to the necessity of advancing the best officers only, but he would make no changes. The division commander promoted only those that I had approved, much to the surprise and annoyance of the regimental commander.

THE SHORTAGE OF FOOD

The ten of us Americans, nine officers and Boob McNutt, had a separate mess, one of the officers electing himself cook. He was quite good when he had anything to cook, but shortly after I returned our total accumulation of canned goods had dwindled to nothing. Since we were with a Philippine Army division, we were at a considerable disadvantage in having no established mess, so we had to look after ourselves.

We were receiving considerably less than one-half a ration, part of it being poor quality rice. A few times per week we received a small piece of meat, but we never knew whether it was going to be horse, mule or carabao. We were interested, because we soon decided that horse was better than carabao, and mule was better than horse. The slaughtering was done at night and delivery started early in the morning, but we received the meat in the late afternoon after it had been transported, without refrigeration or covering, throughout the fly infested tropical day.

The first little piece of meat we received became alive with maggots when it was placed in water. The vote among us was ten to nothing against the meat, so we threw it away. Before we received the next meat, we had learned that meat submerged in water a short time loses its inhabitants, which come to the top of the water ready to be thrown away. Thereafter, we threw away the worms, instead of the meat.

The shortage of food was becoming acute. Flour for the bakery ran out, so we ate our last bread. There had been a few wild pigs and carabao and lots of monkeys when we went into Bataan, but the dumb and unsuspecting animals were killed early. Meanwhile, the smart ones merely stayed a little deeper in the jungle. Even so, shots of hunters could be heard all through the daylight hours.

On a business trip to Little Baguio, Charles gave me a bottle of one hundred multi-vitamins, and suggested that I go see our friend, Colonel McConnell, a real gentleman from Indiana, who had charge of food supplies that had been brought in from the south by a blockade runner.[5] When I told McConnell of the sorry state of our small mess, he grinned and said, "Well since you just made the headlines in Aglaloma, I think you deserve a handout." He gave me an order on the quartermaster for the following:

1 Australian ham
1 #10 can jelly
5 cans evaporated milk
2 #10 cans green beans
5 lbs. flour
2 lbs. dried beans
2 lbs. coffee

When I brought the food into our camp that evening there was great joy in our mess. A coffee can was opened to give us a cup of coffee to drink to our good fortune before we went to bed. The vitamins were rationed out one per man per day, because [Lt. Col. Charles S.] Lawrence had told me he had some more he had salvaged from a partly sunken boat in the bay.

Our imported food was wonderful while it lasted. Someone produced a can of Australian rashers of bacon, which made him very popular for a couple of days. [Capt.] Al [Negley] came in from an inspection trip one evening with six chickens, which he had brought from a Filipino family he had stumbled onto along a trail behind his battalion area. The chicken was fried for the next night's meal, and I can assure you that there were no absentees at our crude table when the chicken was served.

Just as we were helping ourselves to the unusual delicacy the priest, who was the regimental chaplain, came to see us. Sherry, who was a good Catholic, was the only one of us with any manners that day, but his manners were not appreciated by a one of us when he invited the padre to supper. The priest's eyes were wide with astonishment, but that did not keep him from accepting promptly. He had his share of that chicken and enjoyed it as much as anyone. After the padre made an effusive departure, Sherry looked as if he was waiting for the storm to break but, to my knowledge, nobody ever mentioned the subject.

Another business trip to Little Baguio gave me an opportunity to visit Charles at mealtime, get a bite to eat and add to our vitamin supply. Looking at my shoes, Charles directed me to come with him to the clothing supply tent. I got a new pair of shoes, because as Charles told me, my old ones were shot and the supply was almost exhausted.

A QUEST TO MAINTAIN

On the way back to my headquarters, after passing through the rubble of what was left of Mariveles, I had a grandstand view of a Nip air attack without any of the worries that usually accompany them. A half-mile in front of us, our engineers had almost completed the construction of an air strip astride the road, but there were still a number of pieces of heavy machinery and, possibly, a hundred men at work.

Without warning, two Nip planes, flying perpendicular to the road, made a low-level attack on the field. They released their bombs too late, and they fell harmlessly about four hundred yards beyond the target. There were several bursts of anti-aircraft shells when the planes reached the edge of the bay, and the leading plane dropped in the water. The remaining plane must have gone on home. At any rate, it departed.

I stopped at the air strip to talk to an officer I knew, and while there I heard, for the first time, the so called ballad about "Dugout Doug."[6] It was not particularly vicious, but it had been composed to represent the Bataan-ite's resentment that he saw so little of the general and his staff, and that he imagined the inhabitants of Corregidor were living off the fat of the land and enjoying a safe invulnerable retreat.

General Casey drove up to inspect the progress of construction, so I had to congratulate him on his recent promotion.[7] The general, with his usual easy courtesy, replied that he would have the opportunity of return-ing the compliment before long. A couple of weeks later, we were electri-fied by the news that General MacArthur and a part of his staff, including General Casey, had gone to Australia. Of course, there was a great deal of resentment among those left behind, and the expression "Ran out on us" was on many tongues, but if there was a single officer who would not have given his right arm to have gone with him, at least he would have settled for his left.

I can never forget my elation when Ted came to my headquarters to tell me that General MacArthur intended to send for the remainder of his staff, and alerted me to be ready to go to Corregidor at an hour's notice, for he and two others were scheduled to go with the next group of staff officers for the purpose of setting up a supply system in Australia. It was our misfortune that our call never came.

It always surprised me, on Bataan and later in prison camp, how few people knew that General MacArthur had been ordered to Australia by the War Department, but that he had delayed his departure until an order, direct from the President of the United States, made his prompt compli-ance mandatory. General MacArthur's transfer moved General Wainwright to Corregidor as the high commander in the Philippines, and General King received command of the forces on Luzon.[8]

Our empty stomachs were beginning to tell on us, in that at the end of our day of inspections and other duties we could hardly drag ourselves home. The adulteration of gasoline with kerosene, and ever drastic rationing, had forced us to use "Shanks Mare" many times where formerly we had been able to ride.

Sammy, who had been with us at Stotsenburg, dropped in to our head-quarters to see Hugh and me one day. He heard us complain of our fuel difficulties and promised a little relief. He meant what he said, for the next day a truck stopped by our little camp to leave a fifty-five gallon drum filled with gasoline. The arrival of the gift brought a suggestion from Griff that he and I take a ride to Little Baguio early the next morning in search of food. He complained that before the war started he had been a member of an engineer officer's mess at Little Baguio that filled its storeroom with food the day before Pearl Harbor. Many of the officers had, like Griff, been transferred to combat units, so that Griff felt sure he had an interest in a sizable amount of food as the few officers who remained with the mess could not have eaten it all.

Our breakfast the next morning consisted of the last of our coffee, so Griff, Boob, and I took immediately for the engineer mess, with many expressions of good luck from the other seven to speed us on our way.

We drove along past the air strip, through Mariveles and started up the Zig Zag without incident. Close to the top of the hill we met a bus pulling into a ditch, all of its occupants of Filipino soldiers piling out the rear end. We saw no reason for their haste but, as a matter of caution, Boob stopped on the side of the road, allowing us to get out.

We had almost decided to continue the journey when twelve bombers floated over the hill. Our sudden twinge of fear began to fade, because there were no bombs in sight and the planes looked perfectly peaceful. We were rudely interrupted in our contemplation by heavy explosions, out of sight up the hill but rapidly nearing us.

Griff and Boob were under our car quicker than it takes me to tell it. Their undebated action, added to the approaching explosions, convinced me that I was in the wrong place and in the wrong position. The road under the car being well filled, I chose the ditch which was, I thought, the next best place.

As no bombs exploded in the road, it turned out that there was no choice between our selections of cover. We had resumed our journey before I gave Griff and Boob the devil for taking up all of the room under the car. They merely looked sheepish and had nothing to say.

Before we came in sight of it, we knew from our location of the clouds of smoke and dust that Hospital No. 1 had been hit.[9] It was an anxious ride up the mountain until we came in sight of the hospital to learn that it was not badly damaged, as most of the bombs had fallen outside the hospital grounds.

We stopped at the entrance, where a soldier was standing looking across the road at the smoking steel scraps of an automobile. The soldier, pointing to the scanty scraps, related how he had been flat on the ground looking at the car when a direct bomb hit and reduced it to nothing, along with the five Filipino and two American soldiers who were sitting in it.

We examined the area carefully, but we could not find the least trace of human remains. [While examining the bombed out car] a Nip photographic plane came down low over the area, sending us to the ditch, but soon we felt it was safe to go over to the hospital.

At the hospital one ward had been damaged, but the losses had not been great; as I recall two men [were] killed, one of them being a Nip prisoner, and several persons [were] wounded. One of the most painfully wounded was the tall nurse who was at Stotsenburg with us.

Griff led the way to the engineer office, near the hospital, where he had ample opportunity to use his persuasive powers. I was not surprised at Griff being successful [at acquiring food for our mess], but the extent of his success staggered me. Bringing the car up to the storeroom, Griff, with the help of the mess officer and Boob, loaded it down with loot. As a I recall we acquired, among other things:

20 lbs. flour
5 lb. can bacon
4 #10 cans corned beef hash
6 #10 cans vegetables
6 #10 cans fruit
1 gallon molasses
5 lbs. coffee
10 cans evaporated milk

At the engineer office, I saw Colonel Fertig, who had been at Stotsenburg several times before the war on construction matters.[10] Before the fall of Bataan, General Casey sent for him to go to Australia as his assistant, but he was not able to get any further than Mindanao.

He was home in Mindanao, where he had been an engineer for gold mining interests there before the war. His familiarity with the country and the people enabled him to escape to the hills when the Nips arrived, and to engage in guerrilla activities during the remainder of the war. He made quite a name for himself throughout the Philippines before and after the Americans reoccupied Mindanao, so much so that reports of his exploits filtered into our prison camp on Luzon.

The engineer mess being near to General King's headquarters, I felt I should pay him a call. Griff, with the safety of our valuable food supply on his mind, decided to stay with Boob, so I went to the general's office by myself. When I congratulated him on his elevation to the Luzon Command, he sat me down by his desk and smiling wanly he answered, "It is an empty honor."[11]

We discussed the supply situation and the tactical situation for about a half-hour. He told me that we were nearly out of quinine, but that we had been able to fly some in from Cebu.[12] He further told me that the food situation was critical, but that we had been promised two shiploads of food as soon as air cover could be made available, and that he hoped it would be soon. He inquired if I had planned to see Charles before I left, and when I assured him I did, he told me I could get more details about the supply situation from him.

His remarks on the tactical situation were most interesting to me, for he gave me the news that the Nips had constructed an elaborate defensive position near San Fernando, occupying them with part of the troops which, until recently, had been on our front.[13] It was his opinion that the time was right for us to counterattack if we only had sufficient offensive troops, supplies and air support, none of which we had.

I asked him how many casualties the Nips had suffered on Bataan.[14] He answered that, of course I knew of the more than three thousand men the Nips had lost on the west coast and, while he could not say how great the losses were on the front of II Corps, they had been considerable.

He told of the several assaults of the Nips which had been stopped by our defenses, and of the several engagements in which our artillery had taken advantage of favorable opportunities. For instance, our World War I "Long Toms" (the Nips called them "Devil Guns") had, by constant interdiction of the main road, denied it to Nip transport, forcing the construction of a new road through the jungle out of range of our guns.[15] Even though our old artillery was outranged by the Nips' modern guns, we had given a good account of ourselves.

The general added that the extensive time the Nips had been campaigning in malaria- and dysentery-infected country had, undoubtedly, cost them many men. I commented that it looked like the Nips did have a force strong enough to knock us out, that they were waiting for reinforcements, and that if the reinforcements did not arrive until after the rainy season began, we might have a chance provided we could get food. [The general acknowledged] that I had the complete picture [of the situation].

An officer interrupted to advise the general that eight enemy bombers were heading in our direction. General King insisted that I go with him to the bomb shelter, for he wanted to show how a general officer took cover. He was proud of the shelter [that] his engineers had dug into sloping ground so that he could walk into it and have standing room. I had to admit it was a very fine shelter but, with so many people in it, it grew hot very quickly.

An officer kept us amused with new expressions which had been coined during our little war. One that he told us I had never heard before, but I heard it many times later on the Death March and in prison camp. I believe the exact words were, "We are the Battling Bastards of Bataan; No Mother, No Father, No Uncle Sam."

After the raid, I took leave of the general and stopped by Charles' tent. Charles was talking to another officer, who kept an uneasy eye on the sky. He saw a lone Nip plane some distance away and rushed to the dugout, where he stood in the doorway while Charles and I sat in the tent talking. Charles gave me a resume of the food situation from the start of the war based on Colonel McConnell's report.

He stated that there had been very little food on Bataan when the war began but that McConnell had been directed to hold up heavy stocking of food, because it might tend to convince the Filipinos that we had no confidence in the ability of the Philippine Army to hold the Nips at the beaches.

I do not know where the order came from, but it was almost unbelievable, for I did not know a single officer who was familiar with the state of organization, equipment and training of the Philippine Army divisions who believed that they could cope successfully with trained Nip troops. McConnell, on his own initiative, sent a number of [shipments] loaded with food to Bataan, but he could not get authority to start shipping on a big scale until the twenty-third of December [1941], which allowed him only two days of shipping before Manila had to be abandoned.[16]

He said that General MacArthur's order of the twelfth of January [1942] to start issuing half rations was the result of a report he received that day advising him that the quartermaster [only] had twelve days' rations for the troops on Bataan. Every possible source of food had then been exploited in an effort to build up our food reserves. Blockade running of small ships from Cebu had been successful for a short time, deep sea fishing had added little, all the horses and mules had been slaughtered and either fed to the troops or stored in refrigerators at Corregidor, rice mills had been set up and all of the rice on Bataan had been salvaged.[17]

Filipino smuggling had been encouraged. Some carabao had been driven through the lightly held center of the Nips' lines and some had been rounded up on Bataan, all of which did little more than meet our current expenditure.[18] By the first of March [1942] most of those sources had been dried up, and the situation was becoming desperate. Hunger pangs were largely responsible for a minor crime wave in which two trucks loaded with food had been hijacked the previous night. It was going to be necessary to provide armed guards for each ration delivery.

We had been told that we had had a considerable amount of rice in storage near Tarlac when the retirement into Bataan started, but that it had been left behind.[19] He told me that he had been informed that recommendation had been made to USAFFE to remove that rice supply and others, plus all carabao that could be rounded up during the withdrawal, to add to our food supplies, but that the recommendation had been disapproved.

According to the story, Mr. Quezon personally had insisted to General MacArthur that the removal of staple foods from the Filipinos would result in their starvation. At any rate, the food was left for the Nips and I doubt that the Filipinos gained very much, while our loss was tremendous.

Sometimes it is difficult for the man on the ground to see the whole picture and to understand the reasons for decisions which seem to be insupportable. Many of the decisions made by General MacArthur which seemed to be contrary to military interests became understandable when we assumed that he well knew the Philippines were lost but that, above all else, his mission was to leave the islands a loyal mass of citizenry which had every reason to believe that the commonwealth had been more than fairly treated by the United States of America.[20] Actually, the majority of the Filipinos did remain loyal to the United States, and no persuasion of the Japanese could change that loyalty.

Our pilot friend, who had been in Australia, dropped in to see Charles primarily to find out if his bottle of scotch was empty. The little Charles had left did not last long, but it was long enough for us to hear a story. The pilot said he came from Australia in a navy flying boat which had made a night forced landing along the coast of Zamboanga.[21] With the help of some Filipinos, they had concealed the plane, repaired it in one day and continued the journey the next night.

The friendly Filipinos started to tell about a plane which had bombed the nearby town the week before, when one of the crew said, "My God, I was on that plane when we made a hurried run and dropped our load [on] a Nip ship in the bay, but our bombs overshot and hit in the town."

The Filipino continued, "Americans, damn smart. Japanese think Americans not know they all leave ship and hide in school house." When the Filipino was questioned he insisted that the Nips were the only ones killed in that attack, because the Filipinos had run away when the Nips landed.

Charles and I had a good laugh, and the pilot continued, "The Americans in Australia are all crying in their beer, 'What a shame it is those nice guys on Bataan had shot their wad and we can't do a thing about it. Too bad.' We did not laugh so loud at our friend's last offering.

As I left, Charles gave me another bottle of vitamins, which I added to the food supply when we got back to camp. While the cook prepared some of our newly acquired food, the boys at camp had a story to tell about a soldier who had been clever enough to kill a snake, cook it and have it for supper the previous night before, only to die in agony before morning. Somebody remarked that the story had been so thoroughly spread throughout the regiment that no snake need worry about his life from then on.

A rumor to the effect that in the 31st Infantry almost 50 percent of the men were on sick report, due largely to malaria, dysentery, diarrhea, and nutritional disease, was so alarming that I had a check made of the records of the regiment.[22] The sick reports did not approach that percentage, but a survey by the battalion's surgeons indicated that many more men should have been on sick report, and they further stated that there were numerous cases in which men were beginning to show symptoms of nutritional diseases which were not disabling at the moment, but soon would be.

In a few days we received a note from the division commander to the effect that he had been notified officially that the Nip commander had apologized for the bombing of Hospital No. 1. Notification of the Nip apology was received with some divergence of expression; a few of us announced that the Nips were not so bad after all, while the rest of us merely grunted "Nuts."

A LAST STAND

During the months of January and February [1942] we had witnessed many Nip air attacks on Corregidor. It was quite a sight to see formations of ten to twenty heavy bombers flying at an altitude of about ten thousand feet down the entrance of Manila Bay toward Corregidor. The first knowledge we had of an approaching attack was [an] unsynchronized hum of many motors. In a matter of seconds the planes came in sight, flying peacefully until they arrived within the range of anti-aircraft guns in positions on Bataan and on Corregidor, then the air around the formation was angry with the puffs of bursting shells.

The planes always continued through the anti-aircraft fire until their bombs were released, after which they veered to the south. The bomb explosions must have been terrifying to the inhabitants of the tunnels, for they were disturbing to us and we were twenty miles away. Huge clouds of smoke and dust arose from those parts of the islands where the bombs had hit, and the smoke continued to rise for days in areas covered by wooden buildings.

Many Nip planes were reported shot down; however, in two months of watching, I saw only one leave its formation to head north in the direction of Clark Field, streaming smoke and losing altitude. Their photographic plane, which we dubbed "Photo Joe," flew over our area at dawn each day, spending an hour or more with us.

Occasionally small groups of light bombers, flying freelance missions, attacked positions of our anti-aircraft guns, supply establishments and other points which, from a study of their aerial photographs, appeared to be inviting targets. It was not uncommon for a single light bomber to fly along the highway until it found an attractive target to greet with a bomb or two.

Our headquarters being near the highway, we became well acquainted with the noise and excitement of casual bombings. That did not bother us much, because we had a dozen or more holes dug around our little camp area for our protection when we needed to use them. Those holes were about four feet deep, and just large enough to permit a man to squat down and pull in his head. The holes were excellent and we found them quite adequate [to hide in when] highway traffic passing near our camp caught us [off guard].

The scurrying, confusion, and competition for holes which resulted taught us a good lesson. At first explosion one young captain, who already had a reputation for being "windy," started running around in circles shouting, "Where's my tin hat?" Several of us started for the same hole, and two officers actually jumped into the same hole so that neither one could get his head and shoulders below the ground.

After the raid was over, there was great hilarity among us and more than one red face. I assigned a definite hole to each man that very day, which solved the problem.

Collectively, we had had a great number of valuable experiences during the short time we had been in contact with the Nips. Pooling those experiences, so that logical conclusions could be drawn, I was able to establish a number of innovations which strengthened our position.

For instance, using dynamite, caps and fuses packed with coarse sand into joints of bamboo, we made a plentiful supply of hand grenades; and with bombs and mortar shells, we set booby traps at strategic locations. We organized an anti-sniper platoon, and we obtained a few more machine guns [to make] slight changes in our defensive positions. The changes strengthened our defenses, but I was more concerned in improving the fighting spirit of our soldiers than in strengthening our mechanical setup.

I started a program of training small units designed to improve the leadership of junior officers. I was convinced that in jungle fighting, where visibility was so poor, the leadership of small units was more important than in open country operations. Most of all, I wanted to instill in the mind of the individual soldier that he was as well armed and trained as the Nip soldier, and that he could engage in close combat with a Nip on at least equal terms.

We had noted that the undersized Filipino found the recoil of the rifle so jarring to his slight frame that he was prone to put the butt of the rifle on the ground to save his shoulder the blow of recoil, which resulted in his shot going high. We had noted also that when the Nips landed near small units in position, our troops had given ground. In order to assist the men in gaining confidence in themselves, and to improve their offensive quality, I requested the division commander to borrow, for one week, sixteen scout soldiers who had distinguished themselves in hand to hand combat against the Nips.

They arrived the next day and, assembling them, I explained that I intended to send four of them to each of the three battalions, and the other four to the headquarters units, to live with and talk to the men about combat as much as possible. During the training hours I wanted them to conduct bayonet practice and give as much instruction as possible in personal defense, but, above all, I wanted them to talk about their personal experiences and to convince the soldiers that the Nip was no better and perhaps not as good as they [were]. The battalion commanders and the American officers supervised that week of instruction and when the scouts had to leave I was able to congratulate them on a job well done.

You remember, of course, when we were in Stotsenburg how King Tomas used to bring his little negritos down from the slopes of Pinatubo on New Year's Day and whenever he was requested to demonstrate the skill of his warriors in the use of knife and bow and arrow.[23] The demonstrations were held in front of the officer's club so that at their conclusions the club presented the King and his contestants with all the food they could carry away.

On New Year's Day negrito women and children ran swiftly from house to house to receive a handout of canned goods, bread and soap. According to popular rumor the soap was considered more a delicacy for their holiday feasts than the other items. Establishing well guarded caches of their treasures on the parade ground until they had completed their visits to all of the houses, they loaded each person down with his share and started the trek back to their mountain fastness.

Willie became quite friendly with King Tomas, and on at least two occasions he paid him calls at his retreat in the middle of the jungle.[24] Before we evacuated Fort Stotsenburg, Willie hauled several cases of canned goods to King Tomas' domain and buried them at a place recommended by the King. Willie went to Bataan with the rest of us, going to the west coast. On a reconnaissance during the latter part of January [1942], he was ambushed by a Nip outpost and shot in the leg, but he yanked out his pistol and, going into action, he killed three Nips and got away.

As soon as his leg was healed, he headed a large patrol of Americans and Filipinos which started to make its way through the Nip lines en route to Pinatubo. When they crossed the road the Nips were using as a supply line, Willie laid an ambush which caught and annihilated a truckload of Nips. Moving rapidly, the patrol arrived at its destination without a loss. The patrol, with the help of the negritos, made a number of important reconnaissances and continued to make radio reports of Nip activities until after the fall of Corregidor. A short time later Willie was caught in a Nip ambush, to be jailed in Manila and later executed.

Our larder being empty again, Griff asked permission to pay another visit to the engineer mess. Boob already had started the car, so as soon as Griff got his permission they were on their way. Boob came back late in the afternoon with a sad looking Griff. Griff's clothes were dirty, his face lacerated, and his head had a couple of fairly long gashes. He hobbled out of the car swearing, "Those G—damned Nips were after me, they promised they would not bomb Hospital No. 1 any more just to get me in there."

Griff had run out to the engineer office when the explosions started, just in time to be blown over an embankment, where he had stayed until the bombers had disappeared. When Griff reappeared at the engineer office looking so dilapidated, he had no trouble getting another handout of food, although it was not as generous as the first one had been. I sent Griff to the regimental surgeon, who dressed his wounds and made out the report which gave Griff his first Purple Heart.

The damage to Hospital No. 1 was about the same as it had suffered in the first bombing. Colonel Duckworth, "a Gentleman from Indiana," cleaned out the debris, and his hospital continued to function as before.[25] Later, after the fall of Bataan, it was that same hospital which was visited by a Nip general. Colonel Duckworth met the general in front of the hospital, leading him through all of it but stopping first at the ward where the Nip wounded were located. The general, obviously astonished at seeing the Nips, asked them how they were treated, and upon learning that they were treated the same as Americans he went on.

The colonel ended his inspection tour at the cemetery, pointing out the graves of a few Nips buried with our own dead, and referring to the graves of those killed in the bombings of the hospital. They returned to the ward where the Nip injured were. Calling for transportation, the general had all of the Nips, even those with limbs in traction, removed to Nip control. We never knew what happened to them, but we heard they were all courtmartialed for surrendering. It is not unreasonable to assume that the majority of them were executed.

The colonel made such a good impression on the Nip general that the general gave him a written safeguard, and posted sentries to prevent the hospital from being overrun. Apparently, the general made a most favorable report to his headquarters, for the preferential treatment lasted until the hospital was closed.[26]

Our days of peaceful quiet had to come to an end. For several days we had been hearing reports of increased vehicle activity moving west along the new road just out of our artillery range. What was going on behind Mt. Natib was not known to us, except that somewhere the trucks were being unloaded and sent back along the road. Then the attack started on the center of our defensive line with an extremely heavy artillery preparation.[27]

There was increased activity in the air, largely of reconnaissance planes dropping leaflets. There were several different kinds of pamphlets, some of them being addressed to Filipinos and others to Americans, but they all stressed that Bataan was about to be captured and offered good treatment to any soldier who surrendered himself with that slip of paper. As far as we could tell the soldiers paid no more attention to them than General Wainwright had to a Nip surrender invitation he received.[28]

Before the end of the artillery preparation the Philippine Army Division in the center of the line had ceased to exist; consequently, the Nip assault troops pushed through the gap without opposition. There being only one improved road around Bataan following close to the coast, the center of our defensive line could be reached only by trails that, on the map, resembled a spider web stretched between the east and west coasts and held up in the middle by [the] Mariveles [Mountains].[29]

Down these trails from both coasts went infantry regiments of the American Philippine Division, but there were too many Nips, too many trails and too few regiments. A call came from the division commander advising me that the regiment had passed control of Luzon Force, and that it was directed to proceed to a road junction a little north of Little Baguio.

The regimental commander and I were to precede the regiment and report to General King at his headquarters as soon as possible [once we got there]. I gave Sherry instructions to get the regiment under way, and before the regimental commander and I moved, I remarked to our few Americans that it looked as if we were going to have our chance to see how the regiment would react in offensive combat. There were no cheers.

We rode along past Mariveles without incident, but when we started up the Zig Zag we met a solid column of vehicles of all types coming down. The traffic on our side of the road soon slowed down until the columns were slowly crawling by each other. Many of the vehicles coming down the hill were buses loaded with Filipinos.

From the snatches of conversation which we were able to pick up, we surmised that the Nips had made a complete breakthrough forcing all units, except those actively engaged with the enemy, to retire. From what we saw and heard we did not know the situation definitely, but we knew we were headed for a hot spot.

It was long after dark, but a half moon dipping in and out of cloud banks kept changing the road from a clearly illuminated line to an almost dense cloud [so] our driver turned on his dim lights. He had hardly turned them on when out of a car we were passing leaned the tall figure of John[30] shouting, "Turn those damn lights out, don't you know there are enemy planes overhead?" I laughed aloud as our lights went out, for I had seen a different John than I had ever seen before. In all the years that we had known him, I think you will agree, we had never heard him raise his voice or use a strong word.

With traffic stopped on the road some two miles away from General King's headquarters, the regimental commander and I set out on foot. From a position close by, a six-inch artillery piece fired periodically and it continued to fire throughout the night. I learned that it was interdicting the highway to discourage a Nip dash from that direction.

General King was busy at the time we arrived, so I telephoned the division commander to find out how the regiment was faring. He told me that the first battalion had been held up at Mariveles because of the traffic jam, and that the second battalion should have reached Mariveles, but that no transportation had arrived for the third battalion. He further told me that he had ordered the regiment to leave Mariveles without his authority, and directed that I keep him advised of developments.

When General King finished his business, he sent for me. First, he asked me if I was the regimental commander or the senior advisor, and when I replied, "senior advisor," he snapped, "That makes your job just twice as hard," but he did not send for the regimental commander. He wanted to know where the regiment was, and how long it would take to assemble it near a trail junction he located on the map for me. When I explained the traffic problem to him and that, in my opinion, the regiment could not arrive before dawn, he asserted, 'That's too late,' and directed me to remain nearby where he could reach me quickly.

Outside the office I met Charles, who was discussing the details of the evacuation of all the nurses from Bataan to Corregidor. They were then on their way by bus to Mariveles, where they were to be transferred to Corregidor by boat. We learned later that night there was no hitch in the plans, all nurses arriving at Corregidor safely. Turning to me, Charles recommended that I pay attention to what General King was doing, which I did for the remainder of the evening. The general listened to reports on the tactical situation, looked at his map and then called General Jones at I Corps, asking him if he had any troops that were capable of launching a counterattack.[31]

THE SURRENDER

As soon as he hung up, General King sent for General Parker and his [King's] chief of staff, telling them that General Jones reported he did not have a single organization that was capable of making a march followed by an attack.[32] Then he announced, "I have decided to surrender Bataan, for I have nothing left with which I can block the Japanese advance."

He telephoned Corregidor, asking for General Wainwright, but the general not being at his desk, General King apparently speaking to the chief of staff[33] [said], "All right I'll talk to you. Tell General Wainwright for me that I have decided to surrender Bataan. The Japanese attack has broken through the center of the line, they are pouring on all trails toward both the east and west coasts and I have nothing to stop them. This decision is solely my own, no member of my staff nor of my command has helped me to arrive at this decision. In my opinion, if I do not surrender to the Japanese, Bataan will be known as the greatest slaughter in history."

General [King] listened for a moment then sharply asked, "With what!' When he had hung up, General King announced, in explanation of his "With what!", that General Wainwright had wanted a counterattack launched from the west coast, and added that the chief of staff had gone to inform General Wainwright of the telephone conversation.

About fifteen minutes later General Jones called General King to inform him that he had received a call from General Wainwright's chief of staff. As I recall, based on what I heard General King say, General Jones had been urged to launch an attack from the west coast, and he had been advised that, possibly, he might be detached from General King's command.

The general was quite perturbed as he hung up and looked around. Seeing me, he directed that I stay here, for if General Jones was removed from his command our regiment would remain with him instead of reverting to I Corps.

Calling General Wainwright's headquarters again, he demanded to know what the decision was with reference to I Corps, in view of the fact that General Jones had reported to General Wainwright exactly as he had to General King that he could not launch an attack. General King continued, "I want a definite answer as to whether or not General Jones will be left in my command regardless of what action I may take."

There was a considerable pause, during which I assumed that a discussion was going on at the other end of the line. Two or three minutes later General King said, "Thank you very much" and hung up. Turning to his staff, he reported that General Wainwright could not agree to a surrender of Bataan as General MacArthur had ordered him to hold on, but that if General King did surrender on his own authority there would be no interference with any element of his command. Someone remarked, "That's good," but the general went on to say that if he survived to return home he fully expected to be court-martialed, and he was certain that history would not deal kindly with the commander who would be remembered for having surrendered the largest force the United States had ever lost.[34]

To a staff officer he directed, "Find out the hour the ordnance officer will be ready to blow up our ammunition stores and let me know." With a sigh, he told me that I could take the regiment back to its former location after the arsenal had been blown up. I immediately called the division commander, bringing him up to date on what had gone on. He advised me that he would take care of the regiment, so all I had to do was to report to his headquarters when I got back.

General King sent for Colonel Williams and a young major, briefed them on the current situation, and informed them that he had selected them to drive north on the main highway until they contacted the Nips to advise them of the decision to surrender.[35] He told them that he wanted their car to fly a large white flag and proceed cautiously to avoid being fired on. A staff officer reported that the arsenal would be ready to be blown up at 3:00 A.M. General King thanked him and directed Colonel Williams to proceed at 4:00 A.M.

Charles and I followed a trail to a dugout so that we would know where to go before the arsenal was destroyed, because we had been warned that the camp area was in the danger zone. A violent earthquake, coming at that time, took our minds off the war. The trees around us swayed and groaned, and the earth tremors rising through our feet gave us a queer feeling of insecurity. One tremor followed another for an interval of about two minutes.[36]

I went back to headquarters where I sat down to wait the danger-hour. At 2:55 [A.M.] I started slowly ambling toward the dugout. I was about halfway there when it seemed to me the whole earth blew up. The explosion was so breathtaking, the shaking of the earth so violent, that [I] could not go on. Throwing myself flat with my head between the roots of, and close against, a big tree, I waited for I did not know what as rain of steel pattered through the leaves.[37]

Several hot pieces fell on my legs, forcing me to scramble until I shook them off. One explosion followed another, each of them shaking the trees much more violently than the earthquake had, as I wondered if a large piece of steel might not be following the small pieces and hunt me out. But all things come to an end in time and, eventually, I was at headquarters to see Colonel Williams and the major taking their leave of General King.

On [the] morning of April 9, 1942 I had a chance to shake hands with the general before I picked up the regimental commander and [moved] back to our camp. Upon leaving his headquarters, I had nothing but admiration for General King. During the year I had served as a staff officer under his command at Fort Stotsenburg I had known he was a fine officer, and there was never the slightest doubt that he was a gentleman through and through. But not until those last eight hours had I suspected the strength and depth of his character. In spite of the certainty that his name would be forever linked with the disgrace of the surrender of the greatest force that the United States had ever lost, and the belief that he would be court-martialed at the end of the war, he had had the courage to do what he thought was right. In this action, he had not relied on the support of any member of his command and he had been actively opposed by higher authority. It is my honest opinion that there was no greater hero on Bataan than he.

If you recall the press and radio reports from the Philippines, and from other sources which were available to you in the early stages of the war in the Philippines, you will realize that you were led to believe that an invincible combined force of American and Filipinos, numbering one hundred thousand men, was defeating the Nips in every engagement and that our final victory was never in doubt. Actually, the victory of the Nips was never in doubt, because the bulk of our forces was inadequately prepared for combat.

At the time of the surrender of Bataan, there were in the Luzon Force approximately ten thousand Americans and less than sixty thousand Filipinos. The American combat units consisted of the infantry regiment, one anti-aircraft regiment, and a tank group, totaling about four thousand men, the remainder being dismounted air corps and service troops.

The scout combat troops, not counting the artillery, totaled about four thousand men, and the infantry troops, both American and scout, barely exceeded five thousand. All of those men were half-starved, and at least forty percent of them were ineffective because of sickness. The Nips brought fresh, well trained troops from Japan for the attack on our defenses, and the power of their attack had been overwhelming on our starving, untrained and depleted Philippine Army Divisions.

General King had nothing left to stop the Nip attack when he decided to surrender. He well knew that the Nips were on the verge of overrunning Bataan and, judging from his knowledge of Japanese history, he believed the Nips would kill every man on Bataan, unless he forestalled the assault by surrendering. A number of years have passed, adding immeasurably to my knowledge on Nip character, and somewhat to my general knowledge, but I have learned nothing which would cause me to doubt that General King's estimate of the situation and his resulting decision were the best he could have made.

Shortly after daylight we passed the junction leading to the boat-landing at Mariveles. We could see several boats waiting there and some soldiers aboard. How I wanted to go aboard one of those boats and escape to Corregidor, but I could not quite submerge my conscience for I had been ordered by the general to return to my outfit and, besides, I could not run out on my friends and comrades.[38]

We passed the smoking remains of a sub-arsenal to hear a series of explosions along the road ahead. The road was blocked because an artillery dump on fire was going up one shell at a time. A single Nip plane dropping occasional bombs along the road drove us into the forest. The lone plane reminded me that our last P-40 had taken off just before dawn for the comparative safety of the islands farther south. I heard later that Thorne, who had commanded one of the squadrons in my section of the west coast, had been the fortunate pilot.[39] He was the officer you talked to in Texas after he got back, giving you the most recent news of my war activities.

The regimental commander and I sat on a log waiting for the ammunition dump to burn out. I made some reference to the difficult position General King had been in from the moment he took command of the Luzon Force until he had to surrender. The regimental commander shouted, "What did you say?" total disbelief written all over his face. I explained the situation to him, whereupon he burst into tears. The incredulity on my face surely matched his, for it was inconceivable to me that he could have been at General King's headquarters the night before, heard and seen the destruction of a vast amount of ammunition and seen the disorderly traffic snarls without realizing that our part of the war was over. Apparently he was still planning a "victory parade" in Manila, as it never occurred to him that Bataan could be lost.

On our arrival at camp, I took a few minutes to relate the important news to Sherry and the others before going to division headquarters to see the general. The division commander informed me that, by direction of the Nips, General King had gone to Nip Headquarters for a conference.[40] I informed the division commander that most of my American officers and a number of the best Filipinos had spoken of going to the hills instead of surrendering. I suggested a possibility of the general leading a picket detail through the Nip lines following Willie's trail to Pinatubo, but he answered, "If the commanding general had wished that I take a patrol to the mountains he would have told me. I received orders from my commander to surrender myself and my command and I am a soldier who carries out orders." I asked him if he would authorize the immediate departure of a patrol if someone else led it, to which he answered, "No!"

Up until 3:00 P.M. [April 9, 1942,] we received no news, then the I Corps commander called to say that no word had been received from General King while the Nips on his front were attacking. He had given orders to resist, and he directed our division commander to block the highway coming from Mariveles so as to prevent any advance from that direction pending further information. The division commander directed that I take the regiment, and one battalion of scouts that had just arrived, and block the road about a half-mile in front of our camp.

Returning to camp, I directed that one battalion report to me at the road junction where I intended to place the defensive position. The remainder of the regiment also was directed to take up a position in reserve near our camp. The scout battalion was at the defensive position when I arrived, but what a battalion it was. The men had been informed before noon that the war was over, and they had thrown their arms away, substituting white flags for their guns. I tried to get them off the road into the jungle before our battalion arrived, but I was not successful.

The story of surrender spread like wildfire, so that the newly arrived men started to throw their arms away. When I appealed to the battalion commander he did get his companies into position, but I knew there was no fight left in the men. I returned to camp to report my action and the quality of my troops to the division commander, his answer being, "You know the orders, you will comply."

Back with the forward position, I spent the next two hours literally sweating out an impossible situation. General King had surrendered us, yet I had command of a defensive force which was practically useless, under order to allow no Nips to pass our position. The American officer with me tried to reassure me by telling me that there would be at least one man to back me up when I started shooting. It was the greatest relief to me when orders came down at dark to withdraw and go into bivouac at our permanent camp.

I assembled all the Americans at supper to repeat my conversation with the division [commander] relative to taking to the hills. I told them that I was not in good enough physical condition to try to pass through the Nip lines to reach Pinatubo. I further told them that, under the circumstances, I saw it my duty to stay and accept surrender, but that I would order out a patrol consisting of all those who felt that their chances were better in the hills. Moreover, that I would take full responsibility for their absence in the event they were cut off and did not come back. After brief discussion among themselves, every man decided he would stay.

That night was a hectic one for us, because the traffic both ways on the highway outside our camp was quite heavy. In the middle of the night we could hear the explosion of firecrackers all up and down the road. The firecrackers were obviously Nip property, but we concluded we had a number of Filipino spies among us who were using them instead of the Nips.

The following morning we destroyed or buried all of the guns and other mementos of our victory over the Nips and, telling our Filipino friends goodbye, we [then] joined the division commander at his headquarters. He could tell us very little, except that a Nip representative was expected any time to give us detailed instructions. We heard Nip tanks and trucks on the highway, but we remained quietly where we were, to be missed for the entire day.

An interpreter arrived late the second day, [April 10, 1942,] to tell us that the following morning we would proceed to Mariveles. The last two meals were combinations of the remains of Griff's last handout and the bottom of the general's larder. During our last night of freedom we discussed our war, particularly with respect to accomplishments. We wondered if we had fought in vain, or if we had made even a slight contribution toward a favorable end of the war.

Cadet Irvin Alexander,
West Point Class of 1919.
COURTESY OF SARA SPINDLE.

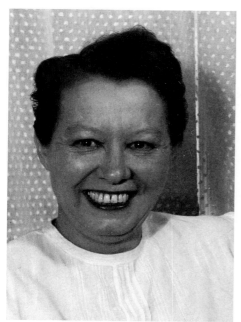

Lucile Alexander at about the time she
departed the Philippines in May 1941.
COURTESY OF SARA SPINDLE.

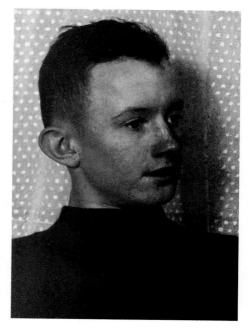

Sammy Alexander in the mid-1940s.
COURTESY OF SARA SPINDLE.

Fort Stotsenburg, 1941 Quartermaster officers. Left to right: Lt. Col. Charles S. Lawrence. Col. Irvin Alexander, and Col. W. E. "Pop" Durst. Note the newly issued olive drab helmets. This photograph was printed in San Antonio newspapers to indicate that three San Antonio natives wer prisoners of war in Bataan. COURTESY OF SARA SPINDLE.

Maj. Gen. Edward P. King, commander of Luzon forces surrendering to Lt. Gen. Masaharu Homma's operations officer, Col. Motoo Nakayama, at Lamao at 12:30 A.M. on April 10, 1942. COURTESY OF THE NATIONAL ARCHIVES.

A prisoner on the Death March in April 1942. Notice that the American has his hands tied behind his back. COURTESY OF THE NATIONAL ARCHIVES.

This photograph, captured from the Japanese, shows American prisoners using improvised litters to carry comrades who, from lack of food or water on the march from Bataan, died along the road. COURTESY OF THE NATIONAL ARCHIVES.

Chaplain Quinn outside the Cabanatuan Library in 1942. COURTESY OF THE NATIONAL ARCHIVES.

Lt. Col. Carl Englehardt in front of the Cabanatuan barracks, some time in 1943. Englehardt was a language officer and was used as an interpreter by the Japanese. The tables behind him were owned by prisoners who had a garden for rice and corn. COURTESY OF THE NATIONAL ARCHIVES.

Maj. Jim Neary standing beside a surface well and working in the garden at Camp Cabanatuan. In the garden is okra, eggplant, and pigweed. Neary died at Fukuoka, Japan, on January 5, 1945. COURTESY OF THE NATIONAL ARCHIVES.

Lt. Col. Moe Daly, an all-American football player at West Point, in Cabanatuan holding an axe. Daly died on a prison ship en route to Japan on January 21, 1945. COURTESY OF THE NATIONAL ARCHIVES.

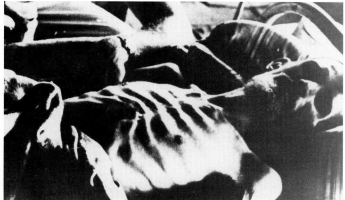

An American prisoner of war dying of dry beriberi. COURTESY OF THE USMA SPECIAL COLLECTIONS SECTION

An American prisoner with wet beriberi. COURTESY OF THE USMA SPECIAL COLLECTIONS SECTION.

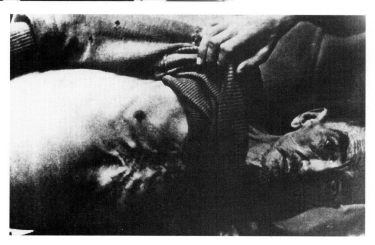

The Oryoko Maru *prison ship being sunk off Olangapo, Luzon, on December 15, 1944.* COURTESY OF THE NAVAL HISTORICAL FOUNDATION.

Cabanatuan Camp No. 1 on January 31, 1945, after the Rangers liberated the prisoners of war. COURTESY OF THE USMA SPECIAL COLLECTIONS SECTION.

Gen. Jonathan Wainwright pins the Distinguished Service Cross on Col. Irvin Alexander after the war, at Brookes Field, Texas. COURTESY OF SARA SPINDLE.

Lucile and Irvin Alexander on their trip to Mexico after his repatriation. COURTESY OF SARA SPINDLE.

Alexander with his granddaughter Julie in 1960. Alexander passed away three years after this photograph was taken. COURTESY OF SARA SPINDLE.

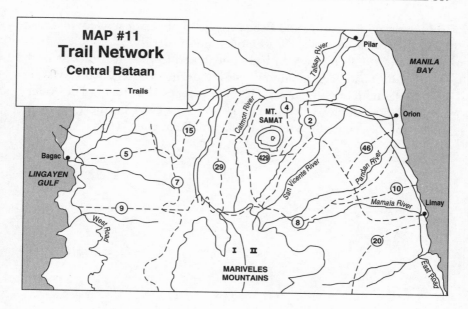

We older officers knew that, in the estimate of our planners, Manila Bay could be closed to an enemy for six months. Now that Bataan had fallen, we were well aware that Corregidor could not last much longer. We had lasted on Bataan a little more than four months, and Corregidor actually kept up the defense for almost another, extending the time to an even five months, or one month short of our plans.

What would be the effect of a five-month delay in opening Manila Bay we did not know, but we knew that we had delayed the Nips' timetable, and that it had been necessary to land several new divisions in order to crack the nut of Bataan. We had heard from Nip prisoners, later we heard it many times during our first months in prison, that the Nips were on the way to Australia. We hoped that our efforts had delayed the Nips long enough to allow a sufficient time to prepare defenses. We had been an outpost, posted to project the main body. We had been an expendable force with a delaying mission to perform. Perhaps we had fulfilled our mission.

We wondered, also, what had been the effect on the Filipinos of our military effort. Most of us were convinced that, in general, it had been excellent. With the exception of a few instances of inability and cowardice, the leadership and example set by Americans had been superb. Time after time, under the most difficult and trying circumstances, young Americans had fought with a daring and a total disregard of personal safety that made them an inspiration to all who saw or heard of them.

One of the factors which had contributed to the great success of the scout soldiers had been the fine leadership of their officers, who well merited the faith and confidence their soldiers reposed in them. The Americans set an example which, for years to come, will be the goal of the officers of the army of the infant Philippine Republic.

Chapter 8

Overcoming Temptation
in the Eye of a Storm

One Autumn morning, the sun was shining brightly into the bedroom and the warm air felt almost like spring had arrived. A glance out of the window told him that it was still fall, for the trees were beginning to look lean with their colored leaves half on and half off.

His head was clear and he felt stronger than he had for a long time. His feeling of well being was accompanied by a craving to go outside and lie in the sun. He called down the stairway to his wife that he was hungry for a change and strong enough to sit at the breakfast table.

She came to the foot of the stairs to answer, "You may come anytime, breakfast is almost ready." Wearing slacks and a sweater and carrying a blanket, he eased down the stairs.

She met him at the bottom, her hands on her hips as she questioned, "Where do [you] think you are going?"

"After breakfast I would like to lie out by the side of the house in the sun," [he replied].

"Getting pretty frisky for an old bird, aren't you?" [she answered with a smile].

After breakfast they both went outside the house where they sat on the blanket in the warm sunshine. Pointing down the hill, he called her attention to the fair V-shaped trace of a deer trail, which came up one side of the draw, crossed at the top and then ran back toward Salt Creek[1] on the other side.

"That is where I saw the big buck outfox a foxhound last summer," he said. "I had heard the hound barking on the trail for some time. I knew he was following his nose and, as he gradually came closer, I suspected that he was trailing a deer. Suddenly, a big buck appeared out of the woods and came bounding along the trail, stopping at the tip of the V.

"His antlers, which were huge, must have been still in velvet for they looked almost black. He was truly a magnificent creature, and he made an unforgettable picture as he stood intently watching along the trail until he saw the hound emerge from the woods. Then he jumped across the ditch and bounded, unhurriedly, down toward Salt Creek, flying his huge white flag. That flag was not a surrender flag, for he soon reached the creek to double back on his trail, leaving it so confused the hound could not follow.

"The buck appeared proud to be alive and he certainly was determined to stay FREE. Today I, also, am glad to be alive and I strongly hope that all Americans are determined to stay FREE."

After a while she mused, "You were so peaceful last night you probably had no bad dreams at all."

[He pondered her remark for a moment and replied,] "If I did I do not recall them."

"The last time you talked about Bataan you mentioned the pretty nurses; why don't you tell me about some of the ladies who came into your life during the war years?"

"There you go,"[he answered.] "That curiosity of yours is certainly chronic. Did I ever ask a single question about *your* war activities?"

"Of course not," [she confidently snapped,] "Because you knew my so-called war activities were not worth talking about. *So,* if you had any interesting experiences with the ladies, I am impatiently waiting to hear them."

[Immediately he responded with equal confidence.] "You heard too many tall tales about the gay Spanish girls in Manila, the *lavenderas* moving into houses vacated by the wives when they came home, about the unprecedented sale of dress goods, and about the chaplain who turned up in the hospital as a venereal patient five days after he put his wife aboard for home."

[Pausing for a moment he then continued.] "You forget that we fought the war on the hard side of this world. We had no London, no Rome, no Paris, no Berlin and no Vienna to help us forget the war. Also you forget that we were considerably handicapped by being prisoners of war for almost three and one-half years. When one reaches a certain stage in starvation, the usual subject for stag conversation changes from females to food. Blondes and brunettes are pushed into the background by such rivals as bread and beef. I can see that you are in no mood for alibis, so this time I am going to tell you one or two tales which I do not guarantee to be true, and I want you to remember, if you do not like them, you asked for them."

[Cautiously, she said,] "I am listening."

"Before the war began, Swede[2] arranged a Saturday evening party with two very nice Spanish girls. We took them to 'Jai A Lai' for dinner, going to the dance at the Army and Navy Club afterwards.[3] When we arrived at 11:00 P.M., the club was crowded. Most of the male faces of the dancers were familiar ones but, except for one nurse who went over to the islands on the boat with us, I did not know a single woman. It was pretty obvious that the rule restricting the club to the white races had been relaxed, insofar as it applied to females. The girls with us wanted to dance, so we danced.

"As you are too well aware, I dance so poorly that it takes a very good dancing partner to keep dancing from being work to me, and neither of the girls was that good. That night grew hotter as the orchestra played on, and the girls showed no inclination to leave. We got away from the club at 2:30 A.M., where we left them, just about three hours later than I would have liked to. I stayed away from Manila from that time until the war started."

[Listening intently she responded almost in a soft but somewhat sarcastic manner,] "How very exciting."

"The next Saturday evening, I walked up the line to play poker with friends. There being plenty of good scotch, it was a pleasant, if unprofitable, evening. After the game, it was raining cats and dogs, so being invited to occupy the extra bunk, I spent the night. Sometime in the wee small hours, I was awakened by a strange noise out in the hall. I slid out of bed and slipped along the hall toward the front porch. Reaching the porch, I stood in the doorway peering out into the dripping, but otherwise uneventful, night for a long time. I started to go back to bed when, with a sudden scream, a small feminine figure in a nightgown ran by me back into the house. She was so close to me when she screamed so unexpectedly that I almost jumped out of my skin and my pajamas at the same time. I never found out who the girl was, or where she was bound, but obviously she was not looking for me"

[In response to this his wife replied,] "That was terribly impersonal."

[He continued on, ignoring her remark,] "One evening sometime later, I was alone at home, reading in my bedroom. A gentle tap at the door startled me. There stood a dainty Filipino girl dressed in a bright new evening gown. Her hair, arranged very carefully, shone like polished ebony. She had tucked a lovely mimosa in her hair over her right temple. Her face, which was powdered to a mestizo shade, was fixed in a demure smile.

"'Who are you?' I asked as soon as I had recovered from my astonishment.

"'Nita,' was her answer as she stood motionless except for a slight lift of a tiny graceful hand.

"I thought of many things, especially of the moral relaxation to be expected with a war almost upon us. Vaguely, I wondered who had sent this pretty expectant vision, for she obviously knew who I was. She moved a step, and then I noticed her feet. They were large for such a small girl, and they were bare. Somewhat darker than the girl's face, they were covered with bruises and calluses. [She probably] had never worn shoes. Instantly a spasm of nausea came over me and as soon as it was gone I told the girl that since I was very busy that night she would have to excuse me. She disappeared, and I never saw her again. You know that peculiar fastidiousness of mine or, if you prefer to call it, my aesthetic sense."

"Yes," [she answered him, obviously happy to hear the outcome of the conversation]. "And you certainly are consistent, in your stories; anyway I might as well go see about lunch."

Chapter 9

The First Prison Camp

SETTLING IN AT CAMP O'DONNELL

In the late morning sunshine, which had removed all trace of the heavy frost, the young pines dotting the hillside looked more like Christmas trees than ever. There was [a] Christmas feeling in the air which the sunshine could not remove. The smoke, drifting slowly from the chimney of the house on top of the hill, was in keeping with the scene and it promised a more comfortable warmth than the sun could provide. As he wearily climbed the hill, he mused that the pines seemed to have grown enormously since the grass and vines around them had faded, and that they were furnishing all of the green which showed on the hillside. After he had reached the top of the hill, before going into the house, he looked back over the forest-covered hills beyond.

She came to the door to announce that lunch was almost ready and, as he started to come in, she said, "I agree with you that, even with all those trees looking like dreary skeletons, the hills are still beautiful."

During lunch he assured her that he had not overdone his exercise, that he felt fine and that he had planned to talk to her about Japanese prison camps if she felt like listening.

Choosing his easy chair by the window, he began.

Although we had passed through a series of Nip prisoner enclosures, Camp O'Donnell was our first permanent [POW] camp. The word "permanent," as I just used it, must be loosely defined as "non-transient," for the camp had been constructed prior to the war as temporary housing for one of General MacArthur's Philippine Army divisions.[1] Even the word "housing," as it applied to the camp, must not be given its usual interpretation for it consisted, in general, of a limited number of primitive kitchens designed for steaming rice, and barracks which were nothing but simple thatch-covered sheds, designed for sleeping quarters.

The sheds were possibly twenty-four feet wide, the center one-third being floor and the outside two-thirds being platforms raised one and one-half feet and covered with split bamboo. The raised platforms formed the combined living and sleeping quarters for the occupants, each man lying with his head to the wall and his feet to the center, having a space [of] eight feet for himself and all his possessions unless the building was crowded, in which case he was lucky if he had enough room to stretch out. The sides of the buildings were hinged to stay open, except during the hardest rains.

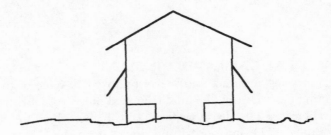

Alexander's sketch of the outside of the barracks at Camp O'Donnell.

Due to the tropical climate, there was no need for a heating system or [such] luxuries as doors and windows. Crude and uncomfortable as the living quarters were, they were better than we had had for almost two weeks and far cleaner.

We were marched directly from the welcome speech by the commandant to a barracks where we had the pleasure of stretching out on a clean surface in the shade. Charles came in carrying a blanket, which he had seen I needed at the time the Nips were inspecting us. He insisted that I go to his shack the next day for a complete change of clothing. He was one of the lucky ones of General King's headquarters staff who had the unbelievable good fortune to be loaded in a truck with all of his baggage one morning, and to be dropped at Camp O'Donnell the same afternoon. He was already an old timer at camp for he had been there ten days.

At his shack the next day, I borrowed Charles' equipment to give myself a shave and a sponge bath, after which he provided a clean suit of underwear, a pair of socks and a clean cotton uniform to replace my filthy rags. I did not put on the uniform immediately, because I saw one object in his footlocker which promised more in the nature of comfort than everything else. That was a hot water bottle with an enema attachment. During the previous thirteen days of little food and extreme exhaustion, I had not had a bowel movement. I was beginning to feel somewhat uncomfortable and, if it had not been for the low residue diet that had been forced upon me, I might have felt considerably worse.

Having made good use of the valuable equipment, I dressed in my new clothes, combed my hair and returned to my shack with a feeling that I might surmount whatever came my way. My feeling of well-being even survived the next meal, which consisted of a too small amount of steamed rice and a small steamed *camote*, the native yam. That meal was not as good as the normal one, for usually in the evening we had a thin watery soup[2] made from whatever vegetables had been issued to us the day before.

Twice the first month, our soup was faintly reminiscent of beef, as a matter of fact one time I found a piece of beef a wee bit larger than my thumbnail. The Nips were munificent in their issue of beef for they gave us two whole calves that dressed out a total of two hundred pounds of meat and bone to flavor the soup of ten thousand men. You can visualize the strength of the soup much better if you realized that the soup of each fifty men contained a whole pound of carcass beef.

After I had recovered enough strength to become curious, I noted that Camp O'Donnell was divided into three parts, the Nips occupying the middle part along the east and west highway for their headquarters, barracks and storehouses. That part of the camp to the south of the Nip area was an enclosure for the fifty thousand Filipinos, leaving the north part of camp as an enclosure for the ten thousand Americans.

Within the strict limitations of Nip orders, the operation of the Filipino camp was under the direction of the senior Filipino officer, and the operation of the American camp was the responsibility of General King. The Nips delegated responsibility to the generals only insofar as they could shed work and undesirable duties from themselves.[3]

For instance, General King was authorized to maintain order and police within his area. Such food as was issued by the Nips, he could have prepared and served to the men. In a building set aside as a hospital he could collect the sick, but he had almost no medicine with which to treat them. He could [also] send out burial details and dig latrines under Nip supervision, and he could select the personnel for such labor details as might be required.

We had to admit that the delegation of authority was not very extensive, but to us it was an important one, in that we were removed a little from the weight of oppression of a race whose language and customs were so different from our own. The Nip commandant published a list of major offenses, the penalty for most of them being "DEATH." Upon his order that poorly translated, poorly printed document was posted at various prominent places in the camp, more for the purpose of showing the power of the commandant than to prevent individuals from committing offenses.

For about a week after I had been welcomed at O'Donnell, another contingent of Americans arrived each day. Pop came with the last group, in much better condition that I had been when I arrived; in fact, except for his hair, he did not look his almost sixty years.

The incoming men were lined up for inspection[4] as we had been, and then marched to the platforms where they were to be greeted by the commandant. At the end of inspection, one of the civilian interpreters, a Japanese boy of sixteen who had been born and raised in the Philippines, came into one of our storage rooms asking for a match. He then proceeded to burn a handful of Nip money, explaining to us that he was burning it secretly to save the life of the POW on whom he had found it.

The day after Pop arrived, dysentery overtook him. His barracks building was only twenty-five yards from the latrine, but it was too far away. When a spasm of pain overtook him he was unable to control himself until he could reach the latrine, and he got back to the shack only to start the run again. He became so weak that he had to take his blanket to the *cogan* grass twenty feet from the latrine. With a little bush for shade, there he lay, when not visiting the latrine, for three painful days.

On the second day I persuaded a doctor to go look at him. When we were out of Pop's hearing, the doctor told me that there were hundreds of cases of dysentery in camp with not nearly enough medicine to go round. He said that Pop's age was against him, which made him doubt the wisdom of giving him any medicine that might be better utilized by a younger man. He finally did agree to provide Pop with about one-third of the amount of sulfa pills he should have had.

Pat and I actually gave him the pills at the proper intervals with amazing results, for he was sitting up showing an interest in life the next day. Alas, we were too optimistic, for on the following day he had a relapse. The doctor provided a few more pills, which he insisted were the last he had. That time fortune smiled on Pop, for he recovered completely to resume his normal prison life. Although we did not think much of his chances at the time, he survived the hardships of our prison years to return home, where he now leads a pleasant peaceful life.

After the war started, the Nip civilians in Manila had been apprehended and placed in a detention area with Sherry in supervisory charge.[5] He had performed that unpleasant duty so efficiently that he had won the respect of the more important Nips. When Manila had been evacuated the civilians had been released, Sherry going on to Bataan. Sherry's previous duty had been forgotten, so it was a surprise when one day two of the Nips who had been in the detention camp came to O'Donnell to see him, bringing a fat hen in token of the Nips' goodwill and esteem.

There I go again, using an adjective in the Philippine sense instead of its accepted American sense. The hen was as fat as hens get in the islands but it never would have passed as such in one of our meat markets. The Nips who brought the bird were no sooner gone than Sherry hunted us all up to invite us to share it that night. There were no refusals, so our friend, Kips, who had been a cook in his youth, stewed the bird which we all divided equally, even to the gravy. There was not a one of us who did not swear that it was the most delicious bird in his life, but I doubt that there was anyone who did not tell himself he could have eaten it all without help. Sherry's generosity that night erased any resentment which may have existed since he had invited the chaplain to help us eat the fried chicken that Al had brought us on Bataan.

About two weeks after we arrived at O'Donnell, the Nips notified General King that, beginning the next morning, the officers would be interrogated by groups of intelligence officers of the Imperial Japanese Army. We were somewhat apprehensive for we had no idea what the scope of the interrogation would be. The next morning, when I walked into the room occupied by the group to which I was assigned for questioning, my heart had increased its tempo somewhat, but I concluded very soon that I did not need to be greatly concerned.

The three Nips at the table were young, well dressed lieutenants of such affability and intelligence that I suspected they had been in civil life until very recently. They gave me a cigarette and, in perfect English, they talked about trivialities for a time in order to put me at ease. Their only military interest seemed to be about Corregidor, so when I answered the first question by stating that I had never been to Corregidor and was not familiar with any details of its defense, they lost interest in me.

My interview lasted not more than fifteen minutes, during which time the Nips learned exactly nothing. One American colonel decided he would stand on his rights, so when the first military question was asked him, he answered that according to the Geneva Convention and International Law he was required to give his correct name only; therefore, he would decline to answer any other questions. The group of young officers released him after a few moments and let him go back to the camp feeling that he had won a great victory.

The following morning the colonel received a message from the Nip commandant that he would be given one more chance to answer questions. The vivid memory which the colonel had of Nip brutalities, and the posted list of the crimes for which the punishment was "Death," convinced him that he did not have to stand on his rights after all.

THE ENEMY GARB

During our combat days in the jungle we had seen very few live Nips; most of them being prisoners who were half-naked when they gave themselves up. Before the start of the Death March we had seen very few Nips in uniform. The period between the surrender of Bataan and the arrival at Camp O'Donnell was such a strenuous time that it was not until after we had been at O'Donnell a little while that we acquired a comprehensive picture of the Nip in his military clothes.

The general impression we received from a casual glance at a Nip uniform was that it was made up of a conglomeration of articles procured in a military [costume] shop. I believe you will understand better what I mean if I describe some of the articles of outer apparel.

The color of the uniform varied considerably, and so did the tailoring, but the articles I shall describe were typical. The cap was something like an overseas cap with a small visor, but in its shape it reminded me of the fur cap for winter wear which our army issued many years ago to troops stationed in cold climates. The Nip cap also had earflaps and a flap that hung down at the back of the neck but, instead of being made of fur, they were made of very light cotton, so light that they waved with the wind and with the motion of the wearer. The purpose of these strange flaps was to protect the face and neck from the sun.

The shirt looked like the old-timers designed for detachable collars and cuffs, most of them having only one pocket. They were fastened by cloth toggles instead of buttons, down about a foot and a half from the neck, for that was as far as they opened, from which we inferred that the coat type shirt had not met favor in Japan.

The breeches, which were held up by tie strings instead of a belt, had a right hip pocket, some of them having side pockets as well. To make up for the lack of pocket space there were several small neat packages of the same material as the uniform hanging from the waist, reminding us of the packages of possibles which our pioneers carried.

The enlisted men wore wrap leggins like those worn by our army in World War I, while the officers and some of the noncommissioned officers wore leather riding boots of the same general vintage. One of the Nip soldiers who spoke English told a work party he was guarding that the shoes came in two sizes. If the small shoe size was too small, it was necessary to wear the large size, filling in with rags or cotton as needed.

The private soldier carried a rifle and bayonet, except when he went to town on pass he left his rifle at home.[6] All noncommissioned officers wore swords of the heavy two-handed Samurai type. Sometimes in camp, when not a part of a military formation, an individual might leave his sword at home, but he never left camp without it.

Many of the officers' swords were of fine workmanship, some of them were quite old and, therefore, expensive. One of our interpreters told me that when an officer was commissioned, he had to pay at least as much as one month's pay for his sword. The weapon was adopted to maintain esprit de corps, because it was the weapon that had been used by the ancient and greatly revered nobles of early Japanese history.

DEATH BECOMES AN EVERYDAY OCCURRENCE

One of the first formations we saw, as we were marching into O'Donnell, was a funeral detail of men with picks and shovels carrying crude litters of dead as they moved slowly, under Nip guard, toward the burial ground. We were to see the same sight each day during our stay there, but I am sad to say that the size of the parties and the number of litters were always on the increase.[9]

Many men had arrived at the end of the Death March so far gone that they never recovered. There were many cases of malaria for which there was no medicine, and there were many new cases of dysentery occurring each day that we were at the camp. It was not uncommon to find a few men dead in barracks when we got up in the morning. Even though medicine soon became practically nonexistent, General King established a hospital under the care of the American personnel in camp. He directed that all sick men in the camp be taken to the hospital, where he hoped that something could be done for them and because he hoped to reduce the alarming increase in infectious diseases.

During the first few days after the sick were collected and brought into the hospital, the starving hospital personnel were very busy for not only were there many dead and dying men in the hospital, but a number of them crawled outside to die, and a few bodies were found under the building when the odor of decay brought out searching parties. The hospital became known as the "Pest House," into which many entered but few returned.

Sometime later, after we had received orders to move, a friend of mine insisted that I go through the hospital to see for myself the terrible conditions there which he stated were beyond description.[7] I had to go tell Griff goodbye anyway, for malaria had laid him low, so I made the visit. Griff was in one of the cleaner rooms, among men who did not have dysentery and who were strong enough to visit the latrine.

Although all the patients were sleeping on the floor, they were as comfortable as they would have been in barracks. All of the rooms were filled with large green mosquito nets of squad size, large enough for eight or more men to lie without crowding, protected from the attacks of mosquitoes by night and flies by day. We told Griff that we expected him to join us soon, which he did, he being one of the small number to survive the Pest House.

After leaving Griff, we entered what must have been the dysentery ward for the floor was covered with emaciated bodies in various stages of undress, lying in their own filth. I do not believe any one of them could have stood on his feet, and most of them did not appear to be aware of where they were, nor of the seriousness of their condition. There were no bedpans but, if there had been, the men could not have used them. Not only the clothes of the men, but the blankets and the floor around them were soiled. The physical state of the men was so pitiable, the living conditions so frightful, and the odor so overwhelming, that I could not take it any more.

Outside, one of the doctors told me that there had been more than a thousand deaths in the first forty days at the camp and, furthermore, if that rate continued the last man of us would be dead before the year had passed by. The death rate among Filipinos in the southern part of the camp was considerably higher than in ours, but I have forgotten the figures. There were so many deaths that the Nips insisted on the burials being made in mass graves, which was a practical solution to the problem, there being so few men who were capable of performing hard labor.

PRISONER–CAPTOR RELATIONSHIPS

The Nips issued an order that there would be no association or communication between the Americans in the north part of the camp and the Filipinos in the south part. The Nip section being in between the two prisoner sections, the order was pretty well enforced, but the work parties of Americans and Filipinos met frequently at the burial ground, at the ration warehouses and at other work projects.

Whenever the work parties met there were always many questions asked by both groups. We learned that the death rate among the Filipinos was even higher than among the Americans. We also learned by reports and observations that the attitude of the Japanese toward the Americans differed from their attitude toward the Filipinos. That was understandable in view of the fact that Americans were permanent captives whereas the Filipinos, after indoctrination, were expected to return home and assist the Filipino people [in becoming] loyal serfs of Japan.

The object of Japan being to develop the Philippines into a vassal state, it was difficult to understand why the Japanese were so openly contemptuous, cruel, and arbitrary in their treatment of the Filipinos. The Nips made no attempt to conceal that they considered the Filipino soldiers the scum of the earth, unworthy of any respect or consideration. While the same cruelty and starvation diet was meted out to the Americans and Filipinos alike, the Nips could not conceal a certain respect and admiration for the American soldier which was in sharp contrast to their attitude towards the Filipino soldier.

CORREGIDOR FALLS

Early in May [1942], we were showered with Manila newspapers, our first and only issue made at Camp O'Donnell. Huge front-page headlines announced the capture of Corregidor,[8] and every article starting on the front page related impressive details of the military action which clearly showed the superiority of Japanese arms. Even the editorial page was filled with authoritative comment on the release of "Greater East Asia" from the domination of the decadent Western Powers to assume its rightful place in the world under the guidance of the generous and omnipotent world power, Nippon.

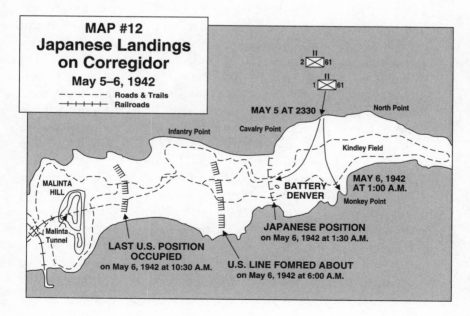

MAP #12
Japanese Landings on Corregidor
May 5–6, 1942
- - - - - - Roads & Trails
+++++ Railroads

Some days later, General King was advised that the American generals and colonels would move the next day to Tarlac,[9] where General Wainwright and his "Brass" had been taken. When Sherry, who was a major at that time, was added to the list of brass to go to Tarlac, most of us had very grave doubts about our future because it appeared that the purpose of the Nips was to repay him for his consideration of their civilians in Manila by sparing him whatever they had in store for us.[10]

Upon being informed by the Nips that he would be in charge of the American enclosure at Camp O'Donnell, General King had designated Charles as his representative in supply matters. As supply officer, Charles had the daily task of drawing food in bulk for use the following day. The food was issued at the Nip storehouse in the form of a pile of *camotes* or squash and sacks of rice. The issue clerks were two Nip corporals who alternated with each other daily in the issue of food and the purchase of vegetables in the nearby towns.

The corporals were quite different in personality, as I came to know after I had regained enough strength to assist Charles in his daily drawing and issuing [of] food. One was young, clean-looking and businesslike in the issue of supplies. He was rigid in his insistence that we draw exactly the amount due us and no more; however, he was scrupulously honest, for in every instance that I was able to show a partially filled bag, or return him a bag of moldy rice, he never failed to make proper replacement. I was very careful to be scrupulously correct in my dealings with him and, occasionally, I thought he showed a slight regard for me. The other corporal was middle-aged and lazy, somewhat dissipated in appearance, indifferent and easygoing in his dealings. Both men spoke a few words of English, being able to read a list of common articles of food.

I went to considerable pains to study the two corporals because I was hungry for something besides rice, and I thought one of them might make purchases for me during his trip to the market. Four of us amassed the huge sum of twenty pesos, almost all we had, and I was commissioned to give it to one of the Nips, along with a list of canned fish, hard boiled eggs and fruit which we hoped he would purchase for us.

The day I took the money and the list with me to the food warehouse the young corporal was on duty. After the issue of supplies, I showed him the money and the list, asking him in English if he would make the purchases for me the next day. He looked at the list long enough to see what I wanted, then he shouted, "NO!" and stalked angrily away. The letdown to my morale was tremendous, so much so that I gave up hope of adding to our food supply through assistance of the Nips, but when I reported the incident to my friends they reminded me that the other corporal would be on duty the morrow.

I was reluctant to ask a favor of another Nip for I had already tried the best prospect, but we were so hungry I could not give up; therefore, after the issue of food the next day I repeated my request to the middle-aged corporal. He merely grinned, putting the money and the list in his pocket. My trip home that afternoon was far more pleasant than my return of the day before. We all talked of the food we were going to get until our mouths watered, even though we knew I could not see the corporal for two more days.

We had a long impatient wait, but the time finally arrived when I went to draw our supplies from the Nip who had taken our money. The supplies were no sooner issued that day than the corporal departed in a hurry without saying a word to me. I did not dare stop him, so I went home again, dragging my feet, to meet a waiting expectant delegation.

My arrival brought gloom to the three other for, at that moment, we had little hope that we would ever realize anything out of our investment. Two days later the middle-aged corporal issued supplies again and started away after he was through, but that time he turned back to tell me to come with him to his quarters. I waited outside while he entered, and came out with two sizable packages. My *arregato* was very warm, if brief, as I grabbed the package to run at my best speed to the shack where I lived.

All the co-owners being present, we opened our bundle to find the eggs and canned goods as ordered, but the bananas were almost rotten. Apparently, the food had been bought three days before, but the corporal had forgotten to give them to me on his previous issue day.

That evening we each had half of a can of pilchards[11] without rice, which made the day one to go down in the record books. After filling my stomach with the best food I had eaten in some time, I reluctantly admitted to myself that I was not the expert judge of character I had believed myself to be.

On the first of June [1942] we started to move to a new camp at an unknown location, and on the next day all of us, except the hospital personnel and the sick, left Camp O'Donnell for the same destination. We arrived at Camp Cabanatuan, where many of us were destined to remain for the next two years, on the afternoon of the second of June [1942].

Chapter 10

Moving to Cabanatuan

SAME STRUGGLE—DIFFERENT PLACE

I arrived in Cabanatuan[1] as one of a truckload who were packed in so tight we could hardly get out, and when we did reach the ground we could hardly stand on our cramped legs. We had lost interest in the camp when one of the officers on our truck, who had been there before the war, told us the Filipino government had built it at the same time as Camp O'Donnell, using similar plans and materials.

The lack of interest was very noticeable when we unloaded from the truck to lie in the grass resting our weary legs. After a while the Nips moved us to join the group which had departed from O'Donnell on the previous day. Those men told us that they had suffered through a long rail trip, arriving at the town of Cabanatuan at sundown the day before. They had been herded into the town's schoolyard to spend the night, marching the seven miles out to the camp the following morning. Apparently the Nips had been waiting for us all to arrive, for as the last truck pulled up we were ordered to form in groups of a hundred in columns of fours to be counted into the new camp.

While everyone had been lying down we had not suspected that there were many sick in the large group, but when we got up to form columns, fifty men or more could not stand up. Most of those appeared to have dysentery for their clothes were smeared with filth. That sight was definite proof that the dread dysentery had not been left behind.

A Nip officer who became very indignant at so many men disregarding the orders of an officer of the Imperial Japanese Army rushed to the area, possibly for the purpose of making an example of someone, but when he discovered the condition of the men on the ground he beat a hasty retreat, holding his nose.

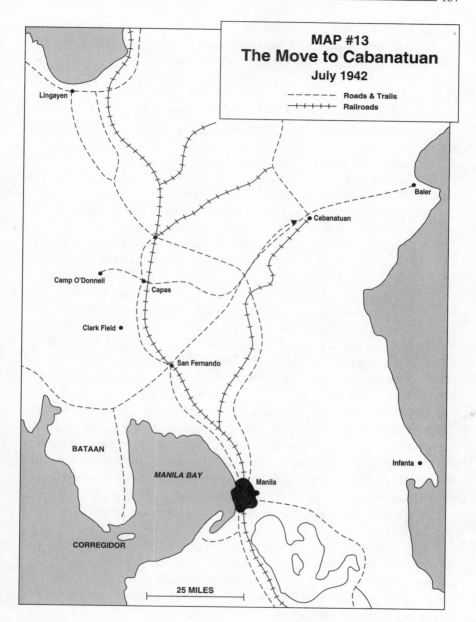

MAP #13
The Move to Cabanatuan
July 1942

- - - - - Roads & Trails
+++++ Railroads

Lingayen

Baler

Cabanatuan

Camp O'Donnell

Capas

Clark Field

San Fernando

BATAAN

MANILA BAY

Manila

Infanta

CORREGIDOR

25 MILES

More than an hour was necessary to verify the count, but we were finally released in time to find shelter before dark. The sick were carried in to live among us until the hospital began functioning a few days later.[2] The western end of camp was already occupied with a group of more than a thousand men who had been brought in by rail a few days before. Some of them had been captured on Corregidor, and some of them were walking cases released from our hospitals on Bataan. All told, we numbered more than nine thousand men.

On our second day the Nips divided us into three groups in order to facilitate the operations of the camp, each group drawing its own supplies and dealing directly with the Nips without any central agency.[3] After a month or two an American central control was established to be maintained for the length of our stay, with two, three, or four subordinate groups varying with the number of men in camp.

The Nips were in the process of modifying the camp when we arrived and, although they continued to make changes as long as we were there, Camp Cabanatuan was roughly a half-mile square, situated on the east side of the Cabanatuan-Cayagan Valley Highway about seven miles north of [the town of] Cabanatuan.

The north one-third of the area ringed in barbed wire was our prison enclosure, the south one-third being a similar enclosure designated as the hospital. Immediately south of our enclosure ran the camp road and south of the road was the Nip area. In between the Nip area and the hospital was a sizable unoccupied area which the Nips considered necessary to protect themselves from the contagion with which they knew our hospital was seething.

Apparently the original arrangement of the camps had not pleased the Nips, because they were in the process of making some changes, using native labor. The Filipinos working inside the camp were under Nip guards who understood no English. Employing all kinds of subterfuge to lull the suspicions of the guards, such as talking from behind a partition and strolling slowly past working parties while apparently talking to a companion, the Americans were able to carry on a satisfactory conversation with the workers.

The quality of food at Cabanatuan being similar to [what] we had received at O'Donnell, the conversation was mostly about chow. The Filipinos agreed to bring in food under their clothes, purchased with the money that had been left by Americans in convenient places where the Filipinos could pick it up without the knowledge of the Nips.

For several days the system worked so well that a surprising amount of canned goods was brought in, but the Nips, becoming suspicious, searched the Filipinos one morning, confiscating all of the food found on them.[4] The Nips held the Filipinos involved for several hours, finally releasing them with a warning, thereby ending that method of food smuggling.

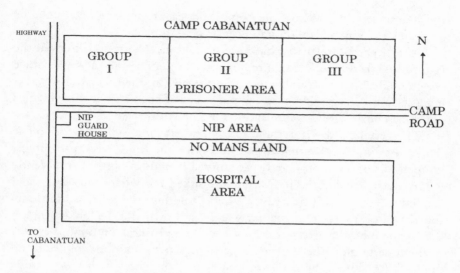

Alexander's Sketch of Camp Cabanatuan.

A friend of mine, who had lived in Manila for several years before the war, convinced several of us that food could still be obtained provided that we could make up a total of forty pesos. Borrowing from friends who had succeeded in bringing into camp plenty of money, we collected the cash which our Manila friend gave, together with a list, to one of the Filipinos.

Two days later we were informed that our food purchases had arrived at the house of a Filipino who lived just across the highway from the main gate. It was our big problem to get the food to our side of the fence, for everyone who entered the camp was searched by the Nip guards. Since we considered it too dangerous to try to go get the food, and the Filipinos considered it too dangerous to try to carry it in, the only solution we had left was to induce the Nips to bring it in.

A hasty review of the Nips at Cabanatuan, who stood out as individuals from their fellows, was enough to cause us to eliminate from consideration all but one of them as a possible benefactor. He was a Nip doctor who held the rank of first lieutenant in the Imperial Japanese Army. He was an easygoing, quiet, and indifferent-looking officer who spoke fair English. His below average military appearance and the fact that he had bought some can goods for our doctor friend, Bob, led us to believe that he might help us out.

After much prodding from my friends, I explained our situation to Bob, asking him if he thought the Nip doctor would consider helping us.

Bob was uncertain as to how the Nip would react to the proposal but, as he said, the only way he could find out was to ask him.

After I left Bob, I had a bad case of cold feet, because I knew if the Nip turned us down he could report me to the Nip administrative office which might have most unhappy results for me. In other words, I was taking a serious risk, gambling on my judgment of character of an individual Nip. I had been wrong before and I could be wrong again.

The very next day Bob came after me to take me to the doctor's office where the Nip was waiting to ask me some questions. My heart almost jumped out of my mouth and it continued to pound somewhat violently for the next half-hour. The Nip doctor asked me where the food was I wanted to get, and if I owned it. When I told him the food was just outside the gate a fourth of a mile away and that I owned it, he looked toward the Japanese headquarters as if he was contemplating taking me there for further questioning, then, apparently making up his mind, he told Bob and me to follow him as he strolled toward the main gate which was guarded by a squad of Japanese soldiers.

I do not know what was on Bob's mind, but I had grave doubts that I had used good judgment in soliciting Nip assistance. I can assure you that the expressions on the faces of our friends inside the fence as they watched us pass by did nothing toward dissipating my doubts.

We did not slow down at the gate but went on to the hut across the road. The Nip guards [at the gate] paid no attention [to us] because we were with a Nip officer. A Filipino at the hut produced a large well-filled jute[5] bag when I asked for the food. The Nip assured himself that the bag contained nothing but food, then he asked me how I had known the package was there. My poor brain was sorely pressed to think of a reasonable explanation, but I finally told him that a Filipino, who I did not know, had passed the word to me that someone from Manila, whose name I had forgotten, had sent the food to the hut in the hope that it could be delivered. How much of the story our Nip friend believed I do not know, but he told me to take the sack with me.

We passed the Nip guards again, going directly to the shack where we lived. The Nip sat down while we unpacked all of our treasures which consisted of several cans of fish, a quantity of home-cured pork and carabao meat, two dozen native bananas and several containers of various spices. The bananas were rotten and the meat smelled like it was too, but at least the steamed rice was palatable.

I asked the Nip if he would like any of the food, but he shook his head and departed without a word. Bob would take nothing but a share of the spices, which we thought was very poor recompense for what he had done for us. We were happy to learn that the jerked meat swelled like it always did, and after sampling a skillet full of it that very night we were sure it was our prize purchase.

For a whole week after we had acquired our food we ate very well indeed and, since we escaped Nip complications for the unusual way in which it was obtained, Bob and I gradually forgot that our heads had been in a very vulnerable position.

At breakfast time on the eighth of June [1942] we had our initiation into the Nip celebration of Imperial Rescript Day. It was on the eighth of December [1941] that Premier Tojo had obtained the Emperor's signature to the document which authorized Japan's entry into the war.[6] In order that the officers and soldiers might not forget how fortunate they were that the "Prince of Heaven" had thus given his permission for Japan to assume her rightful position in the world, they celebrated the anniversary every month.

On those occasions every Nip who was not on guard duty attended the formations, at which time they all repeated the words of the order at the top of their lungs, ending with a cheer for the Emperor. It is my belief that no Japanese troop unit ever missed celebrating that day regardless of circumstances up to the very end of the war.

We had been in Camp Cabanatuan less than a week when we had to form [a] line along the fence of our enclosure facing the camp road to be reviewed by General Count Terauchi [who commanded] all of the Japanese forces in the south.[7] The general, who was a member of the royal family, cousin of the Emperor I believe, came over from Indo-China to see at first hand what his army in the Philippines had presented him with. By the time the review started, we had been standing in line for some time; rather, those of us who could stand up had been.

We must have looked like human scarecrows, some of whom the wind had blown over, the others swaying with the breeze. If that is the way we looked to the count it probably was the way he wanted us to look, for as he rode slowly past us he kept his head out the car window, smiling broadly and saluting continuously.

Shortly after the inspection by the prince, we heard a report that General Homma, the Nip commander in the Philippines, had been replaced.[8] From the information that we received later, he was recalled to Japan in disgrace and removed from the active list of the army. Japanese papers, which we received later, had a news article about him showing a recent picture in civilian clothes. We asked a silly young Nip soldier, who had the habit of hanging around our camp, why General Homma had gone back to Japan. His very prompt answer was that Homma had let too many Japanese soldiers die.

Our conclusions, based on our observations, the reading of the news-papers the Nips gave us and the remarks of a number of Japanese officers and soldiers, were that he had underestimated our defensive strength on Bataan and had released several combat divisions soon after his landing in the Philippines. When he failed to take Bataan with the troops left at his disposal, he had to call for help. Three or more fresh divisions arriving from Japan about the first of April [1942] gave him enough strength to finish his task, but by that time he had materially delayed the timetable of the Nips' advance to the south. The Nip soldier may have been right because the Nip casualty rate must have been higher than had been expected.[9]

NONE OF THE LUXURIES OF HOME
After the Nips had completed their utility improvements, we had electric lights in the kitchens, warehouse buildings, and headquarters buildings only. Consequently, our reading time was limited to the daylight hours. Even the use of lights in the buildings where they were installed was severely regulated, because the power of the generator was limited and gasoline short. An additional water tank was erected so that, soon after our arrival, we had plenty of water from numerous faucets located along the south side of our enclosure, which was our kitchen line.

A primitive purification system was installed at the tanks, but our doctors reported that it was far below the standard that Americans considered necessary in the tropics. Before the war, the water in the Philippines had not been considered potable by the army until after it had been boiled. When the war began we had been forced to use unboiled water, which may have been one reason why we developed so many cases of dysentery.

[Since there was] no plumbing in the camp, open latrines were constructed immediately after our arrival. As soon as material became available, covered boxes were constructed in order to reduce the huge fly population.

The rainy season had started before we left Camp O'Donnell but, as you recall, the early part of the season is characterized by one or two hard rains each day.[10] The daily rains brought to our notice the repairs needed by our barrack buildings, and various improvements needed in the camp, such as ditching and draining in sections of the camp and building paths in others. This work was done by our POWs when the Nip materials and permission could be obtained. As a matter of fact, we had the camp in livable condition before the heavy rains of the typhoon season began to hit us in September [1942].

As soon as our hospital was placed in operation, we removed the worst cases of our sick from the camp area to the hospital area. For a long time after the hospital was opened, thirty or forty more sick men were transported to it each day and, in addition, there were many deaths in the POW enclosure. There being no medicine to give the sick, the death rate at the hospital almost equaled the number of newly arriving sick. Some of the surgical equipment from one of our hospitals on Bataan had been brought in with our medical personnel, but our doctors were not authorized to perform surgical operations.

An American boy who developed an acute appendix was taken by the Nip doctor to a rude shack, which served as the Japanese army hospital in Cabanatuan. There, with an American doctor observing the operation, the Nip doctor removed the diseased appendix. The boy was given a hypodermic injection, and carried to a wooden table by four husky Nip soldiers who held him during the operation. When the doctor started cutting, the pain was so intense that boy mercifully fainted. The Nip, needing plenty of room to work in, made an incision about a foot long, but he did remove the appendix.

After the wound was sewn up the patient was dumped on the floor, where he remained without attention until the next afternoon. He was given some water that day and a little rice gruel the next day. [On] the fourth day he was given more rice than he could eat and [on] the fifth day he had to get up and climb into a truck by himself in order to return to the prison camp hospital, where he made an uneventful recovery under American care. [Eventually,] authority was granted to the American doctors at the hospital to perform essential operations before another one became necessary.

A large percentage of the POWs in the hospital and out of the hospital had malaria. In the Philippines malaria is a dread disease which does not always respond to treatment, even when there is adequate medicine available for the patient. The type commonly known as cerebral malaria is particularly feared because of its high death rate; death [usually] occurring within the first few days after the disease appears.

Some cases [of malaria] seem to respond to quinine only when it is injected into the body, and others recur at periodic intervals. The American quinine had been almost exhausted at the time of the surrender of Bataan, so there was no means of treatment for malaria cases until the Nips produced a small amount of quinine in the late fall of 1942. Up until that time, a fair share of deaths that had occurred had been sufferers of malaria.

Dysentery was another exhausting disease which required medicines for its proper treatment.[15] A large percentage of us suffered from either dysentery or an extremely persistent type of diarrhea, but it made little difference which it was [since] there [was] no medicine available for either. Our doctors advised us to use willpower and reduce the number of trips to the latrine, so that the irritation to our inflamed intestines might be reduced. Those of us who thought the advice of value spent many long hours lying on our sides to give what assistance we could to the tortured valve in our lower bowels. Thus by the exercise of willpower, and the absorbing of some internal punishment, our conditions did improve slowly and surely until our troubles practically disappeared.

We had been in prison camp for seven months before any sulfa drugs became available so, there being nothing to treat the disease, many of our early deaths were attributed to dysentery. The Nips had captured a quantity of evaporated milk in Manila, which they set aside for use of the sick in the hospital. As the food issued by the Nips was not particularly suited for sick patients, the addition of a few ounces of evaporated milk was not enough to be of great assistance to the very ill patients.

THE WALKING DEAD

As the months dragged on, starvation came closer and closer. Many advance cases of beriberi and pellagra appeared, while most of us were showing some of the symptoms of malnutrition.[11] Two distinct types of disease known to us as dry beriberi and wet beriberi were common. The dry beriberi cases suffered from sore legs and feet so much that they could barely hobble around. Usually they had to lie down to take the weight off their legs, but the rest was only a temporary alleviation.

Occasionally, a slightest movement of the victim would make him cry out in pain, and the soreness was so intense that, at times, it was impossible for him to sleep. Most of the men I knew who had the dry beriberi recovered, aided, perhaps by the acquisition of a few cans of fish. The wet beri beri cases suffered from grotesquely swollen legs and feet. The legs became so large that the skin was stretched to the breaking point and beyond. Apparently, the swollen legs were not painful, for it was common to see men walking around paying no attention to their deformities, except that they had to wear shorts. Almost all of the men with swollen limbs died.

One man, whose legs were badly swollen, realizing that his chances were poor, requested his friends to fill a barrel about a fourth full of water and build a fire under it. When the water started to heat, he was helped into the barrel where he stayed, at his own request, until he fainted. The drastic sweating process may have saved the man's life; at any rate, he did recover.

The picture of one officer who suffered from wet beriberi is indelibly impressed on my mind. In addition to being handicapped with oversized legs, one of his testicles had swollen to the size of a twelve-pound shot. The unusual size and weight of the organ had stretched his scrotum until it reached his knees, so that when he walked it was necessary for him to lift the big ball in his hands and carry it. That unfortunate man was one of those who did not long survive his infirmity.

One of the hospital wards, called the "Zero" ward, was reserved for the desperately sick who could not help themselves. Most of the inmates of that ward, which was nothing but a thatch-covered shack with raised split bamboo sleeping platforms, were so wasted that they were literally skin and bones, with the bones beginning to protrude through the worn skin. That ward had more than its share of dead each day, as a matter of fact, a mere handful of the patients who entered the Zero lived to go on their own feet. The deaths were by no means confined to one ward, however, because many patients in all the wards were in only slightly better shape than those in the Zero ward.

Except when it was raining, the weather was so warm that no clothes were needed; consequently, it was normal to see many naked men in the hospital area, especially at the latrines and on the paths leading to them. Most of the naked were so emaciated that their skin hung on them like translucent parchment. The weaker men fell frequently, or had to sit down to rest before they traveled the fifty yards between barracks and latrine. Many a man was too weak to reach the latrine before his weak functional muscles gave way, making the remainder of the journey unnecessary.

A case of diphtheria[12] appeared in the hospital, followed by several others. The Nip doctor was urgently requested to provide the appropriate medicine, there being none in camp. An entire week was required to obtain the medicine, during which time several men died, but after the inoculations were given, all of the other cases recovered.

On the fourth of July 1942, I observed an orderly, from a Nip kitchen across the road from our area, carry a garbage bucket to our enclosure fence and dump it inside. There was an immediate rush of half-naked, half-starved American prisoners, who fought over the scraps of garbage like dogs fighting over the supper scraps outside the kitchen door.

[Additionally,] by great good fortune a boy, who had brought into camp a considerable sum of United States currency, feeling that he had more than it was wise to try to keep himself, consented to let me have two hundred dollars on my personal check. Through devious channels I was able to have that money exchanged for currency of the Philippine government, at a loss of course.

With the exchanged money I made purchases, from time to time, in a commissary which the Nips allowed us to operate beginning in August

[1942]. At first, Filipinos were permitted to bring canned goods and fruit at infrequent intervals; however, there never was enough to go around. Later, the intervals were decreased and the amount of food for sale was increased. Without the purchases made with the money I had borrowed, I do not believe I would have survived 1942.

THE BREAKING POINT AND BEYOND

In our early days at Cabanatuan, because of the numerous Filipino laborers in camp, many contacts were made by mail and messenger between our POWs and well-to-do acquaintances of theirs in Manila. As a result of those contacts, large sums of money were smuggled into camp to provide the means by which individuals continued to make commissary purchases. Unquestionably, if it had not been for the opportunity to buy food of heavy protein content, our death rate would have been much higher.

One hungry American sneaked through the barbed wire one night in search of food. He [sneaked] into a hut occupied by a Filipino family, finding some canned goods, which he was in a process of dumping into a gunny sack when he was discovered. He ran with the food he had in the bag, reaching the hole in the fence which let him back into the enclosure safely.

The Filipino who owned the food ran to the Nip guard at the main gate, making a report on the theft. A patrol of the guard detail came into the enclosure immediately to make a search and, by chance, they found the sack of food in a ditch near one of the barracks. The guilty man was found in the barracks with his shoes still on and his clothes spattered with mud. The next morning, after the culprit had been identified by the Filipino, he was marched through the camp to the cemetery where he was shot without receiving a trial. When the hungry boy, for he was clearly not old enough to vote, marched by us to his death he laughed as if he was embarrassed at being caught, but he did not appear to be concerned about losing his life.

Another boy, who had been under observation for mental derangement, disappeared. Although he was in poor physical condition, as well as being a mental patient, searching parties could not locate him. Almost a week later, he crawled up to the enclosure fence where a Nip guard picked him up. The man, who was in the last stages of starvation, could walk only a few steps at a time, and he was obviously not mentally competent, but he had disobeyed a Nip order for which he had to pay the death penalty. A giant Nip sergeant had the escapee carried to the cemetery where he shot him in the head with a pistol while he was lying on the ground.

The sergeant, known to us as "Big Speedo" because of his liberal use of the Nip slang word for hurry, "speedo," had been a Tokyo policeman before he came in the army.[13] He had been in charge of American work details for a considerable time, during which he had been tolerant and patient and unusually efficient. He always accomplished his job, but he was well liked by American interpreters and laborers. The dispatch and disinterest with which he disposed of the mentally incompetent American brought home to us the fact that even the best of the Nips were perfectly capable of taking the lives of any or all of us without the slightest qualm.

It was our misfortune to be *guests* of a small, poorly fed, and underprivileged race whose conceptions of human dignity and human life were diametrically opposed to our own. Once when we were drawing our food issue, talking through an American interpreter, I tried to explain to the Nip making the issue that the food we were getting was not enough for our average American. I told him that, while the food might be adequate for our smaller men, it was insufficient for the larger ones, and I tried to show him through the analogy of the difference in feed required by a small horse and huge draft animal. The Nip became so enraged that I narrowly escaped being beaten, because I had inferred that the Japanese were small-sized people.

The Nip officer could not understand why Americans were starving to death on as much food as many Orientals have throughout their lives. They would not admit that large men required more food than small ones, and they did not understand that men who had been accustomed to [a] heavy protein diet all their lives needed time to adjust their systems to a diet which was devoid of animal protein.

The tall sergeant, who had charge of the food stores and made the daily issues, was an unusual character for a Nip.[14] He did not smoke nor drink, and [judging] from his lean healthy appearance he did not indulge his appetite as most Nips did. He was one of the first Japs seen at work in the morning, and one of the last to leave his job [at night]. He was unsmiling, quiet, and businesslike, speaking no English and speaking Japanese only when necessary, never saying an unnecessary word. He was honest in his dealings with Americans, but he was always insistent that they receive no more than his issue slips called for. Apparently, he was just as meticulous in his dealings with Nip kitchen details, the only concession to them being that they did not have to accept moldy rice.

He never struck a prisoner, no matter how much the provocation, although immediate physical punishment was an approved and much used method of the Nips for dealing with malefactors. Several times I saw the sergeant, normally quite placid, go into a rage at some act of a prisoner which irritated him, but he merely let out a blood curdling yell and gave the man a murderous glare. The Nip might have been a member of some ascetic cult, for most of the time he appeared to be in contemplation of unworldly things; as a matter of fact, [he] was seen a number of times, on his knees, his eyes closed and his face contorted, presumably in worship of his deity.

Another sergeant, who had overall charge of the repair work and the utilities of the camp, differed so much in character from the one I have just told you about that I shall try to describe him also. Although not more than five feet four inches tall, he was an extremely muscular human dynamo who could do any kind of manual labor as well as any man, and do it as long. He could carry an unbelievably heavy load, and he never asked an American to carry a heavier load or do more work than he.

Knowing exactly what he wanted to do and how he wanted to do it, he was never handicapped by his meager English in the working of prisoners because he could always show them exactly how he wanted a job done, to the accompaniment of voluble Japanese. He carried a sturdy club which he used only when he thought a prisoner was not doing his work or had taken advantage of him in some way, but when he did lose his temper and use it, he did a thorough job.

Once when he was moving a building by manpower, using all of the POWs who could get a hand on it, he had the building almost in the position he wanted it but, the [weight] of the burden becoming intolerable, the prisoners started to let it down too soon. Flying into a rage, the sergeant screamed directions, at the same time belaboring all of the carrying party within his reach with the cudgel he always had with him. As soon as the building was in position, he became his usual laughing self again.

He was a man of strong appetites, [a] heavy eater and drinker when he had the means to gratify his wants, and he always went in to visit the "ladies" on his holiday. We suspected that he was a product of the slums of one of the larger cities of Japan, for the lines in his thirty-five-year-old face clearly told of a hard life.

One day, during the absence of the storekeeper, he made the ration issue. After the rations had been carried away he led John,[15] for whom he showed an unusual attachment, and me to the next warehouse where he gave us each a bottle of warm beer from the Nip stock. Then he took us to the shack where he lived with another noncommissioned officer, for what must have been the equivalent of afternoon tea. Opening several cans of evaporated milk he sweetened it, adding a touch of spice. Sweetened milk was a luxury for us which we enjoyed much more than you can ever imagine.

While we [were] partaking of our repast we had to tell about our children, and John, who was fortunate enough to have photographs, had to show them. The sergeant appeared to be much interested in each family and, in every way, he exerted himself to be the perfect host.

We each had two glasses of milk before we bade our host farewell with many *Aregatos*. We had gone only a few steps when we heard the sergeant roar and rush up to a work detail of POWs who were waiting to be checked into our enclosure. We stopped to see the sergeant, who, in his rage, was spouting unintelligible Japanese to a feeble, half-starved, gray-haired American prisoner. The miserable prisoner had a short piece of plank which he had planned to take to his shack to make improvements, but the sergeant jerked it out of his hand and knocked him down. The American got up with difficulty, to be knocked down again. He struggled to his feet again to receive a vituperative lecture of which he did not understand a word, but at last he was released to enter the enclosure with the other men of his detail. We returned to [our] barracks taking with us another vivid object lesson of how affable a Nip could be one moment and how murderous he could be the next.

The archbishop of Manila, or a Catholic organization of Manila, we never knew which, obtained permission for a priest of German nationality to visit Camp Cabanatuan with much needed clothing and several packages of food for individuals. The Nips let the clothing come in and, after a long conference, they allowed the food to enter, specifying that it go to a kitchen instead of to an individual.

The person to whom the package was addressed probably got his package from the kitchen. The priest's driver, who had worked for an American business concern in Manila before the war, had several letters with considerable sums of money which he managed to slip to prisoners undetected. He also held long distance conversations, without benefit of telephone, with a number of individuals while the Nips were devoting most of their attention to the priest, passing on to us the war news in general.

The good father, having a German passport, was entitled to some consideration as an ally or he would not have been able to visit our camp. The Nip interpreter, speaking for the commandant,[16] asked specifically why it was that a German was befriending his enemies, the Americans. The priest tried to explain that he, as a man of God, had an interest in all humanity and, moreover, if we had been his enemies at one time, we had ceased to be such when we were captured, but his explanation was not understood by the Nip mentality. We enjoyed several visits from those two friends, being the gainers of a great deal of money, some clothing and authentic news.

One day when the priest arrived with his car loaded with clothing, he started toward the Nip headquarters to find the interpreter. His driver, thinking he was unnoticed, tossed a bundle to an American who purposely was passing by. A Nip sentry, observing the incident, held the American with his bundle until the priest returned with the interpreter and the Nip adjutant. The adjutant, who had appeared friendly with the priest, became incensed at the report of his sentry, directed the priest to leave immediately and take all his baggage. The priest tried to explain, pleading with the adjutant, but he stalked off in the usual Nip rage.

Our friend had to return to Manila with all his packages, where he was notified that his permit was revoked. When he returned to Manila at the end of the war, we were informed that some time after their last visit to us the priest and his driver were both arrested and executed for their activities on behalf of American prisoners.

BROTHERS OF BLOOD

Several work parties had gone out from our camp to establish camps of their own near airfields and other work projects. One of the camps, which was located in an isolated spot of the mountains, was attacked one night by guerrillas.[17] After the attack was over the prisoners were formed in line in front of their barracks building and held there under guard until daybreak. At the morning roll call it was learned that a Nip guard had been killed and that two American prisoners had gone to the hills with the attackers.[18] The Nips were enraged, of course.

The Nip commander walked down the line of prisoners, arbitrarily selecting eight men. Those men were marched out in front of their companions a short distance, their hands tied behind them, and a Nip firing squad was brought up. The other American prisoners could hardly believe their eyes when the firing squad, at close range, shot the eight men without further ceremony.

One of the Americans had to see his own brother killed without being able to do anything for him. Another American who witnessed those murders, and who was returned to our hospital because of a disabling attack of malaria, described the shootings to me. He told me of one of the victims, a corporal of Norwegian ancestry who had been under my command at Stotsenburg, [who] had stood erect looking directly at the firing squad, his expression showing nothing but contempt and defiance for his executioners. The witness reported that even the Nips were impressed by the manner in which the corporal died.

The repercussions of the guerrilla attack, escapes, and execution episode were soon felt by all American POWs in the Philippines. By order of the headquarters of the Imperial Japanese Army in Manila, all prisoners were divided into groups of ten or less, depending on the number occupying a particular building as all men in the same group lived in the same place, and if the building was so small that less than ten men lived in it, the actual number living there constituted the group.

In Camp Cabanatuan a camp roster, divided into groups listing each prisoner by name and building, was required to be submitted to the Nips. The Nip commandant then assembled the entire camp to explain that the system had been directed by higher authority which had established the policy that each member of a group would be held responsible for the actions of each other member, and that if any individual should escape all other members of the group would be executed as punishment for their failure to prevent the escape. Thus, by direction of the Nip commandant, we became our brothers' keepers.

The commandant directed that the personnel of each barracks would set up a system of night guard duty, and that the highest American administrative office would establish a perimeter guard. The guards were established that very day, and lists of individuals by groups were posted in each barracks. We called those groups "shooting squads," and we all became extremely well acquainted with the particular squad to which we belonged.[19]

We may have had no previous interest in the nocturnal activities of certain individuals of our squads, but our attitudes in that respect underwent a radical change. In many instances, prisoners were not permitted to go to the latrine at night without being accompanied by another member of their squads.

A very few nights after the establishment of the shooting squads three American officers, who were members of a group occupying a small building, tried to escape. They were unsuspected by their companions as they left the barracks separately, but they were discovered soon after dark by the American perimeter guard as they approached the barbed wire fence of the enclosure. The guard gave the alarm and, with the help of additional guards, the three officers were caught. The Nip sentry outside the fence gave the alarm to the Japanese guardhouse at the main gate, which brought a Nip patrol into our enclosure on the double.

The three officers were taken by the patrol to Nip Headquarters where they were interviewed briefly by the commandant himself. At his direction they were beaten unmercifully at intervals all night long. The next morning they were marched down the camp road for us to see the kind of punishment which attempted escapees could expect. Their faces were covered with bruises, one officer had a broken jaw, and they could hardly walk. They were all tied to posts by the main gate near the guardhouse where they were severely clubbed and beaten every time a sentry came by.

A typhoon struck us at that time, enveloping us with the first torrential rain of the season. The officers remained tied outside in the icy rain for three days, their only attention being additional beatings. On the fourth day when they were united, one officer, who had a broken leg, could not walk and the other two could barely hobble. They were loaded in a truck to be hauled among some trees just out of sight of our camp where they were executed and buried in unmarked graves. We heard the shots and a half-hour later we saw the execution squad march back to camp carrying a few muddy spades. A day or two later the Nip interpreter reported that one of the executed officers had been beheaded because he had been defiant.

Since the three officers had not made their escape their shooting squads were not executed, but they were confined to their barracks for one month as punishment for not preventing the attempt. You may be sure that each and every POW in camp became more acutely interested in his own shooting squad because of the object lesson we had just received.

A week or two later an American doing perimeter guard in the hospital area was caught outside the fence. One of our officers who made an investigation reported that the Nip sentry who caught the American had been engaged in smuggling and that he had helped him go through the fence. When a Nip patrol approached, the Nip grabbed the American and held him outside the fence, while he yelled loudly for help. We had no way of knowing whether the Nip was surprised or whether he was trying to make a reputation for himself with his superiors, but the fact was very clear that he had helped the American outside the fence and had held him until the Nip patrol arrived to arrest him. By direction of the commandant the POW was executed the same morning.

RICE BRAIN SETS IN

The prolonged deficiency in food, both [in] quantity and quality, was largely responsible for our ever-increasing death rate. The rapid physical deterioration in those of us who were left was so obvious that no one could doubt it. We understood the physical deterioration, but were shocked to find that it was accompanied by a mental and moral deterioration. Men who had wasted away in body usually had wasted away in mind so that they could not concentrate on any subject for very long and they could not think clearly at all. That condition was commonly called "Rice Brain."

The moral lapse was the most difficult for us to understand. We saw men, whom we had known to be of the strictest rectitude, become as cunning as animals, capable of doing anything to gratify their one remaining passion—HUNGER. We had only to indulge in the mildest sort of introspection to see that we had fallen almost as low ourselves. It was our conclusion that the veneer of civilization was much thinner than we had suspected, and that it could not resist starvation successfully.

We thought of the severe property laws of England and the United States, and we shuddered to contemplate the punishment which they inflicted on the victims of hunger who were caught tampering with the property of others in an attempt to ease their gnawing pangs. The viewpoint of a starving man became permanently etched in our minds.

In the early days at Camp Cabanatuan, during the time when work details were few, an effort was made by a number of officers to occupy the minds of the POWs through the organization of various activities. Athletic diversions had to be dropped from consideration, less because of a shortage of equipment than because of a shortage of food, for one cannot afford to throw away his energy when his food intake does not average fifteen hundred calories a day.

Schools were organized in a variety of subjects, including the Japanese language, and a comprehensive schedule of lectures on various subjects was arranged. Frequent religious services were held by representatives of the various faiths. All of the activities were brought to an abrupt end by order of the Nip commandant when the shooting squads were formed. The order directed that there would be no meetings for any purpose, including religious meetings, until further orders.

After about two weeks, religious services were permitted on Sundays provided a scenario of the proposed services had been submitted to the Nips and had been approved by them during the preceding week. A Nip interpreter attended the services with a copy of the script to be sure it was followed.

While I am on the subject of interpreters, I might say that I believe many of our difficulties were due to the poor quality of Nip interpreters[20] we had to deal with. Only a few of them had more than a schoolbook knowledge of the English language, but they all took great pains to conceal their lack of knowledge from their superiors. Some of them spoke English with reasonable fluency [but] had acquired an active hatred of Occidental which colored all their actions. Others had such a craven fear of their superiors that they always felt it safer to put the Americans in the wrong, while a few sadists enjoyed the unexcelled opportunity of inflicting punishment on other human beings without fear of reprisal.

Our American interpreters had a much keener understanding of the Japanese people than the Nip interpreters had of Americans, and I am convinced that their knowledge of the Japanese language was more adequate than the average Nip interpreter's understanding of English. Unfortunately, in every case of importance the Nips insisted on using their own interpreters.

Chapter 11

As the Years Come and Go

KEEPING IN TOUCH AS BEST WE COULD

In October [1942] some three thousand of us were moved to Mindanao.[1] The detail for the move [was] made up of volunteers as far as possible, the others being chosen by the American administrative headquarters. A large part of us were undecided as to the advantage of one camp over the other, and some of us were simply averse to volunteering for anything. I think you can guess that I did not volunteer, for I could not forget that I had volunteered for duty in the Philippines.

For a few months of 1942, the Nips loaned us a low–powered radio receiver, equipped with a high powered amplifier, but set to receive the Nip broadcasting station in Manila only. An electrical engineer devised some sort of a coil designed to make the set receive San Francisco, but the Nips took the set away before we got any benefit from it.

Beginning in July 1942, the Nips gave us a limited distribution of the Manila English-language newspapers. Even though the news items on the war were doctored insofar as they concerned the Japanese, the reader could, by making his own corrections, arrive at a reasonably accurate estimate of the progress of the war. Very little correction of facts was necessary in reading the news of the war in Europe because the Nips seemed to get some enjoyment out of the reversals of their Axis partners. Probably half of the news pages were devoted to anti-American statements of Mr. Laurel and his satellites, some of whom had been comrades of ours not long before.[2]

In view of Mr. Laurel's long record of pro-Japanese and anti-American activities, it was not unexpected to read such pronouncements of his, but the articles by some of the others were truly surprising. The editorial page, of course, was always devoted to the future glories of the "Greater East Asia

Co-Prosperity Sphere" under the safe and enlightened guidance of God given Nippon.

The papers were valuable in other ways, one of the most popular of which was their utilization as toilet paper. The Nips, with their usual beneficence, had authorized each American prisoner to receive the normal allowance of toilet paper for an individual of the Japanese Army, which was three thin sheets per day. Although it was called to the attention of the Nip headquarters that, in view of the many prisoners who had to visit the latrine from ten to fifty times each day, the allowance was slightly under our needs, no material increase was granted. The last quotation I remember in the market was one roll toilet paper—fifty pesos.

From the newspapers we learned that the *Gripsholm*,[3] loaded with Red Cross supplies for American prisoners, would reach Manila in early November [1942]. An officer friend of ours, who had been a civilian in Manila prior to the war, had received a note via the underground from his wife who was in Santo Tomas Concentration Camp in Manila[4] informing him that she had been selected to return to the United States on the *Gripsholm*. The officer collected short notes from several of his friends addressed to their families and, making them up into a small package, he sent them through the underground to his wife with the request that she mail the letters when she reached home. Either the letters never reached her, or she found that she could not fulfill the request, for they were not delivered.

Early in November [1942] an American truck driver, who had driven a Nip sergeant to Manila for some electrical supplies, reported that he had seen the prison detail in Manila unloading large quantities of Red Cross food packages. His story ran like wildfire through the camp, disbelieved by some, but believed by most of us who were convinced that only the problem of distribution remained to be overcome before we tasted real food again.

Very few prisoners listened to the truck driver's other stories. He had been sitting in his truck watching the people walk along the *Escolta* when he saw a Japanese officer push a white-haired Filipino out of his way. The old woman almost fell, but she recovered to spit on the Nip as he was passing her. The officer pulled his sword and scabbard loose from his belt and beat the woman to death on the sidewalk of the busy street.

After the Nip sergeant finished his business, he took the truck driver with him to visit his lady friend in one of the brothels run by the Imperial Japanese Army! The sergeant disappeared with his Filipino girl, leaving the American talking to another one. The second girl advised the driver that it was too bad she was diseased because, having both gonorrhea and syphilis she would not consider going to bed with anyone but a Japanese. She vehemently insisted that she was doing her part by disabling an untold number of Nip soldiers.

Sometime during the month of November [1942] we were informed that we had graduated from our captive status to prisoner of war status on the first of August [1942], if I recall correctly. We were further informed that we would be paid each month, and be permitted to correspond with our families, in conformity with the Geneva Convention which the Nips had not ratified.[5] All of which was good news but it put no food in our bellies; however, we had only a short time to wait, for many truckloads of Red Cross supplies arrived during November [1942].

THE RED CROSS, RICE, AND RESUPPLIES

About the first of December [1942] we were issued our first boxes,[6] one whole box going to each man at once, the others going into storage for future issue. No children anticipating Christmas, when they could actually gain possession of countless long-wished-for articles, ever suffered any more than we did while we were waiting for the distribution of our packages, and no small children ever appreciated their presents more than we did ours.

Some of the boxes were British, packed in Canada, and there were three or four slightly different kinds of American packages. As soon as we had eased our immediate hunger, we had a most enjoyable time exchanging articles of food which did not appeal to us particularly for others which we liked better. A few men could not control their appetites, a number of men eating so much [that] they became sick, and one Marine soldier ate his entire box in one day only to die most uncomfortably the next day.

We were overjoyed to receive our second food box on the afternoon of the twenty-third of December [1942] in order that we could have the materials for a pleasant Christmas. We ate well that Christmas day, but I am sure that the keenness of our appreciation did not quite reach that which we had at the receipt of our first package.

Our third package was delivered in January 1943 and [the] fourth, plus a small part of another, came in February [1943]. Before all of our Red Cross food was gone, the Nips altered our ration by increasing the rice component and by adding a considerable amount of meat. For the first time since we had been in captivity, we were issued a diet which was perfectly satisfactory in quantity, if not in quality.

The Nips bought all the old broken down carabao in the immediate vicinity to establish a herd which was to furnish our meat supply. A butchering detail selected by our veterinarians went to work every morning at daybreak to provide our meat supply for the day. Carabao meat is dark, about the same as liver in color, and the meat of old work bulls is extremely tough, but carabao meat is beef which, you know, has a high protein content.

The increase in calories from approximately fifteen hundred to about three thousand, the latter figure being about what a man needed if he was not working too hard, made a rapid change in our physical appearances.

During the long years of our imprisonment, rice was the main component of the ration, taking the place of bread, potatoes, and meat of the American diet.[7] The change to a rice diet was so drastic that many of us had difficulty in forcing the limited amount of rice we received down our gullets. In order to add what little variety that was possible, our mess officers tried giving us porridge rice, called *lugao* by the Filipinos, for breakfast instead of the usual steamed variety.

The Nips were induced to provide a large cooking range for each kitchen so that individuals might fry their rice and cook the food purchased from the commissary. Pepper, garlic, onions and other condiments were obtained in order to make the food more palatable. Many men became experts at preparing dishes which tempted them to relish their last bite of rice. The word commonly used for the cooking activity of individuals was borrowed from the Tagalog language. I am doubtful of the correct spelling but if it is spelled phonetically it should be "*Cuan*."[8] I have been told that it is a "catch-all" noun commonly used to designate indefinitely an object which is not well known or which cannot be well classified. The English words "thing" and "gadgets" are sometimes used similarly. We adopted the word and used it both as a noun and a verb, and also as an adjective when talking about individual cooking. For instance, the words *cuan, cuaning, cuan kitchen,* to *cuan* and *cuaning* hours were all well used words of our prison vernacular.

Everyone who was able to obtain non-ration food and many others who merely hoped to change the taste of their rice came to know and appreciate the *cuaning* privileges, for even though we were half-starved our jaded appetites oftentimes needed stimulation. The Red Cross supplies contained a considerable quantity of Atabrine and sulfa drugs which were exactly what we needed.[9]

The result of additional food and medicine was a steady drop in the death rate, which had been close to twenty a day in October [1942], until on one memorable day in March 1943, there was not a single death.[10] By the time our death rate was back to normal, more than two thousand men had been buried in our cemetery, which made our ratio of deaths greater than one to four within a space of only nine months.[11]

In addition to food and medicine, the *Gripsholm* brought us several thousand new pairs of shoes, a quantity of shoe repair materials, and some cobbler's sets. The selection of shoes and repair equipment could not have been better for many men had substituted wooden clogs for shoes, and many others had worn their shoes almost out. The most surprising of the articles we received were several thousand copies of well selected books, including many novels which had been published in 1942. When those books were added to our little library they made it an entirely adequate and much patronized establishment.

With our improved physical condition, our minds grew more active, we read the Nip newspapers more critically and we discussed among ourselves the Japanese-American military situation. The consensus of opinion, to which I subscribed, was that the Nips had reached the limit of their expansion, the success of which they were justly proud, and that they expected to hold most of what they had gained until the United States grew tired of fighting a costly war and concluded a negotiated peace. They were, at that time, filled with optimism that was reflected in the improvement of our rations and in the change of our status from captives to prisoners of war. Unfortunately, the change in their feelings from optimism to pessimism, which came later, was also reflected in the treatment we received.

We had entered into the Golden Age, or rather the Age of Plenty, if any part of our imprisonment could be so considered. We were no longer captives, we had books to read and shoes to wear. We were getting paid a little money, we had reached a normal death rate and we were growing fat on a diet of plenty of rice and carabao, a small bun a day and what duck eggs and evaporated milk our little money could buy. At any rate, we had entered a year of freedom from physical pain and the specter of death had moved back almost out of sight.

The story of how we acquired the bun or roll of wheat bread a day for six months may interest you. The Nips produced the flour probably from a Manila warehouse that had been bombed. Some of the flour was in good condition packed in the original Minnesota milling company's bags, but almost half of it had been resacked in hemp bag of local manufacture.[12] The resacked flour was full of dirt, rat droppings and debris of all sorts just as if it had been swept up from a floor where it had been for some time.

To utilize the flour, American prisoners built ovens, making containers and baking pans from scrap materials. Other prisoners grew cultures of yeast in sufficient quantity, while still others constructed sieves with which to remove the filth, pebbles and splinters of wood. The finished product which resulted from all of that work as a very fine bun that was highly prized by Americans and the Nip officers and noncommissioned officers who were able to horn in on our supply.

LABOR DETAILS AND MAKING DO AT THE CAMP

After the fall of Corregidor, the Nips initiated various projects on which they used prisoner of war labor. A few of these projects which I shall relate were salvage details on Bataan and Corregidor, stevedore details in Manila, and construction details on new and existing air fields in central Luzon. Usually after a project was completed the men returned to Cabanatuan as there were, during our stay at that camp, frequent changes in [the] size of our population.

In the fall of 1942 the first work detail of several hundred men was sent to Japan, followed by others every few months.[13] The men on outgoing work details were required to be in sufficiently good health to perform hard labor. Because of the heavy drain on the reserve of healthy men and the increasing demands for labor at Cabanatuan, we were hard pressed to protect the men who were really sick.

In the early days the Nips followed the Geneva Convention with respect to officers being exempt from work details, but as time went on more and more officers were included with the daily labor parties.[14] At first the Nips had defended their use of officers by referring to the large number of sick men who could be sent to work in place of officers, but later they frankly insisted that officers had to work the same as enlisted men.

At Camp Cabanatuan there were enough healthy prisoners to fill the local demands for labor until in the latter part of 1943 the strength was greatly reduced by requisitions for several outgoing details. The improvement in our health was paralleled by a marked improvement in the condition of the camp. Each major improvement which required Nip approval was opposed as a matter of principle, necessitating time and effort on the part of the Americans to get permission to start it.

An American officer, after much effort, got permission to construct a septic tank in connection with one of our box latrines.[15] One month after it was finished the Nips were convinced of its efficiency and authorized septic tanks for all latrines, thereby saving considerable labor and eliminating all of the fly-breeding places in camp. We had been infested with swarms of big blue-bottle flies that put up a tough battle to take our meals away from us. They were so persistent in their pursuit of food that they had to be evicted by force once they had made a landing on a messkit.

Upon recommendation of our surgeon, a campaign had been started to kill off the fly population by means of numerous traps and a compulsory swatting "fest" participated in by all men who could walk, but the flies won the battle. However, they could not solve their propagation problem after we had converted our latrines to septic tank equipment. There were latrines in the Nip area that continued to serve as breeding places but they were so few that the flies almost disappeared from our area.

Shelves and racks were built in barracks, tables and chairs were constructed and vegetable gardens began to fill the empty spaces around the barracks. There did not seem to be any lack of inventiveness on the part of the prisoners as a whole and there were many artisans among us, some of them being very skillful.

Materials of all kinds, rope, pipe, tin, iron, paper, and wood, could be used for something by the person who had the necessary imagination and skill. Labels from tin cans were carefully saved and utilized for scratch paper, of which the Nips had very little. As a matter of fact, the records of the hospital and our administrative headquarters could not have been maintained without [using the] labels [as paper].

Most of us were unable to recognize the value of seemingly worthless objects which we had always thrown away at home and oftentimes we did not have the skill to convert them to use after we had been shown how to do it. We came to the conclusion that our civilization had taught us nothing about adjusting ourselves to conditions which were foreign to our experience. I do not mean to infer that we learned definably what the essentials of life are, but we certainly revised our opinions as to the importance of many items.

For instance, a number of articles, hitherto considered worthless, assumed vast importance in our struggle for existence, and many other articles depreciated in value by being eliminated from our acquaintance. We did learn that some people can live on very little for the Nips did not spend more than $15.00 per month on us all told, and that included food, clothing, shelter and medicine. We were astonished the first time we saw a man obtaining his own thread by unraveling a sock to make a creditable repair job on his dilapidated articles of clothing.

After a long time the Nips were induced to bring us a couple of tailor's sewing machines which permitted us to greatly improve our appearance. Two men who could repair false teeth were discovered in the hospital and from then on they led a very busy and lucrative life. Not all sets of teeth could be repaired, which greatly handicapped the owners [since there were] no new ones on our market. I remember one instance in which a man without teeth had a true friend who, after eating, carefully washed his teeth and loaned them to his friend.

Numerous improvisations by our doctors and dentists went almost unnoticed.[16] When there was no material for filling teeth, fillings from silver coins were used to good advantage. Although drills were operated by foot treadles, with the help of an assistant our dentists took care of our needs together with those of the "mooching" Nips who had no dentists of their own.

Money, medicine, and mail between camp and Manila continued in spite of the efforts of the Nips to stop it. Typewritten copies of San Francisco news broadcasts, heard on secret Filipino radios and taken down in shorthand, found their way to us on the average of once a month.

Probably the most ingenious of all the articles constructed in camp was a tube radio receiver which brought in broadcasts from San Francisco nearly seven thousand miles away. This set was built by Lieutenant Hutchison, an engineer officer and an electrical engineer by profession, out of salvage materials except for the tube which was smuggled into him.[17] He cut the bottom off a regulation army canteen and built his set small enough to fit into the canteen. When the set was not in use he wedged the canteen tightly into the cup to reduce the chances of it being discovered. After he had the set in operation he was moved to a barracks which had not been furnished with electricity, but he solved that problem by building a battery from scraps of copper and zinc using the acid stolen from the battery of a Nip truck and zinc buttons cut from trouser flies.

At the risk of his life, Hutch heard the news several times a week and kept us up to date on what was going on in the world. Thus, by means of Nip newspapers, information from the Filipinos, information from individual Nips and the news which Hutch picked up, we were surprisingly well informed about the war.

RELAXING BUT KEEPING REALITY IN SIGHT

Beginning sometime in 1943, the Nips ran a free movie in our area once or twice a month. The majority of the pictures were old American productions but a few were poor Nip films made for propaganda purposes. One film, which was proclaimed to be the camera record of Pearl Harbor, was particularly poor as the scene of the harbor before and after [the] bombing was obviously a mock-up prepared for the filming.

A film representing the advance through Malaya was much more realistic for all scenes appeared to have been taken on the Malayan Peninsula. One scene of a heavy artillery piece going into action was unusually impressive. The big gun was being moved into position by a large number of Japanese soldiers pulling tow ropes. Two soldiers, who appeared to be completely worn out, dropped in their tracks before the gun reached the desired position.

An officer, overcome with fury at the soldiers' shirking duty, rushed to them, drawing his sword. Apparently he ordered them to continue dragging at the rope but, when they did not move fast enough to suit him, he beheaded them one after the other with two mighty blows of his sword. That picture helped us understand why the Nip soldier was so much afraid of his officers.

In 1943, the Nips relaxed their prohibition on assemblies to permit a comic dramatic production by POWs one evening per week provided the script had been approved at Nip Headquarters. There was plenty of talent available for producing the shows, although very little of it was good. But, regardless of the quality of the shows, they were tremendously popular.

[Lieutenant] Colonel O. O. Wilson, generally called "Zero," was in charge of the productions, and appeared occasionally in a monologue on the order of Will Rogers.[18] He had a low dry voice which was well suited to what he had to say and he had the faculty of talking in a smooth unhalting delivery which I thought was an improvement over Will Rogers himself. Many others must have thought so too for his offerings were always the most popular of the evening.

The actors were striving to bring out a belly laugh from the crowd, and they frequently did. One of the biggest laughs they ever got was in a show in which one of the characters was [a] thick-witted oaf who could hardly be induced to make a move. After a good buildup when there was no doubt as to the lethargy of the actor, another actor turned to a friend to say, "He is slower than the second coming of MacArthur."

[While the prisoners entertained themselves, the reality of the situation they were in never escaped them.] There were persistent rumors of guerrilla activities nearby, one of them being to the effect that an attack was planned on our camp. The attack did not materialize, but there were a few incidents which indicated that there were guerrillas in the vicinity. A Nip truck was ambushed at night on a lonely road [and] a Nip officer [was] killed in the action. [Additionally,] two barrios within sight of the camp were bombed by Nip dive bombers about a month apart.

[The Japanese did not let these actions go unanswered.] A Nip patrol left camp one morning in full field equipment, returning that evening with the heads of two Filipinos on poles. They tied the poles to the gate of our enclosure, leaving them there two days for the morale effect. The object lesson was not effective, for two days later a prisoner disappeared from a detail working on the farm. He went to a barrio where he expected to receive aid but he was held by the inhabitants until the Nips could send a patrol after him.

The Filipino who had reported the prisoner to the Nips had the pleasure of receiving a twenty-five peso reward and the opportunity to see him beaten to death by the patrol. The patrol was composed largely of recruits who were required to use the American as a dummy for bayonet practice, as a part of their hardening process. Due to the fact that the prisoner had escaped from the farm his "shooting squad" was not punished, but a group of American officers were required to view the mutilated body in order that they might explain to the other Americans the penalty that was the inevitable result of escape.

The Nips finally got around to making a movie, dramatizing the "Conquest of Bataan." Several hundred American officers and men were taken from Camp Cabanatuan to Bataan, where they represented the United States Army in the Nip film version of the fighting and surrender of Bataan.[19] None of our boys were highly paid stars, but they had three weeks of better food and less work than if they had stayed in camp.

One day, Nip Headquarters sent an order to our enclosure to have a medical officer with his equipment ready to go to a small camp in Luzon within an hour. The officer selected to fill that order was not very happy about it but he had to go. Two months later he stopped by to see us for a couple of hours while the Nip truck driver who brought him attended to business. The doctor told us that he was the only American officer with a work party of two hundred men and he described what he had to do.

He said that the Nip officer in charge of the project had a very bad case of gonorrhea, so he had requested that the officer with the American detail be a doctor who could serve as the Nip's personal physician, in addition to his other duties. The day the doctor arrived in the work camp the Nip officer regaled him with accounts of [the] charms of his Filipino girlfriend, whom he saw every time he went to Manila, which was at least once a week. He was quite frank about his affliction which he definitely expected the doctor to cure. The doctor went with him to Manila where they obtained the necessary medicine to begin the cure, but before they started back to camp the Nip paid his lady friend a two hour visit.

That evening when the doctor gave his first dose of medicine he explained that the disease was a difficult one which would require the Nip to practice continence for some little time in order to permit the medicine to effect the cure. The Nip officer, who was a little drunk at the time, let out a roar and announced that he expected his physician to bring about a cure in the earliest possible time without any inconvenience to him. Five days later, another visit to the lady friend partly undid some of the good the medicine had done. The doctor was of the opinion that the Nip was somewhat better than he had been at first, but he was doubtful that a complete cure would ever be achieved.

One night some tires were stolen from a truck which was parked on the edge of the unlighted camp. The Nip officer sent a patrol to the nearby town to arrest the thieves. The patrol came back in a short time with four Filipinos whom the Nips condemned to death without any loss of time. He directed the doctors to come with him as a witness to the executions. The Filipinos, who were tied hand and foot, were raised to a kneeling position while he drew his sword and examined it carefully. Apparently he was satisfied with it for, choosing the first Filipino, he raised his sword with both hands and brought it down on the back of the poor man's neck.

The neck of the Filipino was cut deeply enough to kill him, although it was not completely severed, which seemed to make the officer very unhappy. Handing his sword to the doctor, the Nip insisted that he try the next man and see if he could do a better job. After some embarrassing difficulty the doctor begged out of being the executioner and as the Nip officer was tired he directed the guards to shoot the other three Filipinos, which they did without delay.

THE UNDERGROUND STRUGGLE

Late in 1942, the Nips gave us two bundles of newspapers printed in English. The two papers, *Nippon Times* and *Tokyo Times and Advertiser,* were much better edited than the Manila papers.[20] From them we collected a great deal of world news and many more details on the war in the Pacific. Unfortunately, we were to receive them only once per month for the next year. When, in early 1944, the Nips discontinued the delivery of the Japanese papers we missed them sorely but, by that time, we were definitely aware that the war was becoming more complete [and from the actions displayed by our captors, the Allies must have been doing well].

We were not surprised at our rations being cut drastically, nor at various economy measures which the Nips had to adopt [as a result of their struggle against the Allies in the South Pacific]. That knowledge was not gained from written generalities, nor from the semi-news articles written from propaganda experts in Tokyo, but from the personal experience articles of which there were many. Those articles always ended with a statement of how brave the Japanese soldiers were and how well they were doing, but, for the most part, the articles definitely told of defeat.

We read accounts of the sky being full of American airplanes so that Japanese air and ground troops were always fighting at a disadvantage, *but successfully,* of course. We saw sketches of new landing crafts and amphibious vehicles, and read of the great disadvantage in which the Nip defenders were placed by the American use of new equipment, but they always fought to win in spite of their difficulties. We were left with the impression that the personal experience writers would not object to resting in Tokyo permanently, permitting others to gain all the glory of defeating the Americans.

At the end of 1943 or the beginning of 1944, a drastic gas shortage forced the Nips to operate a carabao cart train daily between our camp and the town of Cabanatuan. The train consisted of a Nip corporal and two guards, an American train master, and an American driver for each cart. The train operated six to ten native carts, each pulled by a single carabao, and transported whatever supplies the Nips had to be hauled, going the seven miles to Cabanatuan in the morning and returning in afternoon.

Our underground mail system, which had dwindled to a trickle, had a great revival when the carabao train started operations. All outgoing mail was placed in a container hidden under one of the carts where it could be released by a string on the cart when a known Filipino was seen loitering in a rice patty near the road. The carts having passed on, the Filipino recovered the mail and forwarded it to Manila. The incoming mail was picked up on the return trip from a stump where it had been hidden.

The train master always made the authorized halt on the return trip near the stump so he could sit on it and rest. During the rest period he managed to transfer the incoming package to his shirt when the Nips were not looking. In that way letters, news, medicine, and money in thousands of pesos started to flow regularly into camp again and it continued to come in for several months.

We did not know all the details of the underground system from Cabanatuan to Manila, but we knew the names of a number of people working in the underground, most of whom were women. We knew that a woman messenger traveled between Cabanatuan and Manila and that she dealt mostly with women in Manila. Some of those women were Filipinos and Spaniards and a few were of other nationalities.

These women were utterly fearless, extremely efficient and devoted to Americans and the American cause. Thousands of Americans who are alive today would have perished if they had not received the medicine and the money which those gallant women sent in. I have often wondered if our war would have gone differently if the men of the Philippine Army had been as gallant and capable as their women in the underground were.

One unlucky day the carabao train stopped in its usual place for the rest period on the return trip. The train master, who had become a bit careless, was detected by a recruit guard as he lifted the mail package from the stump. The guard called the corporal, gave him the package, and showed him were it had been hidden. The corporal had been friendly with the train master but he did not dare disregard the incident because, if he did, and the recruit's gossip reached Nip Headquarters, he was in a bad predicament for having shown a favor to an American.

When the train reached camp the package was delivered to Nip Head-quarters and the train master was sent to the guardhouse. The loss of the two or three thousand pesos in the mail package was not serious, but the names of addresses and the writers of the letters were. The train master was painfully beaten, in order to improve his memory, and more than twenty other prisoners were arrested for questioning. The questioning was inter-spersed with beatings as the process went on for several days.

About half of the prisoners interrogated were incarcerated in the guardhouse, the others being returned to camp. The prisoners remaining in the guardhouse were crowded into a cramped, uncomfortable room where they were poorly fed but not neglected for they were beaten at irregular intervals during the day and night.

The Nip Headquarters at Cabanatuan made a full report to the Imper-ial Headquarters in Manila, thereby bringing about the arrest of a number of our underground friends. After a week of questioning and investigating in Manila, a group of Nip intelligence officers arrived at Cabanatuan to continue the questioning of the prisoners held in the guardhouse. From the nature of the questions asked it was clear that the Nips were trying to con-nect our POWs with an American intelligence organization on Luzon, which was making periodic reports to the American Armed Forces.

Many of us were extremely worried about all the proceedings for we had corresponded with persons in Manila and had received money and medicine at various times. After a month of investigation we were cleared of everything except unauthorized correspondence and the smuggling into camp of a large amount of money.

For several months the Nips had allowed the hospital commander to buy a number of carabao which provided much needed meat for the sick. The money to purchase those carabaos came from Manila through the underground, although the Nips had been led to believe it came from contributions of money which had been brought with us when we entered camp. The officers who were discovered to have been connected with that importation of money, including the senior medical officer and at least two chaplains, were given jail sentences in the guardhouse which was uncomfortable and sometimes painful, but they survived and returned to duty somewhat the worse for wear.

Many of the civilians arrested in Manila were released after suffering considerable torture, but a number of them were executed. There were isolated cases of correspondence afterwards and considerable money continued to come into [the] camp, but it was introduced by Nip soldiers who were well subsidized for their trouble [and what became known as the activities of the underground at Cabanatuan all but ceased to exist].

THE FARM

In the fall of 1942, one of our officers, who claimed to know something of gardening in the Philippines, talked the Nips into providing some vegetable seeds to start a modest garden. The officer enjoyed some success and became known to the prisoners as "Farmer Jones."[21] The Nips thought so much of his efforts that they expanded his program tremendously by ploughing an extensive area outside the camp which they called "the Farm."

Due to the fact that all work after the original ploughing had to be done by hand, and due to a shortage of tools, the manpower requirements eventually became inconveniently large. As the healthy manpower in camp was drained to fill requisitions for local work camps and for shipment to Japan, it became necessary to send workers to the garden who were too weak and too ill to work.

Protests were made to the Japanese, but they were denied because we were told that the work was beneficial for the men, besides they were receiving the products of the garden. It did us no good to point out that the garden produced more than we could use, whereas the work was really injurious to the health of many of the men. Actually, it made no difference how much food was grown in the garden for we were not permitted to use as much as we needed.

A large amount of the garden products went to the Japanese, some of it being shipped to their headquarters in Manila, but there was always a considerable portion left in the garden until it was definitely past the eating stage. Once we received our allowance we could have starved to death while food spoiled in the garden, and no matter how much more food was grown than was needed the Nips would not reduce our acreage to ease our labor problems.

It was natural that with such a high percentage of sick men among the workers the Nip overseers should be dissatisfied with the general performance of the daily work because, as far as they were concerned, all workers were able-bodied and the Nip authorities held the overseers responsible for the results. The overseers were lowly Nip privates, some of whom were Formosan recruits, the lowliest privates of them all.[22] They were intelligent and brutal, with little knowledge of English, trying to carry out their orders to bear down on the Americans as much as necessary in order to get the work out of them.

Those men, nicknamed "Donald Duck," "Laughing Boy," "Base Ball," "Four Eyes," and others, all carried strong cudgels which they arbitrarily used on any prisoner who displeased them without making an attempt to obtain an explanation.[23] The beatings usually were brutal, not infrequently being of such severity that the victims had to be hospitalized. As the war came close to us and Japan's sun began to look more like a setting sun, the brutalities became worse, giving us plenty of cause to ponder over our future treatment.

The waste of food on the farm when we were hungry was not the only example of starvation amid plenty. The stock of prize cattle from the Philippine Commonwealth's Experimental Farm was brought to a large corral adjoining the Nip part of camp. We were told that the cattle were ours, but we were never permitted to kill more than one animal per week, and the Nips received a considerable part of that. When we left Cabanatuan for good most of the cattle were left behind. The Nips didn't even permit us to slaughter one animal a day before we left.

ENTER 1944—NO CHANGE

Perhaps I neglected to tell you that our food was cut to the original ration before the end of 1943. We did have a Red Cross Food Box for Christmas and little more than two others early in the year [1944], but by March many of us were beginning to show symptoms of dietary disorders. Practically all of the carabao, except those being used as draft animals, had been consumed.

A small amount of granulated fish was issued in place of meat. It was very dry and salty and smelled so rotten that I had to hold my nose when I ate it. Some of the Americans who had been in the Philippines a long time insisted that the fish had been processed for use as fertilizer, and judging from the looks, taste, and smell of the product we could not deny the statement. I can assure you that it was not brook trout.

Food was scarce in the commissary as well as in our kitchens for the supply of canned goods in the Philippines had been practically exhausted. Inflation had affected the value of Japanese script so much that the little money we received could buy very little except bananas and corn which had to be ground into meal by hand.

Duck eggs skyrocketed from one and two pesos to five pesos and sometimes a fourth of them were rotten. The Filipino who brought a truckload of corn to the commissary told our commissary officer that the guerrillas were in control of the roads in the northern part of Luzon, and that they prevented the Nips from acquiring food from their areas. He stated that if he could get a pass from the commissary officer he could buy several bags of mongo beans for delivery the next week. The pass was duly prepared and signed by the American officer with [little hope], but the beans were duly delivered the following week as promised, much to our pleasure and merriment.

As inflation increased, our expenditures in the commissary rose to twice our payroll receipts, which became a matter of some concern to the staff of the Japanese commandant. The only thing we could tell them was that everyone[24] was dipping into the money he had brought into camp with him. The Nips were not convinced, but they did not pursue the subject further.

Before the close of 1943, we knew that one end of the warehouse was full of mail for us but the Nips announced that it could not be delivered until it had been censored. There being only two Nip interpreters at the Nip camp headquarters, it did not look as if we were ever going to see very much of it. Even after three additional Nips reported for duty as assistant censors the number of letters reaching our part of the camp did not average a hundred a day.

Some of the early restrictions must have been lifted for at the end of a month censors were processing several hundred letters a day. None of us ever figured out the method of distribution for some men received twenty letters at a time, while others of us did not receive a single one during the first six weeks of censoring. One man received more than two hundred letters, whereas a few men did not receive any; probably, the twenty that I received were more than the average.

The letters were dated during the period May 1, 1942, [to] October 1, 1943, so they were approximately from six months to two years old. There was no system in the manner in which the mail was sorted for we might receive a recent epistle one day and an old one the next.

We received our last letters in June 1944; it really was the last for we received no other mail during our imprisonment. Estimating the average number of letters in a mail bag, and knowing the number of bags in the warehouse, we were convinced that fewer than half of the letters delivered to the Nips ever reached us.

For those of us who heard no bad news the letters were comforting in that we knew our families were safe and settled for the war. Many men received word of the deaths of members or their families, some of the deaths being battle casualties. The number of cases of marital troubles was surprisingly large. One wife wrote her husband that he had been reported dead and that she had married again, but just as soon as she heard that the report was a mistake she had left the second man, and she promised faithfully she would never do it again.

During 1943 we were permitted to send four postcards on which we could type fifty words. The Nips gave us rigid instructions that we had to use simple language limiting our subjects to personal matters in no way referring to the Nips, the war, nor prison conditions. Many cards, which the interpreters considered violated those conditions or which were not understood, were thrown in the wastebasket.

In 1944 a revised card was adopted which limited us to twenty-five words, but we were allowed one card a month.[25] In March 1944, delivery was made of the one and only personal Christmas package which had been authorized to be sent by the immediate family of each of us the previous fall. As in the case of letters, a number of men did not receive packages but, through some means that we did not understand, a few men received two and one man got three.

The packages were practically all of the same size, but [that's where] their similarity ceased. My box, if you remember picking it, contained a thousand multi-vitamin tablets and some powdered soup for my unhappy stomach. The fact that the box contained no more food was a disappointment but, actually, nothing you could have sent would have been of more value than the vitamin tablets. I had begun to show alarming pellagra and beriberi symptoms which disappeared two weeks after I began taking the globules. There were so many that I gave half of them to my friends who prized them highly.

Some of the vitamins I gave to Pat, who had been a faithful friend since our Stotsenburg days. He had come to see me several times during the bad days, bringing me a can of evaporated milk almost every time.

I do not know where he got the milk, but I do know how much I appreciated it.

You included an undershirt, a pair of shorts and a pair of socks, all of which were very useful. When the socks arrived I put them on and discarded a pair of Nip socks, which were nothing but a cloth tube with a toe formed at one end, the heel having been omitted. The shorts being size 40 did not need a gusset, inasmuch as my waist was a scant 28. I got a big kick out of the shorts because I could see you believed I had grown fat on the prison diet.

With the aid of a safety pin, I was able to fit the shorts and wear them instead of the Nip G-string, which never did feel comfortable. The Nips do not have to worry about their underclothing very much because, with primitive socks and a G-string, they are very simply equipped; no undershirt being required.

My new undershirt was a convenience for, since it was a size 42, when I put it on it hung down to my knees so that no other garment was needed. The deck of cards and the cribbage board were well-worn objects before they were lost on the *Oryoko Maru*.

By the middle of the year 1944, another draft of laborers had been sent to Japan and many work details from projects on Luzon had been returned to us. A large part of the detail that had gone to Mindanao in October 1942 returned. Rusty and Johnny joined us in the prison camp at Cabanatuan in the spring of 1944, after having spent the war up to that time in Mindanao.[26]

Rusty had been in command of an infantry regiment and Johnny had commanded an artillery regiment which had acted as infantry because they had no cannon. Both of the regiments were poorly trained and ill equipped organizations of the Philippine Army, similar to the Philippine Army regiments on Luzon. Although their troops were always outclassed in training, equipment, and strength by the Nip troops they encountered, both gallant officers, by their courage, skill and experience, led their regiments extremely well and made enviable records. They were old friends, so I spent many hours talking to them of their combat experiences.

It is one of the tragedies of the war that those officers are not here to tell their own stories, but both of them were killed later in the bombing attacks we underwent while in the holds of prison ships on the way to Japan. Their stories were corroborated by several other officers who had knowledge of their activities, and I believe them to be substantially correct.

Inasmuch as they were friends of ours, and their stories present fine pictures of the war, I shall tell them to you as well as I can recall them.

THE STORY OF THE DEFENSE OF MINDANAO

Early in the war [Brigadier] General William F. Sharp, the Commander of the United States Army Forces in Mindanao, sent Rusty's regiment of a little more than one thousand men to the vicinity of Cotabato to protect the south flank.[27] The main body of the troops on Mindanao was held in the northern part of the island, particular attention being paid to the protection of the airfield at Del Monte and the approaches thereto.[28]

Del Monte was extremely important because it and Clark Field on Luzon were the only air fields in the Philippines which could accommodate B-17 planes and, in addition, without Del Monte as an intermediate base, air communications between Luzon and Australia by ground planes was impossible.

Del Monte and Cotabato were connected by approximately two hundred miles of unimproved road which wound around and over hills and through heavy jungle growth of the lowlands of southern Mindanao. Cotabato is a port location about halfway between Manila and the equator, so the jungle growth in that part of the Philippines is more luxuriant and more nearly impenetrable than it is in Bataan.

Immediately after he arrived at the coast near Cotabato, Rusty made a reconnaissance to select defensive positions for his regiment in order that he might contest a landing in case the Nips came that way. He found that the possible landing places were so numerous that he could not cover them all, for which reason he decided to occupy a position covering the road to Del Monte with the main part of his regiment and put small outposts at the other places along the beach.[29]

The regiment had been occupying its position for some time before a Nip landing force arrived in the area. After a study of the situation the Nip commander decided not to try a landing in front of Rusty's regiment, but to move by motorboat up the Cotabato River which wound through the tropical jungle on a course roughly parallel to the road. The Nips had sufficient boats and plenty of guides composed of pro-Japanese natives and of Japanese civilians who had resided in that area until shortly before the war began.

They moved out from the ships standing off on shore in a sizable flotilla of boats one night and penetrated the river for several miles before daybreak. In order to carry out his mission, Rusty had to withdraw his force from its position and move back toward Del Monte so that he could remain between the Nips and the air field.[30]

The Nips continued their advance for several days and each day Rusty moved to an intermediate position. The jungle was so heavy that he did not feel that he could risk an attack against the Nip flotilla. After the Nips had proceeded up the river a hundred miles or more, the river became so difficult to navigate that they landed and tried to continue their journey overland, but they did not get very far until they were stopped by Rusty's regiment which was in position blocking the road. Rusty continued to hold the Nip force a safe distance from Del Monte until after the surrender of Mindanao when he was ordered to rejoin General Sharpe's main forces.

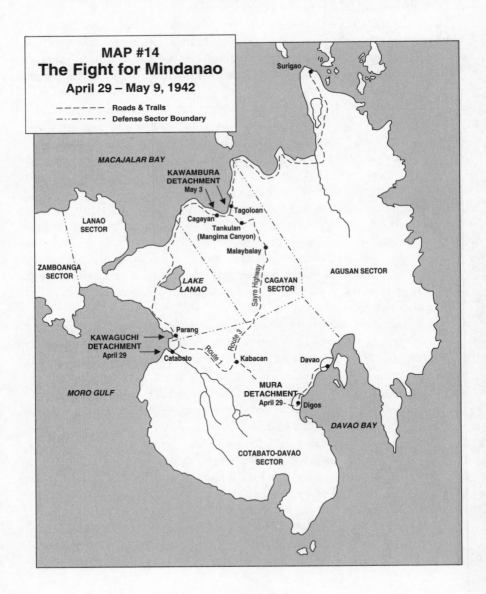

MAP #14
The Fight for Mindanao
April 29 – May 9, 1942

– – – – – Roads & Trails
– · – · – · – Defense Sector Boundary

MACAJALAR BAY

KAWAMBURA
DETACHMENT
May 3

Tagoloan
Cagayan
Tankulan
(Mangima Canyon)
Malaybalay

Surigao

LANAO
SECTOR

ZAMBOANGA
SECTOR

LAKE
LANAO

Sayre Highway

CAGAYAN
SECTOR

AGUSAN SECTOR

KAWAGUCHI
DETACHMENT
April 29

Parang

Route 3

Catabato

Route 1

Kabacan

Davao

MORO GULF

MURA
DETACHMENT
April 29

Digos

DAVAO BAY

COTABATO-DAVAO
SECTOR

During the time he had protected the approach to Del Monte from the south, all our serviceable airplanes had been sent to Australia and General MacArthur, [President] Quezon, and others had been evacuated. Much has been written of the escapes of General MacArthur and his staff, but nobody has ever told how much Rusty contributed to the successful air operations.

The undersized regiment which Johnny commanded was composed of less than a thousand men armed with Enfield rifles and a few machine guns.[31] It was assigned to defend a sector of the coast which included the port [five miles northwest in a straight line distance] of Del Monte. The airfield was connected with the port by a winding mountain road some thirty miles in length. The road constituted the easiest approach to Del Monte, except by air, so Johnny had the dual mission of keeping the road clear for our use and keeping the Nips away from it.

Early in March 1942, Johnny received confidential information from General Sharp that General MacArthur and party were about to arrive by boat en route to Del Monte airfield. In order that no "trigger happy soldier" would fire on the approaching boats, he directed that all troops on beach defense for a mile on each side of the port [be] withdrawn until after General MacArthur had landed and proceeded to the airport.

Johnny was also directed to take such other measures as might be necessary to insure the safety of the party during their short land travel. In compliance with orders, Johnny met General MacArthur when he landed and accompanied his motor convoy to Del Monte, where he saw him take off for Australia.

Johnny told me everything worked out perfectly except that he was not invited to join the party on its trip to Australia. Some time later, President Quezon and party came through [Del Monte] en route to the United States. Again, Johnny furnished the protection, his orders being to deliver Mr. Quezon safely, in the quickest possible time, to the airfield and to guard him closely until his plane departed for the south.

General Sharp made it quite clear to Johnny that it was important to our government to remove the president of the Philippine Commonwealth to the United States [for protection]. Again, the mission was completed and Johnny was left behind when the big planes took off. A few more individuals, including a number of army nurses, came through on their way to the Del Monte airfield before the Nips started landing operations on the west coast of Mindanao. A landing was attempted in the vicinity of the port sometime later, but the Nips suffered such heavy losses that they made little progress until Johnny withdrew his regiment after General Sharp ordered the surrender of the island.[32] As in the case of Rusty, nobody has written of Johnny's contribution to the operations in the Philippines.

LOOKING TOWARD THE UNPREDICTABLE FUTURE

From the news which we gathered from many sources, we concluded that the Nips expected an early attack on Mindanao, and that they were going to send more prisoners out of the danger zone to Japan if possible.

Prisoners who had been working on Nip air fields reported that poor quality gasoline required the lengthening of runways, and they further reported an increase in operational accidents. One truck driver, who had been driving in the mountains of Northern Luzon for two years, reported that all prisoners had been ordered to the main camps. He told a story about picking up a Filipino priest not long before when he was driving a loaded truck from the railhead up the mountain to Baguio.

During the course of the conversation, the American asked the padre what the Filipinos thought of the return of General MacArthur. "Young man," the priest answered, "If my people had as much faith in Jesus Christ as they have in the return of MacArthur, I would be the happiest man in the world."

After I got back from a short stay in the hospital,[33] I went to work in our library. A surprising number of men had carried books into camp and the Nips had brought in a truckload from the Army & Navy Club in Manila. After the addition of the new books which came on the *Gripsholm*, the library, as far as fiction was concerned, would have done credit to a library of a fair-sized city. I enjoyed my association with [the library] greatly for, not only was I able to catch up on my reading of old books, but I had an opportunity to read many new books of the fiction published in 1941 and 1942.[42]

One morning in August 1944, I was working in the library when the room started going around so fast I had to lie down to keep from falling. After I recovered I made my way back to my shack to rest. Sitting in the shade of the shack next door was Colonel Duckworth, a regular army medical officer who came originally from Martinsville, Indiana. He had commanded the hospital on Bataan which had been bombed by the Nips, and it was he who made such a good impression on the Nip general that his hospital had received [the] protection of Nip guards.

I visited him to ask what was the cause of my fainting spell. He told me our diet was the cause of my trouble in that my system was being deprived of badly needed sugar or salt, or both. His advice was to take life as easy as possible until we got back on a normal diet, after which my troubles would be at an end.[35]

I came to know the colonel quite well during the many times we talked in the shade. He told me that he had gone to O'Donnell with a part of his hospital personnel less than a month after we had left there. He had been able to get little medicine from the Nips so he had been forced to see many men die who might have been saved. When they finally closed the camp more than fifteen hundred Americans had been buried there, which made the death toll for O'Donnell and Cabanatuan exceed four thousand.

I was greatly interested in many of his observations for he was a medical officer of wide experience in administering to the sick. One of his remarks I remember was that, in the care of the very sick, the worth of a good doctor was about 25 percent, whereas after the doctor had done his part, the care of a good female nurse was worth 75 percent.

He added that many lives could have been saved in our prison hospitals with good nursing even though there had been no medicine available. As I look back on my hospital experience, I am forced to conclude that, if the colonel was right concerning the importance of nursing, the trend in hospitalization today is going the wrong way for the nurses, more and more, are becoming fully occupied in relieving the doctors of administrative details.

The last memory I have of the colonel was one afternoon, just before I left Cabanatuan, when he and I were in the open-air showers at the same time. He had been a decidedly portly man before the war but the Nip diet had pulled him down to a mere shadow of his former self. As his stomach receded, his skin had not kept up with it but had fallen down in wrinkled folds which reminded me somewhat of an elephant's wrinkles.

Stepping out of the shower, he pulled the folds of his belly skin out as far as he could and announced, "It is a good thing for me that I had all of that fat to live on."

A few of my close friends used to discuss the advisability of remaining in the Philippines or going with the detail to Japan in view of the rapid approach of the American forces.[36] Most of us were of the opinion that the Nips would take such steps as might be available to prevent us from falling into the hands of our own troops. On the other hand, a sea journey in a Nip ship was hardly the safest way to insure a long life, and it was a most uncomfortable way to travel.

There were many arguments pro and con, usually ending with the admission that we did not know the odds well enough to decide the question, but most of us agreed that as far as we were concerned there would be no volunteering to go to Japan, or to stay at Cabanatuan either.

We distrusted our own judgment to some extent, but the real reason we did not care to volunteer was that we were just superstitious enough to want someone else to make the decision for us. Actually, when the time came, the choice was not left to us. All during our long years of imprisonment, we discussed some phase of the war whenever two or more of us were together, except during those periods when the subject of food could not be shaken off.

The most important phase of the war to us was, of course, the future, for we could only be satisfied with such military events that would result in our release from Nip control. There was never the slightest doubt in my mind nor in the minds of the majority of prisoners that the Philippines would be retaken, but during our early days in jail there was a great variance in opinion as to how much time would be necessary for the United States to achieve that much success, the estimates ranging all the way from three months to never.

Those enthusiastic proponents of freedom within three months displayed much more optimism than military knowledge, whereas the "never boys" insisted that they were not pessimistic but merely realistic in their evaluation of Japanese power. Some of us did not feel that we could make a reasonable estimate of the time element without more knowledge of the amount of damage our navy had suffered at Pearl Harbor and without some clue as to whether our national strategy called for our initial main attack on Europe or Asia.

After consulting with our navy friends we were convinced that the navy could not have any great offensive strength for more than a year, which put a decided damper on our hopes. The boys who really brought us down to earth were our strategists who convinced us that the United States had to concentrate her efforts in Europe to defeat Germany before she could bring her full strength to bear on Japan.

Once the Germany First theory was accepted our term of imprisonment extended into the unforseeable future and our interest in the war in Europe soared.[37] Of course, there were not many who discussed global strategy, and the majority of us had no very definite ideas of how long the war might last.

Some of us were of the opinion that it was a mistake to suggest the possibility that the war might drag on a long time because of the lowering effect of the morale among our starving men. One chaplain even went so far as to prepare fake reports of broadcasts which reported allied military successes and quoted favorable predictions by prominent politicians and generals.

I am sure that many men died because they gave up hope, but I am doubtful that any permanent good came out of reports that aroused false hopes. A considerable number of men were bitter about our lot; they insisted that we had been betrayed by our politicians and money grabbers who had let us take the punishment for our lack of preparedness. They said that we had, by treaty, cut our navy and permitted Japan to build one our equal, and that we had let Japan take and fortify islands strategically located in the Pacific while we had refused or failed to fortify those which we occupied. They called attention to the pitifully weak combat units, both ground and air, in the Philippines which had invited the Japanese invasion.

Other men were more optimistic; they admitted that the leaders of our country had made mistakes but that the mistakes had become so obvious that a valuable lesson had been learned for the future. One young man, who failed to survive our imprisonment, was frank in his doubt that he would return home, but he was never in any doubt that the United States of America had already gained, from our fate on Bataan, the knowledge which would save her from making a similar sacrifice of her young men. He repeated over and over again that our deaths would not be in vain, and he believed it so much that he included his thoughts on the subject in a letter to his mother. That letter was buried in a bottle at Camp Cabanatuan, where it remained until the recapture of Luzon, after which it was dug up along with many other letters and forwarded to the boy's mother.[38]

Our long sojourn at Camp Cabanatuan gave us ample opportunity to discuss many problems with our navy friends and to ask them innumerable questions. I remember we particularly wanted to know why our submarines had not attacked the Nip landing force when they came into Lingayen Gulf to land on Luzon. The answer was that our submarines were in position and did release their torpedoes but they were defective and passed under targets without scoring a hit.

The closer the war returned to us, the more concerned some of us became about the reaction of the Nips after our troops had made a landing on Luzon. Several of my very close friends and I were of the opinion that the Nips had no intention of leaving us behind when they retreated, but we were careful to discuss that problem among ourselves. Our experiences with the Nips left us no doubt that they were capable of murdering every one of us if they thought we were in immediate danger of recapture.

A few of the more hardheaded of us, Dinty and I particularly, thought we should prepare a plan designed to resist any such drastic attempt to eradicate us.[39] We knew that, through our secret radio, we could keep well informed as to the movement of our troops. We [also] thought we would always be pretty well informed about the local Nip activities through the efforts of the Americans who worked on the Nip side of the fence.

We knew we could accumulate a number of clubs and a few tools such as axes, picks and shovels, and we were confident that, at night, we could overpower one or two Nip guards in a hurry to add a rifle or so to our accumulation of weapons. Several small buildings, which housed Nip officers and noncommissioned officers, were near enough to be rushed for the purpose of netting us a few more firearms.

We believed that if we selected the right leaders, prompt execution of a good plan could, with a little luck, permit us to get control of the camp before the Nip guards could interfere, after which we would have a fight on our hands. While the fight was going on we visualized that our POWs would be crossing the fence trying to reach the cover of the hills before daylight, where we knew the guerrillas had become more active. We contemplated the plan as an emergency one, which would not be put into execution except as a last resort, because we estimated that not more than half of us might get away.

We selected an emissary to sound out the senior American officer in camp regarding the proposal but, as he was violently opposed to making any plans, we suspended further action pending developments.

THE RETURN OF THE ALLIES

After Leo rescued me from the hospital to take me into his shack, I became well acquainted with Hoppy and his garden which was directly in front of the shack. I did not know where he learned about gardening, and none of us knew where [Hoppy] got his energy. He borrowed a wheelbarrow to haul manure from the carabao pen and by skill, plus a lot of hard work, he raised some really fine vegetables which he shared with all of us who lived with him, although he did as much work as all of the rest of us put together.

One bright morning in September 1944, I was hoeing in the garden, my "rice brain" at rest except for the feeble effort it was making to think of a legitimate excuse to give my hoe a rest. At the end of the row I stopped, conscious that for perhaps a minute I had been hearing a faint unrecognized humming. Looking around, but finding no reason for the sound, I glanced idly overhead, only to blink my eyes and stare in unbelieving amazement. Directly overhead at an altitude of six to eight thousand feet was the beginning of a wave of airplanes which extended to the east in an irregular line as far as my eyes could see.[40]

Leading that wave, which was headed in the direction of Manila, was an advance formation of fighter planes weaving back and forth in pairs. They were too high to distinguish any markings and there did not appear to be any other means of identification. The first hopeful thought that they were American planes was sternly rejected as not being within the realm of possibility. The only logical conclusion seemed to be that the Nips were holding large air maneuvers.

A pilot friend of mine standing outside a nearby shack shouted, "They are Americans. Those two-ship fighter teams weaving in and out, [I can] definitely identify them [as American planes]." I was not convinced, but when another similar wave appeared before the first one was out of sight, making the total number high in the hundreds, I began to be a believer.

Less than an hour after the second wave passed by we heard the rumble of bomb explosions in the direction of Clark Field. We watched anxiously for the return of the waves, but instead of waves we were treated to visits from numerous low flying fighters, always in groups of two. They hit the Nip field about five miles away with light bombs and machine guns resulting in, according to the laughing report of our Nip transportation sergeant, the destruction of two planes on the ground and the death of eight Nips.

Two planes flying at not more than one hundred feet altitude flew directly toward our camp but, apparently recognizing it for a prison camp, they banked steeply to pass along one end of it. The markings of the planes were plainly visible and, as they were the new navy ones, they would have added to our confusion if we had not recognized the ships as being Grumman carrier-based fighters.[41] In order to give us something to remember them by they shot down a Nip bomber in sight of the camp where it was hedge-hopping, trying to keep out of sight.

There being always at least one Nip soldier who liked to talk, we soon had a sketchy report of the first Manila air strike which hit the shipping vessels in Manila Bay and the flying fields near Manila, including Clark Field. Within the month we witnessed a repeat performance by the second mass air strike on Manila and vicinity. Those strikes were a tremendous boost to our morale because they spelled the end of Nip air supremacy. The second one added greatly to our merriment also, because several fighter planes flew over our work parties sending the shaky Nip guards to the ditches while the prisoners jeered at them.

Rumors of an early trip to Japan for all of us were very persistent, causing much discussion about the relative chance of survival in the Philippines and in Japan. The discussions were at their height when more than a hundred Dutch prisoners joined us.[42] They were the survivors of a thousand prisoners aboard a prison ship which was torpedoed and sunk off Luzon while en route from Java to Japan. The stories we heard firsthand from the survivors were conclusive proof of the dangers and discomforts of sea travel as a guest of the Nips. We need not have worried about the choice we should make if we had the opportunity to stay or go to Japan for, when the time came to decide, the Nips made the decision for us.

THE TYPICAL JAPANESE

The alert for our move to Bilibid Prison[43] in Manila, which came in October [1944], directed the transfer of all of us except the sick, some medical personnel and a few utility men. Quite a number of us, who knew that the odds of returning home were against us from then on, wrote our last farewells to our families and left them with friends who agreed to bury them and try to get them out if the opportunity ever came.

Chaplain Borneman, who took my letter, accepted many others which he buried and had no time to retrieve when the prisoners at Cabanatuan were rescued by the Rangers several months later, but he reported to the American authorities the locations of various caches of papers at the camp.

After Cabanatuan was recaptured, a bulldozer excavated most of the hidden containers. The contents of the containers were sent to the War Department for distribution to the addressees. I believe that you told me that you received my letter in July 1945, which was pretty fast time.

The departure from Camp Cabanatuan was a welcome move for most of us, largely because of the increase in Nip brutalities there. The beatings on the farm had been increasing in number and brutality for some time. A young American lieutenant, who was working in a garden near a sentry box, was shot and killed by the Nip sentry because he claimed the lieutenant went too close to the fence.

There were some pleasant memories at Cabanatuan; such as the unauthorized classes in Spanish conversation, which Pancho, Alva and I indulged in, the fine library we finally achieved, and our heated cribbage games in the barracks.[44] Leaving behind Hoppy's garden and our papaya trees, which were beginning to bear, we considered a calamity [since] food [was] so scarce.

The morning arrived for us to bid farewell to the shack where Leo, Hoppy, Long, and I had lived as pleasantly as it was possible to live under the circumstances.[45] We were crowded into trucks to leave Camp Cabanatuan for the first time in more than two years. Beginning the three-hour ride to Bilibid Prison someone remarked that most of us were about to have another first experience—confinement in a penitentiary.

At Bilibid we had plenty of time to review our experiences of the last two and one-half years. During that time we had been in contact with a large number of Nips under such trying conditions that our estimate of Nip character as applied to an individual was always of great importance, and occasionally it was a matter of life or death.

There was, of course, a wide range in intelligence, education, and temperament of individuals but, with the exception of a few outstanding examples, they fitted pretty much into a common mold. On the whole, they were under-privileged, ignorant, unimaginative, sensitive, and excitable. Almost without exception, their deep feelings of inferiority when in association with the white race was the source of suspicion and it oftentimes resulted in rage and uncontrolled brutality.

With few exceptions they were lacking in character and they were totally lacking in human feeling. Greed, graft, and venality were attributes we soon learned to expect in all our dealings with the Nip soldiers. The Nips were especially avid for watches, small manufactured articles, and anything of gold.

In our early days of imprisonment it was not uncommon to see Nip soldiers wearing two American wristwatches, and one hard-looking private who was looking for watches was already wearing five of them, three on his right arm and two on his left. Many of our difficulties with the Nips were aggravated by their jealousy and hatred which, they being in the driver's seat, resulted in their prompt indulgence of an inexperienced opportunity to punish white men.

Hatred of the white race was not the whole factor, however, for in general there appeared to be a marked sadistic trait in their character which was noticeable in their dealings with each other. Whereas the white race almost always can be counted on to champion the underdog, the Orientals only seem to regard him with contempt.

Those of us who went back to Japan as witnesses in the war trials[46] were surprised at the willingness of the Nips in general to testify against another Nip even though their testimony might be the immediate cause of his execution. There was seldom any evidence of reluctance to see another fellow citizen punished for any offense.

The small size of the Japanese race was a matter of such painful concern that all Nips always obtained a keen pleasure in inflicting bodily punishment upon a big man. Usually the man chosen for punishment as an example to the others was the largest man present. They invariably resented any suggestion by an American for a change in method of doing any work. It made no difference how primitive the method or the tools employed, the Nips never failed to insist that they could not be improved upon. The Nips always suspected and sometimes they were almost certain that the Americans were indulging in unauthorized activities, but, although they made numerous inspections, they lacked the imagination to visualize where to look or what to look for.

The Japanese military system differed materially from ours in that their army delegated extreme authority to each individual in their chain of command. For instance, each officer and each noncommissioned officer held the power of life and death over all of their subordinates. The same authority over prisoners of war was granted to each Nip sentry; consequently, one cannot imagine a more unenviable position than the prisoners held at the bottom of the ladder. Our position at the foot of the Nip system was the reason for our poor ration allowance, for we had to receive less than the lowest prison guard whose living standard was very low indeed.

The fear which all Nips had for their superiors was obvious when the power and cruelty of the superior was known. The power of the officers and noncommissioned officers insured the existence of three distinct castes, the unrated soldier occupying the third and almost powerless order of the system, except when there were prisoners of course.

One incident I saw is demonstrative of the military system. A guard company that was undergoing training on its return from drill one day had to double-time the last mile while wearing gas masks. Going up hill two hundred yards from camp a young soldier stumbled out of column to the ditch where he jerked off his mask and lay gasping. The Nip commander, who was running at the rear of the company, rushed up, ordering the soldier to get on his feet and double-time on in to the barracks. When the young soldier did not move fast enough the officer drew his samurai sword with every intention of using it but the soldier, upon seeing the sword, struggled to his feet in a panic and, with the assistance of another Nip, ran on to complete the march.

The Nip soldiers received almost no medical treatment from their doctors who were poorly trained, poorly equipped and, not infrequently, sadistically inclined individuals. The doctors were so greatly feared that they were called upon only [in] cases of last resort.

Venereal diseases were common among the Nip soldiers, but no treatment was ever given as long as the sufferer could perform [his] duties. The Nips no sooner learned that our hospital had received a supply of sulfa drugs than the American doctors were besieged by Nip soldiers seeking cures for their infirmities, because they insisted that they would only be beaten if they visited their own doctor for treatment.

The apparent immaturity of all Nips was commented upon by everyone. To us, the soldiers armed with rifles were irresponsible children playing with dangerous weapons, the result of which was too often fatal to an American prisoner.

It is extremely difficult for Americans to understand the difference between our people and all Orientals, including the Russians. Not only is their standard of living far below ours, but their conception of and attitude toward life and death is radically opposed to ours. Life for them is nothing but a bitter struggle from their first day to their last and, too often, death is a relief from their miserable existence. They are generally fatalists, accepting whatever comes their way without emotion. There is no compassion in them, consequently, they make no effort to alleviate human suffering. The loss of human life or even the taking of a human life is of no more importance than swatting a fly.

In their lack of conception of chivalry and in their entire attitude toward women, the Japanese are as far away from the English-speaking people as it is possible for them to be. In her family life, the Japanese woman occupies the lowest position in the group, being merely a servant of the man. A man's wife is the slave who takes care of his house and raises his children without sharing his pleasures and his confidences.

By his many mistreatments of women in the occupied areas the Nip soldier demonstrated that women were to be taken to gratify his appetite and immediately afterwards discarded. After he was through with a woman she was dropped back to her low social position to be recalled again momentarily at his desire.

I have listened to many people, possibly a hundred, who have returned from occupied Japan during the last two years.[47] Most of them were eloquent in their praise of the Japanese; insisting that they are the most kindly, friendly, and honest people they have ever met. Those extravagant expressions go a long way toward convincing me that our people, perhaps all human beings, learn little except by personal experience.

Everyone who has been in Japan since the war has seen the Japanese when they were the underdogs who had everything to gain by showing their best sides, while those of us who were prisoners of the Nips saw them as top dogs who were determined to get the most out of the situation.

We learned much about the Japanese through hard experience, but our experience is of little value to others who are sure that the kindly people they knew could never have been the savage people [known to us].

PART 3

The Final Year

Chapter 12

The Trek Beyond Bataan

He was faintly conscious of his wife's voice intoning, "Wake up! Wake up! Wake up!" Then as her voice came more clearly he heard her words continuing, "Get a move on you; here is your coffee; if you don't shake a leg we shall be snow bound."

He groaned, opened one eye, sat up, reached for the coffee cup and looked out of the window all in one operation. His astonishment at the white-covered expanse of his familiar hillside was so great that he forgot his coffee until its aroma brought him back to life. As he gazed out of the window, he thought that the pines and the barren trees had become albinos and that, by acquiring a mantle of white, the hill below the house appeared to have changed its shape or, rather, it was more clearly defined than it had ever been before. It reminded him of a huge plump bird resting peacefully on a platter after having been shorn of all its fine feathers.

Handing her the cup with his first real display of energy he announced, "Fortunately, the car is packed; if you will give me a half-hour I'll be ready. We should have no trouble getting down the hill in this light snow."

After they had arrived at the comfortably warm hotel room he said, "That was such an exciting trip, I have the urge to tell you about my trip to Japan if you would like to hear it."

She answered, "The last time you talked you left yourself in the penitentiary at Bilibid, and I think it is about time you got out."

THE BILIBID PRISON
We got out of jail finally, but not as soon as we had expected because our naval planes continued to make life miserable for the Nips in the vicinity of Manila Bay. During our trip down from Cabanatuan we had seen a number of American planes flying in small groups, for Nip opposition in the air was practically non-existent.

For a month after our arrival at Bilibid, those attacks continued, sometimes several of them a day, concentrating on the Bay and air fields nearby. There were no Nip planes in the air to oppose them, except in the late evening and at night when the American planes were all back on their carriers. Our fliers did have to combat fairly heavy anti-aircraft fire and a few of our aircraft were shot down, but the guns did not interfere with their effectiveness.

One of our prisoners who had been on a working party in sight of the Bay stated that there were many many Nip ships in the harbor, but that they were all on the bottom, only their masts showing out of the water. One of our officers who had remained at Camp Cabanatuan a few days later than most of us brought the good news of our landing on Leyte. He had been listening on the secret radio Hutch had left behind at the time General MacArthur announced the landing in his famous *I HAVE RETURNED* speech. Regardless of what anyone may think about the general's exclusive use of the first person, the announcement was perfectly designed to stir the imagination of the Filipinos and to fan the impotent guerrilla movement into effective activity.[1]

The landing in the Philippines explained to us the reason for the daily air attacks on the Manila area. There did not seem to be any prospect for a cessation of the attacks so we did not see how the Nips were going to bring in a ship to take us to Japan. Apparently, the Nips did not see any immediate opportunity of starting us on the way, because week after week went by without any issue being made of woolen clothing which was always made a day or two before sailing time.

In the meantime, Hutch, who had felt that it would be tempting fate too much to take his radio receiver with him to Bilibid, decided to build another one. Starting with one tube, a few condensers and a doctor's stethoscope, which he made into an earphone, he built, with a limited number of tools, a satisfactory receiver with which he got the reports of the world for us every night.

You remember Hutch and his wife, who were staying at the club in Texas when we were there in 1946. [He] brought the radio receiver to our apartment so we could examine it. I recall distinctly that one of your San Antonio girl friends who was there at the time, after one incurious look at the radio, asked Hutch, "Oh are you mechanically inclined?" Hutch swallowed his drink the wrong way, but recovered to reply, "Lady, I didn't come here to be insulted."

The food at Bilibid was so short that Hutch began to lose weight rapidly. A mutual friend of ours mentioned one night that it was obvious

Hutch could not keep up his nightly vigil much longer on our diet. An officer who was with us said, "Hell, Hutch is risking his neck to get us the news, let each of us give him one tablespoonful of our rice every evening." After that the special messkit that went around our barracks every evening, collecting from volunteers who were in the know, never failed to be filled to overflowing.

The American surgeon[2] at the prison hospital, knowing that Hutch was in such bad shape that it was doubtful he could survive a trip to Japan and wanting to keep him for the news value anyway, removed his appendix so that he would not be in physical condition to go to Japan for some time. The plan worked out perfectly, for Hutch survived his operation and remained at Bilibid until he was released by the American occupation of Manila the following April [1945].

The heavy weather which set in about the end of November [1944] was so bad that for more than two weeks Manila was not visited by our planes. During that period several ships came into the bay and unloaded. About the tenth of December [1944] we were issued our [woolen] clothing and given postcards to write home; sure signs that we were to leave soon.

On the twelfth of December [1944], we were informed that we were sailing the next day and directed to report to the infirmary where an American doctor would examine us to determine our physical fitness to make the trip. At the infirmary we received the chair test, which consisted of walking into the room, around a chair placed in the middle of the room and then out again, while the doctor sat at a desk talking to a friend.

On the starvation diet at Bilibid, my fainting spells had increased in number so that I was having several of them a day, but I was fit to travel because I could walk. Of the several men I saw walk around the chair a number were in poor physical condition, but not a one of them was asked a question by the doctor who surely must have had the most stringent orders from the Nips to except litter cases only.

On the night of the twelfth, Hoppy and I, who were messing together, cooked and ate our last mess of mongo beans which we had been hoarding. I had acquired those beans with my last money soon after we arrived at Bilibid, or rather John had got them for me through a Nip guard with whom he had been friendly at Camp Cabanatuan.[3]

That last night most of us shaved and bathed because we had no idea what time we might depart the next day. The following day, Friday the thirteenth of December 1944, one thousand six hundred and eighteen[4] of us marched through Manila to the pier where our boat was docked. How strange Manila looked to us who had not seen it for three years. The street-cars had disappeared and the heavy motor traffic of prewar days had dwindled to a trickle, the majority of the vehicles being buses which, our noses told us, were burning alcohol.[6]

The little merchandise that was being moved was in push carts of various designs, most of them being two wheeled affairs mounted on old automobile tires. The open areas in the parks were pretty well potted with sandbag-ringed anti-aircraft, which had been idle during the previous two weeks. We halted on the pier in front of our ship where we sat for three hours until the Nips finished their loading.[5]

THE *ORYOKO MARU* LOOKED HOPEFUL

While we were waiting we had an opportunity to look the ship over and to discuss it with friends of ours who had been familiar with the Japanese passenger vessel of some eight thousand tons. Our friends told us she was the *Oryoko Maru,* the speedy popular liner which had operated between Yokohoma, Shanghai, and Manila.[6] All of the information sounded so good that most of us were optimistic about the impending voyage.

There was a large number displayed on her deck, similar to numbers we had noticed on other ships tied up at the piers. We learned later that all those ships were in the same convoy headed to Japan and during the night, after the convoy was out in the bay, the numbers had all been changed around, presumably to confuse identification, in the event our intelligence agents were reporting the ships by number.

Late in the afternoon, the column of which I was a member marched alongside with the head of the column near the gangway, awaiting the order to go aboard. We were surprised to see that the top deck was crowded with civilians—men, women, and children. We had seen some Nips in uniform going aboard early in the afternoon, but as they were nowhere in sight we surmised that they were somewhere in the hold of the ship, which was a clue to the class of accommodations we could expect.

The head of the column started to move up the gangplank and over the deck out of sight. Very few of the people on deck paid any attention to us, but one very nice and intelligent looking Japanese woman stood by the rail at the head of the gangplank holding her two-year-old daughter. For the half-hour that I saw her, she could not keep her eyes, friendly ones by the way, off the prisoners.

As I passed her I noted that she was blushing faintly, and I heard her tell the child to say, "Hello Americans." If I remember correctly she was the only Japanese I saw during the war who showed an honest friendliness toward Americans.

We marched across the deck to a small hatch from which a ladder led almost straight down to the bottom of the hold three decks below. Before I started down the ladder I saw another line of prisoners from our group moving toward a similar ladder which led to a hold on the other end of the ship.[7] Reaching the bottom of the ladder I stood waiting for Hoppy to come down when Dinty and several other friends of ours, who were sitting with their backs to the side of the ship, called us to join them, which we did.[8]

It was a most fortunate move for without that wall at my back I doubt that I could have endured all the torture we had in store for us. Sitting with my back to the side of the ship I could not see out the hatch because it was such a small boxed chute, some thirty feet long and twenty-five feet square, which connected the well deck with the ceiling immediately above our heads.

After my eyes had become accustomed to the dim light in the hold, I noted that the space we occupied extended about thirty feet forward of the hatch and sixty feet aft of it. To the aft of the hold, extending to the rear bulkhead, a platform four feet high had been constructed to increase its troop-carrying capacity. The idea might have been a good one if the rear part of the hold had had its own air supply, but the pure air coming from the hatch was insufficient to supply a proper amount to the men at the extreme back end.

A DEATH CRUISE IN THE HOLD OF A SHIP

The steady stream of men coming down the ladder gradually forced more and more of them to go under and on top of the platform and move back toward the rear. The intense heat and the lack of pure air under and on the platform made those positions so uncomfortable that everyone who went very far back tried to get out again within a short time. The crowding at the foot of the ladder caused the line coming down to halt, which infuriated the guards on the deck.

Since their shouting in Japanese accomplished nothing, they began pounding the men on deck with the butts of their rifles. The innocent men who were absorbing the punishment on deck begged for help from those of us who were already down. Finally all nine hundred of us got down the ladder, but there was little more than standing room for anyone except those who crawled back along the platform.

As a matter of fact, those of us who had our backs to the wall could squat down provided we allowed the men in front of us to sit on our knees or, if that arrangement was not suitable, we could stand. Actually, we alternated standing and squatting, each change being made by the mutual consent of the man in front.

I think I can truthfully say that I had never previously had a one hundred and sixty pounder on my knee, and I know I had never been so hospitable to a male. With that much weight pressing on the knees they begin to ache surprisingly soon but, if through willpower or necessity, the position could be tolerated, the pain gradually became less acute. I might add that, regardless of how well I was able to endure the weight on my knees, I was never impressed with that method of entertaining a guest, of either the male or female sex.

At dark the Nip guards turned on the lights in the hold in order that they could see down among us from their positions at the top of the hatch. To our great surprise, they lowered several large containers of rice and drinking water and more rice for our supper. Each of us received a canteen cup almost full of water and more rice than we had received at one meal during the past year.

The rice was of good quality, well cooked and extremely well seasoned. It tasted so good someone commented that we might get to Japan if the food held out, if the ship wasn't sunk, and if she left the convoy to make a fast trip to Japan [by herself]. There were too many "ifs" in that surmise, all too many, for none of the conditions were fulfilled, and more than half of us did not live to reach Japan.[9]

When we first arrived in [the] hold it had seemed reasonably fresh and cooler than the pier, which was blistering under the tropical sun, but the first two hours of occupancy by nine hundred men [in that particular hold] made a considerable difference in the atmosphere of the place.

The hatch seemed to be inadequate because of its size, location, or design, or because of all three, to provide fresh air for the crowded occupants below. The temperature of the occupied space rose steadily until it reached a level very close to body heat. It would be a gross understatement to say that we were uncomfortable after six hours aboard ship, but the vibration of getting underway about that time caused so much excitement that temporarily we were not acutely aware of our discomforts.

I know that, in spite of my cramped position, I slept fitfully for several hours. Sometime during the night we stopped for perhaps an hour, presumably near the mouth of Manila Bay, and then proceeded at normal speed shortly before dawn. Just after dawn we had our second issue of water, which was a great help for me for I had foolishly consumed all of mine, even borrowing a few swallows from a good friend who had exercised more self-discipline than I had.

One experience of a water shortage due to my own lack of self-control was, perhaps, the hard lesson I needed. With the vivid recollection of it to help me, I rationed my supply so carefully that I never again ran out entirely, although there were many days of water shortage before we reached Japan. After the water had been issued, we waited in anticipation of the arrival of our breakfast of delicious rice which we knew had been prepared in the galley, but, as it turned out, we had eaten our one and only meal aboard the *Oryoko Maru* the night before. Unknown to us and the Nips, of course, General MacArthur chose to make his landing on Mindoro the morning of the fourteenth of December, 1944.[10]

Our naval planes, which were covering that landing, upon sighting our convoy leaving Manila Bay early that morning, attacked immediately. At first, we heard a few rounds of anti-aircraft fire from some of the more distant ships which was called a practice drill by Mr. Wada,[11] the Nip interpreter, who was looking down the hatch into our hold at that time.

The heavy increase of gunfire, interspersed with numerous bomb explosions, gave us all the information we needed to know that, contrary to Mr. Wada, we were in the midst of a powerful attack. Soon the gun mounted just outside the hatch almost directly over our heads joined in the heavy fire. If there had been any lingering doubts about the seriousness of the attack, they were completely dispelled by the first dive bomber's attack on the *Oryoko*.

The bomber came in [with] its engine roaring at full throttle and all of its 50-caliber machine guns firing. The gun overhead was shooting as fast as it could, but the plane did not falter. It passed over us with a roar that was followed almost at once by the heavy explosions of bombs which hit close alongside the ship giving us a considerable jolt.

We underwent similar attacks all day until the late afternoon, during which time the *Oryoko* was hit by several light bombs. She did not appear to be badly damaged but she had slowed down. The explosions of near misses during the last attack of the afternoon showered us with sand and gravel, leading us to believe that we were close to shore.

We hoped that we were near the beach because we knew that we might need to abandon ship. We were well aware how lucky we had been that day, and we were uncertain as to how long our luck would last. We had learned from the Dutch survivors of a sunken ship who had joined us at Cabanatuan that the percentage of prisoners saved from a ship sunk at sea might not be very great. They had been on an old steamer in a hold which was similar to the one we occupied on the *Oryoko* when she was torpedoed off northern Luzon. None of them had been killed by the torpedo, but only about 25 percent of them had been able to get out on deck before their ship sank and only about one-half of those who started to swim reached shore.

All day long, while we were under attack, we could only hope that if the ship was sunk she would go down slowly enough to allow us to climb on deck. The end of the bombing in the late afternoon brought us a twelve hour respite from the perils of shipwreck, provided of course, that a submarine did not attack us during the night.

About dark, Mr. Wada, who had been elsewhere during the day, came to the top of the hatch to order six of our doctors topside to give first aid treatment to the Nip wounded. The doctors, who were gone an hour or so, returned with firsthand information of the results of the air attack. They reported that they had been seriously handicapped by an almost total lack of facilities and medical supplies, but that they had given some treatment to two hundred Japanese, many of them women and children.

They estimated that they had treated not more than half of the wounded, and that there were approximately a hundred dead bodies stacked in two large rooms which made the estimated total of casualties, killed and wounded, around five hundred. They reported that the *Oryoko* was better off than most of the other ships close around us.

On our second night aboard there were no lights in the hold. The darkness left us as much dependent on our hearing to estimate what was happening among us as we had been on what was going on outside the ship during the day. Several men who had been talking incoherently for some time grew weaker and weaker until their voices could no longer be heard, and a few of them made strange noises which we concluded were death rattles.[12]

A dozen men, who seemed to have gone mad, tried to walk over the heads of the crouching men to the ladder which led to the top deck. Most of them were thrown back, but one man who fought like a demon was beaten to death by the men over whom he tried to walk.

Many screams from various parts of the hold were confusing because we could not tell whether they were made by demented men or by men who had been attacked. It was reported that in at least two instances friends, who were tortured by the lack of water, had sunk their teeth in the necks of weaker companions to drink their life blood. We were uncertain of many of the activities of the second night, but the following morning when we went ashore we left the bodies of a number of men who had died from unknown causes.

Suffering much more from the heat and my cramped body during the second night than I had during the first, I removed my shirt and shoes to get a little relief. Although I thought I had put them carefully beside me, I did not find them when I looked for them at daylight.

After the search, I found my shirt and a pair of shoes which no one claimed. The shoes were not mine but, being almost my size, I put them on and wore them until after the end of the war. Mr. Wada informed us early in the morning that we were at anchor in the Bay of Olongapo, but that we could not go ashore until the Nip officer in charge of us authorized it.

AT OLONGAPO

About 9:00 A.M. [December 15, 1944,] we were greeted by another low-flying bomber which came at us with all of its machine guns roaring, but that time there was no answering fire from the ship's anti-aircraft guns.[13] The plane had barely passed overhead when we were almost stunned by the explosion of a bomb which hit the opposite end of the ship. A Nip soldier, who appeared at the head of the hatch with the long awaited permission for us to go ashore, arrived so soon after the air attack that I suspected he had been directed to hold us aboard until after we had been bombed again.

The announcement of the evacuation order caused a great stir throughout the hold. There had been almost no indication of fear among the prisoners during the many bombings we had undergone, so I was somewhat surprised to note how many men wanted to be among the first to leave the ship.

The senior officer requested that the stronger men wait until the sick and weak could be sent up the ladder, which was our only means of leaving. Hoppy and I, along with many others, sat back down by the wall to wait until the press of outgoing traffic had lessened. The movement toward the hatch had given us enough room to stretch out our legs and gently exercise our aching joints.

When only about fifty men were left with us we hobbled over to the foot of the ladder where we received a heaping tablespoonful of sugar before we started the climb.[14] Until I started up the ladder I had not realized the combined strength of my legs and arms, pushing and pulling, to go up that fifty feet, but I finally stumbled over the collar of the hatch and fell on deck.

The sun and fresh air felt so good that I just sat there enjoying them. Actually, the transition from the dark, hot, and painfully cramped insides of the ship to the balmy pure air of wide open space was such a sudden relief from misery that for once in my life my cup was running over and nothing else seemed to be of great importance at that moment.

A friend, who stepped on deck beside me, suggested that it might be better for me to get on toward shore. I was walking slowly and uncertainly toward the rail when one of our low flying naval planes came over with a roar. It never occurred to me that the pilot could not recognize me standing in the middle of deck so I waved and did my best to cheer loudly. Why did he not fire his machine guns or drop any bombs is a mystery, but if he had left his calling cards, I would not have come home.

After the plane had gone I went on to the rail from where I could see the half mile stretch of the bay between the ship and shore. The water was well filled with small boats, swimmers, and well-patronized improvised rafts, but I did not recognize anyone until shouts from alongside the *Oryoko,* accompanied by splashing and waving arms, caught my attention.

There were Pat, Art, Al, and Hoppy holding on to a board of a hatch cover, yelling for me to jump overboard, but the idea did not appeal to me. Looking around I found a rope over the side, so I climbed over the rail and slid down it amid the cheers of my watching friends below who, apparently, judged from my appearance that I was incapable of doing anything more complicated than falling off the deck.

They met me with the heavy board, which we held onto while we paddled ashore. Before we reached the beach the Nips opened up with a heavy machine gun, which they fired intermittently for the next half-hour. They were firing at prisoners who strayed away from a direct line to land and, in that way, they killed several men who had no idea why they were being fired on.

One very good friend, who was an exceptionally strong swimmer, jumped off the far side of the ship, and when last seen he was well along toward the other side of the bay more than a mile away. Nothing was ever heard of him except that he did not get back home.

Most of us experienced a feeling of relief at reaching dry land for our voyage of less than two days had been somewhat unsatisfactory. Without bestowing a farewell on the *Oryoko Maru,* we followed slowly after our fellow prisoners who were headed toward an assembly area that the Nips had designated. The area being plentifully supplied with water, we gorged ourselves with it to relieve our dehydrated systems and to gain whatever relief it would give us from our hunger pains.

There having been no toilet facilities on the boat, we had not relieved ourselves for almost forty-eight hours. We had not suffered greatly on that account, because we had received very little to put in our stomachs and the heat had been so great that much of our body liquids had been exhausted through perspiration. I have a vivid recollection that when I did urinate with some effort, the liquid had the consistency of maple syrup, the colors of sorghum, and the soothing effect of carbolic acid.

While resting there we learned that the bomb which had hit the ship that morning had exploded in the hold occupied by the other group of prisoners, killing approximately three hundred of them. Several of my very good friends were among the known dead and others were missing.

Well before sundown the Nips herded the twelve hundred odd of us who had survived inside the fence of a double tennis court.[15] There we had almost enough room for all of us to lie down on the comfortable concrete courts at the same time.

The utilities were limited to one water faucet and an open trench latrine outside the fence. As the Nips would allow no more than a half dozen men outside the gate at the same time, we had to establish a waiting line for the latrine as well as the usual one at the water line. We had hardly got inside the fence when we had it impressed upon us that however suitable concrete may be to sleep on, it is not desirable material in which to dig air shelters with one's fingers.

We had seen a few planes, all American, since we had been ashore but they had been operating as singles or in pairs; therefore, the appearance of a formation of about twenty planes almost overhead caused considerable excitement. They were flying at about two thousand feet when they were first sighted, then they circled and, following the leader in single file, they dived to a thousand feet before they dropped their sticks of bombs and banked sharply.

The bombs were dropped on one side of us, passed overhead and then exploded in the dock area three hundred yards away. We had a grandstand seat for a superlative performance which did nothing to detract from our admiration of Uncle Sam's naval aviation, but there was a moment of suspense from the time the bombs left the planes until we were sure they had passed safely overhead.

The Nips defended themselves as best they could with their light anti-aircraft weapons but no damage was done to the planes. A few shell fragments fell in the area where we were, slightly wounding a few of us. During the next two days, the Nip installations and the *Oryoko* were bombed several times, the ship finally being sunk.

The five days we spent on the tennis court were all hot and sunny, but it rained every night, which greatly varied our comforts from a broiling tropical sun at 3:00 P.M. to a shivering tropical rain at 3:00 A.M. There were no cooking facilities made available for us, but the thoughtful Nip officer in charge provided us with a tablespoon of uncooked rice twice a day.

My attempts at masticating the hard dry grains were not very successful, but many men swallowed all the rice issued to them and all they could beg besides, some of them paying for their greed with the suffering accompanying a severe diarrhea.

An arm of one boy had been badly lacerated by a bomb fragment on the morning we left the ship. It had become so badly infected that our doctors were convinced that it had to be amputated immediately to save the young man's life. The arm was so painful that the boy agreed, although he knew there were few instruments and facilities and no anesthetic. The operation was one of the usual successful ones, but the patient survived it only two days.[16]

At 11:00 A.M. on the twentieth of December [1944], on the hour as well as the day of our thirteenth wedding anniversary, we boarded trucks en route to an unknown destination.[17] I said we boarded but, actually, I was thrown aboard, because I had fainted while I was standing in the hot sun waiting for my turn to climb over the tailgate of a truck.

You probably never knew what a lucky day your thirteenth anniversary almost was. The rough vibration and stir of air which accompanied the progress of the truck quickly revived me. Although I still felt ghastly, I sat up because the truck was so crowded that I had been stretched out on the knees of my fellow passengers. I might not have been able to remain seated if I had not been wedged in so tightly, but a compelling curiosity to see Olongapo and the road over which we were passing helped considerably.

My eyes were focusing so poorly that I had only a hazy vision of Olongapo as we passed through, but gradually my sight improved until I could see the country through which we were passing quite clearly. Shortly after leaving Olongapo we started to climb the Zig Zag road which crosses the mountain connecting the west coast with the central plain of Luzon.

The road was badly in need of repairs for no work had been done on it during the three years of war. If you remember the Sunday automobile trip we made to the beach at Olongapo in 1941, you will recall what a narrow thread the road appeared to be struggling through the jungle. That impression was even more vivid in December 1944, for the ever-aggressive tropical jungle had taken over the drainage ditches, encroaching on the roadbed itself in places. How near and how friendly the bamboo thickets looked to me. A leap from the slow moving truck and a few yards of struggle into the jungle were all I needed to gain my freedom, but, alas, I did not have the strength to stand up in the truck.

In the spring of 1945, a few months after our ride over the road, the 152nd Infantry of the Indiana National Guard went over it, but they went on foot, fighting bitterly most of the way.[18] We passed through Dinalupihan, the road junction to Bataan and Lubao, arriving at San Fernando, Pampanga in the late afternoon.[19]

SAN FERNANDO

[At San Fernando] we were divided into two groups, ours being quartered in the compound of the police station, and the second one in the movie theater. Our group had a court and a number of jail cells to sleep in and, what was more important, a kitchen for steaming rice. That day about dark we had a hot meal of rice, exactly seven days after our first and last one on the *Oryoko.*

Our doctors set aside a small area for twenty or so of the more seriously wounded and sick, but there was little that could be done for them. After two or three had died, the Nip officer in charge directed that the ten worst cases be selected for transfer to the hospital at Bilibid prison, which was only forty miles away.

The men were loaded into a truck and taken away, but they never reached the hospital. We learned after the war that they were taken to a field just outside San Fernando where they were executed and buried in a ditch because the Nip officer did not want to bother with them anymore. The Nip officer and his sergeant, who did the executing, were tried by a Military Commission after the war and, according to an American who attended the trials, the officer was sentenced to be hanged, the sergeant escaping with a long term of imprisonment. The officer well deserved his sentence because, by his cruelty and lack of consideration during the six weeks he was in charge of us, he contributed in no small way to our huge casualty list.[20]

San Fernando was so near to Clark Field that the bomb explosions of numerous air attacks on the field could be heard and almost felt. To the half-dead derelicts that we were, lying practically motionless on the concrete floors of our cells, the faint noise of bursting bombs set up a pleasant trend of thought which was much more soothing than any radio program I have listened to during my prolonged convalescence.

After only three days in the city jail, [on Christmas Eve] we were marched to the same railroad station [at San Fernando] from which we had started on the last leg of the Death March. Again, we were loaded into steel boxcars, eighty-seven of us and two Nip guards to a car, so there was standing room only for all of us, except the guards who sat in one doorway, the other door being closed. About 10:00 A.M., as we started to crowd into the cars, Clark Field was heavily bombed.

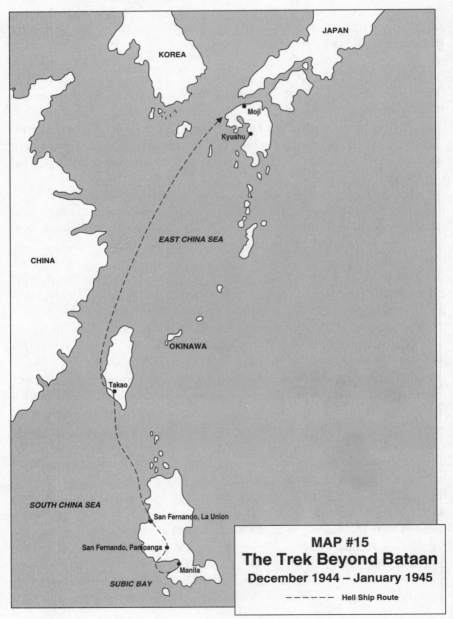

JAPAN

KOREA

Moji

Kyushu

EAST CHINA SEA

CHINA

OKINAWA

Takao

SOUTH CHINA SEA

San Fernando, La Union

San Fernando, Pampanga

Manila

SUBIC BAY

MAP #15
The Trek Beyond Bataan
December 1944 – January 1945

– – – – – – Hell Ship Route

The Nips, fearing that our train might be attacked, selected a half-dozen Americans to ride on top of each car, directing them to wave wildly at any plane that came near.

We did not know until the train started whether we were going north or south because the Nips had refrained from informing us of their plans. As soon as we had cleared the yards at San Fernando, heading north, I announced as my opinion that we were going to San Fernando, La Union, for the purpose of being loaded on another ship to continue our journey to Japan.[21] A few of the prisoners agreed with me, but most of them could not believe it; nevertheless, we were en route to that northern port for the purpose of resuming our postponed travels. The decision of the Nips to follow their original plan was in keeping with our observations and the reports which we had received from newspaper and radio, in that we knew they hated to be forced to make a change in plans and that they always retaliated with the best means left at their disposal regardless of consequences.

The door on the west side of the car being open, we had a fair view of one end of Clark Field as we passed by it. Huge columns of smoke and dust rising from the field and numerous wrecked planes on the ground were muted evidence that the Nips were doing poorly throughout the Philippines. A few miles north of the field, hundreds of laborers were busily honeycombing the mountainside with caves. All of those activities told us plainly that the Japanese High Command anticipated engaging in hand to hand conflict with the Americans very soon.

As the steel cars grew hotter, the discomforts of heat, poor air, and aching bones were reminiscent of the *Oryoko Maru,* but not quite as bad. Darkness brought us a little ease, the only relief we got during the sixteen hour train ride. We arrived at the station of San Fernando, La Union, at 2:00 A.M. on Christmas Eve 1944, going to a nearby enclosure where we spent the remaining hours of darkness.

At daybreak we marched to the municipal school area where we received our first food and water since breakfast the previous morning. We rested quietly in the school yard that day and Christmas, but instead of big turkey dinners we were fed our usual sparing meals of steamed rice. That was another Christmas Day during which we were not plagued by indigestion.[22]

HELL SHIP NO. 2

About 10:00 P.M. of our second day, [December 25, 1944,] we marched again and after some counter-marching we camped in the sand of a broad beach, where [we] stayed until the night of the twenty-ninth.[23] That night we marched to the port area, waiting there until two shiploads of Nip soldiers were brought ashore, after which, just at dawn, we were transported in landing boats to the waiting ships.

The ship my group boarded was a rough, ugly, wartime-constructed freighter which, being empty, was standing high out of the water and bobbing like a cork.[24] Due to our weakened condition and to the length of the ladder up which we had to climb, it took us until almost 8:00 A.M. [on] December 30, 1944 to complete loading the group.

We had no sooner settled down in our hold than the ship got underway for which we were thankful, for we had no more desire than the skipper to stay in the harbor until it was visited by American bombers. We had ample room to lie down and plenty of fresh air; in our opinion, the two most essential requirements for travel as guests of the Japanese.

Within a half-hour after leaving the harbor our lightly laden ship was bounding so wildly that most of us had to lie down to reduce the effects of seasickness. By the time the first food and water distribution was made in the middle of the afternoon, I had recovered sufficiently to eat my rice, and by dark I felt almost normal again.[25]

That night a young naval officer startled us all by climbing the ladder to the deck like a squirrel going up a tree, rushing past the surprised sentry and jumping overboard. The Nip sentry fired into the darkness, and the interpreter notified us that the foolish American had been shot, but we did not believe it. The shore was no more than a mile away so we chose to believe that the officer made a successful escape.

We were awakened in the middle of the night by several shots fired by the bow gun, and we thought we heard the distant explosion of torpedoes. Shortly before daybreak [December 31, 1944,] a Nip seaplane joined the convoy, flying around us for about two hours. All of the unusual activity was enough to convince us that there had been submarine [activity] near us during the night and that we had been lucky once again.

No toilet facilities of any kind existed in our hold, which would have been a major calamity if the feed boxes and water containers had not been left in several horse stalls vacated by four legged prisoners a few hours before [our boarding]. Those containers were set up in a small area designated as the latrine, and were emptied each morning but never until after they had overflowed. The same ropes that were used to raise and lower the latrine buckets were used to lower and raise the food and water containers, which made us wonder if the ropes were not as dangerous as the bombs and torpedoes.

One adventuresome American discovered that, by moving a hatch cover, he could get into the hold beneath us where the Nips had stored, according to his report, a thousand bags of sugar. Soon a way was devised to raise unopened bags to our hold where the contents were distributed among us. Thus, unknown to our Japanese brethren, we added all of the sugar we could eat to our scanty two meals of steamed rice a day.[26]

In addition to the floor of the hold, we were permitted to occupy the U-shaped balcony twenty feet above us which was all there was of the next deck. I investigated the balcony, but one look over the unprotected side to the bottom of the hold below made me so dizzy that I lost no time in taking the ladder to the lower level.

A hundred or more fearless souls who bedded down on the higher level had no trouble until the fifth night, [January 3, 1945,] when a naval officer missed his step in the darkness and fell off the rim. He landed on the chest of a man sleeping below, injuring them both so badly that they died the following morning.

When we woke up on the fifth of January [1945], our senses told us the ship was lying peacefully at anchor in smooth water. Later in the morning a work detail of prisoners that had been out on deck returned with the news that we were in the harbor of Takao, the southernmost port of Formosa.[27]

After three days of inactivity, we were crowded onto a section of the top deck to spend the afternoon in the sun. It was pleasant to be topside, and we enjoyed the sunshine and the opportunity to rest our eyes on distant objects. The majority of us were amazed at the size of the huge horseshoe shaped bay which was ringed for miles with factories and warehouses.

There were hundreds of vessels of all types at anchor but there was little activity usually accompanying loading and unloading operations, which gave us the impression that they had merely sought refuge in a safe harbor. A sister ship to the one we were on eased alongside and the two were tied together, making us very unhappy for it seemed to us that, in the event of an air attack, the two ships together offered a distinct and inviting target.

We were glad to escape the chilling air that followed sundown when our turn came to go below. The group I was with was shunted into a strange hold where we had to sweep the residue of a recent cargo of coal before we could sit down comfortably. After some milling around and a little work we cleared enough space to permit us to sleep without lumps of coal for mattresses, although we had plenty of dust. The coal dust did not keep us warm that night, so we were glad to get an issue of steaming rice early the next morning.

On the morning of January 9, 1945, I had finished the original rice issue and was about to start on a sizable portion of seconds when we were greeted by a heavy volume of anti-aircraft fire. I took a hurried spoonful as the gun over our heads opened up, but before I could swallow the food the familiar roar of a bomber with all guns firing drowned out all lesser noises.

A bomb burst close alongside, blowing a hole in the hull as big as a door and scattering small fragments of steel over the hold. A number of men were killed and Hoppy, sitting on my left, Leo on my right and another officer in front of me all were wounded.[28] We straightened up to survey the damage which was really distressing, but I recall that, at the moment, what seemed a greater calamity to me than anything else was the sight of my portion of rice spilled on the floor and thoroughly mixed with coal dust with the messkit upside down beside it.

Several planes honored us with attacks, a bomb from one of them exploding on deck just outside the far corner of the hold. The heavy steel crosspieces were blown down on top of the men who were lying in the middle of the hold, and fragments of steel were generously sprinkled over most of the hold.

After the attack was over I walked around as best I could through the debris. The entire hold was filled with dead and severely wounded, some of the dead being so badly mutilated that they were unrecognizable. Several of the stronger men were moving the bodies of our dead from the central area to one side of the ship.

Although I looked everywhere, I did not find my missing friends, either because they had been moved to the side of the ship or because I could not recognize their bodies. I encountered two ghouls who were searching the bodies for jewelry and other valuables. Hoppy, who was with me, spoke harshly to one of them, whom he recognized as a soldier who had been a member of his command during the war. The man snarled wickedly, telling Hoppy to shut his lousy mouth, and went on with his revolting search. The following day, Hoppy and I could not escape a feeling of satisfaction when the rude despoiler sickened and died in the short space of a few hours.

Among the seriously wounded were a marine corps captain and a Catholic chaplain, each of whom had lost a leg below the knee. Although those two brave men were in great pain and shivering from the cold, they sat up and talked to me cheerfully, making no reference to their injuries which they knew were fatal.

The four army and navy doctors who had escaped injury worked all day long trying to ease the suffering of the wounded, their gallant efforts sapped their strength so much that they all died before we left the hold. Hoppy, who had been wounded in the cheek by a steel fragment, recovered, but Leo and the other men near us passed quietly into a coma and died the second day [January 10, 1945].[29]

At night there were always a few demented men who wandered through the darkness for no good reason. It was impossible for them to go very far without stepping on or adding to the pain of some of the wounded who littered the floor. Ordinarily, the wounded men made no noise at all, but when they were cruelly hurt by the night prowlers they could not help crying out, sometimes shrieking with pain.

One officer who knew that I had lost my glasses on the *Oryoko Maru* handed me his spectacle case. As I remember his words he said, "Put these in your pocket. I have a feeling I am not going to need them anymore but, if I do, I'll know where to find them." I knew he was dying but I thanked him, assuring him that he would get his glasses back when we reached Japan. The lenses were not exactly the same as mine, and one of the side pieces was broken but, with the help of a string which I looped over one ear, I used them until I could buy a new pair at the end of the war.

Of the four hundred Americans in the hold, many of them old friends, more than a hundred had been killed outright, and as many others died of their wounds within the next two days. In addition, nearly a hundred men who had not been injured, and who had appeared to be in as good health as any of us before the bombing seemed, within an hour's time, to have contracted some incurable malady which deprived them of all hope and the will to live.

On the evening of the eleventh [of January 1945], not many more than one hundred of us were able to climb the ladder and return to the hold we had previously occupied. Back with our fellows, we learned that some of the bomb fragments had penetrated into the main hold where most of our companions had remained, killing a few and wounding several others. The Nips provided no medicine or medical supplies that might have saved the lives of some of the less seriously wounded.[30]

THE THIRD BOAT TO JAPAN

On the thirteenth of January [1945], as the ship was too badly damaged to continue the journey to Japan, the survivors were transferred to an old troop transport, on which we completed our travels.[31] Our number had dwindled to less than a thousand, which may account for the fact that we were not crowded in our new quarters.

Even though we had plenty of space and a sufficient amount of fresh air, we were not comfortably situated for probably half of us had to sleep on the steel deck of the hold we occupied. We did not miss our woolen clothing, which had been left on the *Oryoko Maru,* until we reached Takao but, from then on, we suffered acutely from the cold, especially so during the last two weeks of the journey.

We had abandoned the *Oryoko* with what we were [wearing], a number of our men being shirtless and barefooted. A few pairs of shoes and a little outer clothing had been salvaged on the second ship, but not nearly enough for our needs. All during the trip from Takao north, as the weather grew colder, we were to regret that we had not saved all of the clothing which was of no more use to our many dead.

Immediately after coming aboard the transport, Pat, who always had demonstrated a nimble brain, acquired a ragged section of straw matting and a gunnysack. Pinning the sack to the matting with nails, we used the combination as a community bed covering for the four of us, who occupied a square of the steel deck which under normal circumstances would not have been considered too large for one man.

We sailed from Takao on the fourteenth of January [1945], heading generally north into winter weather with ice and a little snow. Pat's friend, Pat, Hoppy, and I huddled together, depending on the body heat of each other to keep us from freezing.[32] At first I thought we were like puppies of a litter, but, as time went on and we became dirtier and more ragged, I concluded that we were more like pigs in a dirty strawless sty.

Having almost no fat to protect my bones from the icy floor, I suffered so much at night that I could not stay in one position long enough to get much sleep. From a nearby partition I acquired an eight inch board which, used as a mattress, was a big help to me as long as I could stay on it. After a few days of experimenting, we learned to stay on one side as long as we could, then the four of us would turn to the other side at the same time with a minimum loss of community heat.

Most of the exercise we got on the trip was from scratching lice, with which the transport was alive, a form of vermin new to us up to that time. Our food on the third ship consisted of a half messkit of rice and a pinch of soy sauce twice a day. With each meal, we were issued about one-fourth of a cup of water, but never more than a pint on any one day.

The shortage of food was not as bad as the shortage of water. Several men were able to sneak on deck to the winches where they filled their canteens from the condensed steam they drained through the peacocks. After one man was caught at that heinous crime and clubbed down the gangway, the Nip guards kept such a close watch that, for all practical purposes, the extra source of water was eliminated.

The number of deaths increased alarmingly from a few to forty a day; the sick and wounded being among the first to go, followed by the older men and then the large, muscular, and athletic ones. Perhaps the metabolism of the individual had a great deal to do with it; at any rate the little scrawny light eaters, who quietly conserved their energies, fared better than the others.

Many, many men suffered from diarrhea, so much so that the containers used for temporary latrines were always overflowing, adding more refuse to the already filthy hold. Conditions grew steadily worse for as the men grew weaker, the less necessity they felt to visit the latrine when the frequent cramps of their tortured bowels called for relief.

The actual process of dying did not seem so unpleasant, on the contrary, it oftentimes seemed easier to die than to live. Many men who appeared tired [lay] down to a sleep [and then] passed peacefully into a coma from which they never awoke. Frequently, men died so peacefully that their companions sleeping alongside of them did not know that they had passed on until their bodies grew cold.

There were many instances when it seemed that lack of a will to live was the immediate cause of death but, even in those cases, we had to admit that we were as much confused as to which was cause and which was effect as we had been many times before. Each morning the bodies of the dead were carried to a platform at the foot of the gangway that led up on deck. I tried to go by the platform each morning to see the remains before the Nips removed them because that was my only opportunity to bid many old friends a last farewell.

Toward the end of the journey we all had lost so much weight that the dead were harder to identify than usual so that at times I failed to recognize men I had known for many years. For several days after we left Takao, the Protestant and Catholic chaplains had said a word over the remains, but after a time there was no one left with the energy to conduct a service.[33]

The Nips required our men to move the remains topside, then they sent our labor detail below before they committed the dead to the sea. Before the completion of the journey there were very few left who did not expect to go over the side in due time.

One day Hugh,[34] who had been painfully wounded at Takao, called me to tell me that he had reached the end of his rope. When I demurred and tried to encourage him he waited patiently until I had finished, then he continued in his usual matter-of-fact manner to tell me that he would like for me to go see his mother, if I was fortunate enough to survive. He asked me to tell his family how we had enjoyed performing the tough combat job we had been called upon to do. I assured him that I would, which pleased him greatly. He acted perfectly normal when I left him that evening, but the next morning he was dead. I did go to see his mother, telling her all I could about Hugh. The last thing I told her was that, when my time came, I hoped I could be as much of a man as Hugh had been.

WILL JAPAN EVER COME?

It was most discouraging after we had a submarine scare, with guns firing most of one night, to find the following morning that we were speeding toward the south. The next day we were headed north again, but later we took a disabled freighter in tow for a full day. Apparently, as far as the Nips were concerned, there was no hurry about our reaching Japan, and, furthermore, if any ship was to be torpedoed they preferred it to be the one carrying us.

I was fortunate in not having diarrhea, even though I went to the opposite extreme with the low residue diet we were on. Late in January [1945,] I became alarmed by the fact that I had not enjoyed a bowel movement for twenty-two days. Fearing that it might be dangerous to prolong that period, I borrowed a bath towel that Pat pinned around my shoulders, and then I ventured forth on the ice encrusted deck to visit the outside latrine, which was hung over the rail for the use of the able-bodied.

The latrine might have been called a two-holer for it was nothing but a box lashed to the side of the ship, a box divided into two compartments two feet wide by three feet long. A ten-inch strip in the middle of the floor looked large enough for a man to drop through but, of course, there were the waist-high ropes along the side to hold on to if a foot slipped.

On that particular day the wind was blowing a gale from the north pole, encouraging me to waste no time hopping into the box.[35] The roll of the sea was so heavy that the box was almost on top of the ship at the end of the roll to the west, and it almost touched the angry-looking icy sea at the eastern end.

After a few rolls I became accustomed to the unusual experience and felt pretty confident I could escape the sea unless we were torpedoed. Being out of practice at the job I had set myself to do, I rode that box for a half-hour until success crowned my efforts. When I climbed back over the rail my teeth were chattering so that I could not whistle; nevertheless, I returned to my sty well pleased with myself.

Hoppy found a way to trade his ring to a Nip guard for drinking water, generously sharing the proceeds with me. He received only two canteens full of water and two packs of Nip cigarettes, which had become legal tender, for his hundred dollar ring, but he may have saved his life and mine as well.

On the morning of January 30, 1945, we woke up to learn that the four hundred odd of us who were left had arrived at Moji, Japan.[35] After breakfast, we filed through a room on the top deck where we were issued woolen uniforms of the type issued to Japanese soldiers. In the middle of the morning we were ushered down the gangplank and directed to assemble in the waiting room of a shipping company building a hundred yards away.

Hoppy and I were hobbling along when we met a soldier we were both very fond of who had gone to Japan six months before. We were such disreputable-looking scarecrows that he did not recognize us until he identified our voices. It was not until I saw the look of horror on his face that I fully realized how far gone we were. He hurried up and, taking each of us by the arm, he helped us on our way until a Nip sentry we passed sent him back to the work he had been doing when he met us.

Leaving the docks where we avoided small patches of ice, we faced a stiff wind that brought a tingle to our ears while we were crossing the hundred yard space to shelter. Arriving at the revolving door leading into the building, we hurried inside expecting to enjoy the comfort of a steam-heated waiting room but, instead, we found the inside temperature only a little above freezing.

The huge waiting room was supplied with a heating system that was valueless without fuel. Thus, on our first day in Japan, we noted the first incident that demonstrated how desperately short of fuel, food, and supplies of all kinds the nation was.

It took the Nips several hours to divide us into three groups and make rosters of each. Except for an ordinary meal of steamed rice, we had nothing to do but sit on hard cold seats and shiver. One group, made up of the weakest men, left us first to be loaded into ambulances for transfer to a hospital in Moji.[36] The second group went by truck to a nearby camp while the third group, of which I was one, marched through the streets to the railroad station a half-mile away.

Due to our poor physical condition, we moved so slowly that we had time to see the sights, and several belligerent small boys had time to follow along throwing stones at us. The sidewalks were pretty well filled with men and women who were going home after the day's work. They were uniformly well fed and well dressed, except that no one wore topcoats although it seemed plenty cold to me.

The adults appeared to be interested in nothing but getting home for they showed little interest in us and certainly no animosity. I do not remember passing a single shop with wares displayed in the windows, and the only traffic in the streets consisted of a few heavy carts, each of which was pulled by a raw-boned horse led by a rough looking laborer. The railroad station looked modern, as did the coaches except for their wooden seats, but, in spite of the seats, everything about the railroad was surprisingly reminiscent of home.

An hour after dark we arrived at Fukuoka where a mixed party of Nip guards and British POW truck drivers awaited us.[37] They had made two large bonfires which gave them light enough to issue a captured British overcoat to each of us. There were sufficient trucks to haul one-half of us to Camp Fukuoka, a mile away, giving the others an opportunity to toast their lean behinds by the fires.

Hoppy and I were fortunate in being members of the rear truck of the second group, for, the buildings which had been allotted to our party having been filled, the last truckload of twenty men were assigned to one end of the barracks occupied by Dutch prisoners.[38]

Those forty odd men were all young Eurasians, sons of Dutch fathers and Javanese mothers. They were in quite good physical condition and, having been at the Fukuoka Camp for some time, they knew all of the ropes. The twenty of us were in such bad shape that we were hardly able to take care of ourselves, but we did not need to with the Dutch boys there to look after us. They welcomed us with open arms, building up the fire in the little sheet iron stove, distributing blankets, helping us make bedrolls, dishing out the food and even carrying out the "honey bucket" which served as a latrine.

It is hard to see how, under the conditions that existed at that camp, anyone could have looked after us any better than those boys did. Fifteen minutes after we arrived they served each of us a messkit of steaming porridge rice and a full cup of hot tea with plenty of sugar in it.

You may be surprised to hear that at the time we considered the meal a sumptuous one. Not until our bellies were full did we begin making bedrolls out of the seven heavy wool blankets issued to each of us but, with the help of our Dutch friends, we soon had respectable looking beds which we lost no time crawling into.

By morning we were almost as cold as we had been during our coldest nights on the ship so, as soon as the fire had been built, everyone rushed to the stove to thaw out. I had been too tired and too busy to look around much the previous night but after breakfast I went all around the building inside and out. It was somewhat [similar] to the Filipino barracks in that there was a center aisle running the full length of the one room. The center, which was two feet lower than the platforms, was not floored, and the building was of the lowest grade, full of knotholes and cracks.

Tar paper had been used to seal the original cracks but there were plenty of new ones. The roof at the sides came down to within four feet of the sleeping platform, rising to nine to ten feet over the center. The earth outside had been heaped along the sides of the building a foot or two above the level of the sleeping platforms, providing a wind break of sorts. As late as 9 A.M. [every morning] there was still a trace of ice on the ground which made the heaps at our heads almost as comfortable as cakes of ice.

Hoppy and I had a council of war, the result being a decision to build a double sleeping roll out of our fourteen blankets. All of the others followed our example and the second night was a much more comfortable one for two men supplied about the same amount of body heat that one man would have furnished if he had been in normal condition.

After a little experiment we found that by taking off most of our clothes at night we saved a considerable part of the heat of our bed fellows so by stripping down to our shirts, long Nip drawers, socks and anything that served for a night cap we slept as warm as toast. The Dutch boys who were in fairly good health did not seem to mind the cold but they were fat compared to us.

I did not have the opportunity to weigh myself until we had been at Fukuoka almost a month, at which time I tipped the scales at a strong ninety-six pounds, and with that weight a basis to start from, I estimated that at the time of arrival in Japan I had not weighed more than ninety pounds. At any rate, I was convinced that the lack of meat on my bones was largely the cause of the intensity of my suffering from the cold.

Upon recommendation of the Nip doctor, who had listened to the American, British, and two Dutch doctors in camp, we received an issue of Red Cross food boxes. The issue was in keeping with most other actions of the small-minded Nips who could not bear to be generous, in that we received one box for each three men.

At the time we were dividing our boxes, the Dutch doctor, who was the attending surgeon of our barracks, warned us to go easy on the heavy food because he insisted that our stomachs were in no condition to handle it properly. A few men who paid more attention to their appetites than they did to the doctor paid for their folly with cramps and diarrhea. Even the more cautious men who ate only two small slices of Spam, one at breakfast and one at supper, had ample reason to respect the doctor's judgment.

One scene, which perhaps I should have forgotten, gave the doctor the satisfaction of at least thinking "I told you so," for he arrived while it was in progress. Six or eight men were standing in line awaiting their turn to occupy the seat over the "honey bucket," all of them urging the man sitting on the seat to hurry.

Usually the man leaving the seat went to the foot of the line which remained almost constant all morning long, providing an effective object lesson for all of us who wanted to eat more than we could handle. We had long since been aware that a weakening of body muscles was accompanied by a weakening of the muscles which controlled the bodily functions so that we were able, with a little care and foresight, to save ourselves embarrassment.

Three of the twenty Americans deteriorated in strength instead of gaining, and gaining, and they all died before the end of February [1945], their deaths possibly being hastened by intemperance in eating. About the middle of February we enjoyed our first baths since we had paddled ashore at Olongapo two months before.

Unless you can visualize the conditions of extreme filth in which we had existed, without even a drop of water that could be spared from our drinking allowance, you cannot realize how long overdue that bath was. In addition to supplying an urgent need, that particular bath was a memorable experience in itself. On our first bath day the temperature was a little above freezing and a bitter gusty wind made it a decidedly uncomfortable one.

Taking advice of our friends, we undressed in barracks, wearing only our breeches, shoes, and overcoat to the bathhouse, which was not much more than a hundred yards away. That short journey was a long one to us who were torn between the insistence of our weakened muscles to take it easy, and the insistence of the bitter penetrating wind to hurry.

The bathhouse did not offer us as much protection as we had expected because it was unheated and honeycombed with more and bigger cracks than the sides of our barracks. The floor was concrete in appearance but it felt like ice. In fact, to all of us who stood naked and shivering waiting for our turns in the bath, it felt like we were waiting in an icehouse.

There were some twenty-five of us standing there at that time presenting a collective picture of physical deterioration which surprised and shocked me, although I had seen most of the individuals every day for a long time. I had forgotten how much a starving human being looks like a horse of skin and bones on his way to the boneyard, especially when viewed from [the] rear.

My curiosity taking my attention from our infirmities to the bath, I noted that it consisted of six watertight boxes approximately five feet square and four feet deep running along one side of the building. A soldier had been firing the grates outside the building with good results, for a heavy vapor hung over the water-filled boxes almost to the top when they were full of men.

There were nine men in the tub when I reached it so I waited until one man got out and then I clambered over the side. The water felt so hot to my cold feet that I had to ease into the water gradually, taking a minute or more to get down to my neck, but after my body had become accustomed to the warm water I experienced a feeling of well-being, and before I left the bath a half-hour later there was no trace left of the chill that had been in my bones for a month past.[39]

When I did try to get out I was astonished to find that the bath had been so enervating I did not have the strength to climb out. After I had made a few futile efforts, two friends, who had dressed and started to leave the building, laughed at my predicament and helped me out. Putting on my few clothes, I stumbled toward the barracks for what seemed like an interminable time before I got back to my bunk.

We missed our daily radio news of the world but we were not left entirely in the dark for our work parties met Koreans who told them what they knew and gave them Japanese newspapers to bring back to camp. We had several officers who translated them for us and, while we were a little behind time, it is my belief that our knowledge was more complete than that of most of the Nips.

We heard details of the Battle of the Bulge and of the rapid approach of our forces in the south. There [was] so much cheering news on the sixteenth of February [1945] that we sat around the fire discussing it most of the evening. I was more optimistic than I had been at any time during the war and I predicted that the end was in sight.[40]

Monte,[41] who was a bit more pessimistic, asked me what I meant by the end being near, to which I replied that six months from that day, the sixteenth of August, *your birthday,* was a good day to set. We ended up by my making a wager, and he accepted it, that the war would be over and we would be under American jurisdiction by your birthday.

EVERYONE HAD DIFFERENT NEEDS

About the first of March [1945] the Nips had us divide into two groups, one of sick and the other of able-bodied men. Hoppy and I could walk, which must have been the reason why we were classed as able-bodied, for that was about all we could do. We did not have the Dutch boys to look after us in the new barracks but we had nothing to do except to attend morning and afternoon roll call in the Nip part of the camp a quarter of a mile away. Actually, that long trip down and back at dawn and dark each day was plenty of work for the weather was so cold we had to wear all of our clothes.

Because we were so weak, the Nips decided that we needed conditioning so they established a twenty minute routine of setting-up exercises each morning and afternoon. Those exercises were just plain drudgery because of the weakness of our muscles. Hoppy, in particular, was very caustic about that work for he insisted that the regular rice diet we were on was just enough to furnish the energy for the exercises, leaving nothing to build us back up to strength. He was very nearly right, but we did, week by week, gain a little in strength and put on a little weight.

As I recall, when we weighed [ourselves] late in March [1945] I gained ten pounds. Almost all of us were suffering from ulcers, on our hands and legs in particular. When we went to the infirmary, the Dutch doctor scraped the scabs off with the scalpel and wrapped the sore with a flimsy bandage which was expected to give them a little protection for twenty-four hours. There was no medicine and the scraping was downright unpleasant but it was effective. After a few treatments the huge sores started to heal. For a long time I thought the scars on my hand were permanent, but they have completely disappeared.

About the middle of March [1945] the winter officially ended for the Nips, wherefore, there being no further need for heat in the barracks, the stoves were taken out regardless of the near freezing weather. Those of us who were living in [the] able-bodied barracks were most unhappy when we lost our stove, but our unhappiness did not return it. During the daytime, especially when the sun was shining, it was warmer outside than inside the barracks.

Hoppy and I made a determined effort to get rid of our bugs through washing and sunning our clothes frequently. We enjoyed weekly baths which did something to improve our appearance and we kept our clothes clean, but we never did completely rid ourselves of our lice until we left the Nips at the end of the war.[42]

The prisoners in the camp before we arrived consisted of two Dutch doctors and the Dutch soldiers I have already told you about, one American doctor, a number of American soldiers, about twenty British officers and several Australian and English soldiers.

Being handicapped by our infirmities, the only original inhabitants we became acquainted with during the first four weeks were those who came to the barracks to see us. After we moved to a barracks for the able-bodied, we quickly became acquainted with the others through visits, contacts with work parties, and meeting with them at the roll call formations.

One of the British officers, a young Scotchman whom everyone called Robin, became a great favorite of ours because of his personality, his close contact with the news sources and his readiness to discuss the progress of the war. Many of us acquired the habit of contacting him daily in order to keep abreast of the news.

Robin, and the other British officers who worked in the garden not far from our barracks almost every day, came to know me by my beard. I had not shaved since the twelfth of December [1944] because it was much easier to let my beard grow, everyone being short of razor blades and I being short of energy. The barber clipped my mustache close and trimmed my beard into the nearest copy of a doctor's goatee that I could grow. The beard, which might have been pure copper in my younger days, was pretty heavily flecked with gray, but the gray was certainly in keeping with my overall appearance of advanced senility.

Toward the latter part of March [1945] the Nips gave us forty-eight hours to get rid of our beards, probably in conformity with their spring housecleaning or, possibly, because with the advent of spring we had no further need of winter clothing. Whatever the reason, I felt almost naked for a day after my beard came off, and the change in my appearance must have been great, for the first time I saw Robin after I had shaved he did not know me until he recognized my voice. He and the other British officers with him had a good laugh, telling me that I had shed a good thirty years. Alas, how sad it is that one cannot shed his years with his beard.

One does not have to be in a prison camp where tobacco, as well as food, is a shortage to learn that many men consider tobacco an essential component of the ration. However, the actual observation of starving men trading food for cigarettes is a distinct shock.

The cigarette issue at Fukuoka being only about thirty a week, and there being few articles available that money could buy, cigarettes became the commodity which passed as legal tender among the prisoners. Even as scarce as food was, there were always men who were willing to sell their issue of rice at one meal for ten cigarettes and, frequently, men who felt too ill to eat sold their rice for the legal tender which could be used to buy food or other things later.

Even mittens, caps, and other articles of clothing had a price tag of cigarettes, as did the barber and laundryman for their services. Inasmuch as I did not smoke, I was able to buy some additional food [with the selling of my cigarette ration] for which my stomach was calling most urgently, as well as pay for services which I could not render myself. With the assistance of one of the original occupants of the camp, I bribed one of the guards with Nip currency to smuggle in a small queer sea animal similar to a squid which Hoppy and I cooked and shared. Starved as my body was for protein, I considered the addition of seafood a most acceptable one but Hoppy did not agree with me, so a week later when I arranged for another delivery Hoppy declined to join me.

An officer friend who followed my example and obtained a squid for supper made the mistake of allowing a Nip sergeant to catch him cooking it.

The Nip was so incensed at discovering an American with contraband that he took him to headquarters and reported him to the commandant, who threw him into the guardhouse. The weather was near freezing and the guardhouse was a drafty shed which would have been uncomfortable under any conditions. But, for the American officer, who was deprived of his overcoat, gloves and shoes and of his noon meal besides, the ten day sentence was nothing less than a calamity. At the end of his sentence he returned to [the] barracks more dead than alive, and he was months recovering from his punishment.

Early in April [1945] a plant, commonly called "dock" at home, sprang up in abundance along the garden fence. Having seen an officer eat some of it as a salad, I harvested a hat-full which Hoppy and I both found to be a welcome addition to our rice, so much so that we repeated the performance many times.

Dock, supplemented by the occasional leeks I was able to steal when the Nips were not looking, added the green vegetables not provided in our diet. Normally, with our rice supper, we were given a soup made largely from a mild radish called *daikon* by the Japanese. Once a week the soup was ungenerously flavored with meat and our tea was sweetened and, except for a small bun substituted for rice at the noon meal, our diet consisted solely of an inadequate amount of rice.

About the first of April [1945], we able-bodied Americans were put to work alternating working in the garden with our British friends and emptying the camp latrine pits or, as it sometimes happened, carrying contents of the latrine to the garden to fertilize each hill during a transplanting operation.

You probably know that the Nips, in order to waste nothing, use human excrement for fertilizer. For that reason they frequently build their latrines with concrete pits that can be reached from the rear by raising a hinged drop. The contents of the latrine are carried in traditional Oriental "honey buckets," tall wooden kegs holding in the neighborhood of fifteen gallons.

The bucket has a bail made of rope through which a twenty foot bamboo pole may be passed to provide a two-man carry. The transfer from latrine to bucket is made by means of a long handled ladle holding a gallon, more or less. I think you will agree with me that the occupation of honey bucket attendant is not one of the most desirable, but I know from my considerable experience at the job that one can become accustomed to it, as many Americans would learn for themselves if the United States were ever invaded by an Oriental nation.

Although we were kept on our feet a number of hours a day, neither the work in the garden nor with the honey buckets was hard because we were not closely supervised. We learned quickly how full to [let] the buckets [fill], how to carry them with alternate shoulders and the need for the man in rear to keep step with the lead man. As a matter of fact, Hoppy and I became so adept that we could make our living that way if circumstances should ever require it.

A honey bucket was placed in our barracks every night to serve as a urinal because the latrine was fifty yards away and all of us, due to our weakened muscles and the substitute of water for food in our diet, had to use it several times a night. Because the bucket became filled about midnight, two of the stronger men were detailed to perform the duty of emptying and replacing it each night.

One night Carl and I were called at 2:00 A.M. to do our stint.[43] Out of our warm beds we crawled, jumped into our overcoats and shoes, found the carrying pole and started on our way with Carl in front. We got outside without trouble, although we had to go slowly because we were both pretty weak and the load was heavy. After the door to [the] barracks had closed, we were alone in the cold moonless night with only a faint distant light to guide us. We had gone about half of the distance when Carl, tripping over a root, fell to his knees. Luckily for him, he still held the pole on his shoulder until after I had eased the bucket to the ground so he escaped the unwanted baptism. We finished our work and got back to [the] barracks where we found four men in line waiting for the return of the urinal.

JUSTICE COMES FULL CIRCLE

I do not know the exact number of deaths we had while we were at Fukuoka, but forty is pretty close to the number.[44] Additional food and medicine were requested with little results. The Nip doctor appeared to be indifferent, but his hands may have been tied by the orders of the Nip commandant, a very tough character.

One day when I was passing the washrack I saw the commandant talking to a gray-haired British soldier who was cleaning the place. The soldier did not understand how the commandant wanted the work done, which infuriated the Nip so much the entire camp heard him roar. Finally, giving up hope of getting the work done the way he wanted it, he kicked the old soldier as violently as he could in the seat of the pants, reminding me of a football player getting off a booming punt.

The outside work-party interpreter was a short burly Nip who somewhat resembled the commandant in appearance. It seemed to me that he was always trying to ape the "Old Man," his name for the commandant, especially in his shortness of temper and his lack of consideration for Americans. Nevertheless, at every opportunity he loved to brag, in his east side New York English, of the years he had spent in Oklahoma and in New York City as a taxi driver.

I never heard of him doing anything for a prisoner, and I do know he was cordially hated by the work details. On the evening of the day the Old Man received the news of President Roosevelt's death, he had us assembled at the roll call area for a song session to celebrate the occasion.[45] The interpreter, who acted as master of ceremonies, was effervescent and gay, but his manner and taste were atrocious. I do not know how he learned that *Home on the Range* had been one of the president's favorites, but he surely did for he had it repeated by the crew two or three times. The few prisoners who had been doubtful about the character of the interpreter lost all doubt that night.

The interpreter was tried [after the war] by a military commission for specific acts of violence against prisoners and convicted, his sentence being set at twenty years of imprisonment. Monte, who was present at his trial, told me that when his sentence was announced our Nip friend jumped and shouted, "It can't be so! Why I thought the United States would give me a medal!"

Mr. Wada, the interpreter who had made the trip to Japan with us and who, through fear of the Nip officer or through ineptitude and indifference, had failed to help us when so many of us were dying, was also brought to justice at the end of the war, receiving, I am told, life imprisonment.

It may be interesting to note the difference between the two interpreters. Mr. Wada was a wee man in mind as well as in body. Almost four feet and a half tall, Mr. Wada had been afraid of everyone and himself for the thirty or more years he had worked for a mercantile firm as an English speaking clerk. Not until he became an interpreter in a prison camp did he acquire a position where he could call in someone to listen to his childish ideas.

He interviewed each of us at Bilibid before we sailed in order to complete our records, and after he had finished his work he smiled benevolently while he told us in detail what an important and fine person he was. We had some difficulty in reconciling his own estimate of himself with his actions on the *Oryoko Maru*. On one occasion, upon being told that the conditions in our hold should be changed for many of us were dying, he replied, "Let them die." It is my belief that Mr. Wada was not a brutal man like the interpreter at Fukuoka, but his lack of moral courage at critical times had been far more costly in human lives.

While we were at the camp, a few of us were interviewed twice by a young staff officer of the Imperial General Staff, the last interview being about the time of the landing on Okinawa.[46] At the second session, he related briefly how Napoleon had advanced on Moscow only to find that he had gone farther than his lines of communications could support him, thereby having to make a disastrous retreat. Then he asked us if, in the military teachings of our army and navy, there was any point beyond which it was not safe to advance because of [an] inability to continue the supply lines. I answered the question immediately, assuring him that there was no such teaching in our service, because I knew that was what he did not want to hear.

The only other question that I can remember he asked me was why our aviators fought so fearlessly when they did not want to die, whereas the Japanese fliers were only too happy to die for the emperor. My answer to that question did not please him either, for I told him our pilots, knowing that they had the best planes and the best guns in the world and believing themselves to be the best pilots in the air, went into each action with the certainty that the enemy, not the Americans, were going to be killed. The Nip made no comment, but when he left us he looked so sad that I concluded we had obtained more information than he.

ON TO KOREA AND CAMP JINSEN

During April [1945] there were several air alarms, each one resulting in our being crowded into a dark unpleasant air shelter which would have been little protection against anything except fire bombs. One day we sighted a B-29, so high up that it was hardly visible, even after we had located it by its vapor stream.[47] On that day and on several others, we heard the distant rumble of explosions, but no bombs fell in Fukuoka while we were there.

The landing on Okinawa was the final straw that caused the removal of all excess officer POWs to the mainland of Asia. The survivors of the two

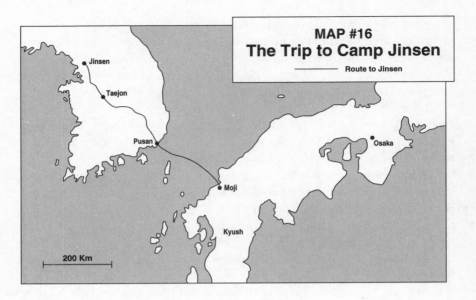

groups we had left at Moji rejoined us early on the twenty-sixth [of April 1945]. Late that afternoon our officers and our British officer friends marched through a part of Fukuoka to the docks where, about 9 P.M., we went aboard a large Fusan Strait ferry.[48]

We made ourselves comfortable and were beginning to think of going to sleep when, because of an air alarm, the Nip commander ran us out on the dock where we shivered in the cold until after midnight although the only explosions we heard were miles away. We had no sooner gone back aboard the boat than she put to sea, arriving at Fusan without incident shortly after daylight the next day.

We could not escape some feeling of satisfaction upon reaching the mainland, because we had heard rumors of the operations of our submarines and our mine-laying planes in the waters we had just crossed. As we had already been sated with firsthand experiences of abandoning ships at sea, we were most willing to forego being blown up by either a mine or a torpedo.

After being divided into two groups, we were marched to a large theater where we received a bountiful rice breakfast. The group I was in occupied the balcony, from where I [was able to inspect] the group in the pit below. Seeing a number of friends I had missed before, I went down and visited with the other group until the noon meal was brought in.

While we were eating, an interpreter gave us the news that we were going to Korea and that the other group was going to Manchuria.[49]

We departed that evening, [April 26, 1945,] on a train almost identical with the one we had ridden from Moji to Fukuoka three months before. Hoppy, Art, Dinty, and I, who occupied a double seat together, were not very happy when the seat in front of us was taken by two Nip officers and an interpreter, but we were unduly alarmed because they did not trouble us. Actually, they proved to be an asset at meal times for they passed their unwanted food boxes to us.

On the trip we were introduced to "binto" boxes, which are attractively prepared individual meals consisting of steamed rice, pickles, and a small piece of fish or meat. Those boxes, especially designed for travelers, were always freshly packed with steaming rice, and they certainly made a hit with us because they contained a piece of meat and more rice than we normally received at one meal.

All during the next morning, we skirted a long low mountain ridge which had been completely denuded of trees for a long time as erosion had brought all of the soil down to the valleys. The valleys, luxuriantly green with grass, were surprisingly free of all animal life and of human habitation. Occasional roads, which could be seen from the train, were nothing but ruts across the unfenced pasture land. Our early impression of Korea, that it was cold, bleak country, remained constant during our six months in the land and even now, years later, the impression is still unchanged.

At noon [on April 27, 1945,] we arrived at Seoul, where we stayed in the yards near the railroad station for several hours. All of the window shades were drawn, but we had no trouble seeing the big airfield near the track and noting considerable air activity. Late in the afternoon our cars were added to another train that brought us into Jinsen a little after dark.

A short march took us to Camp Jinsen,[50] where we were glad to retire in barrack buildings equipped with the familiar sleeping platforms. A Nip bugle call [woke] us at reveille on our first morning just five minutes before we had to be outside to form in line for morning roll call, a practice which we kept up until the end of the war.

Our first full day in camp being the emperor's birthday,[51] we participated in the usual munificence of the emperor, receiving one cigarette each for our very own. The building to which I was assigned was occupied on one side of the aisle by the twelve British officers who had come with us from Fukuoka, and on the other side by sixteen American officers.[52] We lived there in close proximity until the end of the war and became quite good friends. Robin had remained at Fukuoka in charge of the detachment of British soldiers, much to our disappointment because he was very popular. I came to know Copper,[53] the senior British officer, very well, for not only did we live close together during our leisure hours, but we were frequently on the same work details.

It was with deep regret on my part that we were separated to go our own ways at the end of the war, for I had become very fond of him and I had developed a very high regard for him as a man. We frequently talked of the world to come, as we visualized it after the war, and discussed what we considered were the principal lessons of the war. Seldom did Copper fail to voice the hope that Great Britain and the United States would stand firmly together in undivided friendship, thereby providing a wholesome stability among the world powers that would insure peace for the future.

The operating personnel of the camp were British soldiers who had been on the same job with a work party for a long time. After we were ordered to Korea, the work party had been transferred to another camp, leaving only their overhead to operate the camp for us. We found the soldiers friendly and helpful and very efficient in the performance of their duties. We learned about the kind of work we would have to do,[54] about the eccentricities of various Nips we were likely to be in contact with and, what was most electrifying, that a Red Cross food box was issued to each two men twice a month.

Almost to a man, the Americans were pessimists, predicting that no more food packages would be issued. The subject became the one most commonly discussed during the next ten days while we waited the issue date, but the issue was made at the proper time, much to our joy, leaving us free to talk of other things. It would be difficult for anyone who has not been hungry to really understand how much pleasure the coffee, sugar, Spam, butter, and all of the other wonderful articles brought us. We gloated over our possessions on issue day, we hoarded them like misers constantly and we tried numerous experiments to make concoctions with which to delight our long-starved palates.

For the noon meal we were served a bun made of wheat flour instead of rice. The cooks, who were extremely accommodating British soldiers, were always willing to mix into a bun whatever ingredients, such as sugar, butter, and raisins, that any individual might have ready for them at morning roll call. Some of the cakes produced by a suitable amount of those few ingredients available to us were truly amazing. A few enterprising men, desiring to celebrate future occasions, by foregoing buns for a day or two or trading rice for buns, were able to have as many as four or five buns available to them on the desired day when the persons with whom they had traded had to forego theirs.

With the dough for two or more buns going to one man, the cooks used small rectangular cake pans and produced cakes which resembled closely what we knew as poundcake. The Nip rice ration was even less than it had been in Japan, and the growing season being late we received little benefit from the garden until well into June [1945].

One day a week was meat day, the meat usually consisting of fried fish, each man getting a piece about half as big as a slice of bread. Every piece of fish that I received had its share of bones, but even bones have some food value, and I, being a stubborn soul, found that they could be masticated if they were mixed with rice and chewed long enough.

One week when the fish was spoiled, the Nip mess sergeant sent a work party to the garden for a heaping basket of leeks. That night for supper we were treated to a generous helping of fried new onions, tops included. We thought we were being cheated until we tasted the new dish, but after the meal was over the only complaint I heard was that there were not enough onions.

In keeping with the common practice in the other camps where we had been, workers were provided with a small increase in rice. Some of the men volunteered to work in the tailor shop sewing buttons on new shirts, but most of us preferred to work in the garden where we could help grow the food we ate. The work was a little harder, but the weather was so cold that, except at midday, it was good to be out in the sun.

There were two gardens, a small one inside the high board fence which shut us off from the world, and the other a large one on the edge of the town a half-mile away. Working on the farm we spaded the ground; planted potatoes; set out tomatoes, cabbage, and sweet potato plants; hoed the growing plants and killed the bugs; and, at last, we harvested the fruits of our labor. I neglected to say that we took our turns at fertilizing the land by means of the honey buckets with which we were already experts.

A day at work on the farm was usually good insurance for a good night's rest even though we slept on the floor inside a lighted room. As part of our bedding, we were issued curious looking bolsters which we were required to use as pillows. They were cylinders of unbleached muslin stuffed with hulls of rice, looking like sections of white stovepipe and feeling almost as hard. The sentries, who walked through the buildings periodically at night, enjoyed finding a sleeping prisoner with his head off the bolster for they could wake him with a rough jab or a rifle and order him to go to bed properly.

A Korean who came into the camp on business every week usually found an opportunity to pass on the highlights of the news to a soldier and, frequently, he brought a newspaper which our translator could puzzle out at leisure. Carl was reading one of the newspapers in [the] barracks one day when a Nip soldier, who happened to be passing through, caught him in the act. The Nip took Carl and the newspaper to headquarters where Carl was given a tough grilling and then a severe beating.

Carl and everyone who knew anything about the paper insisted that it was found in the bundle of shirts which had been delivered to the tailor-shop that morning. The Nip did not believe the story, of course, but they could not find out how it came into camp. An official report of the incident was made to the Imperial Army Headquarters at Seoul and Carl was placed under arrest pending a reply. The following morning at roll call, the Nip doctor, who was the officer of the day, gave the senior American officer a painful beating so that all of us could see how the Japanese Army punished offenses, the offense being that of permitting Carl to read an unauthorized paper.[55]

The senior American officer[56] was standing beside me when the doctor started beating him and when he finished his beating he was knocked back down and kicked back up again several times in between. Inasmuch as I was in charge of the small group to which Carl was assigned, I was sure I was next on the doctor's list, so when he walked away without a glance in my direction I breathed freely again for the first time since the beating had started.

We had known that the Nip doctor had no interest in our sick men and that he had positively refused to obtain the medicine they needed, but the beating was the first sample of his sadistic traits that most of us had witnessed. I am inclined to believe that the Nip commandant was not too happy about his medical advisor, for a month after the beatings the doctor was replaced.

We all had to learn to count off in Japanese to our roll call formations which placed an added burden to our rice brains. [Since] I was a group leader, I had to make the reports to the Nip officer of the day in Japanese also. Americans who were not fluent in their reports or who made mistakes were frequently beaten, so we all tried to be proficient. The first day I had to report, I wrote the ten or twelve words on paper and reported to myself for several hours beforehand, but when the officer of the day stood before me I had stage fright and could not think of a word. Fortunately, the Nip officer was the most patient one on duty at the camp so he helped me out and went on his way, leaving me very much in a sweat.

All of the Americans were many pounds underweight when we arrived at Jinsen and the diet was insufficient to do much fattening. The craving of hunger was so constant that most of the Americans spent their spare time talking about food or making menus that they expected to devote their attention to almost exclusively if they ever got home.

Our British friends, who had never been on the brink of starvation as we had been, could not understand why we thought of nothing but food and they had difficulty hiding their boredom when they were queried by Americans about the various articles of English food and how they were prepared.

A few days after the new Nip doctor came to camp, we all had to be inoculated with a Japanese patent serum which was designed to protect us against several diseases, including typhoid. Long before we had arrived in Japan, many men had discovered that their muscular weaknesses extended to those muscles which controlled the emptying of the bladder so that they had to get up as often as every half-hour. The night after we got our inoculation I joined the old-timers in their pilgrimage, making my journeys every hour on the hour.

On the tenth of August [1945], I suggested to Hoppy that, it being about time for us to have a cake, we planned on a big one to celebrate your birthday on the sixteenth and he agreed. So, by foregoing four of our rice issues, we had six buns due us on the big day to which we added the ingredients for a cake.

That morning many of us went to work on the farm. At 10:00 A.M. Alva called me from my job to go back to [the] barracks with him and a Nip sentry on an errand. The sentry released us after we entered the camp gate, directing us to meet him in a half-hour. Outside of [the] barracks we met Jack, looking as if he had swallowed a canary. He lost no time in telling us that the Nip doctor had just informed him that the war was over. He said that Japan had been forced to surrender to escape extermination as a race by the terrible atom bombs which the Americans were using.[57]

We returned to the garden walking on air, where we passed on the news behind the sentries' backs. We were still walking on air at noon on our return for lunch when Hoppy and I had the fine cake to celebrate the occasion of your birthday and the end of the war. Hoppy, who has a considerable technical knowledge, scoffed at the idea of an atom bomb so vociferously that he was a bit embarrassed the next day when we found that he had been wrong.

Our British friends were just as jubilant as we, so between us we were a most elated crowd in barracks that noon. Monte came by to tell me that while, technically, I had not won the bet about the end of the war, I had been so close that he wanted to call it off, but I declined for it was one bet I was glad to pay. The next day our senior officer and the British senior officer were called to Nip headquarters to be notified officially of the end of the war and that the Nips had been directed to keep us in the enclosure and maintain order until further information could be obtained.

WE WERE FREE

Chapter 13

Freedom's at Hand

The long winter was over, he was going back home. When he got out of the car to open the outer gate, the sun felt so comfortably warm and the gentle breeze so balmy that he asked his wife to drive on to the house, leaving him to walk.

He shut the gate and went up the hill a little way where he could see the big gorgeous redbud bush at close quarters. Surely, he thought, the redbud was enjoying its most luxuriant day of the year. The little dogwood tree across the road was in full bloom too, but although its pure white blossoms were quite beautiful, it could not compete with the redbud in show and vigor. Most of the big trees which scorned such feminine displays of red and white were joyfully unfolding their tiny leaves. Slowly, he walked on to the house where he could see over his hill that, wherever he went, always seemed to be calling him back.

She brought out two hickory chairs which she leaned against the house and began issuing orders, "Sit yourself down in the chair. You can see just as well from there. You should remember that, although you are ever so much stronger than you were last summer, you must be careful not to overdo it."

He sat on one of the chairs and tilted back against the house and announced, "Spring is in the air; spring is in my bones; I feel almost as elated as I felt when I heard the wonderful news that the war is over. In fact, I felt FREE."

She interrupted, "You have told me all about your part of the war, except how you felt and what you did during the two months between the end of the war and the day you got home."

"Very well," he said, "The announcement that the war was over did set us free. No longer were we shackled and bound by a ruthless and unfeeling alien foe. We were going home after an infinity of time and suffering; we were only waiting for the means of travel which was on its way."

229

THE BEGINNING OF THE END

While we waited, our immediate concern was acquiring more food. It took us only a day to translate a few pigs from their sty in the garden to our pot. We had all of the vegetables we wanted with no niggardly Nips to limit us. We bought an old bull which was no longer of value to pull a cart because of an injured hip. Contrary to common belief, bull meat is delicious.

The remaining Red Cross food packages were issued, giving each of us two whole boxes apiece and a little more. Every meal of every day we ate all we could hold, concentrating on proteins and articles of food that had become strangers to us. None of us did any work except the volunteers who gathered, prepared, and cooked the huge quantities of food we ate. A few of the more pessimistic men or, perhaps it would be accurate to say a few of the more far-seeing men, began to anticipate a famine.

Then [on August 29, 1945] the B-29s came.[1] The roar of their engines as they flew over the camp at three hundred feet brought every man of us out of [the] barracks to shout and wave wildly. The big ships, flying in column, put on quite a show for us who had never seen more than a glimpse of one at thirty thousand feet. When the planes passed overhead, the final touch of frenzy was added to the howling mob in camp by the sight of the huge block letters on the wings which spelled P.W. SUPPLIES. At the second approach to our camp, the bomb bays of the leading B-29 were open. A little before the plane passed overhead, the bays erupted with bundles and packages of all descriptions, tied to huge parachutes of green, red, white and yellow. Many of the loads which were too heavy for the chutes broke loose to fill the air above us with oil drums, boxes, bales, and various sized cases of canned goods.

The falling articles, which looked so small and harmless at the moment they left the planes, increased in size and speed so rapidly that our feeling was not unlike that of standing on a railroad track and watching an express train bear down on us. In no time we were all running and dodging amid the shower of missiles, displaying as much senseless energy as we had a few moments before but the impelling force had changed from joy to fear. Many of us had close calls, but the only man hurt was an American officer who lost out in a game of tag with a stuffed oil drum, from which he was lucky to escape with a badly crushed leg.[2]

I was standing stupidly in the garden when the second B-29 started its supply run, heading directly toward me. An icy chill, such as I had never experienced in combat, grabbed at my heart. It was very clear to me that while I had come a long way and was free at last, it was entirely possible that I might die ignominiously before I could reach home again.

I wondered if it would not have been better to have been killed in action while facing the enemy. I ran across the garden in a panic, losing my untied shoes in the soft ground, but I was no better off than before because the plane was still coming directly toward me as well as the air full of packages just released. I tried to dodge each individual package until I became as confused as if I were trying to dodge falling snowflakes. Many of the packages fell close but, miraculously, I was untouched.

Running toward the gate, I noted with great relief that Dinty had shown the presence of mind to open the gate and that I was just in time to join the column of prisoners hurrying out to a side street where we watched the remainder of food drop from a safe distance.

After the planes had gone we returned to camp to collect our possessions and check the damage. A number of Nip soldiers had been injured, which bothered us not at all, but we were greatly concerned about a gaping hole in the kitchen roof. The roof was repaired in a hurry, the repairmen being careful not to impede the cooks who had already started to prepare a meal of our newly acquired food. A heavy package had gone through the roof of the infirmary, narrowly missing the injured officer and the American doctors treating him.[3]

Several cartons of canned goods had wrecked the side of the building where our small group of officers lived, so we had to move to another room to escape the debris. We knew that our good luck was still holding for the material damage was not great and only one man had been hurt. After all of our loot had been collected a volunteer detail worked for several hours emptying all damaged cans in order that the cooks might utilize the contents before they spoiled.

There were very few men who did not have the curiosity to visit our collection of stores to read the labels and dream about the near future sampling of items which could not be included in the first meal being prepared from our full larder. There were carton after carton of cigarettes for each man and, what amazed us most, there were cartons and cartons of matches.

All during our imprisonment there had been a painful shortage of matches. Many times it had been necessary for a man to walk some distance to light a cigarette and bring the fire back to [the] barracks. Frequently the light bearer complained that he lost all of his cigarette giving lights to others. During our long period of famine we had not believed there were so many matches in the world.

The bales of clothing contained more than enough outer clothing, shoes, socks, and underwear for everyone. After the clothing was issued our

British friends got even with us for the long period we had bored them with the food. Their subject was clothing. They were amazed at the trim tailoring and good workmanship of all our soldier clothing, especially the underclothing. They frequently held up pairs of khaki drawers to extol their virtues which were previously unknown to them.

In order not to have our camp used for dropping ground again we marked an open field a mile away.[4] The new dropping ground worked out perfectly except for a Korean boy who failed to get out from under a case of canned goods. After all our goods had been loaded on bull carts, the attention of the Nip guard was called to the dead boy, but he merely shrugged his shoulders saying, "Only a Korean."

On the sixth of September [1945,] an American staff officer, who had been flown to Seoul as a member of the advance party of the occupation force, drove to Jinsen to see us and bring us up to date on the news. He also directed that we report to the commanding general of the landing force which was due in Jinsen harbor on the eighth, only two days away.[5] While our clerks made rosters for him, each of us prepared a radiogram to be sent home which became the first news our families received of our rescue.

Upon hearing our story, he confirmed the rumor we had heard that the ship which had preceded ours from Manila en route to Japan had been torpedoed in the China Sea. He also told us of the slaughter at Palawan and Mindanao and of the rescues at Cabanatuan, Bilibid, and Santo Tomas.[6]

Since my return home, I have talked to individuals who were participants of each of those incidents except the Palawan massacre. According to the staff officer's account, the Nip commander on Palawan, believing that he could expect an early American landing on the island, crowded all of the American prisoners, many of whom had been with us at Cabanatuan, into a tunnel which he blocked, and then set fire to the gasoline-filled entrance. I do not know the details except that most of the prisoners perished.[7]

The thrilling rescue at Cabanatuan, at Bilibid, and at Santo Tomas have been related a number of times and need no retelling; however, men who were present at Cabanatuan and Bilibid have told me of Nip plans which miscarried and may not have been known at the time the stories were told. A chaplain who was rescued at Cabanatuan told me that he had good reason to believe the Nip commander there had intended [on] executing all the prisoners and had, in fact, issued the order for their execution but that the providential arrival of the Rangers at the camp had not given the Nips time to carry out the orders.

An officer who remained behind at Bilibid when we left there in December 1944 related to me in detail how Bilibid had been heavily mined so that it might be blown up when in danger of capture. He said that our attack on Manila deprived the city of electricity and proceeded so swiftly that the Nips did not have time to improvise a reserve detonation system before the prison was overrun and captured.

An officer who stayed with a working party in Mindanao told me the ship carrying the last group of Americans away from the island was torpedoed before it had gone very far.[8] Most of the prisoners abandoned the ship and started by raft and swimming toward the shore, scarcely a half mile away. Less than half of the men reached shore as the Nips set up machine guns in boats and on shore and fired on all of the rafts.

A naval officer who survived the October [1944] sinking in the China Sea told me his story. Their ship left Manila in October 1944, with eighteen hundred Americans in the holds, a large number of whom were medical personnel taken from Cabanatuan.[9] The convoy had reached the China Sea somewhere between Formosa and China when there was a submarine alarm. The prison ship immediately slowed down, and in the opinion of the naval officer, deliberately turned broadside to the suspected submarine, inviting a torpedo which was not long in coming.

It was the same story of which we had long been familiar. The Nips [often would] expose prison ships to the most danger and even using them as decoys. The torpedo exploded in a hold occupied by Japanese [and] not an American [was] wounded. The ship was doomed, but she took four hours to sink, which was plenty of time for the Nips to abandon her, leaving [the] Americans to their own resources. The prisoners raided the galley and ate their fill before they left the ship. There was an abundance of life rafts with which everyone was comfortably equipped fully a half-hour before the ship sank.

The Nips had several escort ships nearby but they did not pick up a single prisoner. Their active patrolling of the area seemed to be for the purpose of preventing any rescues by our submarines. At dark there were four men on the naval officer's raft, but at daylight the next morning there were only two and there were no ships nor rafts in sight. That day was one of considerable suffering because of the burning sun, and the night was just as unpleasant because of the cold. On the second morning our naval friend was the only left and he was sure he could not last out the day.

About midday the crew of a Nip destroyer sighted him, pulled him aboard with a boat hook and gave him a little water. As soon as the skipper discovered he was a POW survivor he lost all interest for he had hoped to find a member of a sunken submarine crew who could give him some information. A few days later the boat reached Japan and the naval officer was sent to a prison camp where he remained a sick man until the end of the war. He was one of the nine or twelve survivors of the eighteen hundred to reach Japan and one of six now alive.[10]

On September seventh [1945], Hoppy and I made a pilgrimage to downtown Jinsen. The big reason for the journey was that we just wanted to visit the city, although we told each other that we had to locate the docks and to make some necessary purchases, all of which we did. We were probably more of [a] curiosity to the Koreans than they were to us as we wandered through the streets and shops that day. The shops were practically denuded, the only purchases which we thought worthwhile being several bottles of beer and a very poor pair of glasses that were better then the ones I had.

That day the Nips paid us all of our arrears in pay in Korean currency but, there being nothing to buy in Korea, I brought the money home and still have it because it is valueless in the money market today.

The day of the American landing finally arrived, an occasion which Hoppy and I had no intention of missing. After we had an early lunch we started gaily toward the waterfront. About halfway down we were interrupted by a succession of popping noises which, when we passed a street corner, sounded unpleasantly near. "Firecrackers," Hoppy, who was a big man in the artillery, announced.

"Firecrackers hell," I answered, "Those are Nip rifle bullets." Again that cold feeling seized me around my heart, but the shooting stopped and we arrived at the boat landing without further ado.

There at the docks, we learned that the Koreans had started a parade with banners down the main street contrary to Nip orders, whereupon the Nip police argued effectively with bullets, and after leaving a few Koreans killed, the parade evaporated. Our place at the pier was a very good one, in that we had a grandstand view of the landing of the division which was being made by small boats from the ships anchored in deep water five miles out.

The sight of American troops under arms was a thrilling one, and the way they went about their business left no doubt of whether or not they knew what they were doing. A staff officer informed me that we were not scheduled to go aboard ship until the following day, making me very sad for I was ready to leave Korea.

At that time, Major General "Archie" Arnold, the Division Commander [of the 7th Infantry Division], came ashore and Alva, who knew the General, introduced me.[11] I explained to him that we were living in a hovel and that we had exhausted our supply of food, whereupon he called a member of his staff and directed that we be put aboard a hospital ship that afternoon. Hoppy and I hurried back to camp, where we alerted everyone and started to collect our own belongings.[12]

RETURNING TO THE PHILIPPINES

At 5:00 P.M. on September 8, 1945 we climbed into landing boats that took us to a navy hospital ship, where we were fed, bathed, and our clothes sent through the delouser, after which we were tucked into bed by navy nurses.[12] Those hospital beds with their snowy white sheets were luxurious [and that is something that] had been unknown to us for almost four years.

The last man I saw on the pier when we departed was the commandant of Camp Jinsen, an old gray-haired lieutenant colonel [in] the Japanese Army. Like most of our previous commandants, he had been recalled from the retired list and had been in such poor health that we had seen little of him.

He had come down to the pier, a sad lonely old man, completely ignored by us as we loaded the boats and departed. All night long we dreamed of returning to Manila amid the luxuries of the hospital ship, looked after by the navy nurses but, much to our disappointment, after breakfast the next morning we were transferred to a wartime cargo ship.[13]

Our transfer was not without some compensation, for the small group of which I was a member occupied a part of the petty officer's quarters, next door to their mess, where we were assigned for meals. The skipper may have eaten better and more frequently than we did, but I doubt it, and the skipper liked his chow as well as anyone. He installed a first class ice cream freezer the last time he had been in San Francisco, and he carried enough mix to last for two voyages, just to be sure he did not run out.

For the seven days we were en route to Manila,[14] we had only to go to the ice box to get all of the ice cream we wanted at any hour of the day or night. Perhaps I did not overdo the privilege for I averaged eating not more than a half gallon of ice cream a day.

From a distance, Manila looked the same as it had when the transport brought us into port years before, but the city could not stand close inspection. She was an old lady who had suffered severely from the ravages of hardship and disease, so much so that she had lost all pride, no longer making any attempt to hide her wounds or adorn herself in any way.

A huge section of the city had been burned to the ground, and the buildings on the Escolta were full of gaping holes. The Manila Hotel and the concrete buildings along Dewey Boulevard were patched a little where the damages were most inconvenient, but they still looked as if they needed complete renovation. The utilities had been largely destroyed, no telephone system, except the army's, was in existence and there was no directory of residents.

Through the office of the Spanish Consul, I located my Spanish friends and repaid them for what they had been able to do for me by way of the underground. Through them I learned of the torture and ruthless execution which the Nips had meted out to known and suspected members of the underground who had done so much for us. It would take years for Manila to recover in body and spirit, and for me it would never be the same.[15]

We stayed in a tent camp near Laguna de Bay while we were examined by the doctors and interviewed by several agencies while we were waiting for our orders to be prepared for home.[16] During that period we ate all we could, drew clothing, shopped at the post exchange, and bade our British friends farewell. Being of too little importance to be sent home by plane, we finally sailed from Manila on a slow ship returning via Hawaii.[17]

ON THE WAY BACK HOME

Having been away from the United States of America for almost six years, I asked so many questions about everything that the ship's executive loaned me his copies of the current stock catalogues of Sears and Roebuck and Montgomery Ward. For days, I perused those catalogues, page by page, thereby bringing myself up to date on the material things which our people required to live comfortably and happily. I was impressed by two advances, the greatly improved styling in women's dresses and the great increase in quantity and advertising of articles used in birth control.

Our transport having business in Hawaii, we eased into Pearl Harbor and tied up at the dock about the middle of October [1945]. The war had been etched vividly and permanently into our minds and bodies, so naturally we were extremely curious to view the scene where Japan had struck the first blow. All signs of damage had long since been removed, leaving a peaceful appearance which would have bewildered us completely if a naval officer had not been available to give us a little orientation.

I was amazed that there were no scars left to see, and I could not help wondering if the lessons which might have been gained by the war would not be as quickly and permanently erased. Entering San Francisco Bay under the Golden Gate Bridge, skirting the city to a dock only a little way from the Ferry Building, is inspiring any time, but to us, returning home to our loved ones, after many years of hardship and little hope it was almost overwhelming.

It seemed like a dream to me as we tied up to the dock which was crowded by hundreds of people I did not know. More than two months had elapsed since the end of the war and still we had not reached home. Rapp came aboard and rescued me, leading the way to the gate where you were waiting.[18]

I saw Alice and the kid first, and then your head peeping over the gate with the questioning expression of the city girl who had come to the station to meet a country cousin and was not sure the cousin would be sufficiently presentable to walk down the street in public.

Rapp's driver brought up his limousine, and Rapp pushed you, the kid and me into the back while he and Alice sat with the driver. It was a novel experience for us to ride in style with a major general and his lady acting as footmen.

WE MADE IT AND WHY

Our return to American control in Korea brought forcefully to mind that we would never have started the journey home if it had not been for the failure of the Japanese plan of conquest. In general, that plan contemplated holding the frontiers in Manchuria and China and extending their holdings to the south and east to include the Philippines, Burma, Malaya, Dutch Indies, Gilbert and Marshall Islands, Guam, Wake, Midway, the Aleutian Islands and, if possible, Australia, New Zealand and Hawaii.

Occupying that ambitious perimeter, a safe distance from Japan itself, they could prevent attacks from the air and the sea and make a closer approach to Japan so expensive in time, cost and, above all, in manpower that the materialistic United States would be glad to make a negotiated peace. They believed that they could conduct a successful war on a shoestring.

For assets, [the Japanese] possessed a powerful navy, an air force which was initially potent but incapable of expansion or even of adequate replacement [of] losses in flying personnel and improved equipment. The army was adequate in manpower but weak in artillery and tanks.

In industrial output, Japan was far behind the United States, many of the Japanese factories depending largely on hand labor instead of machines. The homeland being unusually poor in natural resources, dependence had to be made initially on stockpiles of steel, coal, and rubber which came from the mainland of Asia. [Furthermore,] aviation gasoline and airplane parts [could only be] imported from the United States.

After rapid occupation of the so called "Greater East Asia," Japan's merchant marine worked incessantly to replace the rapidly dwindling stockpiles. The factories in Manchuria, which were near coal and steel, were worked twenty-four hours a day. All of the incoming war materials were either stolen outright or paid for with worthless military script.

Industrially, the odds appeared to be all in favor of the United States. On the other hand, Japan had no labor troubles. All her labor was regimented [with] food, clothing, and necessities rigidly controlled, and a minimum wage was paid in script, which probably could never be redeemed.

Discipline among the civilian personnel was almost as severe as in the military services. A worker who was suspected of contemplating a strike in [the] war industry would have been lucky to live twenty-four hours. There are men back home in our country today who were facing the enemy during the times strikes were in progress in essential industries of the United States and have seen their own men die when they might have been saved if there had not been a shortage of equipment. Those men are bitter in their denunciation of a political system that will permit the well-paid workers, who stay safely at home, [to] take any action for their own preferment which costs the lives of the poorly paid young men who are fighting in their defense.

To offset the lack of resources and low industrial development, and to fit the character and temperament of their own people, the Japanese militarists had devised a military system somewhat different from all other systems and vastly different from that of the United States. To the Japanese, being Orientals, human life is an expendable commodity, whereas, to the people of the United States, human life is precious and must be saved, whatever the material cost.

In order to make the most use of human beings, the Nip military system gave the arbitrary power of death over his subordinates to each officer and noncommissioned officer, who thus could, and did, demand explicit obedience regardless of [the] circumstances. Through instruction in the services and even throughout all instruction in the public schools, young Japanese were impressed with the honor of dying for the emperor in time of war. All Japanese, including the women, were taught that surrender to the enemy, and failure to carry out a military mission, except when fighting to the death, were the greatest dishonors that could befall an individual and his entire family as well.

Thus, at the start of the war, the Nips believed that they had built a machine which could be trusted to execute, to the letter, military orders of the higher commanders of the army, navy, and air force, who were, according to their own valuation, the best military leaders in the world. With such leadership and such explicit execution of assigned missions, what difference did it make if, at times, the enemy had a little more and a little better equipment. The main principle was to reach the enemy, whether on offense or defense, and in the ensuing physical contact the superior spirit of the Japanese soldier could not fail to be decisive. Therefore, they would strike fear to the enemy by their unstoppable assaults and, ignoring losses, go on to conquer.

On the defense each unit was a sacrifice force which, by digging in and dying to the last man, would make the capture of any Nip position so expensive in human life that the soft Americans could not long continue attacking. In their limited combat experiences on the continent of Asia they had known very little of artillery and air bombardment. It was with great dismay that they discovered, even in the early days of the Philippines, that the Nip soldiers were as vulnerable to attacks of heavy explosives as those of other countries and, as time went on, the Nips met increasing amounts of heavy explosives.

With each day that the war was prolonged, the odds in wealth in the growing air force and navy and in the improved equipment employed by all our military forces tipped the scales more and more against Japan. The Nips had taught their people that the spirit of the Japanese soldier could not fail to bring victory to Japanese arms, but that spirit did not prove equal to the task of combating the American machine. [As a result,] the "safe" perimeter caved in to bring about the miscarriage of Japan's carefully prepared war plans.

One can only guess how the war would have ended if the odds in equipment had been in favor of the Nips instead of in ours, but everyone of us can see so clearly, out of regard for our boys who must fight the next war, if we have one, that we must never permit a situation to arise in which the material odds are against us.

During the various periods when hundreds of us were dying, and I well knew that the next moment might be the big one for me, it was not hard to make peace with my Maker, even though my understanding was and is today as dim as it always had been. As I contemplated the dead and the suffering, there was no pattern that I could apply to them for they were made up of the good and the bad, even as were the survivors.

Better men than I were dead, and worse men than any of the dead had not been touched. Several times I heard the comment that the many deaths we suffered demonstrated that all life was nothing but a fight for the survival of the fittest. If the fittest survived, I failed to discover what they were fittest for, because they seemed to include the physically strong and weak, the wise and the foolish, and the saints and the sinners.

[I] cannot tell you why I came home, an old derelict of little value to anyone; possibly, I was saved to be hung. Maybe I survived to tell you this story of what it means to lose a war, as we on Bataan lost our war. I know I am too old and too decrepit to fight another war, and I hope, with all my heart, that our young men will never be faced with that necessity. However, I do know that human nature being what it is we must not sell those young men down the river of UNPREPAREDNESS.[19]

There is an old saying that "Away from the battle all men are soldiers." How true that statement is, and today it applies more to men who are lacking in training and equipment than to men who are lacking in spirit. Above all else, I have learned from my experiences that as terrible as war is, it is preferable to loss of FREEDOM.

If I have appeared to you to favor the taking of human life, or if I have seemed callous when discussing that subject, I ask you to remember the words of [Rudyard] Kipling, "If evil men were not now and then slain it would not be a good world for weaponless dreamers."

NOTES

Introduction

1. Professor Michael Howard suggests that a student of history follow three guidelines—study history in width, depth, and context—to gain a holistic view of a war or campaign in order to fully understand the cause-and-effect relationships of the battle while simultaneously delving into the creative intellectual processes of those involved. Inferring that the best accounts of war are firsthand experiences, he says, "The lessons of history are never clear." He then cautions those who study history to be aware that what one is studying is not always what happened in the past but what historians say happened, thus giving relevance to the importance of memoirs or firsthand accounts. See Allen, "Piercing the Veil of Operational Art," 117.

2. *General Wainwright's Story* was first written in 1946 by the commander of forces on Bataan, Lt. Gen. Jonathan Wainwright.

3. Ed Thomas, in *As I Remember: The Death March of Bataan*, often refers to the march as the "hike." He notes that while a POW, he and his fellow captives referred to this trek as the hike, only finding out after their repatriation that the press had labeled it the Death March. He acknowledges that calling it the Death March was by far more appropriate. See Thomas, *As I Remember*, 143.

4. The exact number of prison ships leaving the Philippines for Japan and other Japanese-controlled territories is debatable. Furthermore, the number of prisoners to leave the Bataan Peninsula is not exactly known. What is known is that these prisoners were at sea when their unmarked prison ships were bombed or torpedoed by the U.S. Navy and U.S. Air Corps, causing many casualties. Some reports estimate that as high as 85 percent of all prisoners that left the Philippines aboard these prison ships died either from the naval and air attacks or from starvation and lack of water. One well-researched account is Van Waterford's *Prisoners of the Japanese in World War II*. Waterford cites 56 different prison ships (four with unknown names). Nineteen of the 56 ships were torpedoed or bombed (and sunk) and one was lost in a typhoon. According to Waterford's research these ships held 68,068 prisoners, and 22,001 lost their lives—a 30 percent loss ratio—but Waterford's numbers take into account only

those killed by U.S. attacks. Many more prisoners lost their lives at sea due to lack of food, water, and medical care.

Some of the more written about "hell" ships leaving Manila for Japan include the *Shinyo Maru*, torpedoed off Sindangan Point, Mindanao, Philippine Islands on December 7, 1944, with a loss of 688 prisoners, 83 reaching shore; the *Junyo Maru*, torpedoed in the Indian Ocean on September 18, 1944, approximately 5,500 killed and only 800 surviving; the *Arisan Maru*, torpedoed on October 24, 1944, in the South China Sea, 1,792 lost and only 8 surviving; and the *Oryoko Maru*, bombed by the U.S. on December 15, 1944, off Bataan near Subic Bay. Survivors from the *Oryoko Maru* were later transferred to the *Enoura Maru* and then to the *Brazil Maru*. After 47 days at sea, the prisoners on board the *Brazil Maru* reached Moji, Japan, with only 425 surviving. See Lawton, *Some Survived*, xii, 214; and Waterford, *Prisoners of the Japanese in World War II*, xi, 151–68.

5. Camp Jinsen, now Inchon, famous for the remarkable U.S. landing during the Korean War, was located 50 miles south of the 38th Parallel. See Lawton, *Some Survived*, 223.

6. Morton, *The Fall of the Philippines*, 600.

7. Most of this information is taken from Statement of the Military Service on Irvin Alexander, No. 012414; Palmer, "Be Thou At Peace"; and the Official AOG Records on Irvin Alexander.

8. This information was provided by Colonel Alexander on March 20, 1917, while he was stationed in the National Guard at Columbus Barracks, Ohio. See Personal and School History Sheet (March 1917) and Birth Certificate, Irvin Alexander, November 10, 1896.

9. Villa's band of 500 men made a night attack on Columbus, New Mexico. Surprising the town and its garrison of U.S. cavalry, Villa's men killed 14 American soldiers and 10 civilians while losing 100 of their own men. See Dupuy and Dupuy, *The Harper Encyclopedia of Military History*, 1108.

10. Palmer, "Be Thou At Peace," 110.

11. Statement of Military Service on Irvin Alexander; and *1994 Register of Graduates*, 177.

12. General Orders No. 49, Headquarters United States Military Academy, November 27, 1918.

13. Two hundred eighty-four new cadets arrived at West Point in the summer of 1917 as part of the Class of 1921, but graduated early on November 1, 1918, in order to participate in the fighting in Europe. When the armistice was signed at 11:00 A.M. on November 11, 1918, thus ending the hostilities with Germany, the newly commissioned officers' services no longer were needed for active duty, and they returned to West Point to complete their studies as student officers. The majority of these student officers attended classes from December 3, 1918, through June 11, 1919, thus getting their class designation

as the Class of 1919. From a phone conversation with Dr. Steve Grove, a historian at the U.S. Military Academy, and Roger Nye's *Era of Education Reform (1900-1923)*. Class sizes and dates were taken from Col. Wirt Robinson, *Biographical Register of the Officers and Graduates of the USMA at West Point, New York*, 2112. Information about World War I was taken from Dupuy and Dupuy, *Harper Encyclopedia of Military History*, 1078.

14. Gen. Williston Birkhimer Palmer was a good friend of Alexander, having been his roommate at West Point in 1918. See *1994 Register of Graduates*, 175.

15. Alexander's nickname, Alex (pronounced Aleck), was confirmed in a conversation the editor had with Sara Spindle, Lucile Alexander's sister, on May 24, 1995, and shows up in most personal correspondence received by and about Alexander.

16. Palmer, "Be Thou At Peace," 110.

17. Robinson, *Biographical Register of Officers and Graduates*, 2112.

18. First Lieutenant Alexander returned to West Point to teach law without a law degree, an unorthodox occurrence by today's standards (most instructors at West Point have at least a master's degree and if they teach law they almost always have law degrees) but a common practice in the early to middle 1900s. Because of the postwar drawdown in the early 1920s many officers were rifted a rank, this being the case with Alexander. After being promoted to first lieutenant on January 24, 1920, he was honorably discharged from his commission and appointed to the rank of second lieutenant on December 15, 1922. He was promoted for the second time to first lieutenant, just prior to his tour at West Point, on February 19, 1924. See Statement of Military Service on Irvin Alexander.

19. Matthew B. Ridgway, *Soldier: The Memoirs of Matthew B. Ridgway*, 40–41.

20. En route to Washington via boat down the Atlantic Coast, through the Panama Canal and then up the Pacific Coast, the Alexanders stopped at San Francisco to visit a friend who was in command of the Disciplinary Barracks at Alcatraz, Col. George McDougall Weeks (USMA 1893). From a conversation with Sara Spindle on July 9, 1995 and *1990 Register of Graduates*, 314.

21. In 28 letters prior to the outbreak of hostilities in the Philippines and in a letter over a three-year period while in captivity, Alexander clearly indicates his affection for his son and his wife. Most notable were the excerpts he wrote to his beloved family on each of their birthdays and his anniversary during his tenure as a prisoner on Bataan.

22. Sammy's nickname and its meaning was confirmed in a conversation the editor had with Sara Spindle on May 24, 1995, and in a letter from Sara Spindle to the editor dated June 8, 1995.

23. President Roosevelt's New Deal included the Civilian Conservation Corps (CCC), which gave 250,000 young men meals, housing, uniforms, and small wages for working in the national forests and other government properties.

During this period, Alexander was temporarily working out of a CCC headquarters on Mt. Hood in Portland. From *Compton's Interactive Encyclopedia* and conversation with Sara Spindle on June 30, 1995.

24. From a letter dated November 5, 1941, to Lucile Alexander. In this case the letter indicates the date on which Lucile and Irvin Alexander Jr. left the Philippines. In a letter dated May 16, 1941, Alexander talks about Fort Stotsenburg in the days immediately after the dependents departed. More specifically, he states how "this is about the most quiet place in the world right now—no women or kids around to pester the commissary so the men do not know what to do with themselves." Commenting on the men left behind after the dependents left, he writes, "It has been a pretty sad looking gang here for the last two days."

25. Gen. Edward P. King was an artilleryman of wide experience and a distinguished army career. On September 14, 1940, he was ordered to the Philippines, where he had already served from 1915 to 1917, to command Fort Stotsenburg. Appointed to the rank of brigadier general on his arrival, he later supervised the artillery training for the Philippine Army, commanded the North Luzon Force, and served as MacArthur's artillery officer with the rank of major general. His assignment to command the North Luzon Force in late March 1942, although a recognition of his ability and reputation, was destined to end tragically. On him fell the terrible responsibility for making the hard decision three weeks later to surrender his starved and defeated troops to the enemy. See Morton, *The Fall of the Philippines*, 366.

26. Summary of Commissioned Service Since 1 January 1937: Alexander Irvin, No. 012414.

27. Although the aim of the air strike on Pearl Harbor was to destroy the U.S. Pacific Fleet in its home port, the attacks on the other Southwest Pacific islands were meant to serve as preludes to full-scale invasion and occupation. The well-coordinated Japanese campaign, spread across great reaches of the Pacific, progressed quickly. The U.S. Army and Marine garrisons on Guam and Wake surrendered on December 10 and 22, respectively, and the British forces in Hong Kong on December 26. Singapore, the supposedly impregnable British bastion on the Malay Peninsula, capitulated on February 15, 1942. Only on the Philippines did the combined U.S.-Filipino units mount a prolonged resistance, holding out with grim determination for five months. See Bailey, *Philippine Islands*, 3.

28. On Bataan and Corregidor together there were more than 50,000 military and naval personnel, but actual combatant troops never exceeded 30,000. Of these about 3,200 were hardened U.S. Army Regulars, including 1,200 Philippine Scouts and some National Guard units recently arrived from the states. Later they were joined by a force of marines and sailors from Corregidor, where they had been practically immobilized by lack of equipment. See Monaghan, *World War II: An Illustrated History*, 415.

29. Morton, *The Fall of the Philippines*, 68–71.

30. From a conversation with Maj. Johnny Lock, Engineer, U.S. Army at West Point, on May 30, 1995.

31. Morton, *The Fall of the Philippines*, 105.

32. Captain Colin P. Kelly, Jr. (1915–41), a member of the West Point Class of 1937, was the first West Point graduate to die in World War II. Myth also had it that Kelly was awarded the Medal of Honor. In actuality, he received a posthumous Distinguished Service Cross, the nation's second highest award for heroism and valor in combat. For a concise study of Colin Kelly's life see Dennis E. McClendon and Wallace F. Richard, *The Legend of Colin Kelly*. See also McCombs and Worth, *World War II: Strange and Fascinating Facts*, 301; Powell, *My American Journey*, 13; *1994 Register of Graduates*, 246, 489; and Alexander's letter dated September 10, 1941.

33. Gen. Masaharu Homma was eventually indicted in 1946 for his part in authorizing the Bataan Death March in violation of the Geneva Convention. He was tried, sentenced, and executed. See Yenne, *Black '41*, 99.

34. Bailey, *Philippine Islands*, 8, 11.

35. A battalion of the 12th Quartermaster Regiment was located in Manila, with a platoon of that regiment stationed in Fort Stotsenburg, 50 miles north of Manila. The supply situation on Bataan was serious at the start of the war and worsened as the campaign progressed. See Morton, *The Fall of the Philippines*, 21, 120.

36. General Orders No. 145, General Headquarters: United States Army Forces, Pacific, April 18, 1946. Alexander was originally recommended for the Silver Star by Brig. Gen. C. C. Drake, Office of the Quartermaster General, on March 5, 1946. The request was denied by General Wainwright but overturned on April 18, 1946, by Headquarters, United States Army Pacific Command. Besides the Silver Star awarded in December 1941, Alexander also was authorized to wear the following decorations: the Distinguished Service Cross, Bronze Star Medal, Purple Heart with First Oak-Leaf Cluster (indicating subsequent award), Distinguished Unit Emblem with two Oak-Leaf Clusters, American Defense Service Medal with Foreign Service Clasp, World War II Victory Medal, Asiatic-Pacific Campaign Medal with two Bronze Service Stars for participating in the Philippine Islands and Air Offensive Japan Campaign, World War I Victory Medal, Mexican Border Service Medal, Army of Occupation of Germany Medal, Combat Infantryman's Badge, Philippine Defense Ribbon with one Bronze Service Star, Second Nicaraguan Campaign Medal, Philippine Presidential Unit Citation Badge, and National Defense Service Medal. See Statement of Military Service on Irvin Alexander.

37. The 71st (PA) was commanded by Brig. Gen. Clyde A. Selleck (USMA 1910) who survived the Death March and retired from the army as a colonel in 1947. See *1991 Register of Graduates*, 338.

38. In the spring of 1942 approximately 80,000 Allied troops under the command of Gen. Edward P. King faced surrender en masse to the Japanese when King sent his chief of staff, Col. Arnold J. Funk, to Corregidor to inform General Wainwright, the USFIP commander, that the fall of Bataan was imminent. Wainwright had received direct orders from President Roosevelt and General MacArthur not to surrender the Philippines and to "continue the fight as long as there remains any possibility of resistance." Wainwright, therefore, perceived that there was no other recourse but to tell Funk on April 7, 1942, that Bataan must be held. He therefore gave Funk two direct orders to pass on: first, that under no circumstances would the Luzon Force surrender, and second, that King was to counterattack in an effort to regain the main line of resistance from Bagac to Orion. Funk then returned to the mainland with Wainwright's orders. King believed that if he had, in fact, followed Wainwright's orders he would be accepting the wholesale slaughter of his men without achieving any military advantage. Realizing that his forces had no other means to resist he capitulated to the Japanese the next day, April 8, 1942. See Morton, *The Fall of the Philippines*, 455–57; and Wainwright, *General Wainwright's Story*, 83.

39. Reporting to Bataan prior to the outbreak of hostilities were three regiments of Philippine Constabulary. Although officially designated as the 2nd Regular Division, Philippine Army, they are abbreviated in most places as PC. See Young, *The Battle of Bataan*, xiii.

40. General Orders No. 16, Headquarters: United States Army Forces in the Far East, January 28, 1942.

41. Summary of Commissioned Service Since 1 January 1937: Alexander Irvin, No. 012414.

42. The numbers listed in various accounts and those in the Report of the Liaison and Research Branch, American Prisoner of War Information Bureau, do not coincide. The important fact, however, is that out of 1,619 original prisoners, somewhere around 425 survived the trip to Japan; approximately three out of every four prisoner died aboard the "hell ships." See Feuer, *Bilibid Diary*, 243; Lawton, *Some Survived*, 259; Hopkins, "Prisoner of War," 103; and Waterford, *Prisoners of the Japanese in World War II*, 157.

44. Medical history section of Summary of Commissioned Service Since 1 January 1937: Alexander Irvin 012414, 4.

45. Lawton, *Some Survived*, 219.

45. Again, it is uncertain how many of the original prisoners out of the 1,619 that left Manila on board the *Oryoko Maru* lived to see Korea. Lawton's *Some Survived* states that 271 made it to Jinsen and Waterford's *Prisoners of the Japanese in World War II* has the number at 236. Regardless of the exact count, the important fact is that somewhere around 144 to 179 of those reaching Moji, Japan, lost their lives while captive in Japanese camps in Northern Kyushu,

Japan. Conversely, only one prisoner died while in captivity in Camp Jinsen, Korea. See Lawton, *Some Survived*, 211, 225–26.

46. Palmer, "Be Thou At Peace," 111.

47. Information about the accident was taken from a conversation the editor had with Sara Spindle, May 24, 1995.

48. Special Orders No. 127, Department of the Army, June 30, 1950.

49. Conversation the editor had with Sara Spindle, May 24, 1995.

50. Sammy and his family eventually moved to Dickinson, Texas, but not until 1964, a year after his father's death. Conversation with Sara Spindle on July 9, 1995.

51. Colonel Alexander died of myocardial infarction, or a heart attack, due to arteriosclerotic heart disease. He was never really in good health, even during the time he spent as a POW in the Philippines. According to Hopkins in his memoir, Alexander had a heart attack while at Cabanatuan Prison Camp; however, nowhere in the Alexander manuscript is this stated. The honorary pallbearers at his funeral included the legendary Gen. Matthew B. Ridgway (USMA 1917), Gen. Williston Palmer (USMA 1919), Lt. Gen. Alva Fitch (USMA 1930), Brig. Gen. Ralph Eaton (USMA 1924), Col. Milo Barragon (USMA 1918), and Col. Carl Graybeal (USMA 1927). See Hopkins, "Prisoner of War," 42. Information about Alexander's death was taken from a conversation the editor had with Sara Spindle, May 24, 1995, and by Alexander's Death Certificate, Irvin Alexander, dated December 26, 1963. The pallbearers' names were taken from Alexander's obituary listed in a San Antonio newspaper, title unknown.

52. Irvin and Lucile Alexander are interred at the National Cemetery in San Antonio, Texas. Their son, Irvin Spindle Alexander, is interred at Forest Park East, in Webster, Texas. From a letter from Sara Spindle to the editor dated May 8, 1995, and a letter dated March 29, 1991, from Aaron Cohen, director of the Johnson Space Center, Houston, Texas, to Mrs. Irvin S. Alexander.

53. Written by war correspondent Frank Hewlett. See Daws, *Prisoners of the Japanese*, 67.

Preface

1. This is how Alexander began the original manuscript. Keep in mind that the number of chapters has changed, making some of his comments not applicable in the sense of how the manuscript, in its current form, is presented.

2. The manuscript as described in the introduction was conceived in 1949 while Alexander was recovering from a near-fatal accident in Indiana. He spent seven months in a hospital at Scott Air Force Base, 12 months at Percy Jones General Hospital, and 14 months at Brooke General Hospital in San Antonio, Texas. See Chronological Record of Service Section of Summary of Commissioned Service Since 1 January 1937: Alexander Irvin 012414, 2.

3. The paragraphing, editing, and locations of leading sketches of illustrations, of course, refers to the original manuscript. Most of the leading sketches Alexander refers to have not been located and it is assumed they no longer exist.

Chapter 1: Reflecting Back

1. The chattering of Alexander's teeth signifies a reccurrence of malaria with which he was infected while in the Philippines. People who have had malaria usually suffer from it periodically throughout their lives. See Young, *The Battle of Bataan*, 346.

2. Quinine is a bitter, colorless, amorphous powder crystalline alkoloid used as medicine to treat malaria. The prisoners on Bataan suffered a severe shortage, with practically none available in the later years, causing many POWs to die of malaria. The effects of the disappearance of the drug were felt immediately. On the seventh day after the use of quinine was restricted, nearly 500 men qualified for admission to hospitals suffering from malaria. The daily admission rate continued, rising until it reached the staggering figure of 1,000 by the end of March 1942. Within the combat units more than 70 percent of the men contracted malaria before the surrender and it only got worse thereafter. See Young, *The Battle of Bataan*, 346.

3. Alexander probably meant Joseph in the Book Exodus.

4. Nashville, Indiana, is about 30 miles south of Indianapolis and just east of Bloomington.

5. Photo Joe is a Japanese reconnaissance plane as described in the early parts of the manuscript during the evacuation of Fort Stotsenburg.

6. Meaning, the surrender of U.S. and Filipino forces to the Japanese Army after the withdrawal south to the Bataan Peninsula on April 9, 1942, had taken place in his dream already.

7. Camp O'Donnell is what most historians label as the end of the Death March. It was, in fact, an intermediate prison camp for most soldiers before they were transferred to Cabanatuan and then to Bilibid Prison camps before being transported from the Bataan Peninsula to Japan, China, Korea, and elsewhere. Camp O'Donnell was a Filipino training camp built just prior to the war; its construction was never completed, and it was wholly inadequate in size and in facilities available for the eventual 30,000 tired and ill prisoners.

   From the tip of the Bataan Peninsula near Mariveles to Camp O'Donnell is about 65 miles. Most of the prisoners, including Alexander, made this trek on foot with minimal food and water and were brutalized by the Japanese along the route. See Lawton, *Some Survived*, 25; Martin, *Brothers From Bataan*, 76, 79–80; and Waterford, *Prisoners of the Japanese in World War II*, 252–53.

8. The average Japanese soldier was much smaller than his Western foe. This became readily apparent when the Japanese attempted to take the clothing, especially the shoes, of their prisoners.

Chapter 2: Being Captured

1. Mariveles is at the tip of the Bataan Peninsula. Located south of the city is Mariveles Bay, a U.S. Naval port; therefore, during the war prior to the American surrender the city was guarded by U.S. Naval troops. A few miles inland was the single-lane, badly surfaced West Road, which wound its tortuous way northward from the city. However poor, the West Road was one of the only paved roads on the islands. Many prisoners were transported along it, but most began the infamous Death March on foot from Mariveles. Most of the Americans had withdrawn to the southern tip of the peninsula during the retreat in early April 1942. After the surrender, the Japanese forced the Americans to assemble in and near the city of Mariveles. The Japanese were initially shocked at how many prisoners they had actually captured. Some reports claim that the Japanese expected 25,000 total prisoners or less, and they were shocked to find more than 12,000 American and 65,000 Filipino prisoners assembling in Mariveles. From this point the POWs began the grueling march, mostly by foot, to Camp O'Donnell. After walking 60 miles to San Fernando those prisoners "lucky" enough to survive were then loaded onto boxcars and transported another 20 miles by train to Capas. Finally, after arriving in Capas the prisoners were walked another 10 miles to Camp O'Donnell. The first POWs entered Camp O'Donnell on April 24, 1942. See Martin, *Brothers From Bataan,* 76; Morton, *The Fall of the Philippines,* 296, 298; and Waterford, *Prisoners of the Japanese in World War II,* 255–57.

2. Al is Lt. Albert S. Negley of San Antonio, Texas. Griff is believed to be Lt. Levis E. Griffen. Hugh is believed to be Capt. Hugh H. Fink of El Paso, Texas, and Sherry is Maj. Dean Sherry, an infantry officer and former police judge of San Diego, California. Negley, Griffen, and Fink are all listed as those who survived boarding the prison ships. Their ability to survive while captive on the ships or in the camps thereafter is unknown. Sherry's name was not listed as a passenger aboard the ships; therefore, he may have died prior to the movement out of Bataan or he may have been one of those repatriated at Cabanatuan. Carrothers is Capt. Sam Carrothers who was with Alexander during the Battle of Points and at Cabanatuan during captivity. See Braly, *The Hard Way Home,* 32; Lawton, *Some Survived,* 259–92; and Alexander's letter dated November 5, 1942 to October 15, 1944.

3. Bagac is on the west side of the peninsula located on the South China Sea. It was an important city for both the Americans and Japanese because from it ran a east-west road that cut across the peninsula connecting to Route 110 near Pilsar. Route 110 is a north-south running road on the east coast. The road leading from Bagac cut across the saddle between Mount Natib and the Mariveles Mountains. This road, called the Pilsar-Bagac Road was the only vehicular road providing lateral communications for the forces divided by the rugged heights of central Bataan. Bagac's location was so significant that the Philippine

I Corps kept its headquarters there during the battle up until the surrender in April 1942. See Morton, *The Fall of the Philippines*, 245; and Young, *The Battle of Bataan*, 222.

4. A musette bag is a small leather, and sometimes canvas, bag with a shoulder strap, used for carrying personal items.

5. After the Manchurian Campaign of the early 1930s, the Japanese brought back to honor the Samurai saber, a terrific weapon that was wielded with both hands and whose guard was almost half as long as the blade. If an officer was a descendant of a family of Samurai, he frequently carried the family saber; some sabers were handed down for generations, covering up to six centuries of pride. Some officers, when they had to buy new sabers, were known to throw their entire family into debt in order to pay for these expensive weapons. The big heavy swords were not mere badges of rank but were used skillfully whenever opportunity offered: both the cavalry saber type and the classic single-edged blades of Japan's feudal era could slice a handkerchief in mid-air or part a man's body from collar bone to waist in a single clean slash. See Thompson, Doud, and Scofield, *How the Jap Army Fights*, 23, 36.

6. Colonel Ito, commander of the U.S. prison camp at Mariveles, became the commander of Camp O'Donnell on or about July 6, 1942.

7. The fall of the Bataan Peninsula to the Japanese on April 8, 1942, ended all organized opposition on Luzon, but it did not give the Japanese control of the much-valued Manila Bay. In order to gain control of this vital waterway, the Japanese had to defeat the Harbor Defenses of Manila and Subic Bay to gain control of all American-held island forts in the bay. Of the four fortified forts in Manila Bay, Corregidor, home of Fort Mills, was the largest, measuring three and a half miles in length and one and a half miles at its widest point. Corregidor lay only two miles off the southern coast of Bataan, well within the range of the Japanese 75mm guns firing from Cabcaben and Mariveles. The other bay islands included Caballo (Fort Hughes), located just south of Corregidor, and south of Caballo was El Fraile, which quartered the American post of Fort Drum. The southernmost island is Carabao, which held Fort Frank. Compared with Corregidor, the three other bay islands are extremely small; the largest, Caballo, is only about a quarter of a square mile of land area. All the islands and their host forts, to include Corregidor and Fort Hughes, were commanded by Maj. Gen. George F. Moore, commander of the Philippine Coast Artillery Command. See Morton, *The Fall of the Philippines*, 8, 471–78, 536.

Chapter 3: The Journey Begins

1. Zig Zag is the name given to the road that wound through the Zambales Mountains connecting the southern tip with Olongapo in the north-

western part of the peninsula and across the center of Bataan to San Fernando. The road had been built at the turn of the century when there were no bull-dozers; consequently the work was done with dynamite and picks and shovels. The resulting roadbed followed the contour of the hills, curving around the edges of cliffs, rather than through or over them.

Little Baguio is located on the highlands overlooking Mariveles. Hospital No. 1 was organized on December 23, 1941, at Limay, five miles south of the front near Orion. During the withdrawal it was moved to Little Baguio to minimize the threat of bombing. But a few days after settling at Little Baguio, everyone on the hospital staff realized that they had placed themselves right in the center of one of the choicest military targets on Bataan. On the left sat a huge Philippine II Corps ammunition dump; on the right, a motor pool; on the hill behind was a unit of anti-aircraft; across the road in front, a large quar-termaster supply dump; and down the road a few hundred yards, USAFFE's echelon headquarters. Hospital No. 2 was located about three miles south of Cabcaben, in the bamboo thickets and jungle along the Real River. See Law-ton, *Some Survived*, 175; Morton, *The Fall of the Philippines*, 258, 380-81, 444; and Young, *The Battle of Bataan*, 124.

2. Probably in a location along the eastern coast of Bataan just north of Cab-caben.

3. In the original manuscript Alexander calls Harwood, "Col. H—" Information on Colonel Harwood comes from Morton, *The Fall of the Philippines*, 254.

4. In this case the dump is referring to a former logistical storage area.

5. Many men contemplated taking for the hills. The universal feeling that MacArthur would soon return led many to believe that heading into the for-midable mountains would be better than remaining a prisoner of the Japanese. Hundreds of men, both Filipino and American, escaped to the hills. Conse-quently, many Americans were successful in joining up with guerrilla forces in fighting the Japanese in hit-and-run skirmishes until MacArthur returned nearly three years later. Many were successful for only a short period of time before they were captured or turned in by Filipinos who succumbed to Japan-ese threats or the desire for the bounty monies. The majority of prisoners, being too weak to run, remained captives of the Japanese. See Thomas, *As I Remember*, 150.

6. Beriberi is a disease caused by a deficiency in vitamin B_1. In a diet with high carbohydrates—for example, a rice diet—extra B_1 was needed. There are two kinds of beriberi. The dry kind was terribly painful. Prisoners with dry beriberi were usually very thin, and their chief complaint was lightning-like pains (neuralgia) in their legs and feet. The only relief came from soaking their legs in buckets of cold water, which was impossible to obtain. The wet kind did horrible things to the look, feel, and functioning of the whole body. It caused men to swell up with the fluids of edema. It turned them into blobs,

with distended bellies and huge puffy chests. One distinct characteristic was that many men looked as if their heads were resting directly on their shoulders, with their necks invisible. The arms and legs of a man with wet beriberi were like bags of suet or baker's dough; many claimed that if you poked a finger into a thigh of one of these men it would leave a dent. The doctors told them to sleep sitting up, or with their feet up, but either way the fluid drained back to the middle of their body, so the sack of the testicles swelled like water balloons. The longer they were deprived of B1 the worse they filled up, until fluid began to accumulate in their lungs and suffocate them from inside. A man dying of wet beriberi made a choking noise, and in the camps of Bataan it was called the beriberi song. See Daws, *Prisoners of the Japanese*, 121–22; and Jacobs, *Blood Brothers*, 56–57.

Chapter 4: The "Hike" Continues

1. Orani is located on the northwestern side of the Manila Bay about 85 miles by foot from Camp O'Donnell. During the battle for Bataan an auxiliary field was located in Orani in which U.S. P-40 aircraft were deployed. See Morton, *The Fall of the Philippines*, 524; and Young, *The Battle of Bataan*, 20.

2. In Van Waterford's *Prisoners of the Japanese in World War II*, the captor-captive relationship is explained in terms of sociological, cultural, historical, and political facets. It is important to understand these aspects when discussing the differences between the Japanese and their American prisoners. Waterford summarized them as:

   (1) The economic strangulation of the Japanese by the West after the U.S. announced its 1941 oil embargo against the Japanese because of the controversial Japanese landing at Cam Ranh Bay and subsequent occupation of Saigon and Danang; this action taken against Japan by the West left the Japanese resentful of American authority.

   (2) Stereotyping and racist thinking by the West; the Americans had a long history of segregation and universal poor treatment of Japanese migrants and citizens in the United States.

   (3) Continued colonialism by the West as it sought occupational control of the many smaller islands in the South Pacific.

   (4) The Yamato tribe that unified Japan through the common belief in the superiority of the Japanese people over other cultures, espcially Western cultures.

   (5) The existing cult of *Bushido*, the warrior who believed in honor, obedience, and valor and sincerely believed in the emperor's divinity and that dying for him was glorious.

   (6) The individualism of the Japanese soldier within the framework of group action, causing commanders in the field to frequently disregard orders

from the Tokyo War Ministry, and the belief that they were acting in the emperor's best interest.

(7) The dishonor of being captured, or *horyo*—a dishonored captive—led many guards and camp leaders to be insensitive to their American prisoners who so easily surrendered; the Japanese culture accepted death before dishonor and to surrender was dishonorable.

(8) The insularity of the Japanese soldier; for years Japan had been isolated from the West; isolation from other cultures was the catalyst for their belief that the Japanese were superior.

(9) The emotionality of the Japanese soldier; always trying to "save face" and keeping up appearances.

(10) The tough training of the Japanese soldier; he was trained to believe that loyalty, in all its sacrificial manifestations, was the greatest expression of military spirit. Inflexible duty was its corollary, with a fatalistic bind to a life of service. The Japanese soldier's own outstanding military behavior, even in a life-and-death situation, would be publicized only briefly while he was alive. Lavish praise and great honors came after death. This twofold policy prevented the creation of national heroes, while further underlining the glory of death on the battlefield. Furthermore, the relatives of a captured Japanese soldier were never notified. If they suspected that he was imprisoned, they were obliged to show that he had brought everlasting dishonor to his family and himself and that it would be better if he were dead for he was marked as a traitor to the imperial cause.

Waterford explains that "all of these elements of Japanese and American thinking, in a variety of combinations, greatly influenced the way the Japanese treated their prisoners and the way the prisoners reacted and their behavior toward Japanese and Korean guards." See FitzPatrick, *The Hike into the Sun*, 81; Jacobs, *Blood Brothers*, 17; and Waterford, *Prisoners of the Japanese in World War II*, 15-23.

3. Corp. Wayne Lewis of Company D, 31st Infantry, remembered that "rumor had it that the Japs were checking the numbers in the group, and if at the next check point the numbers didn't match, they'd kill people to even the count. Then we heard for every guy missing in the next check point they were shooting ten guys." Whether this rumor was ever proven or not, the point is that the Japanese captors had very little compassion for their prisoners along the route. See Knox, *Death March*, 125–26.

4. The Japanese were ruthless as they drove by the Americans along the route to the prison camps. Sgt. Ralph Levenberg of the 17th Pursuit Squadron remembered: "The thing that burned itself into my mind for days and days was the imprint of a body in the road that had been run over, I don't know how many times. It was paper thin, but the shape was very clear. It was as if the guy was

still pleading for somebody to reach down and pick him up." See Knox, *Death March*, 125.

5. Not recognizing the rank of their prisoners and the captives' chain of command is in direct violation of both the 1929 Geneva Convention Relating to the Treatment of Prisoners of War document and Japan's own Japanese Army Regulations for Handling Prisoners of War: Army Instruction No. 22, dated February 1904. Signed at Geneva on July 27, 1942, by 47 nations, the Geneva Convention was ratified or adhered to by 34 countries. Since Japan had not formally ratified this Convention before the outbreak of World War II, the Allied powers sought an assurance from Japan in early 1942 that she would adhere to the Convention. Japan replied that she was not formally bound to the Convention, but she would apply it "with changes applied" toward Allied POWs. The Japanese violated not only most of the articles of the Geneva Convention but also the spirit of the Japanese regulations that were reviewed in April 1942 by a Japanese council that included Premier Tojo himself. The council decided that the POWs should be treated in accordance with the Japanese regulation that closely paralleled the spirit of the articles of the Geneva Convention. Among the many violations was the blatant disregard for Article 18, which provides for the provisions of officers while being interned as prisoners. It states that, in short, officers who are being held as prisoners should be given suitable treatment in accordance with their position and rank. This provision is also protected in the Japanese Army Regulations for Handling Prisoners of War, Article 2. The Japanese on Bataan violated this provision as well as numerous others by not recognizing the detained prisoners' chain of command and rank structure and by forcing commissioned officers to hard labor once they arrived at the various prison camps. See Report on the Interpretation, Revision and Extension of the Geneva Convention of July 27, 1929; and Waterford, *Prisoners of the Japanese in World War II*, 34–37, 345–58.

6. The controversial "Bataan Ration," implemented in early January 1942, represented barely half the usual peacetime ration of 4,000 calories or 71 ounces of food per man per day. Although ordered, if the 2,000-calorie daily Bataan ration was ever issued it was most likely to the rear area troops. According to many reports, the ration, from the first day's issue to the last, receded steadily until bottoming out in late March to near 1,000 calories. See Young, *The Battle of Bataan*, 341–43.

7. Daws's *Prisoners of the Japanese* explains that the enlisted men believed that "the officers were the ones who surrendered to the Japanese, and for enlisted men that was powerful grudge material. Early in the captivity, some men came up with a new doctrine: Rank meant nothing anymore; a prisoner was a prisoner was a prisoner. They would bow to the Japanese because the Japanese had the boot and the rifle butt and the bayonet. But no more did they have to pay respect to officers merely out of respect for rank." He goes on to give an

example of a man named Oklahoma Atkinson who, when asked by a marine major if he didn't recognize the stripes of an NCO Atkinson had been sassing, replied, "I don't give a damn if you've got stripes on your underwear, it don't mean nothin' to me." See Chunn, *Of Rice and Men*, 96; and Daws, *Prisoners of the Japanese*, 108.

8. O'Donnell was constructed to hold nearly 8,000 soldiers, but upwards of 50,000 prisoners (mostly Filipinos) were jammed inside the barbed wire in an area of less than one square mile. Of the 9,000 American POWs that reached O'Donnell, 1,547 died and were interred in the camp's cemetery. It is believed that between 10 and 12 POWs were executed and buried in undisclosed places. As a result, it appears that at least 1,564 POWs perished and possibly as high as 1,567. The last known prisoner to die at O'Donnell perished in November 1942. Most of the prisoners to survive were moved to Cabanatuan in May-July 1942. See Lawton, *Some Survived*, 31; and Olson, *O'Donnell*, 1, 2, 5, 66, 152.

9. The Catholic chaplain is believed to have been John E. Duffy of Cleveland, Ohio. He is mistakenly cited as William in some accounts. Duffy escaped on the Death March, only to be recaptured as part of MacArthur's guerrilla forces. He was brought to Bilibid Prison in Manila in July 1941 and then survived the *Oryoko Maru*, but only barely. He was so weak in the Japanese prison camp at Fukuoka 17 after arriving there from the Philippines that he could not minister last rites to the dying Americans of his denomination. A Dutchman, Carel Hamel, who was a Protestant, courageously carried dying Catholics to Duffy so that the priest could offer them their last rites. Colonel Alexander and Chaplain Duffy were friends before the war broke out and he mentions Chaplain Duffy in a letter dated May 18, 1941. See Daws, *Prisoners of the Japanese*, 312; Hopkins, "Prisoner of War," 97; Jacobs, *Blood Brothers*, 63; Lawton, *Some Survived*, 267; Martin, *Brothers From Bataan*, 181, 186; and Alexander's letter dated May 18, 1942.

10. The 17-mile march refers to the foot movement from Orani to Lubao.

11. Lubao is northeast of the Bataan Peninsula. At Lubao the prisoners were herded into a sheet-iron warehouse. See Daws, *Prisoners of the Japanese*, 78.

12. Colonel Alexander is referring to his West Point class ring.

13. Matt is Lt. Matt Dobrinic, the former commander of Company B of the 52nd Philippine Infantry, who fought the Japanese at the Legaspi landing in late December 1941. See Chunn, *Of Rice and Men*, 158; and Morton, *The Fall of the Philippines*, 111–12.

14. There are two towns named San Fernando in northern Luzon, both of which figure largely in the campaign. One is in La Union Province, along the shore of Lingayen Gulf, which will be visited by the prisoners prior to leaving the Islands in 1944 (see Chapter 12). The other, the one Alexander is referring to here, is the capital of the Pampanga Province and is considered, because of

the rail system existing there, the gateway to Bataan. It was more than just a barrio; it was a good-sized town. It had several two-story buildings with apartments upstairs, a few factories, a large school yard, a cockpit arena, and a railroad station. See Levering, *Horror Trek*, 76; Morton, *The Fall of the Philippines*, 102; and Thomas, *As I Remember*, 153.

15. A *calesa* is a small horse, a pony. See Daws, *Prisoners of the Japanese*, 68.

16. The enclosure in San Fernando was a large shed with open ends used as a cockfight arena. The floor was bare dirt and at one end sat some wooden bleachers. Many of the men had dysentery and were defecating in the middle of the crowded shed. Prisoners arriving in San Fernando were also assembled in a local elementary school. See Knox, *Death March*, 149-50.

17. Although there is no known official record indicating the average death rate, many accounts estimate that on average 20 prisoners died a day. A report made after the majority of prisoners left for Cabanatuan in early July 1942 showed that the death rate ranged as high as 35 to 40 in mid-July and fell to 21 a day by August 1. During August the rate varied from a high of 24 on the sixteenth to a low of 5 on the thirty-first, with an average of around 15. Olson, *O'Donnell*, 242.

18. The prisoners marched down Main Street of the city to the railhead while Filipinos looked on in horror at the bizarre spectacle of bleeding, dehydrated, abused men who at one time where their protectors. The rail line was of the narrow gauge type; consequently the boxcars were small—seven feet high, 33 feet long, and eight feet wide. Figuring two feet per person, 50 men could have sat pushed tightly together. The Japanese crowded nearly three times that number into each boxcar and closed the doors. The trip from San Fernando to Capas, 25 miles north of San Fernando, usually took on average about two hours. Most prisoners recall this ride as a harrowing experience. It was worse than the foot march for many, for on the road there was at least fresh air and the prisoners could encourage each other; here was darkness and near suffocation. The POWs were rapidly running out of oxygen by the time they reached Capas. See Lawton, *Some Survived*, 23.

19. The commandant of Camp O'Donnell was Capt. Yoshio Tsuneyoshi, "an insignificant, overage in grade junior officer," who probably was selected because he could be spared at a time when the Japanese needed their best for the attack on Corregidor. Still holding the rank of captain by the end of the war, Tsuneyoshi was well known to all prisoners that passed through O'Donnell. He was nicknamed by the prisoners a variety of names, among them being "Baggy Pants," "Whistling Britches" and "Little Napoleon." At the trials after the war, Tsuneyoshi received a life sentence instead of the death penalty because the jury failed to reach a unanimous vote. See Olson, *O'Donnell*, 41-42, 171-72.

Chapter 5: Building Up a Wall of Fear

1. Mount Pinatubo (Alexander spells it Penatuba in the original mnuscript) is an active volcano rising to a peak of 5,770 feet. Pinatubo is part of the Zambales Mountains, which separate the central plain of southeastern Luzon from the China Sea.

2. Lingayen and Lingayen Bay is located about 75 miles north of the Bataan Peninsula on the China Sea.

3. Located on Subic Bay is the Olongapo Naval Station. Many units used the firing range at the Naval Station prior to the outbreak of hostilities. Route 7 connects Olongapo with San Fernando in the east (the road partially used during the Death March) and north along the Zambales Coast to Lingayen Gulf. See Morton, *The Fall of the Philippines*, 29, 223.

4. During the battle to retake the Philippines toward the end of the war, Maj. Gen. Henry L. C. Jones's 38th Infantry Division, as part of XI Corps, sailed to Luzon and landed on the San Antonio area of the Zambales Province, 40 miles west of the southwest corner of the Central Plains and 25 miles northwest of the northwest corner of Bataan. The 38th secured Subic Bay and San Marcelino Airstrip on January 29, 1945. From here the division drove rapidly eastward paralleling Route 7 toward Dinalupihan. The aim of reaching Dinalupihan with the 38th by February 5 was successful, for the 149th Infantry of the 38th had taken the "high" road bypassing the majority of enemy forces. At Dinalupihan the 149th made contact with XIV Corps, who had cleared the eastern shore of Manila Bay. The majority of XI Corps, along Route 7, had a difficult time clearing the road and sealing off Bataan, for the Americans met head-on a series of mutually supporting Japanese strongpoints along both sides of the road in an area that began approximately three miles northeast of Olongapo and extended eastward another three miles through rough terrain known as Zig Zag Pass. The corps commander, Maj. Gen. Charles P. Hall, dissatisfied at the 38th Infantry's progress, replaced Major General Jones with Maj. Gen. William Chase on February 7 and in short order Chase had reduced the enemy at the Zig Zag Pass. Soon after, the 38th secured positions from which to launch subsequent operations aimed more directly at securing Manila Bay and the Bataan Peninsula. See Smith, *Triumph in the Philippines*, 309–34.

5. Although the U.S. had maintained military forces in the Philippines since their annexation in 1898, including a considerable number of indigenous units, the islands were largely unprepared for hostilities with Japan in December 1941. The total unit strength stood at 31,095 men, a 40 percent increase since September, but the Filipino soldiers as well as the hastily mobilized U.S. forces were inadequately trained. The majority of the Filipino reserves recruited by MacArthur spoke some 60 dialects and it was believed it would take months to train them. Although U.S. forces did bring with them some modern

equipment, including 108 M3 tanks, 107 P-40 fighters and 35 B-17 bombers, they lacked the critical maintenance and repair facilities as well as functional airfields to sustain this equipment. Additionally, the ten Philippine Army (PA) reserve divisions that were mobilized by December 1, 1941, and incorporated into the U.S. defense forces lacked everything from boots to artillery and were armed with the antiquated World War I Enfield and Springfield 1903 rifles. See Bailey, *Philippine Islands*, 4–7; and Jacobs, *Blood Brothers*, 11.

6. During the six and a half months from the time Lucile Alexander left the Philippines (May 14, 1941) until the outbreak of hostilities, Colonel Alexander wrote his wife a note nearly every day, mailing these letters in 28 separate postmarks. In each letter he would conclude with the words "See you all in February," for Alexander firmly believed that he would leave the Islands by February 1942 to attend further Army Officer schooling. Of course, no one was allowed to leave the theater once the onset of hostilities became imminent, but Alexander and his colleagues remained optimistic. This information is found speifically in his letter dated May 26, 1941. Other information found in letters dated May 16, 1941 to November 30, 1941.

7. Initially commander of the forces on Northern Luzon, Major General King assumed command of the Luzon Force from General Wainwright on the basis of his oral instructions on March 21, 1942. See Morton, *The Fall of the Philippines*, 366.

8. The appointment of Gen. Douglas MacArthur as commander of all army forces in the Far East effective July 26, 1941, did much to improve the bleak situation in the Philippines. When MacArthur assumed command of USAFFE, the Philippine Department consisted of 22,532 men, 11,972 of whom were Philippine Scouts. By November 30, 1941, MacArthur had increased that force to 31,095 soldiers, 16,643 being U.S. soldiers and just over 11,500 scouts. He also recruited some 110,000 young Filipinos to incorporate into the Philippine Army, mostly as reserves. An optimist by nature, with implicit faith in the Philippine people, MacArthur was able to inspire confidence and loyalty in his associates, staff, soldiers and, most importantly, in the people of the Philippines. By fall 1941 there was a firm conviction in Washington and in the Philippines that, given sufficient time, a Japanese attack could be successfully resisted. See Jacobs, *Blood Brothers*, 11; and Morton, *The Fall of the Philippines*, 17–19, 21, 49, 64.

9. In early November 1941 the Japanese forces assigned to the Philippine campaign began to move to their designated jump-off points. The 5th Air Group arrived in southern Formosa (now Taiwan) from Manchuria late in the month. On November 23 two of the advance detachments stationed in Formosa boarded ships at Takao and sailed to Mako in the Pescadores. Between November 27 and December 6 the 48th Division concentrated at Mako, Tako, and Kiran. The first units of the 16th Division sailed from Nagoya in Japan on November

20, followed five days later by the remainder of the division. On December 1, when General Homma established his command post at Takao, he received final instructions from the Southern Army to begin the assault of the Philippine Islands on December 8, 1941. See Morton, *The Fall of the Philippines*, 60–61.

10. Baguio (Colonel Alexander spells it Bagio) is located in central Luzon. Camp John Hay, named after President Theodore Roosevelt's Secretary of State John Milton Hay in 1903, was located in Baguio. Official records show that the first attack against the Philippines came on December 9, 1941 (Philippine time), when shortly before 9:00 A.M. Japanese Army bombers were reported by the aircraft warning service on Luzon to be heading south over Lingayen Gulf in the direction of Manila. One group struck Tuguegaro at about 9:30 A.M., while another concentrated on the barracks and other installations at Baguio. Baguio was again attacked on December 13 when 200 Japanese planes attacked Clark Field, Tarlac, and Baguio between 10:30 A.M. and 11:00 A.M. See Jacobs, *Blood Brothers*, 9, 10–11; and Morton, *The Fall of the Philippines*, 77, 84n.21.

11. Don Bell was known as "the Walter Winchell of the Philippines." On the day the Japanese bombed Pearl Harbor, Bell was said to have announced, "Those dirty little bastards have struck Pearl Harbor! Reports remain sketchy, but there is no doubt! Oh God!" He was crying, near hysteria, as he continued, "The yellow-bellied Japs have hit our ships at anchor!" See Hartendorp, *The Japanese Occupation of the Philippines* vol. 1, 5, 470–71; Jacobs, *Blood Brothers*, 10; Martin, *Brothers from Bataan*, 60–61; and *Compton's Interactive Encyclopedia*.

12. After one day of war, the Far East Air Force had been eliminated as an effective fighting force. The U.S. Air Corps forces had been cut in half in less than 24 hours. Of the modern combat aircraft, only 17 of the original 35 B-17s remained. Fifty-three P-40s and three P-35s had been destroyed, and an additional 25 or 30 miscellaneous aircraft (B-10s, B-18s, and observation planes) were lost. In addition, many of the planes listed as operational were heavily damaged. The installations at both Clark Airfield and Iba were either burned out or badly hit. Total casualties for the day were 80 killed and 150 wounded. The total cost to the Japanese was seven fighters.

The Japanese Type O aircraft, or "Zero" known by Americans, made by Mitsubishi, was the pride and joy of the Nippon naval air arm. This fighter could reach speeds of 300 miles per hour and, reportedly, "maneuver like a swallow." In China it flew rings around enemy planes, knocking down Chinese aircraft with ease with its dual machine gun capability and double 20mm weapons systems. See Daws, *Prisoners of the Japanese*, 95; Morton, *The Fall of the Philippines*, 88; and Prange, *At Dawn We Slept*, 195.

13. Most likely the Fort Stotsenburg chaplain, Frederick B. "Ted" Howden, who died in captivity in early 1943. This proves the point that memoirs are merely just that—how well a person can remember what happened. Although Colonel

Alexander wrote this memoir in 1949, there is always the possibility that errors exist in what he was able to recall.

14. Colonel Alexander's son contracted polio as a little boy and had to have surgery to correct a leg affected by the crippling disease. His first operation on June 9, 1941, was five days before his ninth birthday and just three weeks after Lu and Sammy departed for the states. Sammy's illness rested heavily on Alexander's mind in the months preceding the war and throughout his captivity. See Alexander's letter dated June 4, 1941.

15. Joe E. Brown was an American comedian (1893–1973). Dr. Harold "Brick" Mueller (California 1918–22) is a member of the College Football Hall of Fame. See Grun, *The Timetables of History*, 481, 483, 575.

16. "Bull Gang" was a term used during this era to refer to any group that worked extraordinarily hard.

17. Official records claim that Captain Kelly departed on December 10, 1941, at 9:30 A.M. with only three 600-pound bombs. When he was unable to find a carrier, Kelly decided to attack what he thought was a large battleship, later presumed to be the *Haruna*. Of the three bombs, one is supposed to have been a direct hit; two, near misses. As the B-17 flew away, the vessel appeared to have stopped, with black smoke rising in a heavy cloud above it. On the return to base, the plane was jumped by two enemy fighters and shot down. Apparently, Kelly's plane was hit by Japanese ace Saburo Sakai. All of the crew except Kelly bailed out safely. See Morton, *The Fall of the Philippines*, 105.

18. The Japanese Scheme of Operations in the Philippines Campaign called for simultaneous air attacks starting on December 9, 1941, against American aircraft and installations. While the air attacks were in progress, advance army and navy units were to land on Bataan Island, north of Luzon; at three places on Luzon—Aparri, Vigan, and Legaspi; and at Davao in Mindanao. See Morton, *The Fall of the Philippines*, 67; and Young, *The Battle for Bataan*, 241.

19. Aparri (Colonel Alexander spells it Apari in the original manuscript) was a Japanese-maintained trading post in Northern Luzon. Alexander has mistaken the name of what battleship Kelly reportedly sunk; the battleship in the myth is actually the *Haruna*. The Japanese battleship *Kongo* took part in the bombing at Guadalcanal in October 1942, then on November 21, 1942, the U.S. submarine *Sealion* sunk the *Kongo* in the waters northeast of Formosa. See Young, *The World Almanac Book of World War II*, 175, 309, 418.

20. The southern Luzon region had one railroad, controlled totally by the Philippines until the Japanese siege, that extended from Dagupan on the Lingayen Gulf south to Manila and then southeast to Daraga. By Christmas Day 1941 not a single locomotive was operational on the Manila Railroad in Luzon, which was a heavy blow for the Americans, for that single line constituted the chief artery for evacuating stocks from advance depots and combat areas into

the Bataan Peninsula. See Morton, *The Fall of the Philippines*, 109; and Stauffer, *The Quartermaster Corps*, 11.

21. While the Americans watched the skies, thousands of Japanese soldiers poured ashore in Northern Luzon near Aparri and Vigan on December 9 and 10 against a feeble 11th Division (PA). The 48th Infantry reinforced with tanks made up the main Japanese landing at Lingayen on the 22nd. The 71st Division (PA) and the 11th Division (PA) could neither repel the landings nor pin the enemy on the beaches as outlined in USAFFE's defense plan. The 48th Infantry quickly marched south and conducted a linkup with those forces moving from the north and pushed south, reaching San Fernando on the west coast soon thereafter, and then prepared for the offensive on Manila. In the south, the 16th Division voyaged to Lamon Bay, east of Manila. The enemy also assaulted ashore in Davao on the Island of Mindinao and at Legaspi on the southeastern most shore of Luzon. The American naval base at Cavite suffered heavy damage as Japanese bombers hit the U.S. Destroyer *Peary*; Submarines *Seadragon* and *Sealion*, and Minesweeper *Bittern*. The Japanese axis of advance was toward Manila and the heart of Luzon, the Bataan Peninsula, where the American and Philippine armies fought their way rearward. See Bailey, *Philippine Islands*, 11, 14; Hannings, *A Portrait of the Stars and Stripes*, 70–72, 75; Martin, *Brothers From Bataan*, 64; and Morton, *The Fall of the Philippines*, 98–99, 138.

22. The P-40 Kittyhawk manufactured by the Curtiss-Wright Corporation (in its earliest versions) enjoyed speeds of 345 mph and a rate of climb of 2,650 feet per minute. Although a more effective engine, armor protection, and self-sealing fuel tanks had been added to the aircraft, the P-40 could not compete on equal terms with either the Spitfire or the Luftwaffe's Bf-109, so it was relegated to ground support. Nevertheless, the U.S. Army did receive the later marks of the P-40 in quantity (calling them Warhawks) and it undoubtedly helped to sustain American fighter strength during the early months of the war. See Morton, *The Fall of the Philippines*, 42; and Young, *The World Almanac Book of World War II*, 464.

23. Eighty-eight women constituted the U.S. Army Nurse Corps units in the Philippines. They were stationed at various places on the islands including Sternberg Hospital in Manila, Fort McKinley, Fort Stotsenburg, Camp John Hay, and on Corregidor. They had suffered no casualties during the war, and most who were not evacuated to Australia were detained in the Santo Tomas Prison after the surrender. See Hartendorp, *The Japanese Occupation of the Philippines* vol. 1, 174.

24. Alexander still held the rank of major at this point in the war. According to his official military records he didn't receive promotion to lieutenant colonel until September 15, 1941.

25. On December 10, 1941, Japanese planes attacked the Manila Bay area, specifically Nichols and Nielson Fields. They also attacked Del Carmen Field near

Clark and focused their efforts on Cavite. As at Clark, the damage at the rest of these airfields was severe. There were no raids on the eleventh due to bad weather, but on the twelfth and thirteenth the Japanese attacked in force. Hundreds of Japanese army and navy planes struck Iba, Clark Field, and Cavite between 11:30 A.M. and 12:00 P.M. on December 12. The next day 200 Japanese planes struck Clark Field at 11:00 P.M. At about the same time on the thirteenth, Del Carmen, Baguio, and Tarlac were hit. The defense of Clark at this time, as it had been on the ninth, was feeble. About 500 men of Col. Lester Maitland's 200th Coast Artillery Corps Anti-Aircraft Regiment had been moved to Manila on the ninth and redesignated the 515th. Note: The 200th CAC experienced difficulty in defending any and all air attacks because its three-inch ammunition, the most recent of which was manufactured in 1932, had a high percentage of duds and most of the fuses were badly corroded. One observer noted that only one of every six shells fired actually exploded. Therefore, what little anti-aircraft defense Clark had at this time was ineffective. See Morton, *The Fall of the Philippines*, 86–96.

26. Maj. Edward Granade and his wife were good friends of the Alexanders' at Fort Stotsenburg. Granade was a medical doctor assigned to the post. See Alexander's letters dated May 18, June 5, and June 29, 1941.

27. Lt. Col. Wallace E. "Pop" Durst was the post quartermaster at Fort Stotsenburg. Many officers were rotated out of the theater during the summer of 1941. Durst was one who speculated about being sent home in August 1941. Apparently that didn't occur since Durst was there during the war. However, according to Alexander's Summary of Commissioned Service Since 1 January 1937, Alexander worked as the assistant post quartermaster until the latter third of 1941 when he became the quartermaster, taking Durst's position. See letter dated June 24, 1941, and Summary of Commissioned Service Since 1 January 1937, 012414.

28. Pat is believed to be Capt. Pat Byrne, who was with Alexander at Cabanatuan and on the *Oryoko Maru* prison ship. See Chunn, *Of Rice and Men*, 173, 176 and Lawton, *Some Survived*, 263.

29. The actions of bravery in removing the bomb from the warehouse is what earned Alexander the Silver Star.

30. On December 24, 1941, General MacArthur's headquarters ordered the evacuation of Fort Stotsenburg and the destruction of 300,000 gallons of gasoline and large amounts of high-octane fuel. In addition to the fuel, Stotsenburg's stocks included 8,000 pounds of fresh beef, about 100,000 components of dry rations, large supplies of clothing, and air corps ammunition and equipment. When the fort was abandoned, all supplies were shipped to Bataan or issued to troops in the Stotsenburg area. Therefore, nothing was left intact, contrary to much criticism and bitterness by numerous officers who blamed the Quartermaster Corps for their failure in adequately supplying the forces on Bataan.

According to Alexander, "This bitterness continued on into the prison camp and no doubt many survivors believed they were starved on Bataan because of the failure of the QMC to perform its duties properly." The truth is that the QMC was not responsible for the lack of supplies. The chaotic conditions of the battle for Bataan, with the decision made by the higher military authority to discard War Plan ORANGE and fight it out on the beaches, therefore compelling the QMC to disperse food stocks as well as other supplies throughout Luzon, and the need to supply a 60,000-man Philippine Army as well as the 20,000 Regular Army forces, contributed largely to the Quartermaster Corps' inability to logistically supply the force. See Morton, *The Fall of the Philippines*, 179; and Stauffer, *The Quartermaster Corps* vol 2, part 3, 33–34.

31. Brig. Gen. Allen C. McBride, MacArthur's deputy for the Philippine Department. The tip of Bataan south of the Mariveles Mountains was designated the Service Command Area.

32. Alexander was initially assigned as an adviser to the 1st Philippine Constabulary Regiment, which was under operational control of Selleck's 71st Division in the Service Command Area.

33. The commander of the 1st Philippine Constabulary Regiment was Lt. Col. Mariano Castaneda. See Baclagon, *Philippine Campaigns*, 188.

34. Because of censorship during the late 1940s the division to which Colonel Alexander was referring to was omitted from the original manuscript. The original manuscript simply says the "—st Div." It is clear from his records that the division he is indicating here is the 71st Division (PA). The 71st Division was officially given the mission to defend the west side of the Service Command Area of the peninsula. The ground on this side of the peninsula is thickly forested almost to the shore line, where foothills of the central range end in abrupt cliffs. Sharp points of land extend from the solid, curved, dark shore line to form small bays all along the shore. To defend the shore in this area was indeed a formidable task and most of the troop units were taken from Major General Selleck's command. Therefore, the skeleton 71st Division consisted of service troops and one battalion of artillery (two 75mm guns plus one battery of 2.95-inch guns). In addition to these troops, Selleck was given the 1st Constabulary Regiment from the 2nd Division (PA), which had responsibility for the defense of the eastern portion of the Service Command Area. Along with the Philippine Regiment came five grounded Air Force pursuit squadrons. See Morton, *The Fall of the Philippines*, 296–99.

35. By January 22, 1942, Selleck had organized his defense of the coast by incorporating a number of grounded U.S. air crews. The northernmost portion of his sector was defended by 200 men of the 17th Pursuit Squadron. Below it, down to the Anyasan River, was the 1st Battalion of the 1st Constabulary. The 34th Pursuit Squadron, with 16 officers and 220 men, occupied the next sector, which included Quinauan Point. Following in order from north to

south were the Constabulary's 2nd Battalion, the 3rd Pursuit Squadron, and then a naval battalion from Mariveles. The 3rd Battalion of the Constabulary Regiment and the 20th and 21st Pursuit Squadrons were held in reserve. Rounding out the defense of Quinauan Point and the area surrounding it were elements of the 803rd (U.S.) Engineers. These units were obviously not trained to defend the shores. They weren't equipped for the fight either. Some units had .30-caliber World War I machine guns; others had air corps .50 calibers. Lt. Col. William E. Dyess later wrote that "in a group of 220 men there were only three bayonets, but, that was all right because only three . . . men knew anything about using them." See Dyess, *The Dyess Story*, 39, 41; Morton, *The Fall of the Philippines*, 299; and Young, *The Battle for Bataan*, 108.

36. The G3 is the operations officer on the general staff responsible for making the combat plans for the division.

37. A major part of Plan Four consisted of dispatching Alexander with the 3rd Battalion, 1st Philippine Constabulary to thwart any enemy landing. The 3rd Battalion, 1st Philippine Constabulary was commanded by Capt. Apolinar Fajardo. Given the go-ahead by Selleck, Alexander and his forces attacked at 10:00 A.M. on the twenty-third, running into a now dug-in enemy halted 600 yards from the tip of the 1,000-yard-long Quinauan Point. See Morton, *The Fall of the Philippines*, 281, 300–302; and Quirino, *Filipinos at War*, 211.

38. The reserve for this sector consisted of the 1st Battalion, 1st Philippine Constabulary Regiment, the 20th Pursuit Squadron, the 21st Pursuit Squadron, and the Philippine Army Air Corps Battalion (PAAC). Alexander was assisting the reserve unit, the 1st Battalion, 1st (PC) Regiment when he was wounded. See Quirino, *Filipinos at War*, 211; and Young, *The Battle of Bataan*, 101.

39. A Q-boat is a British-built, Philippine-owned, PT-type (motor-torpedo) boat. The defense of the coast line—which was longer than that of the United States—fell to the Phillipine Army's Off Shore Patrol. Thirty-six Q-boats, which were 65 feet long, with a 13-foot beam, three 12-cylinder engines, and a speed of 41 knots, were to be patrolling the shores under the original plan to defend the coast. Armament consisted of two torpedo tubes, depth charges, and light anti-aircraft guns. But by early November 1941 only six boats had been allocated to the fleet defending the islands. See Morton, *The Fall of the Philippines*, 11, 47; and Young, *The Battle of Bataan*, 11.

40. The highway Alexander is referring to is the West Road, just over a mile from Quinauan Point. See Young, *The Battle of Bataan*, 15.

41. The Navy Bluejackets are the grounded naval servicemen from the 16th Naval District at Mariveles. These men formed the Naval Battalion under the command of Commander Frank Bridget. These 120 Marines and 480 shipless sailors were responsible for coastal and anti-aircraft security of the immediate Mariveles area, but they found themselves thwarting the Japanese landings at

several locations north, to include Quinauan Point. See Young, *The Battle of Bataan*, 13.

42. The reserve battalion, the 1st Battalion, 1st Philippine Constabulary Regiment was commanded by Capt. Diosdado Rodriguez. See Baclagon, *Philippine Campaigns*, 188.

43. The unit at Quinauan was actually two-thirds of Lt. Col. Nariyoshi Tsunehiro's 2nd Battalion, 20th Infantry.

44. Alexander surmised that he was facing a reinforced battalion and requested tanks, artillery, and more infantry. Instead he was authorized two Bren gun carriers, sent in lieu of the tanks; also dispatched were elements of the 21st Pursuit Squadron, a company of constabulary troops, and a provisional company formed from Selleck's 71st Division headquarters company. See Morton, *The Fall of the Philippines*, 304.

45. Maj. Gen. Allen C. McBride, commanding general of the Service Command, relieved Maj. Gen. Clyde Selleck as the division commander of the 71st on January 23, 1942, and replaced him with Colonel Clinton A. Pierce, commander of the 26th Cavalry, which was located just north of Bagac. Pierce was promoted to brigadier general six days later. Within 24 hours of the first shot at Quinauan Point, Selleck had his command yanked from him and later he would lose his general's star. After the war, however, a special War Department Board of Officers investigation restored Selleck to the rank of brigadier general retroactive to January 25, 1942. See Morton, *The Fall of the Philippines*, 305 and Young, *The Battle of Bataan*, 109, 111.

46. Most likely Lt. Comdr. Carey M. Smith, a naval surgeon. See Fortier, *The Life of a POW under the Japanese*, 145; and Young, *The Battle of Bataan*, 244.

47. A British Bren Gun Carrier is a four-ton Mark I Bren Carrier. The tank is manned by three men and is able to reach speeds of 29.5 miles per hour. Its operational range was 155 miles without refueling and its armament was one 7.7mm Bren gun, an automatic rifle. See Funcken, *Arms and Uniforms: The Second World War* part 2, 26.

48. Maj. Pelagio Cruz, commanding officer of the Provisional Philippine Army Air Corps (PAAC), was awarded the Silver Star during that battle, as the citation reads, through a "personal display of courage and leadership" while under fire. Time and time again, according to the citation, "despite heavy machine gun fire, he crawled forward to where his foremost riflemen were, thus inspiring leadership." See Young, *The Battle of Bataan*, 126.

Chapter 6: Heroism and Convalescence

1. This is in reference to the difficulty the troops had in traversing the terrain in the area. Col. Samuel C. Grashio of the USAF remembered that "the entire area was covered with the dense forest and thick undergrowth that made all

movement difficult and dangerous. Even without enemy opposition the troops could move through the jungle only with great difficulty, cutting away vines and creepers that caught at their legs and stung their faces and bodies." See Grashio, *Return to Freedom*, 17; and Morton, *The Fall of the Philippines*, 309.

2. Colonel A. Willoughby (Alexander calls him General in the original manuscript) was eventually promoted to major general at the end of the war. Willoughby was the intelligence officer for MacArthur's USAFFE. Ted is most likely Lt. Col. Theodore Kalakuka (USMA 1927) from the USAFFE Quartermaster Section. Kalakuka, a friend of Alexander's from Stotsenburg, later died of malaria on October 30, 1942, while working with the Japanese to secure the surrender of the guerrilla underground forces. See Morton, *The Fall of the Philippines*, 574; *The Wainwright Papers*, 179; and Alexander's letter dated June 1, 1941.

3. Hospital No. 2 was located about three miles south and west of Cabcaben, in the bamboo thickets and jungle along the Real River. See Morton, *The Fall of the Philippines*, 381.

4. Jim was Dr. Jim McClosky, a doctor stationed with Alexander at Fort Stotsenburg. See Alexander's letter dated August 13, 1941, and letter from Sara Spindle to the editor dated June 8, 1995.

5. Capt. Robert Lewis (later major). He survived the war, including the Death March, Japanese prison camps, labor details, and the hell ships. See Jacobs, *Blood Brothers*, 7.

6. "Chick" is Lt. Col. Halstead C. Fowler (USMA 1920), commander of the 71st Field Artillery. See Morton, *The Fall of the Philippines*, 134, 250; Young, *The Battle of Bataan*, 81; and *1994 Register of Graduates*, 180.

7. Tagalog is the official Filipino language (along with English) spoken by the Filipino Army during this period. See *The Cambridge Factfinder*, 448.

8. The initial attack on the Mauban-Abubay line began in the II Corps sector when on January 9, 1942, the Japanese attacked the II Corps with two regiments of infantry, tanks, and artillery. See Bailey, *Philippine Islands*, 16–18; and Yenne, *Black '41*, 90–91.

9. Maj. Alva R. Fitch (USMA 1930). Fitch, a close friend of Alexander's, survived the Death March and was awarded the Distinguished Service Cross, the Silver Star, the Bronze Star, and the Purple Heart during his tour in the Philippines. See *1994 Register of Graduates*, 212.

10. Col. Kearie L. Berry (promoted later to brigadier general) was commander of the 3rd Infantry and was also given command of the 1st Infantry (PA) on January 15, 1942, becoming what Colonel Alexander is calling the force commander. By January 24, 1942, Berry's forces on the front line of the I Corps sector were holding the front line of troops while the II Corps pulled back. Effects of the enemy's hold on almost the entire back side of Mauban ridge, coupled with a desperate shortage of food and ammunition, led Berry, without consulting

General Wainwright, to order the line abandoned that night. By noon on the twenty-fifth Berry's forces had reached Bagac, where by coincidence he ran into Wainwright. Ironically, the corps commander was on his way to order Berry to do the very thing he had just done. A little hesitant to face the general for what he might say about withdrawing without orders, Berry, standing barefoot with a 1903 Springfield slung over his shoulder, saluted. "Berry," said Wainwright, reaching out to shake hands, "I'm damn glad to see you." Berry relaxed and Wainwright recommended Berry for the Distinguished Service Cross later that same day. See Morton, *The Fall of the Philippines*, 280; and Young, *The Battle of Bataan*, 85–86.

11. Capt. Edward Woolery (24th Pursuit Squadron), one of the few pursuit squadron pilots who flew P-40 missions against the enemy in Bataan and Mindoro after most of the aircraft and airfields were destroyed at the beginning of the war. He was one of the seven air corps officers to fly combat missions since the onset of the battle of Bataan, targeting Nichols and Nielson Fields on January 26, 1942. On February 2, 1942, Woolery was killed in a mysterious mid-air explosion during a bombing run over the East Road on Bataan. See Young, *The Battle of Bataan*, 75, 115, 143–44.

12. The official citation, dated January 28, 1942, awarding Alexander the Distinguished Service Cross reads:

> By direction of the President, under the provisions of the Act of Congress approved July 9, 1918 (Bul. No. 43, W.D. 1918), the Distinguished Service Cross is awarded by the Commanding General, United States Army Forces in the Far East, for extraordinary heroism in action to the following named officers of the United States Army Forces in the Far East:
>
> IRVIN ALEXANDER, (0-12414), Lieutenant Colonel, (Infantry), Quartermaster Corps. For extraordinary heroism in action near Agloloma [sic] Bay, Bataan, Philippine Islands, on January 24, 1942. During an attack to expel an enemy landing party near Agloloma [sic] Bay, Lieutenant Colonel Alexander, then on duty with the 1st Regiment, Philippine Constabulary, learning that a company commander had been wounded and that the company was without an officer, went forward to assume command in person. On arrival, he found that the unit disorganized, with stragglers beginning to drift back. He reorganized the unit, and by setting a personal example of courage, pushed the company forward in the face of heavy fire to within thirty-five yards of the enemy position. In spite of the concentration of the heaviest fire in his vicinity, he continued to expose himself, encouraging and steadying his men, although severely wounded in the hand and struck in the chest, continuing to display courageous leadership until he collapsed from shock and fatigue.

See General Orders No. 16, Headquarters: United States Army Forces in the Far East, January 28, 1942.

13. The Voice of Freedom radio broadcast came from Corregidor, broadcasting reports throughout Southeast Asia three times a day on the status of the battles in the Philippines and elsewhere. Col. Carlos Romulo of the Philippines was the newscaster for the Voice of Freedom station. One of the most notable messages sent was Brig. Gen. Lewis C. Beebe's announcement addressed to General Homma offering General Wainwright's surrender of forces on May 6, 1942. See Hatendorp, *The Japanese Occupation of the Philippines* vol. 1, 54; and Morton, *The Fall of the Philippines*, 385, 544, 564.

14. The Rock is the name the troops in the Philippines gave to Corregidor. The tunnels Colonel Alexander is referring to are part of the extensive tunnel system dug on the island to protect the forces from artillery that came in constantly during the battle.

15. The unit of scouts was the 3rd Battalion, 45th Infantry (PS) commanded by Maj. Dudley Strickler (USMA 1927). For four days, despite the addition of a company of 57th Infantry troops, the tough scouts could only account for gains of a little more than 40 yards. The entire 900-yard-wide patch of ground at Quinauan Point had become a living hell during this battle. Young describes, "the putrid stench of rotting jungle and decaying flesh permeated the stifling blanket of humid air that hung over it. Bodies of dead enemy snipers dangling grotesquely from the trees . . . were everywhere." Seeing that the casualty rate was a staggering 50 percent, General MacArthur moved the 192nd Tank Battalion into the fray. This would be the first time in World War II for close coordination between American tanks and infantry in jungle warfare. On the last day of the battle, seven days after committing his forces, Strickler's body was found well inside the enemy position. He had been shot in the head. Strickler was awarded two Distinguished Service Crosses during the battle of Bataan. See Young, *The Battle of Bataan*, 127–28, 130; and *1994 Register of Graduates*, 201.

16. Capt. Ernest L. Brown of the 57th Infantry wrote of the scouts, "They were well-known to the rest of the United States Army for their proficiency in marksmanship and their love of soldiering. Court-martials were rare and insubordination unheard of. Their standard of discipline was among the highest in the army. Their willingness and immediate obedience to orders provided inspiration to their American officers in combat." Lt. Col. Adrianus Van Oosten of the 45th Infantry wrote that just the "knowledge that the Scouts were fighting in the same action" gave inspiration to the Philippine troops. The only all-Philippine Scout combat regiment not attached to the Philippine Division was the 26th Cavalry. This autonomy alone gave the 26th its distinction among the other units in the Philippine Islands. See Young, *The Battle of Bataan*, 4, 6.

17. To the rear of the constabulary was Company A of the U.S. 803rd Aviation Engineer Battalion, which had been working on widening the West Road through the Quinauan area. The battalion also had the additional responsibility of anchoring the right flank of front line of troops engaged with the Japanese as they landed. The engineers suffered 50 percent casualties by January 24, 1942, and less than a week later what was left of the company was withdrawn and sent to Corregidor for the duration of the battle. See Young, *The Battle of Bataan*, 126, 129.

18. Charles Pollard Jones (USMA 1919), an artillery officer stationed in the Philippines. See *1994 Register of Graduates*.

19. Brig. Gen. James R. N. Weaver (USMA 1911) established the Provisional Tank Group consisting of the 192nd and 194th Tank Battalions and the 17th Ordnance Company (Armored). Shortly after the beginning of the war, Weaver's group was augmented with 40 Bren gun carriers. Weaver was awarded the Distinguished Service Cross, the Silver Star, and the Bronze Star for his actions in the battle and as a POW for nearly four years. See Morton, *The Fall of the Philippines*, 33, 121; and *1990 Register of Graduates*, 340. For a good small unit history of what it was like to be part of the Provisional Tank Group and for a concise history and task organization of the group refer to Dale R. Dopkins's self-published *The Janesville 99*.

20. The identity of Sergeant Castro is unknown.

21. The vice president of the Philippines at the time of the Japanese invasion. He and his family accompanied President Quezon on February 20, 1942, aboard the USS *Swordfish* to Del Monte Airfield in Mindanao. Quezon and his party eventually left Mindanao via aircraft for their exile in San Jose, Panay, in the Visayan Islands, some 160 miles away. President Quezon died on August 1, 1944, of tuberculosis and was replaced by Osmena. On October 23, 1945, MacArthur restored the Philippine Commonwealth Civil Government in Tacloban, turning over the leadership of the Islands once again to the Philippines; this time to Osmena. See Hannings, *A Portrait of the Stars and Stripes* vol. 2, 410, 481; and Morrison, *The Rising Sun in the Pacific*, 203.

Chapter 7: Overtures to the End of Battle

1. Most likely Col. Edmund J. Lilly, the commander of the 57th Infantry (PA) from January 29, 1942, until the surrender. See Olson, *Anywhere-Anytime*, 208.

2. The presence of nearly 25,000 refugees on Bataan, mostly located in the three camps along the Real River above Cabcaben, added greatly to the already critical supply problem. Although many refugees volunteered to work for the military, others feared Japanese repercussions and instead opted for the security of the camps. This fear led to a large shortage of labor required by the Fil-American forces to maintain its quartermaster and engineering efforts. See Young, *The Battle of Bataan*, 349–50.

3. Although the first battle for Longoskawayan and Quinauan Points was over, the Japanese renewed their actions and the "Battle of the Points" continued. A company of 200 men from the 1st Battalion, 20th Infantry came ashore at Silaiim Point on January 27, 1942, a mile short of Quinauan Point. The Japanese thought they had landed at Quinauan and mistakenly expected to augment Tsuneyhiro's forces already ashore. Opposing the Japanese landing was the 17th Pursuit Squadron and the 3rd Battalion of the Philippine Constabulary. The Filipinos, at word of the Japanese landing, left their positions in a hurry. The 17th Squadron gallantly tried to repel the Japanese on their own with ground-mounted .50-caliber machine guns taken from P-40 aircraft, but the U.S. airmen were repelled the next day. By daylight on the thirtieth, the 3rd Battalion had returned to the fight, and Colonel Pierce augmented the two battalions with the 2nd Battalion, 45th Infantry, and a battalion from the 12th Infantry of the Philippine Army's 11th Division. However, during the Fil-American counterattack, the Philippine Scout 88th Field Artillery dropped artillery mistakenly on friendly forces moving forward. That very night Brigadier General Pierce, who had just pinned on his general's star, ordered the 57th Infantry (less the 2nd Battalion) to the Silaiim area. By now the Allies outnumbered their Japanese foes five to one, but neither the enemy strength nor its exact location was known. Nonetheless, the addition of the 57th couldn't have been timelier, for on the night of January 31, 1942, the Japanese conducted another successful landing, tripling the size of its existing force. By February 1, 1942, the Americans were again flying P-40 missions against the Japanese along the west coast with limited success. The Japanese commander, in an attempt to save face, ordered another landing at Quinauan. The reinforcements again missed Quinauan, landing at Silaiim, reinforcing the 1st Battalion, 20th Infantry with the remainder of its forces on February 2, 1942. Ensuing attacks on the invaders showed few positive results the next day. Facing this larger force, the Fil-Americans beefed up their infantry forces with two platoons from the 192nd Armor Battalion. By the afternoon of February 6, 1942, the situation for the Japanese was fast becoming desperate. The Japanese commander dispatched a message concluding that his battalion, under attack by both tanks and artillery, was "about to die gloriously." This led the 16th Division commander, Gen. Sasumu Morioka, to order as many boats as possible to rescue the 1st Battalion on February 7, 1942. These operations were futile, and by February 11, 1942, reports had reached Brigadier General Pierce that the points had been secured. The final battle came on the thirteenth when Lieutenant Colonel Lilly's 3rd Battalion, 57th Infantry assisted the 2nd Battalion, 45th Infantry in dislodging the final Japanese siege. By 3:00 P.M.. on February 13, 1942, the scouts had the beach secured. For the first time in more than three weeks, the entire coast of Bataan, from Longoskawayan to Saysain Points, was free of enemy threat. See Young, *The Battle of Bataan*, 134–41, 145–46, 150–54, 158–63.

4. Capt. Raymond "Spud" Sloan was the commander of the 17th Pursuit Squadron. He was killed on February 12, 1942, while pushing the Japanese off Silaiim Point. It is said that his last words were, "A $10,000 pilot shot to hell in the infantry." See Young, *The Battle of Bataan*, 161–62.

5. Charles is Lt. Col. Charles S. Lawrence, a former instructor in the Quartermaster Subsistence School at Chicago and now the commander of Tarlac Depot. Colonel McConnell is Alva E. McConnell, commander of the Philippine Quartermaster Depot. See Morton, *The Fall of the Philippines*, 254, 256; Stauffer, *The Quartermaster Corps*, 10; and Wainwright, *General Wainwright's Story*, 203.

6. The ballad Colonel Alexander is speaking of is a spoof of General MacArthur's departure from the Filipino mainland as soon as the hostilities began.

7. Brig. Gen. Hugh J. Casey (USMA 1918) joined MacArthur's staff in 1937 as an engineer adviser. See Morton, *The Fall of the Philippines*, 10; Young, *The Battle of Bataan*, 337–39; and *1994 Register of Graduates*, 170.

8. The subject of MacArthur's evacuation from the Philippines was first raised on February 2, 1942, when General Marshall outlined two possibilities for MacArthur. The first was his transfer to Mindanao where he would wait out the battle on Bataan and control the forces from the southern island. The second, which he eventually was ordered to do, was to go directly to Australia and resume command of all army forces in the Far East. The order came from President Roosevelt on March 11, 1942, for MacArthur to leave the Philippines. Therefore, on March 12, as darkness fell, MacArthur and his party embarked from Corregidor. They reached the north shore of Mindanao on March 14 and from there flew to Australia. As MacArthur departed for Australia he made the now-famous statement, "I shall return." See Kerr, *Surrender and Survival*, 51; and Morton, *The Fall of the Philippines*, 353–54, 359–60.

9. Hospital No. 1 was located at Limay until January 28, 1942. Following the general withdrawal of forces to positions on the Bagac-Orion Line, Hospital No. 1 was moved down the Mariveles Road past the turnoff to Hospital No. 2, to an area known as Little Baguio. Unlike Hospital No. 2, which had only a vegetative canopy for overhead cover, Hospital No. 1 was able to move into barracks and sheds formerly occupied by prewar motor-pool units. See Young, *The Battle of Bataan*, 345.

10. Col. Wendell Fertig was the chief Bataan construction engineer. On October 7, 1942, he officially assumed command of the Mindinao-Sulu Force, a guerrilla resistance movement. See Baclagon, *Philippine Campaigns*, 281–82; and Young, *The Battle of Bataan*, 338.

11. Wainwright's elevation to the highest command in the Philippines left vacant the post of commander of the Luzon Force on March 21, 1942. Consequently, King became the commander of I and II Corps on the peninsula. It was a hollow honor for King, however, since the Fil-American defense had deteriorated

considerably and the advent of an American surrender was likely at the time of King's assumption of command. See Morton, *The Fall of the Philippines*, 365.

12. Supplies were transported from Mindanao and Cebu throughout the siege. Located on Cebu was the Cebu Advance Depot, the central collection point for supplies shipped to Bataan and Corregidor. See Morton, *The Fall of the Philippines*, 395–96; and Stauffer, *The Quartermaster Corps*, 20.

13. On the morning of March 23, 1942, General Homma called a meeting of his subordinate commanders in his headquarters at San Fernando. Here plans for a D-day were unveiled and the date, April 3, 1942, was announced. The 4th Division was the main effort assaulting the front near Mount Samat. Supporting the 4th was the 65th Brigade. On the left flank of the assault would be the 21st Division, and the 16th Division was given the mission of making a feint attack in front of I Corps. Beginning on March 24, 1942, the 22nd Air Brigade, aided by naval aircraft, would begin an intensive air assault in concert with a massive artillery barrage. King apparently saw this pause to plan for the assault as an opportune time to counterattack; unfortunately the assets to conduct an effective offensive action did not exist for the Allies. See Morton, *The Fall of the Philippines*, 416; and Young, *The Battle of Bataan*, 232.

14. By January 7, 1942, Japanese had lost about 2,000 soldiers since their first landing (627 KIA, 1,282 WIA, and 7 MIA). By March 1, 1942, the Japanese casualties totaled 2,700 killed and 4,000 wounded. Between 10,000 and 12,000 Japanese were down with malaria, beriberi, dysentery, or other tropical diseases. See Morton, *The Fall of the Philippines*, 230, 350, 412.

15. A World War I Long Tom Gun is a 75mm artillery tube. Long Tom was originally a nickname for the British 60-pounder gun and later applied by the western forces to any long-barreled gun. See Griffith, *The Great War*, 216; and Morton, *The Fall of the Philippines*, 29.

16. On and after December 23, 1941, shipments from Manila included approximately 750,00 pounds of canned milk, 20,000 pounds of vegetables, 40,000 gallons of gasoline and 60,000 gallons of lubrication and grease. The movement of supplies to Bataan was difficult, largely because of transportation problems, the brief period of time in which to accomplish the tasks, and the size of the shipments. The only land route to Bataan was the one being used by the retreating troops. There was no time to evacuate the depots in northern Luzon and scarcely time enough to get out part of the reserves from Forts McKinley and Stotsenburg. See Morton, *The Fall of the Philippines*, 254–55.

17. The shortage of rations during the early days of the battle proved to be even more serious than expected, and from the start the scarcity of food was the most alarming fact in the situation for the 80,000 Allied troops on Bataan. The transfer of rice to Bataan proved difficult because of Commonwealth regulations, which stipulated that neither rice nor sugar could be removed from one

province to another. So serious was the shortage of food after the first few weeks on Bataan that the search for food assumed more importance than the presence of the enemy to the front. Every man became a hunter, and the "hunter's" rifle shots could be heard at all hours far from the lines. See Morton, *The Fall of the Philippines*, 256–57.

18. In a report written for Quartermaster Report of Operations titled "Supply Problems," Alexander wrote that "any carabao which was encountered in the jungle was classed as wild and neither his ancestry nor his ownership was investigated. The wild game was not too numerous and it was very shy so that only the cunning and lucky hunters were successful in bringing in meat." See Morton, *The Fall of the Philippines*, 257–58.

19. The commanding officer of Tarlac, Lt. Col. Charles S. Lawrence, planned the confiscation of 2,000 cases of canned fish and corned beef and sizable quantities of clothing, all of which were held in the warehouses of Japanese firms. USAFFE disapproved the plan, however, and informed Lawrence that he would be court-martialed if he took the goods. These supplies were later destroyed during operations. See Morton, *The Fall of the Philippines*, 256; and Stauffer, *The Quartermaster Corps*, 9.

20. In fact, during the return to the Philippines by the Americans, General MacArthur was viewed as an immortal savior. Many believed that many of the actions MacArthur took during the Japanese invasion, and after the fall of Bataan, resulted in the complete trust the Filipinos had for the general upon his return.

21. Alexander spells Zamboanga "Zamboango" in the original manuscript. Zamboanga is the most western peninsula on the island of Mindanao. See Morton, *The Fall of the Philippines*, 509.

22. The 31st Infantry Division was the only all-American fighting unit in the Philippines. At the end of the battle, the 31st found themselves strung out in the II Corps area with the 26th Cavalry on their left and the 57th (PA) Division on their right. See Young, *The Battle of Bataan*, 5, 281.

23. King Tomas was a tribal chief who lived near Stotsenburg on Mount Pinatubo. In the first week of the war he and a procession of his tribesmen brought General Wainwright the severed head of a downed Japanese pilot. See Schultz, *Hero of Bataan*, 87–88.

24. Willie's identity is unknown.

25. Col. James W. Duckworth, M.C., was the commander of Hospital No. 1. He had commanded the hospital in Fort McKinley and the 12th Medical Regiment prior to the war. During captivity, Duckworth was given credit for reducing the death rate of Filipino prisoners from 200 a day to one a day in a two-month time period. See Hartendorp, *The Japanese Occupation of the Philippines* vol. 1, 177; vol. 2, 592; and Olson, *O'Donnell*, 76.

26. On June 30, 1942, Hospital No. 1 was closed, and the officers were sent to Camp O'Donnell; the enlisted men were sent to Cabanatuan and Bilibid. See Hartendorp, *The Japanese Occupation of the Philippines* vol. 2, 592.

27. The expected Japanese attack began on April 3, 1942, after a sustained aerial and artillery bombardment. The strongest enemy push, spearheaded by the 4th Division and the 65th Brigade, was directed against Sector D on the II Corps's left flank, defended by Brig. Gen. Vincente Lim's 41st (PA) Division. The exhausted, malnourished, and dispirited defenders soon gave ground and the entire line began to crumble. In 36 hours the Japanese succeeded in breaching the American line. See Bailey, *Philippine Islands*, 20; and Young, *The Battle of Bataan*, 248.

28. In some sectors, propaganda leaflets were dropped nearly every day. Some had the picture of a Filipino who had been captured, sitting at a dinner table loaded with good things to eat with his wife holding a child in her arms while she waited on him. It said, "You too can enjoy this if you will come to the coconut grove with your rifle over your left shoulder and the barrel pointing down. This leaflet will be accepted as your ticket and any number can enter. You will be treated well." Another of the leaflets pictured a battleground after a battle, with dead men lying all around. A rifle with a bayonet attached was stuck in the ground with a helmet on top of the gun stock. It read, "That is what you will look like if you don't surrender by a certain time." One leaflet had a picture of a beautiful, blond woman. Its caption read, "You too can enjoy this if you will surrender." On March 19, 1942, the Japanese dropped from planes thousands of empty beer cans, to each of which was attached red and white ribbons to make spotting easier. In the cans were the demands, addressed to Lieutenant General Wainwright, saying, in part, "If you do not reply to this [order to surrender forces] by special messenger within three days we will feel free to act in any way at all." It was signed, "The Commanders in Chief, Imperial Japanese Army and Navy Forces in the Philippines." No reply was made by Wainwright or any other Fil-American official. See Coleman, *Bataan and Beyond*, 36; and Wainwright, *General Wainwright's Story*, 71.

29. The Japanese had concentrated a solid square mile of field pieces, spaced one gun every thirty yards, all booming at the Fil-Americans in front and abreast of Mount Samat. Here, "the most devastating concentration of fire seen during the Philippine Campaign" took place. Old-timers with the Americans paralleled the experience with those that lived through the Western Front in France during World War I. Directly in front of Mount Samat was the 21st Division (PA) and to its left was the 41st Division (PA). By sunset on April 3, 1942, the Japanese had forced no less than a two-square-mile salient into the Fil-American line on the southwest slope of Mount Samat. Only the 41st Infantry Regiment (of the three regiments in the division) of the 41st Division

remained intact. The fighting at this point was confined to the trails cutting through the area. Trail 29 led directly south up the center of a ridge dividing the Pantingan and Catmon Rivers. Trail 6 generally followed the steep eastern bank of the Catmon for about a mile and a half. At that point it split southeast from the river, following the lower contours of Samat for another mile, where it intersected Trail 429. Running predominantly east–west, Trail 429 linked Trail 6 with Trails 4 and 2 on the east, and 29 on the west, some three-quarters of a mile behind the front line of troops. See Young, *The Battle of Bataan*, 247, 251–52.

30. Col. John W. Irwin, the commander of the 31st (PA) Division. See Young, *The Battle of Bataan*, 448.

31. At 8:00 A.M. on April 3, 1942, the Japanese artillery opened up the heaviest concentration of fire on the 41st Division. It continued until 3:00 P.M. and then shifted toward other targets. When the enemy attacked, the 41st Infantry withdrew as soon as it grew dark, creating a gap between the 41st and 21st Divisions. On the fourth, the Japanese shifted its attack against the 21st, while more Japanese poured into the gap reaching the San Vicente River. On April 5 the 21st Division's line deteriorated. That same day, the 43rd Division was ordered to establish a road block on Trail 6, but to no avail. Wainwright dispatched all reserves to the II Corps area and on the morning of the sixth, the 31st, 45th Divisions, and the 33rd Infantry of the 33rd Division counterattacked northward. Realizing minimal success, what was left of the Fil-American forces established a hasty defense south of the San Vicente River.

In the I Corps sector, the Japanese 16th Division had been carrying out a feint against the 2nd Philippine Constabulary. The I Corps right flank held out, but by the morning of April 5, it had been considerably weakened by the transfer of troops to the II Corps sector. On the sixth the 4th Division overran the defenses at San Vincente. King then committed the 803rd Engineers and 26th Cavalry to II Corps and moved them up Trails 10 and 2. By the seventh, all forces in Sectors B and D had lost contact with II Corps. On the eighth, King ordered the withdrawal of II Corps to the Alangan River. By noon that day, the 4th Division crossed the Mamala River with the 65th Brigade and occupied Mount Limay and then continued south. All remaining Luzon Force units (the 57th Infantry, 26th Infantry, 14th Engineers, and 31st Infantry), as well as the 1st Philippine Constabulary and Provisional Coast Artillery Brigade, were moved to the high ground south of Bataan Air Field. But before the forces could organize an effective defense, they were attacked, rendering the II Corps combat ineffective.

To Luzon Force, the chief threat seemed to be developing along the East Road, which provided the enemy clear passage to Mariveles. On April 7, 1942, King ordered the beach defense forces that included Alexander's 1st

Constabulary Regiment to the front lines along the Mamala River. On the eighth General King attempted to form a line with the only organized unit remaining, the Provisional Coast Artillery Brigade (AA). At about 7:00 P.M. he directed Col. Charles G. Sage, the artillery brigade's commander, to destroy all his anti-aircraft guns except those which could be used by the infantry, and to form his men along the high ground north of Cabcaben. He then ordered Alexander's unit into position on the left of the brigade. It was evident to King, however, that II Corps had disintegrated and that there was no chance of the 1st Philippine Constabulary Regiment reaching Colonel Sage by daylight. Orders were then issued to have what was left of the 26th Cavalry to fall on the right of Sage's unit, but they never got the order and the artillerymen stood alone on the last remaining line of defense. At 11:30 P.M. on the eighth, Wainwright, following orders directed by General MacArthur himself, ordered King to launch a counterattack with Maj. Gen. Albert Jones's I Corps northward toward Olongapo. Jones replied that his corps was in the midst of a withdrawal to the Binuangan River. King withdrew the order, but Corregidor contacted Jones directly and ordered the counterattack. In his memoirs Wainwright glosses over this conversation as a miscommunication between commands. See Baclagon, *Phillipine Campaigns*, 196–100; Wainwright, *General Wainwright's Story*, 80–81; and Young, *The Battle of Bataan*, 447, 451–53.

32. Gen. George M. Parker, Jr., was now the II Corps commander. King's chief of staff was Col. Arnold J. Funk.

33. Brig. Gen. Lewis C. Beebe was Wainwright's chief of staff.

34. Wainwright was indeed hamstrung at this point. He knew of the grave situation on Bataan, but was being ordered by MacArthur to have the I Corps perform a feint in the form of an "ostentatious" artillery preparation, to commit the II Corps in a "sudden surprise attack" toward the Dinalupihan-Olongapo Road, and to seize Olongapo by simultaneous actions of both corps. "If successful," MacArthur explained, "the supplies seized at this base might well rectify the situation." But Wainwright knew it was an impossible mission. He had already notified the War Department that the withdrawal of both corps was necessary. Even the best of his regiments, he said, "were capable of only a short advance before they were completely exhausted" for they had subsisted for so long on one-half and one-third rations. In response, MacArthur denied Wainwright the authority to surrender and directed him "if food fail" to "prepare and execute an attack upon the enemy." MacArthur then sent a memo to the army chief of staff, General Marshall, stating that he was "utterly opposed, under any circumstances or conditions to the ultimate capitulation of his command. If it is to be destroyed it should be upon the actual field of battle taking full toll from the enemy." When Wainwright's chief of staff, General Beebe, called Jones directly to order the counterattack at 3:00 A.M. on the ninth, King telephoned USFIP at Corregidor to inquire if I Corps had been removed from

his command. Wainwright, through Beebe, assured King that he was still in command of all forces at Bataan. This telephone call was the last conversation Wainwright had with King before the surrender. In his memoirs, Wainwright wrote, "I have no criticism of General King for accepting the situation and surrendering. It was a decision which required great courage and mental fortitude. . . . I had orders from MacArthur not to surrender Bataan, and therefore could not authorize King to do it. But King was on the ground and confronted by a situation in which he had either to surrender or have his people captured or killed piecemeal." See Morton, *The Fall of the Philippines*, 452–53, 455; and Wainwright, *General Wainwright's Story*, 82-83.

35. On the night of April 8–9, 1942, King held a meeting with his chief of staff, Colonel Funk, and his operations officer, Col. James V. Collier. Collier wrote in his notes that the meeting was "a weighty and never to be forgotten conference." Considering that the Japanese would be able to reach Mariveles—from which they could dominate the southern tip of Bataan as well as Corregidor Island—by the evening of the ninth, King decided to open negotiations with the Japanese for the conclusion of hostilities on Bataan. He made the decision entirely on his own and with full knowledge he was acting contrary to orders. This "ignominious decision," he told his staff later that night, was entirely his, and he did not wish anyone else to be "saddled with any part of the responsibility." Contrary to Alexander's statement in this book, as Morton points out in *The Fall of the Philippines*, Wainwright was informed of the decision to surrender; the official report of the principals, most notably Collier's notes, states that King's decision to surrender was not communicated with Wainwright.

  The first task was to establish contact with the Japanese and reach an agreement on the terms of the surrender. Col. Everett C. Williams and Maj. Marshall H. Hurt Jr. (USMA 1930), both bachelors, volunteered to go forward with the white flag to request a meeting for General King with the Japanese commander. These two men would time their movement to arrive at the front lines at daylight, just as the destruction of Fil-American equipment was being completed. In order for the men to reach the front by dawn they would have to leave the headquarters at Little Baguio by 3:30 A.M. At 6:00 A.M. on the ninth, when General King was confident that Hurt and Williams either had or would soon be in contact with the Japanese, he phoned General Wainwright to tell him what he had done. Lt. Col. Jesse Traywick (USMA 1924), Wainwright's operations officer, who took the call, rushed to the commanding general to tell him the news. Wainwright was shocked. "Go back and tell him not to do it," he yelled. But it was too late to call it off; contact with the Japanese was believed to have been made. See Morton, *The Fall of the Philippines*, 457–58; and Young, *The Battle of Bataan*, 295, 300.

36. At about 9:30 P.M. on April 8 an earthquake of serious proportions shook the peninsula at Bataan. Most thought this was fitting for the situation at hand.

37. The units on Bataan were given the warning that if they received the one-word message, "blast," they were to immediately destroy all guns, vehicles, and ammunition. Throughout the evening explosions were heard and felt by all forces on the peninsula. Naval forces at Mariveles sunk the ships *Dewey Dry-dock, Canopus, Napa,* and *Bittern* during the early evening. However, the explosions of the U.S. naval ships were merely a prelude to the force of the destruction felt when the army's ammunition depots were destroyed. Having no time to move the ammunition to a safer place, the TNT and ammunition stored in the congested area adjacent to Hospital No. 1, the engineer and quartermaster depots, and Luzon Force and II Corps Headquarters, near Little Baguio, was blown in place. The headquarters building at King's command post was knocked over by the two massive explosions. See Miller, *Bataan Uncensored,* 208–9; Morton, *The Fall of the Philippines,* 460; and Young, *The Battle of Bataan,* 296.

38. In the confusion and disorganization of the last night of battle, the evacuation of personnel to Corregidor proved difficult if not impossible. Only about 2,000 individuals, including 300 survivors of the 31st Infantry (U.S.), navy personnel, some scouts from the 26th Cavalry, and other Philippine soldiers escaped to Corregidor. See Morton, *The Fall of the Philippines,* 460–61.

39. Thorne was Capt. Hank Thorne, commander of the 3rd Pursuit Squadron that fought at Iba. He flew his P-35 (not a P-40 as Alexander has stated) to Corregidor on April 9, 1942, at about 10:00 A.M. Accompanying Thorne was Capt. Ed Brown. Their commanding officer, Capt. Ed Dyess, ordered Thorne and Brown (although, at first, they refused to go) to depart the peninsula. Capt. Joe Moore took the sole remaining P-40 to Corregidor and, prior to Thorne's departure, Capt. O. L. Lunde and Lt. Randy Keator flew another P-35 to Corregidor. See Dyess, *The Dyess Story,* 64–65; and Young, *The Battle of Bataan,* 284, 291.

40. The signal "crash" (as the signal "blast" was done earlier) was sent to all units by radio, telephone, and courier at 5:35 A.M. on April 9, 1942. This signal indicated that the forces were surrendering and each unit must prepare. Soldiers were fed as much as possible, trucks were hidden for such use as might be possible in the future, and papers and maps of possible use to the enemy were destroyed.

 Meanwhile, Williams and Hurt were proceeding to the front to issue King's offer to surrender. The two men started out at 3:30 A.M. on the ninth, leaving Little Baguio by car. They soon found that the roads were untrafficable so they abandoned their car. Williams then looked at his watch in dismay, grabbed the white flag from Hurt and climbed onto the rear of a passing motorcycle and took off. Hurt followed behind the best he could, attempting to reach the front by daylight. By 5:00 A.M. Major Hurt hitched a few more rides and was within three-quarters of a mile of Lamao. He had been all alone on the road for the last half-hour when suddenly he recognized Williams and a driver sitting in a jeep parked next to Kilometer Post 155. Williams had discovered that the front was less than a mile and half to the north, near Kilometer 151.8. Traveling the rest of the way together by jeep, Williams and Hurt crossed a bridge at the Lamao River. There they met Lt. Col. Joseph Ganahl (USMA 1927) who, with a few tanks and a handful of troops, represented the entire covering shell. When Ganahl heard the news that the battle was over, he turned his forces around and headed south. Williams and Hurt then waited for the Japanese. After waiting an hour they slowly started forward, crossing the bridge over the Alangan River, where they met a Japanese platoon. Williams gave the Japanese noncommissioned officer in charge of the platoon King's instructions. The men were then brought to Maj. Gen. Kameichiro Nagano's command post. At the time, Nagano was leading the Nagano Detachment of the 21st Division down the East Road. An interpreter read the letter of instructions, and Nagano agreed to meet General King at the Experimental Farm Station near Lamao. Hurt went back to meet with King, and Williams remained at the Japanese headquarters. Hurt made it to Luzon Force headquarters by 9:00 A.M., and within a few minutes he; General King; the Luzon operations officer, Colonel Collier; and King's two aides, Majors Wade Cothran (USMA 1918) and Wade Tisdale departed. He felt, he said later, like General Lee, who on the same day seventy-seven years earlier, just before his meeting at Appomatox, remarked: "Then there is nothing left to do but go forward and see General Grant and I would rather die a thousand deaths."

After being bombed and strafed en route to the front, they arrived at Lamao at 11:00 A.M. and met with Maj. Gen. Kameichiro Nagano. Lt. Gen. Masaharu Homma (commander of the 14th Army) refused to meet with King, insisting that he would meet only with his "equal," General Wainwright. Nagano didn't have authorization to accept the American surrender, so they waited a few moments for the arrival of Homma's operations officer, Col. Motoo Nakayama. Nakayama had come to the meeting without any specific instructions about accepting a surrender. The discussion got off to a bad start when Nakayama asked King if he were Wainwright. When King replied that he was not, the Japanese colonel asked why Wainwright had not come. King told Nakayama that he did not speak for all the forces on the Philippines, but only for his command on Bataan. The Japanese did not want to negotiate for only part of the forces in the Philippines, and the Americans weren't willing to give up any other ground. King asked for an armistice and requested that the air bombardment cease. He also requested that his troops be permitted to march out of Bataan under their own officers and that the wounded be transported in the vehicles he had saved for that purpose. Nakayama turned a deaf ear to all proposals, insisting that the cessation of hostilities would be made only after all forces in the Philippines surrendered. Finally, General King agreed, at about 12:30 P.M., to surrender unconditionally, without any provisions that the Japanese would treat prisoners under the terms of the Geneva Convention. Nakayama then asked for the general's saber, but since he had none, he accepted his pistol instead. King, Williams, and the two aides were kept in custody by the Japanese as a guarantee while Collier and Hurt, accompanied by a Japanese officer, returned to pass the news on to General Funk. Upon returning to Little Baguio they were to assemble all troops by unit and move them to a field south of Cabcaben and come under Japanese control. See Grashio, *Return to Freedom*, 31; Kerr, *Surrender and Survival*, 51; Morton, *The Fall of the Philippines*, 413, 461, 463–66; Young, *The Battle of Bataan*, 298–302, 307–11; and *The Wainwright Papers*, 163.

Chapter 8: Overcoming Temptation in the Eye of the Storm

1. Salt Creek is located in Brown County near Nashville, Indiana.
2. Swede is Lt. Col. Kenneth S. Olson (USMA 1919). Prior to the surrender he was with the Finance Department at Manila and Panay. See Vance, *Doomed Garrison*, 13, 30; and *1994 Register of Graduates*, 177.

Chapter 9: The First Prison Camp

1. O'Donnell got its name from a family of early Spanish settlers in the late 1800s. It has been used to hold soldiers ever since its founding and, prior to hostilities, construction was being done starting in September 1941 to make the camp more permanent. Construction work ceased in mid–December 1941 when the troops were sent north to defend against the December 23 Japanese landings. See Olson, *O'Donnell*, 8; and Martin, *Brothers from Bataan*, 79.
2. Called *lugao* by the Filipinos, this thin watery soup was a main staple for the POWs during captivity. See Martin, *Brothers from Bataan*, iii.
3. Rules laid down by the Japanese camp commandant were:
   (1) The Japanese Army does not recognize rank of prisoners of war.
   (2) Prisoners will salute all Japanese officers and soldiers while wearing headgear and bow appropriately when not.
   (3) Daily check-ups will be made [accountability of personnel].
   (4) Men will not leave the barracks between the hours of 7:00 P.M. and 6:40 A.M.
   (5) None will approach nearer than 3 meters to the fence surrounding the compound.
   (6) Water will be economized. Only sponge baths are permitted.
   (7) No smoking within 20 feet of a building.
   (8) All borrowed articles from the Japanese will be carefully accounted for.
   (9) Anyone disobeying orders or trying to escape will be shot to death.
   (10) All requests should be sent through proper channels.
   See Olson, *O'Donnell*, 50.

4. The first act by the captors, after the commandant's address, was to shake down every officer and enlisted prisoner. All prisoners were stripped of their blankets, pencils, pens, lighters, knives, surgical equipment, paper, and tobacco products. Almost everything of value was taken from the prisoners, leaving them with nothing but their canteens and mess kits. See Olson, *O'Donnell*, 42.

5. Maj. Dean Sherry had been on duty in Manila when the war broke out. He was placed in charge of the Japanese Civilian Internee Camp at Muntinglupa, 20 miles south of the city during the battle. See Braly, *The Hard Way Home*, 32.

6. The Japanese rifles, carbines, and machine guns were of 6.5mm caliber and fired the same cartridge. The army's old-fashioned Arisaka (Meiji 38) was the favorite Japanese rifle of that era. The model 1911 Arisaka carbine, which was popular with artillery and cavalry units, differed from the long rifle only in length (it is twelve inches shorter). Finally, more modern (1925) than either the carbine or rifle was the Nambu automatic pistol. Patterned after the German Lugar–Parabellum, it was issued in both 8mm and 7mm calibers. The Japanese also considered the bayonet the most essential weapon they carried and were taught to indulge in bayonet sticking whenever they could close with the enemy. The Japanese bayonet was a 14-ounce, 15 ½-inch bladed knife, often fixed during combat operations. See Thompson, Doud, and Scofield, *How The Jap Army Fights*, 33–36.

7. Olson writes in *O'Donnell*, "Of all the buildings in the camp, none was regarded by the captives with such awe and fatal fascination as was the Hospital . . . if it couldn't be called a 'hospital,' it was merely a place for men to go to die." Master Sergeant Gaston, who saw the ward in July 1942, had this graphic description: "The men in the ward were practically nothing but skin and bones and they had open ulcers on their hips, on their knees and on their shoulders . . . maggots were eating on the open wounds. There were blow flies . . . by the millions . . . men were unable to get off the floor to go to the latrine and their bowels moved as they lay there." Of all those that had it the most difficult was the American placed in charge, Capt. John Rizzolo, who was the officer in charge of the ward from its creation until early May 1942. With minimal supplies and little support from Japanese captors, Rizzolo did the best he possibly could do. See Olson, *O'Donnell*, 109, 111.

8. The fall of Bataan gave the Japanese an excellent location from which to shell Corregidor and a staging area for their final assault on the island. The forces on Corregidor had weathered the blockade better than those on Bataan. They had proportionally more supplies, safeguards against enemy infiltrators, and more disease-free surroundings. But as early as mid–April 1942 the defend-ers were showing the effects of the long siege. The Japanese began their final assaulton Corregidor with a heavy bombardment on May 1, 1942. On the night of May 5–6, two battalions of the 61st Infantry landed on the northeast end of the island. Despite strong resistance, they established a beachhead that

was soon reinforced by tanks and artillery. Artillerymen and other miscellaneous army and navy personnel, fighting as infantry, joined the U.S. 4th Marine Regiment to meet the invasion. The defenders were quickly pushed back toward the island's Malinta Hill stronghold where their position became untenable. Late on May 6, 1942, General Wainwright decided to surrender the Corregidor forces. He ordered Col. Paul D. Bunker (USMA 1903), the commander of the 59th Coastal Artillery, to hoist the white flag over the island. Wainwright then broadcasted a message to General Homma in an attempt to surrender the four islands located in Manila Bay (Corregidor, Caballo, El Fraile, and Carabao) which came under his immediate control. He traveled to Cabcaben to offer the surrender, but Homma wouldn't cease hostilities unless all islands in the Philippines capitulated. Convinced that the lives of the 11,000 men left on Corregidor would be endangered if the forces elsewhere didn't surrender, Wainwright finally capitulated. On May 8 he sent a message to General Sharp, commander of the Visayan-Mindanao Force, and to local commanders in Northern Luzon ordering them to surrender. Meanwhile, the Japanese accepted the soldiers on Corregidor as prisoners. Wainwright and his staff were then moved to the University Club in Manila and, while waiting for word from Sharp and the other commanders, they were able to view the soldiers from Corregidor on the Death March. It wouldn't be until June 9, 1942, that all commands in the Philippines had surrendered. See Bailey, *Philippine Islands*, 20–21; Braly, *The Hard Way Home*, 117; Morton, *The Fall of the Philippines*, 471, 560; Wainwright, *General Wainwright's Story*, 123–25, 131–57; and *1990 Register of Graduates*, 326.

9. Tarlac Prison Camp was in existence for only a few months—from May 20, 1942, to August 17, 1942. It was used for high-ranking officers, including General Wainwright, 4 major generals, 10 brigadier generals, 106 colonels, and a number of orderlies. After the fall of Corregidor, General Wainwright and five of his staff officers were taken to Lamao on the Bataan Peninsula on May 7, 1942. From there the general and his staff were moved to Station KZRH in Manila to broadcast the surrender order to the other commands located throughout the islands. While in Manila, Wainwright sent a letter to General Homma requesting that he send a radio to President Roosevelt, in his name, asking for a ship to be dispatched at once to the Philippines with food, clothing, and medical supplies, for Americans and Filipinos were dying at a rate of 300 a day at O'Donnell. No message was sent. On June 9, 1942, the Japanese captors informed Wainwright that his high command had ceased to exist and then moved him and his staff to the prison camp for senior officers in Tarlac. Wainwright and other senior officers, like General King, stayed at Tarlac until August 12, 1942, when they were loaded on a prison ship (Maj. John Pugh, an aid to General Wainwright, called this ship the *Stinko Maru*) and were transported to Karenko in Formosa. See Braly, *The Hard Way Home*, 268;

Wainwright, *General Wainwright's Story*, 142–73; and *1994 Register of Graduates*, 192, 221.

10. Maj. Dean Sherry was moved to Tarlac on May 20, 1942, presumably because of his considerate treatment of the internees at the Japanese Civilian Internment Camp at Muntinglupa before the surrender. See Braly, *The Hard Way Home*, 32, 266–67.

11. A pilchard is "any of various small marine fishes related to the herrings." See *American Heritage Dictionary*, s.v. "pilchard."

Chapter 10: Moving to Cabanatuan

1. In order to completely segregate Americans from their Filipino comrades, the Japanese began transferring the Americans to the three Cabanatuan prison camps in late May 1942. The town of Cabanatuan, or Cabanatuan City, is located on the Pampanga River, 40 miles from Fort Stotsenburg and 100 miles north of Manila. There were three camps at Cabanatuan numbered 1, 2, and 3. Camp No. 1 was approximately four miles to the east of Cabanatuan City. Camp No. 2 was four miles farther on in the same direction and Camp No. 3 was six miles past No. 2. A small dirt road connected the two camps at No. 2 and No. 3. In addition to those arriving from O'Donnell were many of the Americans in Bataan field hospitals who were brought to No. 3 in late May 1942. Shortly thereafter, the men who surrendered at Corregidor also arrived at No. 3. When No. 3 was filled, the remainder from Corregidor were placed in No. 2. When no water supply was found at No. 2, those in No. 2 were transferred to No. 1 in early June and No. 2 was maintained in the future mostly for naval personnel. In late October 1942, No. 3 was permanently closed and the prisoners located there were moved to No. 1. Alexander was a prisoner in Camp No. 3 and was eventually moved to No. 1. See Chunn, *Of Rice and Men*, 16; Jacobs, *Blood Brothers*, 43; Martin, *Brothers from Bataan*, 83–84; Morton, *The Fall of the Philippines*, 167; and Waterford, *Prisoners of the Japanese in World War II*, 252.

2. The Cabanatuan hospital was first opened in June 1942 under the command of Col. James Gillespie. At the hospital there were 30 wards (made to hold 40 soldiers each), often holding up to 100 patients. In each ward were upper and lower decks made of bamboo slats. Each patient was allotted a two-by-six-foot space. The seriously ill were kept on the lower deck. Fenced off from the hospital was a quarantined area containing about ten wards, called the dysentery section. Within the dysentery section was a building missed when the wards were numbered. Later, it was called the "zero" ward and served as a place to put the seriously ill or dying patients. See Jacobs, *Blood Brothers*, 55–56, 58–59.

3. Camp No. 3 was divided into three distinct groups by the Japanese, mostly for control purposes. The overall American commander at the camp, until he was

sent to Bilibid Prison on August 30, 1942, and then to Karenko on September 27, 1942, was Col. Napolean Boudreau, the former commander of Subic Bay's Harbor defenses. Replacing Boudreau was Lt. Comdr. Curtis T. Beecher, a marine. The commander of Camp No. 1 was Col. Dorsey J. Rutherford. Commander of Group No. 1 at Camp No. 3 was Col. Leo Paquet (USMA 1919). Col. Armand Hopkins (USMA 1925) was the commander of Group No. 2. When many of the prisoners were sent away to become slave laborers for the Japanese, the groups were consolidated into one group, with Paquet in command and Hopkins as his executive officer. Numerous changes in command occurred over the years that the prisoners occupied the various Cabanatuan camps but, for the most part, the chain of command noted above was in place while Alexander was a captive at Cabanatuan. See Braly, *The Hard Way Home*, 66, 269; Chunn, *Of Rice and Men*, 17–19; Hopkins, "Prisoner of War," 32–33, 35, 39; and Kerr, *Surrender and Survival*, 79, 96, 176, 194.

4. There was a very organized underground system at Cabanatuan. Food and money was smuggled into the camp on a daily basis. The principal organizers of the smuggling activities were two American women, Margaret Utinsky ("Miss U") and Claire Philips ("Highpockets"). Both were the wives of American soldiers who died in Cabanatuan during the summer of 1942 and both had avoided confinement in the civilian internment camp at Santo Tomas in Manila. The underground organization received help from local merchants, farmers, and businessmen who provided "baked cookies," or in other words, produce, other foods, medicines, notes, and money to the prisoners. A Filipina mestiza, Evangeline Neibert ("Sassie Suzie") carried the "cookies" by train from Manila to the town of Cabanatuan, where she delivered them to the market. Naomi Flores ("Looter"), a licensed vegetable peddler, hid the loot in the bottom of rice sacks and took them to the camp. Once or twice a week, the rice detail from the camp picked up the sacks of rice and took them to the mess hall, where the goods were removed and delivered to one of six officers designated as "helpers." The helpers then delivered the goods to the beds of those requesting the notes and/or goods. Lt. Col. Harold K. Johnson, an infantry officer in charge of the Cabanatuan commissary, estimated that while the underground was in operation, he spent nearly one and one-half million pesos on food and other items with an apparent income of only one-half million. On May 3, 1944, the Japanese put an end to the underground operations when a group of men were compromised in Manila. Several "ring leaders" and American sympathizers were severely punished, including imprisonment and execution. See Jacob, *Blood Brothers*, 65, 67; and Kerr, *Surrender and Survival*, 152–53, 197.

5. Jute, used for sacking and cordage, is a fiber that comes from an Asian plant. See American Heritage Dictionary, s.v. "jute."

6. For most Japanese soldiers and sailors, their allegiance to the emperor and the state was reaffirmed on a daily or weekly basis when they faced in the direction of the Imperial Palace in Tokyo and recited portions of the Imperial Rescript to Soldiers and Sailors proclaimed by Emperor Meiji in 1875. This particular Rescript was in honor of the six-month anniversary of the Japanese bombing of Pearl Harbor.

7. General Count Hisaichi Terauchi was the commander of the Japanese Southern Army. Under his command was the 14th, 15th, 16th, and 25th Armies, constituting ten divisions and three mixed brigades. See Kerr, *Surrender and Survival*, 163–64; and Morton, *The Fall of the Philippines*, 56.

8. The conquest of Bataan in early 1942 did not progress as rapidly as the Japanese high command had hoped. Gen. Tomoyuki Yamashita was therefore brought in from Malaya to relieve Homma, who left the Philippines in August 1942 and was sent back to Tokyo, where he spent the rest of the war on the sidelines, as a reserve officer. Homma was tried and convicted in April 1946 for atrocities at O'Donnell and Cabanatuan and executed by firing squad. Yamashita was convicted of war crimes and hung in February 1946. See Berry, *Prisoner of the Rising Sun*, 227; Daws, *Prisoners of the Japanese*, 365; FitzPatrick, *The Hike into the Sun*, 111; Kerr, *Surrender and Survival*, 294; and Morrison, *The Rising Sun in the Pacific*, 199.

9. As an example, from January 6 to March 1, 1942, the Japanese 14th Army had almost 7,000 combat casualties and between 10,000 and 12,000 noncombat casualties suffering from malaria, beriberi, dysentery, and other tropical diseases. Homma's army had literally ceased to exist as a combat force by mid-March 1942. See Morton, *The Fall of the Philippines*, 349–51.

10. The Philippine Islands lie wholly within the low latitudes and are surrounded by the warm waters of the western Pacific Ocean. This location insures a constantly warm and moist tropical climate in the Philippine lowlands, where temperatures remain high throughout the year and rainfall is generally abundant. Overall, the average rainfall in the Islands is 82 inches per year. See Morton, *The Fall of the Philippines*, 5–6; *The Cambridge Factfinder*, 300; and *Comptom's Interactive Encyclopedia*.

11. Like beriberi, pellagra is a vitamin-deficiency disease; it afflicted fewer men than beriberi, however. Thomas in *As I Remember* describes one method the doctors at Cabanatuan used to rid a patient of pellagra sores: "The sore was getting worse and worse and there were no salves or powders. The patient was willing to try anything. I was sent to the saddle trench to bring back a few healthy maggots. I found a stick and fished out some of the filth. I washed them [the maggots] off with water and gave them to the doctors. They placed three of them in the pus [of the sore on the patient]. Those maggots began eating immediately. They were eating only the pus. . . . The process was repeated

each day with new maggots until the pus was entirely gone." See Kerr, *Surrender and Survival*, 99; and Thomas, *As I Remember*, 183.

12. Diptheria is a contagious disease caused by infection and characterized by the formation of false membranes in the throat and other air passages, causing difficulty in breathing, high fever, and extreme weakness. Jacobs in *Blood Brothers* talks of an epidemic of diphtheria at Cabanatuan for a short period in which 200 cases were diagnosed and 125 died before the Japanese obtained the antitoxin that would control it. See Jacobs, *Blood Brothers*, 57; and American Heritage Dictionary, s.v. "diptheria."

13. The prisoners had many "affectionate" nicknames for their guards: Big Stoop, Little Speedo, Air Raid, Laughing Boy, Donald Duck, Many Many, Beetle Brain, Fish Eyes, Web Foot, Hammer Head, and Hog Jaw were just a few of the names known to most prisoners at Cabanatuan. Urban McVey, in Martin's *Brothers From Bataan*, said that "Two of the main guards were 'Big Speedo' and 'Little Speedo.' They were called that because if you were too slow in your work they would holler Speedo. 'Big Speedo' didn't beat up the prisoners. 'Little Speedo' did, and he was much bossier than 'Big Speedo.'" See Martin, *Brothers From Bataan*, 99.

14. This guard appears to be First Lieutenant Oiagi, the camp quartermaster. He was tall and had played on the Japanese Davis Cup team in America. Unlike most of the prison guards, Oiagi was relatively fair and pleasant to the POWs. See Chunn, *Of Rice and Men*, 17.

15. John is most likely Lt. Col. (Chaplain) John Borneman, a good friend of Alexander's and who is cited in numerous books on the Death March and POW life. Col. Armand Hopkins describes Borneman in his memoir as "a dignified, intelligent gentleman whom all respected and liked, and to whom any prisoner, regardless of religion, age or military rank, readily went for advice." Borneman sent Lu Alexander a letter, dated April 2, 1945, once he was released. See Hopkins, "Prisoner of War," 58; and letter dated April 2, 1945, from Lt. Col. (Chaplain) John K. Borneman to Lucile Alexander.

16. The camp commandant was Lt. Col. Masao Mori, who operated a bicycle shop in Manila when the war began. He was nicknamed "Blood" and "Bamboo Mori" by the prisoners. Mori, who was in charge of both Camp No. 1 and No. 3, chose to live at No. 3 until he moved to No. 1 in September 1942. He and another guard, Kasayama Yoshikichi, who the prisoners called "Slime," were the terror of the camp. Blood and Slime were punished after the war as war criminals. Blood was hanged and Slime got a life sentence In late October 1942 Mori was replaced (after Camp No. 3 was closed and all prisoners were transferred to No. 1) by Major Iwanaka. Iwanaka was quite old for a major and paid no attention to the goings-on in the camp. In June 1944 Iwanaka was relieved by Major Takasaki, who ruled the camp with an iron fist. See Chunn, *Of Rice and Men*, 16; Daws, *Prisoners of the*

Japanese, 370; Kerr, *Surrender and Survival*, 102, 119; and Miller, *Bataan Uncensored*, 250.

17. The Japanese occupation of the Philippines was opposed by increasingly effective underground and guerrilla activity that ultimately reached large-scale proportions. Postwar investigations showed that about 260,000 people were in guerrilla organizations and that members of the anti-Japanese underground were even more numerous. Their effectiveness was such that by the end of the war, Japan controlled only 12 of the 48 provinces in the Philippines. The major element of resistance in the Central Luzon area, besides those organized by the U.S., was furnished by the Huks, Hukbalahap, or the leadership of Luis Taruc, a communist party member since 1929. The Huks armed some 30,000 guerrillas and extended their control over much of Luzon. See Chapter 1.07: The Commonwealth and the Japanese Occupation. File extracted from Department of Commerce, Economics & Statistics Division's January 19194 National Trade Data Bank (NTDB) CD-ROM, SuDoc C1.88:994/1/V.2, Processed February 16, 1994.

18. The two officers who escaped were Howard Breitung (USMA 1923) and a navy lieutenant. See Hopkins, "Prisoner of War," 42; and *1994 Register of Graduates*, 187.

19. The American prisoners had been severely warned upon entering any prison camp that an attempt to escape would result in death by firing squad. Despite the warnings, a handful of escape attempts from Cabanatuan occurred in the early days of incarceration. If the escapees were captured they were usually tortured and shot to death while other POWs were forced to look on. To prevent any more escape attempts, the Japanese captors initiated what were called "Shooting Squads" or "Blood Brothers." Each POW was assigned to a group of ten. If anyone in that group escaped, the other nine would be shot. When it came to the deed, the Japanese often had mixed feelings about whether to actually shoot the helpless hostages or not. Sometimes they did, sometimes they didn't, but one could never feel any confidence about the matter. Thomas, in *As I Remember*, writes, "You can believe that each man knew where his blood brothers were most of the time and especially at night." Because of the danger to those in the camp, the American leadership took extra precautions by imposing additional rules to prevent escape attempts and to prevent the perception (which had occurred more often than not) of a POW trying to escape. For instance, the Japanese rule was to stay within ten feet of the fence. The American leaders made it 30. In addition, a walking, unarmed patrol of POWs was formed to watch for anything suspicious. The patrol wore white armbands with MP printed on them. See Grashio, *Return to Freedom*, 65 and Thomas, *As I Remember*, 185–86.

20. Chunn, in *Of Rice and Men*, 22, names two of the interpreters as Ito and Masada.

Chapter 11: As the Years Come and Go

1. Mindanao is the largest island in the southern Philippines. More than half the men came from the healthier group at Camp No. 3 with the remainder from Camp No. 1. They were shipped to Mindanao aboard the *Erie Maru*. The rumor was that the group being sent to Mindanao was made up mostly of "technicians," air corps mechanics, and army ordnance men, eventually to be put to work as factory slaves. Most of the men sent from Luzon had little or no industrial experience, however, and were shipped to Davao Penal Colony at Dapecol, to work alongside Filipino convicts on a southern version of the "Cabanatuan Farm." The men from Luzon were joined soon after by another 1,000 shipped from Malabalay. In August 1944, 1,200 of the men from Mindanao were brought to Bilibid Prison in Manila; about 250 sick men were left at Davao. Jones, in *The December Ship*, a story about Lt. Col. Arden R. Boellner's captivity, describes how the newly arrived "battling bastards" looked to those already at Davao. "The men were filthy, most had lice and they were starved and ragged. The Cabanatuan prisoners seemed dazed. They had come from the horror of Camp O'Donnell and Cabanatuan to this paradise." Davao was no such paradise, but in relation to the horrors of the Luzon camps the conditions offered to the Americans were much better. In April 1943 a dramatic escape from Davao, masterminded by Capt. Ed Dyess, took place. Dyess and his companions escaped to Australia and brought to the Americans the first news of the Japanese brutality in the Philippine prison camps. See Daws, *Prisoner of the Japanese*, Dyess, *The Dyess Story*, 148–49; Jones, *The December Ship*, 77; Kerr, *Surrender and Survival*, 111, 165; Schultz, *Hero of Bataan*, 248; and Waterford, *Prisoners of the Japanese in World War II*, 254.

2. Dr. Jose P. Laurel, before being appointed President by the Japanese, was Chief Justice of the Supreme Court in the Philippine Commonwealth. After the fall of the Philippines, Laurel and many of his followers became increasingly anti-American, declaring at Manila City Hall and in a report in the *Tribune* that "America can't come back. . . . Even if America should return here, which I believe she can not do, you [the Filipino citizens] would be the one to suffer by cooperating with the Japanese. . . . But we are ready to make that sacrifice. We are ready to be traitors to America if by so doing we will be of service to you, to the Filipino people." See Hartendorp, *The Japanese Occupation of the Philippines* vol. 1, 226, 450; and Shigemitsu, *Japan and Her Destiny*, 292, 323.

3. The vessel *Gripsholm* was a Swedish liner. Soon after the fall of Corregidor the U.S. government and the American Red Cross, through the intermediation of the Swiss government and the International Red Cross, began negotiations with the Japanese for the exchange of diplomatic personnel and certain civilians who were interned in each country at the outbreak of the war. On July 23, 1942, the Japanese met the U.S. chartered liner, the *Gripsholm*, which not only had aboard Japanese diplomats and civilians, but also a substantial

cargo of food, medical supplies, clothing, cigarettes, toilet articles, and other items. These relief supplies were a combination of contributions by the American, British, and Canadian Red Cross societies. The following is a list of supplies sent aboard the *Gripsholm* destined for the Philippine prisoners: 22,160 eleven-pound food packages; 271 cases of drugs; 219 cases of bulk foodstuffs; 2,220 articles of clothing; 640 pairs of shoes; 3,680 toilet kits; 3,588 toilet articles; 6,129 cakes of soap; 25,000 packs of cigarettes; 4,896 tins of tobacco. In September 1943 the *Gripsholm* made a second transshipment of supplies. Aboard the liner this time were 140,000 food packages prepared by women volunteers in the Red Cross packaging centers in Philadelphia and New York and numerous bags of mail sent from loved ones at home. After the cargo was transfered to the *Teia Maru*, the supplies reached Manila in early November 1943. Japanese inspectors confiscated much of the cargo and prohibited many American newspapers and Old Gold cigarettes because each cigarette pack had "Freedom" printed on its rear cover. Despite the looting of supplies by the Japanese at all levels between the port and the prison camp, the Red Cross supplies immensely helped the Cabanatuan prisoners and those being held captive throughout the Far East. See Chunn, *Of Rice and Men*, 28; and Kerr, *Surrender and Survival*, 90–91, 125–26, 158–59.

4. Located at the 43-acre Dominican University complex, one mile northeast of Manila, the Santo Tomas Concentration Camp kept captive many civilians, including American women and children. Overall, 4,000 men, women, and children from Manila (to include some 100 nurses captured at Corregidor) and the surrounding area lived in the camp until their repatriation in February 1945. While the situation for the prisoners at Santo Tomas was relatively amenable compared to those suffering at Cabanatuan, there were hardships for the civilians interned. Food was, of course, a major shortage. The prisoners kept a garden, however, and in one month, for example, 15,000 pounds of *tolinum* (a green similar to spinach) was harvested. See Schultz, *Hero of Bataan*, 296; Waterford, *Prisoners of the Japanese in World War II*, 2, 183, 254, 257; and Young, *American Ex-Prisoners of War*, 69.

5. In October 1942 the Japanese removed the prisoners from the status of "captive" (criminal awaiting trial) and designated them prisoners of war. Since they were now prisoners the Japanese followed the international law by providing them with a monetary salary. The pay scales were set heavily in favor of officers. In the beginning, enlisted men had to work for their pay; officers did not. At Cabanatuan the pay was 220 pesos a month for a lieutenant colonel, 85 for a first lieutenant, and a working private received only three pesos a month. According to Jacobs, the pay was the same as the Japanese officers and soldiers of the same rank. Jacobs then explains that he would receive 30 yen at the pay window and then had to immediately deposit 20 yen at the Japanese Postal Savings window. He explains that by the time he was

repatriated he had more than 30,000 yen in postal savings that was never returned. Jacobs did say that once he became a prisoner of war, he received a yellow, printed postcard in which he could fill out the blank places, sign it, and it would be sent to his home. The postcards leaving the prison camps were censored by the Japanese, and any card marked "poor health" or "not improving," or containing some comment the Japanese didn't want, would not make it back to the States. Incoming mail came the long way. According to Hopkins, "The mail didn't come to us all at once, nor in any chronological order. There must have been thousands and thousands of letters. The Japanese, at some depot in Manila read them and censored them by cutting out parts. Then every once in a while, when a bag full was ready, a few lucky prisoners would receive a letter or two that had been pulled by chance out of the great pile. . . . Since the order in which our letters reached us was not related to the order in which they had been mailed, the news was often confusing." See Daws, *Prisoners of the Japanese*, 109, 128; Hopkins, "Prisoner of War," 45–46; Jacobs, *Blood Brothers*, 62–63; and Martin, *Brothers from Bataan*, 95.

6. A standard Red Cross parcel contained the following items: Evaporated milk, irradiated—one 14.5-ounce can; Lunch biscuit (hardtack)—one 8-ounce package; Cheese—one 8-ounce package; Instant cocoa—one 8-ounce tin; Sardines—one 15-ounce tin; Oleomargarine (Vitamin A)—one 1-pound tin; Corned beef—one 12-ounce tin; Sweet chocolate—two 5.5-ounce bars; Sugar, granulated—one 2-ounce package; Powdered orange concentrate—two 3.5-ounce packages; Soup (dehydrated)—two 2.2-ounce packages; Prunes— one 16-ounce package; Instant coffee—one 4-ounce tin; Cigarettes—one pack of 10; Smoking tobacco—one 1 2.25-ounce package. See Waterford, *Prisoners of the Japanese*, 42.

7. The following hospital menu from August 1, 1944, points out some of the nutritional problems of prison life.

    Breakfast: Rice, Tea, Limes

    Lunch: Rice, Gravy with Gabi, Corn on the Cob

    Dinner: Rice, Braised Carabao, Boiled Greens, Pudding

    Total Calories: 2,386

    This is what the menu said, but most reports indicate that no one received what was publicized by the Japanese. See Martin, *Brothers from Bataan*, 109.

8. *Cuan* is sometimes seen spelled as *Quan*, and the word is officially spelled *kuwan* in Tagalog. Although it is the Tagalog term for "thing" or "watchamacallit," many prisoners labeled various items and various acts specifically as *Quan*. See Daws, *Prisoners of the Japanese*, 113–14; and Martin, *Brothers from Bataan*, viii.

9. Atabrine is a trademark for an anti-malarial preparation, quinacrine hydrochloride. It is a substitute for quinine and has been known to turn a person's skin a

faint color of yellow. A sulfa drug inhibits bacterial growth and activity. See Daws, *Prisoners of the Japanese*, 352; and American Heritage Dictionary, s.v. "Atabrine."

10. The first day without a death at Cabanatuan is contestable. Alexander states that it was sometime in March 1943. Others, in their memoirs, dispute this. For instance, Chunn in *Of Rice and Men* states, "The first day in prison without a single death was Dec. 15, 1942—a reprieve granted solely by nourishment." Also, Jacobs in *Blood Brothers* credits that, "After the package in 1942, the camp mortality rate fell miraculously from forty deaths daily to one or two a month. December 15, 1942, was the first day in camp in which there was not a single death."

11. During the first eight months of camp in Cabanatuan, deaths totaled 2,400. Some 30 to 50 skeletons, covered by leathery skin, were buried in common graves each day. The Japanese issued documents certifying that each death was caused by malaria, beriberi, pellagra, diphtheria, in fact, anything but the real cause—starvation and malnutrition. Death hit the youngest men the hardest. Of the men who died during July 1942 at Camp No. 1, 85 percent were under 30. Ten percent of the enlisted men died, compared with only 4 percent of the officers. See Jacobs, *Blood Brothers*, 53; and Kerr, *Surrender and Survival*, 96.

12. Flour was procured in greater volume than any other foodstuff. In 1944 alone, the quartermaster corps obtained about 219 million pounds of flour. However, those who baked the bread from the flour recognized that, although the amount of flour obtained was substantial, it made smaller and less acceptable loaves than did the American variety because of its low gluten content. Alexander claims that the flour was from Minnesota, but most of the flour was procured from Australia. See Stauffer, *The Quartermaster Corps*, 116.

13. The Japanese intended, and the Americans expected, that some kind of prisoner labor would become part of the daily routine while at Cabanatuan. Violating numerous articles in the Geneva Convention, however, the Japanese forced the prisoners to work excessive hours (violation of Article 30), and, perform duties directly related with war operations (violation of Article 31), and they used aggravated disciplinary measures in the form of beatings and executions to get the captives to perform in unhealthy and dangerous situations (violation of Article 32). Though most prisoners worked on the "farms," or on wood and rice details inside the camp, many Americans were sent elsewhere as laborers. Details were taken to many places in the Philippines to build and repair roads, bridges, and airfields. Many prisoners also were sent to Manila to load and unload ships at the port. The shipment of men to Japan Alexander is referring to is the 1,500 men transported to Manila from Cabanatuan on November 7, 1942, when they boarded the *Nagato Maru* and set sail for Osaka, Japan. One hundred fifty-seven men died during this movement; seven died en route and 150 dying men were left on the docks of Moji, Japan, and never seen

again. The survivors eventually arrived in Osaka on November 25, 1942, where they were put to work as prisoner laborers at the railroad in Osaka, at the Yodogawa Steel Company, and on various construction jobs in the surrounding area. See Coleman, *Bataan and Beyond*, 105–14; Jacobs, *Blood Brothers*, 53, 55; Kerr, *Surrender and Survival*, 119–22; Martin, *Brothers from Bataan*, 95–97; and Waterford, *Prisoners of the Japanese*, 9, 161–62, 168.

14. Under the Geneva Convention rules, officers under POW status are exempt from labor details. The Japanese often violated this rule, for Premier Tojo had established a "no work, no food" policy for all prisoners. By international law, officers can be put in supervisory positions, but must not be forced to perform hard labor while being held captive. After January 1, 1943, the details in and out of the camps increased tremendously so that even men too sick to work were forced to go to work. At this point, officers were volunteered to work by Lieutenant Colonel Beecher (the U.S. camp commander) to replace sick enlisted men. This practice shortly fell into abuse, and in April 1943 the Japanese had ordered 12 $\frac{1}{2}$ percent of the total work force to be commissioned officers. See Chunn, *Of Rice and Men*, 51–52; and Kerr, *Surrender and Survival*, 178.

15. Lt. Col. Fred Saint is the officer who took charge of this mission.

16. For instance, ingenious American doctors built a camera from X-ray film found at the hospital. With this camera the prisoners took pictures around the camp and developed the film in the hospital X-ray solution. Many of the only photographs found in the archives today were taken with these types of cameras. See Jacobs, *Blood Brothers*, 59.

17. Lt. Homer T. Hutchison, a former mining engineer, built the receiver inside a mess kit while at Camp No. 1, dismantled it when he was moved from that camp, and reassembled it when he arrived at Camp No. 3. He entrusted his tiny radio, small enough to be packed in a corned beef can, to a close friend, Capt. Charles Brown, who hid it in a hole under his barracks. Several nights a week Hutchison would go to Brown's barracks, set up the radio, and listen to station KGEI in San Francisco. See Daws, *Prisoners of the Japanese*, 279–82; Chunn, *Of Rice and Men*, 106; Hopkins, "Prisoner of War," 61–62; and Kerr, *Surrender and Survival*, 160.

18. Col. Ovid Oscar "Zero" Wilson (USMA 1924) organized the stage shows to raise morale. Every Saturday night, starting in October 1942, the camp put on a show under the name of "The Mighty Art Players." Some of the 54 productions included *Casey Jones*, *The Drunkard*, *Gone with the Wind*, *Journey's End*, and *Uncle Tom's Cabin*. Remarkably, most of the plays were rewritten from memory. Most notable was the rewriting and production of *Three Men on a Horse*. One time the performers even enacted an Army-Navy game, which appropriately ended in a tie. Along with the show productions, the prisoners formed a glee club and the camp put together its own orchestra called the "Cabanatuan Cats." PFC Johnny

Kratz, a clerk from Corregidor's coastal artillery, organized the orchestra, which performed in concert every Wednesday night. The Japanese enjoyed music so they permitted those who owned instruments to bring them to the camp after the surrender. The Japanese also enjoyed going to the concerts, so they allowed the orchestra to practice several hours each week. The plays and concerts were extremely important to the prisoners as well; they were a means of escape for the poorly treated captives and it was not uncommon to have 3,000 to 4,000 men watching a show. The men who worked on the shows were exempt from other work in the camp, but the performers did such a good job that the other prisoners didn't complain that they had it "easy." In October 1944 the orchestra was ordered to Japan on a prison ship. After a few days it was sunk and all members of the American orchestra were killed. See Chunn, *Of Rice and Men*, 67, 73; Hopkins, "Prisoner of War," 47; Jacobs, *Blood Brothers*, 70–72, Kerr, *Surrender and Survival*, 153; Knox, *Death March*, 244; Thomas, *As I Remember*, 221–22; and *1994 Register of Graduates*, 193.

19. The official name of this movie was *Down with the Stars and Stripes*. On the first day of the shooting in August 1943, more than one-third of the Americans in Cabanatuan acted in a scene depicting a mass surrender of American troops. After this scene was completed, about 100 men were taken to Bataan for a week's filming. Hopkins in "Prisoner of War" writes that the prisoners were given captured rifles as props. The Japanese soon realized that some loaded rifles belonging to the guards had gotten mixed up with the unloaded prop rifles. This confusion, of course, caused quite a stir with the guards that the prisoners found quite humorous. See Hopkins, "Prisoner of War," 53; Kerr, *Surrender and Survival*, 150; and Levering, *Horror Trek*, 124.

20. The prisoners periodically received old copies of the *Nippon Times* and other newspapers from the Japanese, which usually reported that the Japanese were triumphant throughout the Pacific. While most of the reports about the Japanese success in the Pacific were untrue, the papers were somewhat reliable in their reporting of the events in the European Theater. See Schultz, *Hero of Bataan*, 359.

21. In August 1942, Lt. Henry "Farmer" Jones, who was the headquarters gardener and had planted a small patch of vegetables at the Cabanatuan camp, ventured into Cabanatuan to buy seed. The size of the "farm" grew quickly and, initially, because of the large number of men needed to tend it, it was unpopular with the Americans. Eventually, the farm grew to 300 acres and at its peak nearly 3,000 men dug, hoed, planted, and hauled water to the growing squash, beans, corn, and a variety of vegetables and rice. The workers, for all their efforts, received only a small amount of extra food. The rest of what was harvested went with the Japanese guards to the Manila markets, and they profited greatly from the hard work done by the farmers. See Daws, *Prisoners of the*

Japanese, 163; Chunn, *Of Rice and Men*, 52; Jacobs, *Blood Brothers*, 55; Kerr, *Surrender and Survival*, 149–50, Knox, *Death March*, 229; and Thomas, *As I Remember*, 190–91.

22. In August 1942, in effort to free up Japanese troops for duty in war zones, 600 Formosan nationals arrived for training as guards. The Japanese treated the Formosan guards as second-class citizens and, in turn, the Formosans treated the Americans in the same or even worse manner. See Kerr, *Surrender and Survival*, 104, 110.

23. The Japanese guard called Donald Duck received his name because he stammered and waddled around like a duck. Once he learned of his nickname he asked an American what it meant. The American prisoner told him that Donald Duck was a big movie star in the U.S. That pleased the guard, but only for awhile. He soon learned of the true meaning and went on a rampage. Laughing Boy got his name because he laughed all the time, Four Eyes was called that because he wore glasses; and Base Ball swung his club like a major league ball player. Sgt. Forrest Knox in *Death March*, wrote that all of the guards carried clubs, which the prisoners called "vitamin sticks," for they got more done by beating the prisoners than a barrel of vitamins. See Knox, *Death March*, 230, 232–33; and Thomas, *As I Remember*, 192–93.

24. Alexander is referring to the Japanese guards and other Japanese administrators at Cabanatuan who skimmed money from the commissary account.

25. Although Alexander sent his wife the many postcards allowed, he kept a running note to his wife that dated from November 5, 1942 to October 15, 1944, a total of two years in the making.

26. Rusty is Lt. Col. Russell J. Nelson (USMA 1919). He commanded the 102nd Infantry of the 101st Philippine Division on Mindanao. Johnny is Lt. Col. John P. Woodbridge (USMA 1926), who led Fil-American forces in the fight for Mindanao. Woodbridge was the commander of the 81st Field Artillery and a 65-man detachment from the grounded 30th U.S. Bomb Squadron. See Morton, *The Fall of the Philippines*, 511, 516; and *1994 Register of Graduates*, 177, 198.

27. Brig. Gen. William F. Sharp (Alexander spells his name "Sharpe" in the original manuscript) was the commander of the Visayan-Mindanao Force during the war. See Morton, *The Fall of the Philippines*, 69, 238.

28. Del Monte is the airfield in Mindanao that the planes at Clark Field escaped to and fought from after the bombing on December 9, 1941. The final bomber left Clark Field on March 12 and arrived at Del Monte where the army air corps fought from throughout the remainder of the war. Also located at Del Monte, the town near the airfield, was the Mindanao-Visayan headquarters. See Morton, *The Fall of the Philippines*, 96.

29. Mindanao was dissected into sectors with the boundaries designated by the major roads leading through the island. Route 1 is a northwest-southeast run-

ning road and it intersects with Route 3, known as Sayre Highway, halfway across the island at a town named Kabacan. Sayre Highway is a major north-south running road and is key to the defense of the island. Owning the Sayre Highway basically indicated control of the island, and even more significantly, Del Monte Airfield. Therefore the major fight on the island would be to control the roads and the airfield. See Morton, *The Fall of the Philippines*, 508–9.

30. The initial Japanese landing on Mindanao was on December 20, 1941, when the Sakaguchi Detachment and Lt. Col. Toshio Miura's (Miura Detachment) 1st Battalion, 33rd Infantry occupied Davao and Digos. The Sakaguchi Detachment left the islands in short order for Jolo and Netherland Islands, and the Miura Detachment was joined on Mindanao by the 10th Independent Garrison. In March 1942 the Japanese occupied and controlled Zamboanga and in late April 1942 the Japanese made a series of landings on each coast of the main island with the mission of converging on its center to control the Sayre Highway. On April 29 the Kawaguchi Detachment came ashore at Cotabato and Parang. Opposing the Japanese here was Nelson's regiment, and after a series of fights his unit and the remainder of the 101st were pushed back to Route 1. The Miura Detachment began moving northwest and conducted a linkup with the Kawaguchi Detachment at Kabacan on May 3, 1942. By then the only sector still under control of the Fil-Americans was the Cagayan Sector in the north. Defending the coast was the 61st Field Artillery, the 103rd Infantry, and Woodbridge's 81st Field Artillery. On May 2 the Kawamura Detachment landed basically unopposed in the Macajalar Bay and immediately controlled the area between Tagoloan and the Sayre Highway. By May 3, 1942, all Fil-American forces were forced to withdraw to the Mangima Canyon, just southwest of Del Monte Airfield. By May 9, 1942, the Japanese controlled all sectors of Mindanao. See Morton, *The Fall of the Philippines*, 507–19.

31. Although the troops on Mindanao trained extensively throughout their stay prior to the breakout of hostilities, there was a severe shortage of ammunition for training. One officer noted that "most of the men never fired a round until battle." See Morton, *The Fall of the Philippines*, 508.

32. On May 7, 1942, General Wainwright sent his operations officer, Col. Jesse Traywick, to Mindinao to order General Sharp to surrender his forces and cease the battle for the islands. On May 11, Traywick returned to Wainwright, who was at Manila at the time, with the news that Sharp had agreed with Wainwright's assessment of the situation and had surrendered his forces. See Schultz, *Hero of Bataan*, 307–14.

33. Alexander was in and out of the hospital because of high blood pressure, and Hopkins reports in his memoir that Alexander may have had a heart attack while in captivity. See Hopkins, "Prisoner of War," 42, 91.

34. There is some question as to who began the camp's library. Hopkins indicates that the "Cabanatuan Lending Library" was begun by Lt. Col. Joe Ganahl. Chunn and Jacob both claim that the library was started by Lt. Col. David S. Babcock (USMA 1923), assisted by Capt. J. C. Brunette and Lieutenants L. A. Edwards and Trifilo. See Chunn, *Of Rice and Men*, 78–86; Hopkins, "Prisoner of War," 47; Jacobs, *Blood Brothers*, 72; and *1994 Register of Graduates*, 187.

35. Alexander obviously heeded Duckworth's advice. Hopkins described Alexander as follows: "Alex . . . was patient and practical. He had no illusions about the seriousness of our situation. He realized that we were completely helpless and that we must conserve what little strength we had left until our captors got around to giving us some attention. Within our group of three [Hopkins, Alexander, and Leo Paquet aboard the prison ships] Alex was the wise and fatherly one . . . Alex was the most patient and loyal friend any man could hope for." See Hopkins, "Prisoner of War," 91, 109.

36. In January 1945, after more than three years of war, United States forces returned to Luzon. Prior to the dramatic return of forces to the same place where in 1942 American troops had suffered a historic defeat, the U.S. had to gain control of the South Pacific. By late spring 1943, the U.S. Joint Chiefs of Staff had developed a new plan for defeating Japan, which included a plan to invade the Japanese Islands. Integrating an extensive bombing campaign on Japanese-controlled islands, coordinated with combined surface, air, and submarine operations, the U.S. was successful in cutting off Japan's overwater lines of communications. Most importantly, the Allies determined that to achieve success it must gain control of the South China Sea. In accordance with these 1943 plans, Allied forces in the Pacific had struck westward toward the strategic triangle formed by the south China coast, Formosa, and Luzon. MacArthur's air, ground, and naval forces in the Southwest Pacific Area had driven up the north coast of New Guinea to Morotai Island. Simultaneously, Adm. Chester Nimitz had directed the forces of the Central Pacific Area in a drive through the Gilberts, Marshalls, and Marianas to the Palau Islands, some 500 miles east of Mindanao. Realizing that the seizure of Formosa was a stepping stone to the China coast, and possibly Japan, they almost bypassed the Philippines. However, the joint chiefs had directed MacArthur to be ready to move into southern Philippines before the end of the year (1944) and to make plans to invade Luzon in February 1945. Simultaneously, they ordered Nimitz to prepare plans to invade Formosa in February 1945. By September 1944 the choice to invade the Philippines first instead of Formosa had been made. See Smith, *Triumph in the Philippines*, 3–17.

37. Prior to the bombing of Pearl Harbor, the United States and its Allies worked on plans elaborating its strategy of fighting a possible war in Europe against the Germans and on another front in the Pacific against the Japanese. These plans prioritized the defeat of Germany first while holding Japan in check as best as

possible. In retrospect, this strategic attitude defined the initial demise of the Philippines. The plan for defending the Philippines called for a concentration of defenses on Manila Bay and the withdrawal of forces to the Bataan Penin-sula, with the hope that they could hold out there for half a year until a relief force from Hawaii could reach the islands. See Weinberg, *A World at Arms*, 242, 311, 339, 344.

38. Many letters were buried on Cabanatuan and recovered when the Rangers repatriated the 516 remaining prisoners during their raid on January 30, 1945. Chaplain John Borneman sent a letter to Lucile Alexander on April 2, 1945, explaining that during the raid on Cabanatuan the POWs had buried their per-sonal letters during the raid to prevent their destruction. The letters were dug up later that year and sent to their addressees. See Waterford, *Prisoners of the Japanese in World War II*, 11; Alexander's letter dated November 5, 1942, to October 15, 1944; and letter dated April 2, 1945, from Lt. Col. (Chaplain) John K. Borneman to Lucile Alexander.

39. Dinty is Lt. Col. Dennis Milton Moore (USMA 1925). He was with Alexan-der at Fort Stotsenburg prior to the war. At Cabanatuan he was placed in command of the officers and ran interference for them and gave them direction during captivity. See Chunn, *Of Rice and Men*, 53; Hersey, *Men on Bataan*, 306; Alexander's letter dated May 27, 1941; and *1994 Register of Graduates*, 192.

40. This may not have been the first sighting of American aircraft, for Alexander describes a sighting of airplanes that didn't attack the camp he was in. Breuer in *The Great Raid on Cabanatuan* describes Sgt. William C. Seckinger's initial sighting of American planes that had actually attacked Cabanatuan as follows. "September 21, 1944, dawned hot and sticky. . . . Looking into the clear blue sky, he saw two planes, one on the right on the tail of the other, diving toward the camp. Suddenly, there was a burst of machine-gun fire. . . . Then it struck Seckinger: He had witnessed a dogfight. He had recognized the Zero before it struck the ground. . . . A short time later, waves of airplanes flew directly over Cabanatuan camp." The planes turned out to be Hellcats from Adm. Bull Halsey's U.S. Fifth Fleet 40 miles east of Luzon. Waves of U.S. warplanes swept over Manila, Clark Field, Subic Bay, Nichols Field, and elsewhere during the next two days and pounded the Japanese relentlessly. See Breuer, *The Great Raid on Cabanatuan*, 134–36.

41. In 1939 the U.S. Navy purchased from Grumman Aircraft Engineering Cor-poration 54 F4F (Wildcat aircraft similar to the ones the British had purchased and been using since 1940). This carrier-based, short-winged aircraft had a 1200-hp engine (Wright Cyclone radial). A modification of the aircraft, the F4F-4 with folding wings, was introduced later in the war. It had a top speed of 318 mph, a range of 900 miles, and armament of six wing-mounted .50-inch machine guns as well as racks for two 250-pound bombs. See Young, *The World Almanac Book of World War II*, 505, 508.

42. The Dutch, as part of the Netherlands XV Battalion, were on the island of Java, which capitulated to the Japanese on March 8, 1942. At Cabanatuan, the Dutch had a significant language barrier with the Japanese. Although the Japanese guards could not speak English very well they had grown accustomed to the few English words like "speedo" to convey to the Americans what they wanted. With the introduction of Dutch prisoners the Japanese had to translate what they wanted through a select group of Dutch officers who could understand Dutch, English, and in some cases, Japanese. See Coleman, *Bataan and Beyond*, 128; and Waterford, *Prisoners of the Japanese*, 296.

43. Located in downtown Manila at Azcarraga Street and Quezon Boulevard, Bilibid Prison was formerly an old Spanish penitentiary built in 1805 that had been declared unfit for the incarceration of criminals. It was reopened by the Japanese after the fall of Manila in January 1942 and used as a clearinghouse for men coming in and out of Luzon. At one time about 8,700 Americans and 3,300 Filipinos were at Bilibid. At the end of 1944, only about 800 physically incapacitated men were left in the camp. On January 9, 1945, American forces dramatically liberated the POWs at Bilibid. Note: There was also another camp in Manila called Old Bilibid, where 470 civilian men, women, and children were held captive until their repatriation in February 1945. See Feuer, *Bilibid Diary*, xvi; and Waterford, *Prisoners of the Japanese in World War II*, 251, 259.

44. At Cabanatuan seminars were given by prisoners to other prisoners on numerous topics such as banking, psychology, journalism, French, Russian, Spanish, German, Tagalog, Chinese, and even Japanese. Additionally, photography, mathematics, history, and grammar were all topics of interest, and a "Cabanatuan University" was organized. In fact, each camp in Luzon had its own branch of what the prisoners called the "University of the Far East." See Chunn, *Of Rice and Men*, 64; Daws, *Prisoners of the Japanese*, 124, Alexander's letter dated July 9, 1941; and *1994 Register of Graduates*, 249.

45. Long is Dr. William Long. Long, Leo Paquet, Dr. Merle Musselman, and Armand Hopkins were roommates with Alexander during their stay at Cabanatuan. See Hopkins, "Prisoner of War," 42.

46. At the end of the war the Americans defined three classes of war crimes and criminals. A Class referred to top men like Prime Minister Tojo, policy makers who conspired to wage aggressive war. B and C Classes referred to men who ordered, allowed, or actually committed atrocities. The International Military Tribunal of the Far East (IMTFE) was established in Tokyo after the war to hold the A Class trials. The B and C Class criminals were tried in the area where the crimes were committed. More than 200 A Class criminals were identified but only about two dozen were tried and sentenced. A list of more than 300,000 B and C Class criminals was developed, with about 57,000 brought to trial. Because of such a large number of trials it would be 1948 before any verdicts were handed down. The Japanese, for the most part, did not

understand the war trials and in the end believed that they were unfairly treated by Americans. As late as 1979, the war criminals executed by the Allies were seen as martyrs for the Japanese cause and were enshrined at Yasukuni, close to the emperor's palace, where the spirits of Japan's glorious war dead were gathered. Shigemitsu in *Japan and Her Destiny* writes from his prison cell in Sugamo on March 1, 1950, that "the . . . Tribunal was of course, a military trial of the vanquished by the victors, one-sided, partisan and conducted by those against whom it was submitted that Japan had committed international crimes." See Daws, *Prisoners of the Japanese*, 363–76; and Shigemitsu, *Japan and Her Destiny*, 12.

47. Considering when this manuscript was written, the last two years he is referring to are 1948 and 1949.

Chapter 12: The Trek Beyond Bataan

1. On October 20, 1944, Gen. Douglas MacArthur returned, as he had promised, to the Philippines, stepping ashore on Leyte Island. As Cutler writes in *The Battle of Leyte Gulf*, "It was one of those moments that would become a graven image in the American heritage, photos of which would flash around the world in newspapers and then settle indelibly into thousands of history books as icons of restored national honor." MacArthur theatrically approached a waiting microphone and stated, "People of the Philippines, I have returned." He continued, "By the grace of Almighty God, our forces stand again on Philippine soil—soil consecrated in the blood of our two people." See Baclagon, *Philippine Campaigns*, 321–24; Cutler, *The Battle of Leyte Gulf*, xiii–xiv, 78–79; and Feuer, *Bilibid Diary*, xxii.

2. The chief of surgery at Bilibid from July 2, 1942, until December 12, 1944, was U.S. Naval Cmdr. Thomas H. Hayes. In the second half of his imprisonment he was also appointed senior medical officer of the prison. Hayes was one of the few to survive the sinking of the *Oryoko Maru* as it traveled to Japan on December 15, 1944. However, he was killed on January 9, 1945, when the ship he was transferred to, the *Enoura Maru*, was sunk at Takao. See Feuer, *Bilibid Prison*, xvi xvii.

3. John is Chaplain John Borneman.

4. As stated before, the actual number of prisoners to board the *Oryoko Maru* is in question. While Alexander claims 1,618 boarded, most accounts indicate the actual number is 1,619. See Daws, *Prisoners of the Japanese*, 293; and Kerr, *Surrender and Survival*, 218.

5. Jacobs in *Blood Brothers*, 82, describes the movement to the port prior to boarding the prison ship. "December 13, 1944: . . . our long line moved slowly through the gate and down Rizal Avenue. . . . Rizal Avenue was crowded with sober, gaping Filipinos—not the happy-go-lucky ones we had known before the war. . . . We could see pity on their faces as we passed down the streets, by the Metropolitan Theater and over the Passig Bridge. . . . We went the

long way—through Luneta Park; we saw artillery and anti-aircraft positions there and in the streets."

6. The *Oryoko Maru*, a passenger ship from the Tokyo-South American run before the war, had no markings but it was armed with numerous anti-aircraft guns. See Feuer, *Bilibid Diary*, 218; Jacobs, *Blood Brothers*, 82–83; and Jones, *December Ship*, 99.

7. The first group of prisoners under the command of Comdr. Warner Port consisted of 850 men, shoved into hold No. 5 of the ship. The second group (Alexander's group) of 500 men was placed under the command of Lt. Col. Curtis Beecher, and they were pushed and shoved into hold No. 1 at the forward end of the ship. This space was only 60 by 100 feet and the Japanese had emplaced a horizontal platform about four feet from the floor in order to double the holding space in the hold. The platform was four feet deep and the men were forced to sit four men to a row, each man's back against his neighbor's knees. The men in the center had no choice but to stand and were eventually ordered by the Japanese, no matter how impossible, to sit. A third group consisting of prisoner medical personnel and chaplains was placed amidships in hold No. 2, along with grain that was stored on three sides of the compartment. See Feuer, *Bilibid Diary*, 218.

8. Personally accompanying Alexander were Armand Hopkins, Leo Paquet, Dennis Moore, Zero Wilson, and Chaplain (Capt.) Arthur Cleveland, the former chaplain of the 59th Coast Artillery. See Hopkins, "Prisoner of War" 73.

9. Only 425 of the original 1,619 who left Manila on December 13, 1944, made it alive to Japan.

10. MacArthur's return to the Philippines in December 1944 included the U.S. Navy carrier *Hornet*. It was the *Hornet*'s naval planes from Task Force 38 that, while on patrol from a raid off the east coast of Luzon, spotted the Japanese convoy passing Corregidor and heading north. The strafing on that day caused many injuries to the Japanese passengers above deck. American doctors from the holds who treated the Japanese reported that the carnage was appalling. The American doctors worked for hours on the injured Japanese, were given a drink of water, and then returned to the hold with the rest of the prisoners. See Jones, *December Ship*, 103; and Kerr, *Surrender and Survival*, 220.

11. The Japanese commander of the shipment, Lt. Junsaburo Toshino, placed his interpreter, Shunusuke Wada, in charge of the prisoners. Wada had amassed a gruesome record for cruelty to prisoners at Davao on Mindanao, and he continued his tyranny on the hell ships. See Feuer, *Bilibid Diary*, 217; Jones, *December Ship*, 100; and Kerr, *Surrender and Survival*, 218.

12. The heat was stifling in the holds of the ship, reaching an estimated 100 to 130 degrees. Men began to suffocate and die, and only the man next to those who passed on knew that his comrade-in-arms had died. The first night in the hold took the lives of dozens of men, thirty in the aft hold alone. With the lack of

fresh air, the agonizing breaths of hundreds of suffering men made huge drops of moisture that clung to the bulkheads and were systematically scraped off and drunk in an attempt to alleviate the unbearable thirst. By the time the *Oryoku Maru* was sunk near Olongapo Naval Station on December 15, 1944, 286 men had died. See Jones, *December Ship*, 101–2; and Kerr, *Surrender and Survival*, 226.

13. Shortly after midnight on December 15, 1944, Japanese women, children, and the wounded American prisoners were moved from the ship to the shore, followed soon by the remainder of the Japanese passengers and crew. By 8 A.M. that morning, only the gun crews, the guards, and POWs remained on the ship. The flyers from the USS *Hornet* attacked first with rockets, hitting midship and at the stern. The planes that soon followed carried 500-pound bombs. One hit about midway between the stack and the fantail and then, soon after, a bomb met its target on top of the aft hold, causing the most lethal single blow the prisoners received. See Kerr, *Surrender and Survival*, 223–24.

14. Chaos erupted once the prisoners realized they weren't being guarded. Lt. Russell Hutchison noted, "Everywhere around us there were dead bodies, with blackened faces and purple lips. I soon noticed that the guards had disappeared, so we . . . scooped up sugar from some broken baggage and ate what we could before jumping over the side." See Feuer, *Bilibid Diary*, 223.

15. The prisoners were ordered to swim 300 yards to the shore adjacent to Olongapo Naval Station, as the *Oryoko Maru* was sinking slowly in Subic Bay. Before leaving the ship, the prisoners were ordered to strip off all belongings and jump overboard. No one was to leave from the starboard side and if they went off course the Japanese shot them dead in the water. Once ashore the prisoners occupied a hasty assembly area and then were herded, prior to sundown, 500 yards from the sea wall to a cement slab that at one time had been a tennis court. The heat grew intense during the following days and then dropped drastically at night while the men waited in the open on the tennis court. Because many men shed all their clothes, as ordered, they suffered in the tropical sun with no place to go to shade themselves and, in turn, froze at night as the temperature dropped. Jammed once again into a small enclosure, the men had barely six square feet per man. To add to their misery, there was only one water spigot outside the fenced-in tennis court. The prisoners had to ask permission to use it and endure long lines, as more than 1,000 men attempted to obtain water just to survive. Meanwhile, the prisoners observed the U.S. planes returning to the now-burning wreck of the *Oryoko Maru*. More bombs dropped and secondary explosions were seen as the ship sank sometime between 3:30 and 4:15 P.M. on the fifteenth. See Feuer, *Bilibid Diary*, 225; Jacobs, *Blood Brothers*, 87; Kerr, Surrender and Survival, 226; Lawton, Some Survived, *164, 166, 168; and* Stamp, Journey Through Hell, *85.*

16. Comdr. Thomas Hayes, the surgeon at Bilibid, and his medical unit worked around the clock performing surgery with nothing more than knives and razor blades. One injured prisoner, Marine Cpl. Carl Logan, had a gangrenous arm that had swollen to an astonishing size. Lt. Col. Jack Schwartz amputated Logan's arm with only a knife and without the benefit of anesthesia while two men held him down during the operation. The operation was successful but the marine lived only a few hours, succumbing finally to other injuries. See Feuer, *Bilibid Diary*, 226; and Jacobs, *Blood Brothers*, 89.

17. The mystery of male recollection was not lost with Colonel Alexander during his captivity. Colonel and Mrs. Alexander were married on December 20, 1929, making December 20, 1944, their fifteenth anniversary, not their thirteenth.

18. The Indiana National Guard unit was of interest to Alexander for he had served as an enlisted man in that unit in 1917. Specifically, the 152nd Infantry of the Indiana National Guard was part of the 38th U.S. Division that landed in early 1945 on western Luzon. See Smith, *Triumph in the Philippines*, 324–30.

19. Six hundred eighty-one men left Olongapo on the twentieth, and after traveling 35 miles on a winding and bumpy road, the prisoners were dropped off at San Fernando, Pampanga (the San Fernando near Fort Stotsenburg, not to be confused with San Fernando, La Union which will be the ultimate destination). The 20 trucks returned to Olongapo to upload the remaining 648 on the twenty-first. Of the 1,619 that initially left Manila, 1,329 remained alive; four more had died while waiting on the tennis courts. See Jacobs, *Blood Brothers*, 89; and Kerr, *Surrender and Survival*, 227.

20. The American leadership at San Fernando had appointed Lt. Col. Carl Engelhart (USMA 1920) as their representative, since he spoke Japanese. The Japanese officer-in-charge, Lt. Junasburo Toshino, told Engelhart that the most badly wounded POWs would be moved to Bilibid Prison Hospital. Fifteen men (not ten as Alexander indicates) were selected, and Lieutenant Urabe from the Manila POW headquarters ordered the execution of POWs who could not withstand further movement. Subsequently, at 8:30 P.M. on December 23, 1944, the doomed prisoners were forced to dig their own graves in a cemetery south of San Fernando. Seven of the prisoners were decapitated and the other eight were bayoneted to death. All 15 were dumped into the freshly dug graves. See Kerr, *Surrender and Survival*, 228; and 1994 *Register of Graduates*, 181.

21. La Union is the province where San Fernando is located. This province is in the western part of Luzon that borders the Lingayen Gulf; the same place the Japanese first came ashore nearly three years earlier. During the train ride a number of wounded prisoners were ordered to ride atop the roofs of the passenger cars to wave off any possible air attack by the Americans. See Feuer, *Bilibid Diary*, 229.

22. Kerr in *Surrender and Survival* describes the Christmas meal as "one cup of rice, a piece of camote (sweet potato), and a half a cup of water." See Kerr, *Surrender and Survival*, 229.

23. Lawton in *Some Survived* describes that several men died in the school ground on Christmas Eve and Christmas Day. He goes on to describe the conditions at the beach while waiting for their ship: "As night fell, it grew cold on the beach. To protect ourselves from the chilling wind we dug holes in the sand and huddled together. With our bony frames molded into the soft sand and the hastily constructed dunes breaking the wind, we were more comfortable than we had been on the cement of the tennis courts. Still, we shivered and shook from the cold. Two men died that night, one of them Lieutenant Colonel H. J. Edmonds [*sic*]." Lt. Col. Howard J. Edmands was the former commanding officer of the Cebu Military Police Regiment. See Bartsch, *Doomed at the Start*, 258; and Lawton, *Some Survived*, 179.

24. On December 27, 1944, two ships were loaded at San Fernando, La Union. The *Enoura Maru* (which Col. William Braly dubbed "The Barn," for no one knew its actual name at the time), with 1,070 men stuffed into its hold, to include Irvin Alexander; the *Brazil Maru* carried the remaining 235 prisoners. Although Alexander claims that the loading of the ships went on until December 30, most accounts have the two ships leaving on the twenty-seventh. See Braly, *The Hard Way Home*, 236; Daws, *Prisoners of the Japanese*, 294–95; Lawton, *Some Survived*, 182–83; and Waterford, *Prisoners of the Japanese in World War II*, 156–57.

25. Alexander had linked up with his friends, Paquet and Hopkins, whom he hadn't seen since the tennis courts at Olongapo. Hopkins in his memoir tells of the "bitter irony, to be starving but too seasick to eat" during the first day on the *Enoura Maru*. See Hopkins, "Prisoner of War, " 87.

26. In fact, the Japanese did notice the missing sugar and ordered the Americans to deliver the thieves to the top deck for punishment. Wada threatened to not feed the prisoners until someone confessed to the crime. Sgt. Arda M. "Max" Hanenkrat, of the 31st Infantry, finally stood and announced to his captors that he would take responsibility. Additionally, Sgt. Edwin Trapp, of the British Army, courageously accompanied Hanenkrat. The prisoners in the hold, convinced that the Japanese would execute these brave men, were shocked to see them return relatively unscathed. Perhaps the Japanese admired the raw courage displayed by the prisoners. See Feuer, *Bilibid Diary*, 232; and Lawton, *Some Survived*, 191–92.

27. The prisoners made Formosa in only four days, but on the way, five dead bodies were thrown overboard from the *Brazil Maru* and 16 were tossed from the *Enoura Maru*. See Daws, *Prisoners of the Japanese*, 294.

28. Hopkins, in "Prisoner of War," 89–90, recalled:

Everybody hits the deck, flattens out as flat as can be. And in a moment the attack is over. The silence, for a brief second, seems more complete than complete silence. The sudden weight and fury of that assault had left me dazed. I stood up and sort of checked myself. I seemed to be still in one piece, Alex was standing too. He appeared to be unhurt. Leo [Paquet], still sitting against the bulkhead, said: 'I think I've been hit.' He raised his shirt. There was a small cut on his chest, but very little blood. It didn't look serious. . . . I took some hasty glances at the rest of the hold. Things looked very bad. The steel beams and heavy wooden planks of the open hatch had been blown loose by exploding bombs, and had fallen on the prisoners below. It looked like a lot of men had been crushed. . . . This scene of carnage was mostly towards the center of the hold.

29. According to Hopkins, "The second day, Leo continued to grow weaker. Internal bleeding must have been filling his lungs. His heart simply wasn't getting enough oxygen to sustain life. His breathing became faint and erratic. Sometime in the afternoon it stopped altogether, and Leo's life simply slipped quietly away." See Hopkins, "Prisoner of War," 94.

30. On January 12, 1945, three days after the bombings, a large cargo net was lowered into the hold for the removal of the dead: 295 in total were killed in the latest bombing; 357 had lost their lives prior to the most recent massacre. Thirty-one days in the trek had cost the lives of 40 percent of the original 1,619; a total of 652 men had died to this point. See Lawton, *Some Survived*, 196.

31. On January 13, 1945, Wada informed the remaining prisoners that they were to be transferred to the *Brazil Maru*. Many men were injured so badly that they died during the transfer, about a dozen or so cases in total. The aft hold of the *Brazil Maru* was designated as the prison quarters. The compartment was divided into bays separated by stanchions. Each bay was of a space of about 10 by 12 feet but with less than four feet of head room. Thirty prisoners were assigned to each bay, and the men had either to sit with legs stretched out, or lie down with their knees drawn up. See Feuer, *Bilibid Diary*, 239.

32. Pat Byrne's friend is unknown.

33. As Lawton states in *Some Survived*, "I believe most of the wearers of the cross of the Chaplain Corps who were physically able helped many to face death with hope. Two who were especially noteworthy for their steadfastness came from different sections of the United States and had dissimilar religious backgrounds. Chaplain Robert Preston Taylor, a Southern Baptist . . . [and] Father William 'Bill' Cummings hailed from San Francisco, California." Lawton continues that regardless of their denomination, these two men earnestly believed that confession would save a man's soul. "The important thing to them on the hell ships," he continues, "was to see that no man died alone and uninformed of the

chance of salvation." Additionally, Hopkins, in his memoir, speaks highly of Catholic Chaplain William Duffy: "a few mornings out of Takao, I saw a tall, gaunt fellow, naked to the waist, and barefoot, going from sleeping bay to sleeping bay, anointing the dead and blessing them—the last rites. . . . He told me he was giving them conditional absolution; and apparently his concern was for all of them, Catholic, Protestant or Jew." See Lawton, *Some Survived*, 205; and Hopkins, "Prisoner of War," 97.

34. Hugh is Capt. Hugh H. Fink.

35. Moji (now Kitakyushu), Japan is on the northern coast of Kyushu, the largest island across the Straits of Shimonoseki and south of the Japanese main island, Honshu. It was the dead of winter when the prisoners disembarked the final hell ship. The temperature was just above freezing, dipping below the freezing mark with the wind chill. After leaving the boat, the prisoners were ordered to strip off what little they had on for a delousing. After roll call, the guards made a bonfire and issued overcoats to the prisoners, who crowded around the fire to keep warm. That night the prisoners were herded into an empty schoolhouse. See Daws, *Prisoners of the Japanese*, 301; Hopkins, "Prisoner of War," 103; and Lawton, *Some Survived*, 185, 211–12.

36. Approximately 135 extremely sick men were transported to Moji, where more than 80 eventually died. See Feuer, *Bilibid Diary*, 244.

37. The remaining prisoners were transferred to prison camps near Omuta (Fukuoka No. 17), about 60 miles from Nagasaki; Tobata (Fukuoka No. 3); and, as with Alexander and his companions, the others were transferred to Kashii Camp No. 1 (Fukuoka No. 1). See Feuer, *Bilibid Diary*, 244; and Waterford, *Prisoners of the Japanese in World War II*, 202–3.

38. There were 913 men in the camp with Alexander. Four hundred ninety-three men in Fukuoka No. 1 were Americans, including 100 civilians from Wake Island and 193 survivors from the *Oryoko Maru*; 150 British; 250 Dutch; and 20 Australians. While camp life at Fukuoka was relatively easier than at Camp O'Donnell and Cabanatuan, it wasn't all "fun and games," for the enlisted men worked ten hours a day at hard labor in the construction of an airfield bomb shelter and in the local coal mines. Additionally, the prisoners were exposed to periodic bombing raids and subjected to frequent beatings by the guards and stonings by the civilian population. See Waterford, *Prisoners of the Japanese in World War II*, 202.

39. Hopkins, in his memoir, describes the bathhouse and how he felt after taking this long overdue cleansing.

> In the undressing room there were some wooden basins, sort of miniatures of the old-fashioned washtub. You took one of these, dipped it into one of the deep, steaming tubs where five or six of your friends were sitting, immersed to the chin. You poured the hot water over you, soaped

up well, then rinsed with more hot water dipped from the tub. Then you waited, shivering, until it was your group's turn. When I finally put a tentative foot into that steaming water, I jerked it out immediately. It didn't seem possible that a living thing could get into that water and survive; but there, lobster-red and dripping, were the six friends who had just emerged, and they were obviously pleased with the boiling. So, inch by inch, I got myself in up to my neck; and soon I was completely immersed in the overwhelming physical pleasure of being warm, through and through, after all those weeks of unending chill. And when my time was up, and I had to get out, the warmth had so penetrated to my bones that even the cold air no longer bothered me. It was like a renewal of life.

40. Colonel Alexander was optimistic after hearing about the Battle of the Bulge in Bastogne, Belgium, which began on December 16, 1944, three days after he had boarded the *Oryoko Maru*. What occurred on February 16, 1945, that so elated Alexander is somewhat unclear. Perhaps this was the day he heard of the success the Allies eventually had in Bastogne or it could be the knowledge of the success of the 8th Army on recapturing most of Luzon. By February 16, the Americans had controlled most of the Manila area, to include the bay. Additionally, on February 16, 1945, the Americans re-invaded Corregidor when two U.S. battalions, one seaborne and one dropped by parachute, landed on the island. See Dupuy and Dupuy, *The Harper Encyclopedia of Military History*, 1299–1300; Laffin, *Brassey's Battles*, 51–52; Young, *The World Almanac Book of World War II*, 324; and *American Military History*, 495.

41. The identity of Monte is unknown.

42. Wright in *Captured on Corregidor* writes, "Probably one of the most annoying features of our stay at Fukuoka was the lice. Lice seem to be taken for granted in Japan; we were afflicted with them from the time of our arrival until we were liberated. We never had lice in the Philippines Islands. Lice inhabit clothing, hiding along the seams and laying thousands of eggs, which hatch in only a few days. . . . Boiling was the only way to clean clothes thoroughly, but that privilege was available to only a select few." See Wright, *Captured on Corregidor*, 149.

43. Carl is Lt. Carl Engelhart, the interpreter for the American prisoners who took command of a group of prisoners while in the provincial jail at San Fernando, Pampanga, awaiting transportation to San Fernando, La Union. See Wright, *Captured on Corregidor*, 103.

44. The number Alexander is referring to is the number of men who died in his particular camp while in Japan. Many accounts report only the number of men who died in the specific camp and since the only prisoners that left Japan in April 1945 were those who survived the *Oryoko* and the subsequent hell ships, a count can be taken from identifying how many were transferred to Korea from all camps in Japan. Of the 1,619 prisoners that started the trip to Japan in

December 1944, only 271 remained alive by the time they moved from Japan to Korea. See Lawton, *Some Survived*, 219.

45. Hopkins, in his memoir, writes, "we learned from our gleeful Jap guards that President Roosevelt was dead. The guards seemed to have been told that he had committed suicide or been assassinated for, in passing the news to us, they would run a finger across their throats, or point it at their heads and say with a grin, 'Rooseveltu! Rooseveltu!'. . . . News of the President's death had been a sad blow to all of us. . . . The Japs were unwilling to permit any sign of mourning over what was, to them, a welcome bit of brightness in the increasing gloom." See Daws, *Prisoners of the Japanese*, 317; Hopkins, "Prisoner of War," 111; and Young, *The World Almanac Book of World War II*, 339.

46. The American Okinawa landing, beginning on April 1, 1945, is known as the "greatest land battle in the Pacific War." The 794-square-mile island, off the southern coast of the Japanese Islands, was defended by the Japanese 32nd Army. Fifty thousand U.S. troops from the U.S. 10th Army assaulted the shore on April 1, 1945, and what followed was a fierce battle that included the introduction of the 6th U.S. Marines. Officially, the battle ended on July 2, 1945, and cost the U.S. the lives of 2,938 Marines dead, 4,675 U.S. soldiers killed, and 31,807 Americans injured. On the Japanese side the losses were much greater, accounting for 100,000 Japanese killed or wounded and 10,000 captured. See Laffin, *Brassey's Battles*, 315; and *Campaign Atlas to the Second World War*.

47. A Boeing B-29 Superfortress was a technologically advanced bomber, incorporating such innovations as pressurization and very high wing loadings. It was equipped with a 2200-hp Wright R-3350 Duplex Cyclone engine and had a top speed of 358 mph, a range of 2,850 miles and a bomb load of up to 20,000 pounds. These aircraft were used to drop the atomic bombs on Nagasaki and Hiroshima in August 1945. See Macksey, *Weapons and Military Technology*, 61; and Young, *The World Almanac Book of World War II*, 494.

48. The boat has been described as clean and the prisoners were more like passengers in that they could sit or stand in the large passenger space. They had been issued a rice ration the day before and were quite surprised to receive a third, which included a small amount of soup, once coming aboard the ferry. The prisoners were also allowed to use the ship's lavatory, which was clean with running water. However accommodating the ship may have been, one prisoner did die en route. See Stamp, *Journey Through Hell*, 101; and Wright, *Captured on Corregidor*, 154.

49. At 9:00 P.M. on April 26, 1945, the 270 survivors were divided into two groups once they reached Fusan. The 140 Americans and 10 Brits from Fukuoka Camp No. 1 left the larger group and entrained. The prisoners later learned

that the second group of prisoners to leave Fusan that day were brought to the Hoten Camp located in Mukden, Manchuria. See Waterford, *Prisoners of the Japanese in World War II*, 219; and Wright, *Captured on Corregidor*, 155.

50. At about noon on April 27, 1945, Alexander and his fellow prisoners arrived at Camp Jinsen (present day Inchon), about 50 miles south of the 38th parallel. Altogether, it was a 250-mile, 24-hour trip for the prisoners. Camp Jinsen was about a mile from the main street in the city of Jinsen and the compound was enclosed by a ten-foot-high fence. The fence was so high and the boards were so close together that the prisoners, once inside, could not see out. The compound was a small troop garrison with several small single-storied buildings with one much larger than the rest. Two of the buildings were assigned to the U.S. prisoners; one housed a small hospital and another, at the entrance, served as Japanese headquarters. The other buildings were used as warehouses and work projects. See Hopkins, "Prisoner of War," 113; and Lawton, *Some Survived*, 223–24.

51. On April 29, 1945, Emperor Hirohito's birthday was celebrated by the Japanese and Americans alike. The U.S. prisoners were happy to celebrate the Japanese emperor's birthday for they were given one Red Cross package for every two men. See Wright, *Captured on Corregidor*, 156–57.

52. Until the prisoners arrived at Jinsen they didn't know how many prisoners there were moving from Fukuoka or what proportions of the contingent were American, British, officers, enlisted men, army, or navy. They gradually learned that those who ended up at Jinsen were of an odd mixture, with no logical explanation of why the Japanese authorities had made their selections as to who went where. There were some British prisoners at Jinsen prior to the arrival of the new group, but most of them had been transferred to a camp at Seoul, leaving behind a few enlisted men to run the cook shack. The group from Fukuoka consisted mostly of American junior officers. There were about 50 enlisted men, half of whom were British. The only British officers were the dozen who shared the same barracks. See Hopkins, "Prisoner of War," 114.

53. Copper is Lt. Col. M. D. S. "Copper" Saunders. He was a graduate of Winchester and of Sandhurst (equivalent to the USMA). During the war he had commanded an anti-aircraft unit that assisted the Dutch in the defense of the East Indies. Most of the British soldiers at Jinsen were from Copper's unit. See Hopkins, "Prisoner of War," 114, 118.

54. On May 1, 1945, work in Camp Jinsen began for the prisoners. At first it consisted of cultivating, weeding, and fertilizing the vegetable garden adjoining the camp. On May 3, another work project was begun. A zig-zag slit trench to serve as an air raid shelter was constructed between the barracks and the garden. Many other projects were handled by the prisoners during their captivity at Jinsen, to include a "sew-sew" project, providing work for men who were not physically strong enough to work in the garden. This work consisted of

sewing buttons on Japanese army uniforms. See Wright, *Captured on Corregidor*, 158 159.

55. The Japanese doctor happened to be the camp commandant, Lt. Col. Okasaki. He was an older man who had been recalled from retirement. Although Okasaki was the camp commandant, his executive officer, Lieutenant Isobe, was responsible for the day-to-day running of the camp. Isobe was a reserve officer, a bank official in civilian life. He was middle-aged, slim, and taller than the usual Japanese. Although Isobe was not overly friendly to the Americans, he was approachable and the U.S. liaison officers responsible for reporting the U.S. activities to him could occasionally get permission for days off and additional rations. See Hopkins, "Prisoner of War," 115.

56. The senior American officer was Marine Lt. Col. Curtis Beecher, the former commander of U.S. prisoners at Cabanatuan. See Hopkins, "Prisoner of War," 123.

57. On August 6, 1945, the first atomic bomb was dropped on Hiroshima from the *Enola Gay* of the 509th Composite Group of the 20th Air Force, piloted by Col. Paul Tibbets. The bomb was a uranium fission weapon and the yield was in the region of 20,000 tons of TNT. Sixty percent of Hiroshima was destroyed in the blast and the following firestorm, killing about 80,000 Japanese. The second atomic bomb was dropped on Nagasaki on August 8, 1945 (the same day the Soviets declared war on Japan). This bomb was a plutonium fission device, which killed approximately 40,000 Japanese. After the August 8 bombing, President Truman threatened to destroy Japan with more atomic bombs; the Japanese agreed late that night to accept the Potsdam Declaration, making the surrender announcement on August 10, 1945. However, it was not until August 15, 1945 (VJ Day) that the Japanese finally accepted to surrender unconditionally.

Hopkins, in his memoir, describes Lt. Col. Jack Schwartz's report of the end of the war:

> He stopped me and, somewhat pale and breathless, said, 'The war is over!' I said, 'You're not kidding?' He assured me he was not, that the Japanese doctor had just told him, and that our previous news source had told Major [Alan] Steele. [Steele was the British liaison with the Japanese; the previous news source was a Korean who delivered newspapers to the Japanese, or possibly Lt. Isobe himself.] My chief emotion was a lump in my throat, and it took some effort to keep tears from my eyes. As it was a big secret, I promised to keep quiet, and went back to work. By noon, however, the word had been passed to all the senior officers, and by evening, some of the guards had talked, so that all prisoners knew it. As it had not been officially announced, however, we carried on as usual, maintaining the fiction that they did not know we knew. However, there was very little sleep last night, and this morning, Col. Beecher and Col.

Saunders were called to the J. Hq. where Lt. Col. Osaki [*sic*] told them the news, and gave instructions for our conduct until Allied representatives should arrive to take over. Alex was celebrating his wife's birthday yesterday. It was a happy celebration. Six months ago he had made a bet we would be in the US on that day. Though he lost the bet (a big dinner) he was more than elated that the very next day he picked should bring us the word of peace! For the time being, we are restricted to camp, still have Jap guards, but our food is now adequate, and interior administration is now in our hands. The J. doctor told Jack Schwartz this morning that the Americans had invented an atomic-molecular' bomb having the force of 10,000 ordinary bombs; that two such bombs could completely destroy a city of half a million; that the J. emperor, to save lives, had ordered his troops to surrender. The J. doctor; Lt. Col. Okasaki (commandant); and Lt. Isobe (Asst. Com.), all very considerate & gentlemanly in the past, were in tears. Our people are all behaving very well. The embarrassed J. guards are all smiles.

Hopkins later adds that the prisoners were not actually placed on restriction to the camp, but asked by the Japanese to stay within the camp limits. They explained that Korea was now a Soviet state and that there was rioting in Seoul and Jinsen, and to remain in the camp was the safest thing the prisoners could do. The Japanese went on to explain that the guards were kept in place, not to keep the prisoners in, but to keep the rioters out. Furthermore, when the American rescue teams came it would be best for the prisoners be in the camp where they could be found. See Hopkins, "Prisoner of War," 122–23; and Young, *The World Almanac Book of World War II*, 353–54.

Chapter 13: Freedom's At Hand

1. Hopkins, "Prisoner of War," 127.
2. None of the prisoner of war camps were marked during the war, as prescribed by the Geneva Convention. On August 26, 1945, the prisoners were finally allowed to lay out large POW panels on the roofs of all the buildings in Camp Jinsen. On the twenty-ninth, three B-29s circled the camp low enough to read the panels and then dropped tons of supplies for the prisoners. The supplies were packed in five-gallon steel drums, weighing 400 to 500 pounds apiece. Many of the heavy drums snapped the lines holding them and Capt. Oliver W. Orsen was hit by a drum, fracturing his leg. Other drums killed Japanese soldiers and on the thirty-first a Korean was killed. About 75 percent of the food was destroyed during the resupply attempt. See Hopkins, "Prisoner of War," 127; and Wright, *Captured on Corregidor*, 170.
3. Lt. Col. Jack Schwartz and Maj. Bill North were working on the injured Captain Orsen when a can fell through the roof of the hospital nearly hitting the three men. See Hopkins, "Prisoner of War," 127.

4. Panels were emplaced on August 31, 1945, directing the B-29s where *not* to drop the supplies. Fearing for the loss of their only source of food, the prisoners placed a "DON'T DROP HERE" panel on the camp garden. The camp adjutant gave instructions that he would blow a whistle three times once it was decided the bombers were en route. Once the whistle blew, the camp was evacuated to allow the supplies to fall freely without injuring anyone. On the way out of the camp John Wright was told by the adjutant that they needed all the supplies they could get and to remove the panel from the garden. Wright, knowing he was pressed for time, simply removed the "NT" from the panel, leaving it to read "DO DROP HERE." See Wright, *Captured on Corregidor*, 171.

5. The U.S. landing force in Korea was Maj. Gen. Archibald "Archie" Arnold's U.S. 7th Division, which saw action on Leyte. Lieutenant Colonel Fry and Captain Stengel of the 7th Division were the first to arrive at Jinsen on September 7, 1945. They informed the prisoners that Arnold's forces would be landing in the harbor on the eighth. See Hannings, *A Portrait of the Stars and Stripes* vol. 2, 478; and Hopkins, "Prisoner of War," 128.

6. The massacre Alexander is referring to is the Japanese massacre of American prisoners prior to the U.S. landings.

7. According to Waterford, "In December 1944, perhaps worried the American forces would soon recapture Palawan, the Japanese started to kill the Americans in a day-and-night-long massacre of shooting and bayoneting. Only nine of the 350 men managed to escape the bloody event." See Waterford, *Prisoners of the Japanese in World War II*, 255.

8. This ship appears to be the *Shinyo Maru*, which departed Zamboanga, Mindanao Islands on September 3, 1944. Its destination was most likely Japan; however, it was sunk on September 7, 1944, by a torpedo fired by the USS *Paddle*. Six hundred sixty-seven of the 750 U.S. prisoners on board were killed. See Waterford, *Prisoners of the Japanese in World War II*, 164–65.

9. The name of this ship was the *Arisan Maru*. It departed Manila on October 10, 1944, and its destination was the Japanese Islands. On board the Arisan Maru were at least 1,800 Americans when it was torpedoed on October 24, 1944, east of Hong Kong; 1,792 of the 1,800 on board perished in the attack. See Braly, *The Hard Way Home*, 230–32; and Waterford, *Prisoners of the Japanese in World War II*, 154.

10. The naval officer Alexander is speaking of is CWO Martin Binder. See Braly, *The Hard Way Home*, 230–31; and Kerr, *Surrender and Survival*, 207.

11. Maj. Gen. Archibald Vincent Arnold was eventually named the military governor of Korea from 1945 to 1946. See Hannings, *A Portrait of the Stars and Stripes* vol. 2, 788.

12. The navy ship that the POWs were loaded on was the USS *Refuge*. See Wright, *Captured on Corregidor*, 176.

13. The ship Alexander is referring to, which would eventually transport the prisoners back to Manila, was the USS *Noble*, a navy attack transport. On September 9, 1945, the prisoners were sent to the *Noble* after lunch. Then in the evening, the orders changed and all prisoners were sent back to the *Refuge*. On the following day, the tenth, the orders were again changed and the prisoners were returned to the *Noble* for the last time. See Hopkins, "Prisoner of War," 130; and Wright, *Captured on Corregidor*, 176–77.

14. The USS *Noble* arrived in Manila on September 17, 1945. See Wright, *Captured on Corregidor*, 177.

15. A brief ceremony at Malacanan Palace in Manila on February 27, 1945, restored the Commonwealth back to Philippine control. The damage in Manila was tremendous, however. More than 12,000 Japanese were killed in the fight for the city, and the city stank of decaying human flesh. Manila had not simply suffered the ordinary destruction of war. Rather, large parts of the city had been deliberately and methodically demolished by the Japanese, followed soon by the massive bombardments of American artillery. The largest buildings in the city had been transformed into piles of rubble. The greater and most important part of the city was completely destroyed—its piers, docks, bridges, power, gas, and water plants. Everything from the library to the universities was razed. Manila as it had been known before the war was gone. See Hartendorp, *The Japanese Occupation of the Philippines* vol. 2, 596, 604–5.

16. Once in Manila the prisoners were divided into two groups. The navy and marine ex-prisoners went to Cavite and the army officers and enlisted men went to the 29th Replacement Depot, near Laguna de Bay, for processing. See Wright, *Captured on Corregidor*, 177.

17. The ship the prisoners returned to the continental U.S. on was the USS *Dickman*, which departed Manila on September 24, 1945. Wright, *Captured on Corregidor*, 178.

18. Rapp is Maj. Gen. Rapp Brush, and Alice is his wife. The Alexanders and the Brushes were neighbors and friends while stationed at Vancouver Barracks in Washington state during the 1930s. Conversation with Ms. Sara Spindle on November 7, 1995.

19. Betts, in *Military Readiness*, with extracts taken from Watson's *Chief of Staff*, discusses the unreadiness of the U.S. forces in the Philippines as follows.

> Despite the time before the war in which defenses might have been prepared, the U.S. Army and Navy were unable to hold the Philippines in the spring of 1942. Serious U.S. efforts to improve military capacity in the area had not begun soon enough. . . . By the beginning of 1941 there was still tremendous U.S. tension between the objectives of expanding the armed forces and hedging against an emergency. The latter required keeping 'the best trained units in reserve as an expeditionary force rather than

using them as an ideal training establishment.' A major buildup in the Philippines did not begin until the end of July 1941, scarcely more than four months before the Japanese attack. Thus, by the time war broke out American forces had fewer than 100 modern combat planes in commission in the islands. . . . [When the buildup did occur, it] was rushed, poorly coordinated, and unbalanced. Personnel were sent without adequate preparation, and weapons were sent without supporting resources for their maintenance. As a result, the forces available were only partly serviceable. . . . Some fighter pilots had no more than fifteen hours of flight training before they were thrown into combat. . . . On the ground, raw manpower was not the immediate problem. Combined Filipino and American forces available within a week of Pearl Harbor numbered more than 130,000 men . . . outnumber[ing] the Japanese force . . . at least three to two. . . . But the quality of U.S. and Filipino troops did not match their quantity.

See Betts, *Military Readiness*, 11–13.

BIBLIOGRAPHY

ARCHIVES

Birth Certificate, Irvin Alexander, Local No. 4–9, (State of Indiana, Lawrence County), November 10, 1896.

Death Certificate, Irvin Alexander (State of Texas, Bexar County), December 26, 1963.

General Orders No. 16, Headquarters: United States Army Forces in the Far East, Fort Mills, P.I. (St. Louis: National Personnel Records Center), January 28, 1942. [Orders authorizing Colonel Alexander to wear the Distinguished Service Cross.]

General Orders No. 49, Headquarters, United States Military Academy (West Point, New York; USMA Archives), November 27, 1918. [Orders indicating the delineation of classes at West Point for those graduating in June 1919, June 1920, and June 1921. These orders were necessary due to the integration of the Student Officers who graduated early and returned to finish their studies in December 1918.]

General Orders No. 145, General Headquarters: United States Army Forces, Pacific (St. Louis: National Personnel Records Center), April 18, 1946. [Orders authorizing Colonel Alexander to wear the Silver Star.]

Personal and School History Sheet (West Point, NY; USMA Archives), March 1917.

Special Orders No. 127, Department of the Army (Washington, DC,) June 30, 1950. [Orders indicating Colonel Alexander's retirement due to ninety percent disability.]

ARTICLES AND POEMS

Allen, Ralph L. "Piercing the Veil of Operational Art." *Parameters: US Army War College Quarterly* (Summer 1995): 117.

Almon, William B. "Colin Kelly's Heroism Allowed the Crew of His Stricken Bomber to Reach Safety, and in the Process Launched a Legend." *World War II Magazine* (January 1996): 66–72.

Bloomfield, Gary. "Tokyo on Trial." *VFW Magazine* (November 1995): 36–38.

Caraccilo, Dominic J. "Kasserine Pass: Baptism of Fire." *VFW Magazine* (February 1993): 12, 14.

Comtois, Pierre. "Manila's Bloody Liberation." *World War II Magazine* (January 1996): 40–49, 80.

Haan, Ruth. "Our Colonel." Nashville, Indiana (December 1963). [A dedication to Colonel Alexander after his death that was placed in the local newspaper.]

Palmer, General Williston Birkhimer. "Be Thou At Peace: Irvin Alexander." *Assembly.* West Point, NY, Association of Graduates (Summer 1964): 110-11.

"Report to the Classes: Class of 1919." *Assembly.* West Point, NY, Association of Graduates (January 1994): 45–46.

BOOKS

American Heritage Dictionary: Second College Edition. Boston: Houghton Mifflin, 1982.

American Military History. Edited by General William A. Stoft, Chief of Military History. Washington, DC: U.S. Army Center of Military History, 1969.

Baclagon, Lieutenant Colonel (Philippine) Uldarico S. *Philippine Campaigns.* Manila: Graphic House, 1952.

Bailey, Jennifer. *Philippine Islands: The U.S. Army Campaigns of World War II—CMH Pub 72–3.* Washington, DC: U.S. Army Center of Military History, 1993.

Bartsch, William H. *Doomed at the Start: American Pursuit Pilots in the Philippines, 1941–1942.* College Station: Texas A&M University Press, 1992.

Berry, William A. and Alexander, James Edwin. *Prisoners of the Rising Sun.* Norman: Oklahoma University Press, 1993.

Betts, Richard K. *Military Readiness: Concepts, Choices, Consequences.* Washington, DC: The Brookings Institute, 1995.

Bird, Tom. *American POWs of World War II: Forgotten Men Tell Their Stories.* Westport, CT: Praeger, 1992.

Braly, Colonel William C. *The Hard Way Home.* Washington, DC: Infantry Journal Press, 1947.

Brown, Charles. *Bars from Bilibid Prison.* San Antonio: The Naylor Company, 1947.

Breuer, William B. *The Great Raid on Cabanatuan: Rescuing the Doomed Ghosts of Bataan and Corregidor.* New York: John Wiley & Sons, 1994.

Bulosan, Carlos. *The Voice of Bataan.* New York: Coward-McCann, 1943.

The Cambridge Factfinder: New Updated Edition. Edited by David Crystal. New York: Cambridge University Press, 1994.

Chunn, Major Calvin Ellsworth. *Of Rice and Men: The Story of Americans under the Rising Sun.* Los Angeles: Veteran's Publishing Company, 1946.

Coleman, John S. Jr. *Bataan and Beyond: Memories of an American POW.* College Station: Texas A&M University Press, 1978.

Cutler, Thomas J. *The Battle of Leyte Gulf: The Dramatic Full Story, Based on the Latest Research, of the Greatest Naval Battle in History.* New York: HarperCollins, 1994.

Daws, Gavan. *Prisoners of the Japanese: POWs of World War II in the Pacific.* New York; William Morrow, 1994.

Dopkins, Dale R. *The Janesville 99: A Story of the Bataan Death March.* Self published, 1981.

Dupuy, R. Ernest and Dupuy, Trevor N. *The Harper Encyclopedia of Military History,* 4th Edition. New York: HarperCollins, 1993.

Dupuy, Trevor N., Johnson, Curt, and Bongard, David L. *The Harper Encyclopedia of Military Biography.* New York: HarperCollins, 1992.

Dyess, Lieutenant Colonel William E. *The Dyess Story: The Eyewitness Account of the Death March From Bataan and the Narrative of Experiences in Japanese Prison Camps and of Eventual Escape.* New York: G. P. Putnam's Sons, 1944.

Feuer, A. B. (editor). *Bilibid Diary: The Secret Notebooks of Commander Thomas Hayes: POW, the Philippines, 1942–45.* Hamden, CT: Archon Books, 1987.

FitzPatrick, Bernard T. with Sweetser, John A. III. *The Hike into the Sun: Memoir of an American Soldier Captured on Bataan in 1942 and Imprisoned by the Japanese Until 1945.* Jefferson, NC: McFarland & Company, 1993.

Fortier, Colonel Malcolm Vaughn. *The Life of a P.O.W. Under the Japanese: In Caricature.* Spokane, WA: C.W. Hill Printing Company, 1946.

Fowler, Colonel H. C. and Wagner, Dorothy. *Recipes out of Bilibid.* New York: George W. Stewart, 1946.

Funcken, Liliane and Fred. *Arms and Uniforms: The Second World War, Part 2.* Englewood Cliffs, NJ: Prentice–Hall, 1984.

Garraty, John A. *1,001 Things Everyone Should Know About American History.* New York: Doubleday, 1989.

Grashio, Colonel (USAF, Retired) Samuel C. and Norling, Bernard. *Return to Freedom: The War Memoirs of COL. Samuel C. Grashio USAF (Ret.)*. Tulsa, OK: MCN Press, 1982.

Griffiths, William R. *The Great War (The West Point Military History Series)*. Edited by Thomas E. Griess. Wayne, NJ: Avery Publishing Group, 1986.

Grun, Bernard. *The Timetables of History: The New Revised Third Edition*. New York: Simon & Schuster/Touchtone, 1991.

Hannings, Bud. *A Portrait of the Stars and Stripes: Volume II—1919–1945*. Glenside, PA: Seniram Publishing, 1991.

Hartendorp, A. V. H. *The Japanese Occupation of the Philippines: Volume I and II*. Manila, Philippines: Bookmark, 1967.

Hersey, John. *Men on Bataan*. New York: Alfred A. Knopf, 1942.

Howell, John. *42 Months of Hell: My Life as a Prisoner of the Japanese in World War II*. Self published, 1971.

Jacobs, Colonel Eugene C. *Blood Brothers: A Medic's Sketch Book*. Edited by Sam Rohlfing. New York: Carlton Press, 1985.

Jones, Betty. *The December Ship: A Story of Lt. Col. Arden R. Boellner's Capture in the Philippines, Imprisonment, and Death on a World War II Japanese Hellship*. Jefferson, NC: McFarland & Company, 1992.

Karig, Commander (USNR) Walter and Kelley, Lieutenant (USNR) Welbourn. *Battle Report: Pearl Harbor to Coral Sea*. New York: Farrar & Rinehart, 1944.

Kerr, E. Bartlet. *Surrender and Survival: The Experience of American POWs in the Pacific, 1941–1945*. New York: William Morrow and Company, 1985.

Knox, Donald. *Death March*. New York: Harcourt Brace Jovanovich, 1981.

Lael, Richard L. *The Yamashita Precedent: War Crimes and Command Responsibility*. Wilmington, DE: Scholarly Resources, 1982.

Laffin, John. *Brassey's Battles: 3,500 Years of Conflict, Campaigns and Wars from A–Z*. London: Brassey's Defense Publishers, 1986.

Lawton, Manny. *Some Survived*. Chapel Hill, NC: Algonquin Books, 1984.

Lee, Clark. *They Call it Pacific*. New York: Viking Press, 1943.

Levering, Robert W. *Horror Trek: A True Story of Bataan, The Death March and Three and One-half Years In Japanese Prison Camps*. Dayton, OH: The Horstman Printing Company, 1948.

Macksey, Kenneth. *The Penguin Encyclopedia of Weapons and Military Technology: From Prehistory to Present Day*. New York: Viking, 1993.

Mallonee, Richard C. *The Naked Flagpole: Battle for Bataan from the Diary of Richard C. Mallonee.* Edited by Richard C. Mallonee II. San Rafael, CA: Presidio Press, 1980.

Marquardt, Frederic S. *Before Bataan and After: A Personalized History of Our Philippine Experiment.* Indianapolis: The Bobbs-Merrill Company, 1943.

Martin, Adrian R. *Brothers From Bataan: POWs, 1942–1945.* Manhattan, KS: Sunflower University Press, 1992.

McClendon, Dennis E. and Richard, Wallace F. *The Legend of Colin Kelly: America's First Hero.* Missoula, MT: Pictorial Histories, 1995.

McCombs, Don and Worth, Fred L. *World War II: Strange and Fascinating Facts: 4139 Entries About the People, the Battles, and the Events.* New York: Greenwich House, 1983.

Miller, E. B. *Bataan Uncensored.* Long Prairie, MN: The Hart Publications, 1949.

Monaghan, Frank. *World War II: An Illustrated History.* Chicago: J. G. Ferguson and Associates, 1943.

Morrison, Samuel Eliot. *The Rising Sun in the Pacific, 1931–April 1942 (History of United States Naval Operations in World War II), Volume III.* Boston: Little, Brown, 1948.

Morton, Louis. *The Fall of the Philippines.* Washington, DC: U.S. Army Center of Military History, 1953.

Nye, Roger. *The United States Military Academy in an Era of Education Reform (1900–1923).* New York: Columbia University, 1968.

Olson, Colonel (U.S. Army, Retired) John E. *Anywhere-Anytime: The History of the Fifty-Seventh Infantry (PS).* Self published, 1991.

Olson, Colonel (U.S. Army, Retired) John E. *O'Donnell: Andersonville of the Pacific.* Lake Quivira, KS: Historical Research Study, 1985.

Powell, General Colin L. with Joseph E. Persico. *My American Journey.* New York: Random House, 1995.

Prange, Gordon W. *At Dawn We Slept: The Untold Story of Pearl Harbor.* New York: McGraw-Hill, 1981.

Quirano, Carlos. *Filipinos at War.* Philippines: Vera-Reyes, 1981.

Register of Graduates and Former Cadets 1802–1990: Dwight D. Eisenhower Edition, United States Military Academy. West Point, New York: Association of Graduates, USMA, 1990.

Register of Graduates and Former Cadets: United States Military Academy. West Point, New York: Association of Graduates, USMA, 1994.

Ridgway, Matthew B. *Soldier: The Memoirs of Matthew B. Ridgway.* New York: Harper & Brothers, 1956.

The Second World War: Asia and Pacific. Edited by Thomas E. Griess. West Point, New York: Department of History, 1981.

Shigemitsu, Mamoru. *Japan and Her Destiny:·My Struggle for Peace.* Edited by Major General F. S. G. Piggott and Translated by Oswald White. New York: E. P. Dutton, 1958.

Shultz, Duane. *Hero of Bataan: The Story of General Jonathan M. Wainwright.* New York: St. Martin's Press, 1981.

Smith, Robert Ross. *Triumph in the Philippines.* Washington, DC: U.S. Army Center of Military History, 1993.

Smith, Stanley W. *Prisoner of the Emperor: An American POW in World War II.* Niwot: University Press of Colorado, 1991.

Stahl, Bob. *You're No Good To Me Dead.* Annapolis: Naval Institute Press, 1995.

Stamp, Loren E. *Journey Through Hell: Memoir of a World War II American Navy Medic Captured in the Philippines and Imprisoned by the Japanese.* Jefferson, NC: McFarland & Company, 1993.

Stauffer, Alvin P. *The Quartermaster Corps: Operations in the War Against Japan, Volume 2, Part 3 (The Technical Services).* U.S. Army in World War II series from Washington, DC: Office of the Chief of Military History, Department of the Army, 1956.

Stevens, Frederic H. *Santo Tomas Internment Camp.* New York: Stratford House, 1946.

Thomas, Ed "Tommie." *As I Remember: The Death March of Bataan.* Sonoita, AZ: Edward E. Thomas, 1990.

Thompson, Lieutenant Colonel Paul W., Doud, Lieutenant Colonel Harold, and Scofield, Lieutenant John. *How The Jap Army Fights.* New York: Penguin Books, 1942.

The United Nations War Crimes Commission. *Law Reports of Trials of War Criminals, The Belsen Trial.* New York: Howard Fertig, 1983.

Vance, Colonel (USA, Retired) John R. *Doomed Garrison—The Philippines (A POW Story).* Ashland, OR: Cascade House, 1974.

Wainwright, General Jonathan M. *General Wainwright's Story: The Account of Four Years of Humiliating Defeat, Surrender, and Captivity.* Edited by Robert Considine. New York: Doubleday, 1946.

The Wainwright Papers: Volume II. Edited by Celedonio A. Ancheta. Quezon City, Philippines; New Day Publishers, 1980.

Waterford, Van. *Prisoners of the Japanese in World War II.* Jefferson, NC: McFarland and Company, 1994.

Watson, Mark Skinner. *Chief of Staff: Prewar Plans and Preparations.* Washington, DC: U.S. Army Historical Division, 1950.

Weinberg, Gerhard L. *A World at Arms: A Global History of World War I.* New York; Cambridge University Press, 1994.

The West Point Military History Series, Atlas of The Second World War: Asia and Pacific. Edited by Thomas E. Griess. Wayne, NJ: Avery Publishing Group, Inc., 1985.

The World Almanac Book of World War II: The Complete and Comprehensive Documentary of World War II. Edited by Brigadier General Peter Young. New York: World Almanac Publications, 1981.

Wright, John M. Jr. *Captured on Corregidor: Diary of an American P.O.W. in World War II.* McFarland & Company, 1988.

Yenne, Bill. *"Black '41": The West Point Class of 1941 and the American Triumph in WWII.* New York: John Wiley Sons, 1991.

Young, Donald J. *The Battle of Bataan: A History of the 90 Siege and Eventual Surrender of 75,000 Filipino and United States Troops to the Japanese in World War II.* Jefferson, NC: McFarland & Company, Publishers, 1992.

Young, Colonel (U.S. Army Nurse Corps) Eunice F. *American Ex-Prisoners of War.* Paducah, KY: n.p., 1988.

DOCUMENTS

Daws, Gavan. *Notes from: Prisoners of the Japanese: POWs of the Japanese in World War II.* Unpublished. September 1995.

Hopkins, Armand. "Prisoner of War, 1942–1945: Reminiscences of Armand Hopkins." Unpublished Acquired from the Special Collections Department of the USMA Library.

International Military Tribunal For the Far East. Part of the "Treaties and Other International Acts Series 1589" published by the United States Government Printing Office, Washington, DC, 1947.

Official AOG Records on Irvin Alexander. Cullum No. 6445, West Point, New York: Association of Graduates.

Reports of the American Prisoners Liaison and Research Branch, American Prisoner of War Information Bureau, Washington, DC, Office of the Provost Marshall General, Washington, DC, July 31, 1946.

Report on the Interpretation, Revision and Extension of the Geneva Convention of July 27, 1929. Geneva, 1938.

Robinson, Colonel Wirt. *Biographical Register of the Officers and Graduates of the USMA at West Point, New York.* Saginaw, MI: Seemann and Peters, Printers, 1920.

Statement of the Military Service on Irvin Alexander. National Personnel Records Center, St. Louis, MO: No. 012414.

Summary of Commissioned Service Since 1 January 1937: Alexander, Irvin 012414. National Personnel Records Center, St. Louis, Mo: No. 012414.

ELECTRONIC FILES

Chapter 1.07: The Commonwealth and the Japanese Occupation. File extracted from Department of Commerce, Economics & Statistics Division's January 1994 National Trade Data Bank (NTDB) CD ROM, SuDoc C1.88:994/1/V.2, Processed February 16, 1994.

Compton's Interactive Encyclopedia. Carlsbad, CA: Compton's NewMedia, Inc., 1992.

INTERVIEWS

Gunther, Dick (COL, Retired). Association of Graduates, USMA. Interview with editor on December 6, 1994.

Grove, Dr. Stephen. Officer of the Director of Operations, Plans, and Security, USMA. Interview with editor on December 6, 1994.

Lock, Major Johnny. Executive Officer, 1st Infantry Battalion, 1st Infantry Regiment, West Point, New York. Professional conversations with the editor on numerous occasions.

Russel, Thomas (COL, Retired). Association of Graduates, USMA. Interview with editor on December 6, 1994.

Spindle, Sara. Colonel Alexander's sister in-law. Interviews with editor on numerous occasions. *[Editor's Note: Ms. Spindle has given the editor immeasurable assistance in matters of locating information on Colonel Alexander's life as well as providing letters, photographs, etc.]*

LETTERS

Alexander, Irvin to Lucile Alexander. Colonel Alexander wrote twenty-eight separate letters from Fort Stotsenburg to his wife after she and their son departed the Philippines on May 14, 1941, and before the outbreak of hostilities in December 1941.

Letter #1: May 16, 18, 20, and 21, 1941
Letter #2: May 21, 23, 24, 25, 26, 27, and 28, 1941

Letter #3: May 29, 30, June 1, 2, 3, and 4, 1941
Letter #4: June 4, 5, 6, 7, 8, 9, 10, and 11, 1941
Letter #5: June 11, 12, 14, and 18, 1941
Letter #6: June 18, 19, 20, 21, 22, 23, 24, 25, and 26, 1941
Letter #7: June 26, 27, and 29, 1941
Letter #8: July 5, 8, and 9, 1941
Letter #9: July 10 and 16, 1941
Letter #10: July 17, 1941
Letter #11: July 25, 1941
Letter #12: July 31, August 1, 2, 3, 6, 7, and 8, 1941
Letter #13: August 10, 11, 12, 13, 14, and 15, 1941
Letter #14: August 17, 18, 19, 20, and 21, 1941
Letter #15: August 22, 23, 24, 25, 26, and 27, 1941
Letter #16: August 30, 31, September 1, 2, 3, 4, 5, 6, 7, 8, and 9, 1941
Letter #17: September 10, 12, 13, 14, and 16, 1941
Letter #18: September 18 and 19, 1941
Letter #19: September 20, 21, 22, 23, 24, 25, 26, 27, 28, and 29, 1941
Letter #20: September 30, October 1, 2, 3, 4, 5, and 6, 1941
Letter #21: October 6, 7, 8, 9, and 10, 1941
Letter #22: October 10, 11, 12, 14, 15, 16, and 17, 1941
Letter #23: October 18, 19, 20, 21, 22, 24, and 26, 1941
Letter #24: October 27, 28, 29, 30, 31, November 1, 2, and 3, 1941
Letter #25: November 4, 5, 6, 7, 8, 9, 10, and 11, 1941
Letter #26: November 12, 13, 14, 15, 16, and 17, 1941
Letter #27: November 17, 18, 19, 20, 21, and 22, 1941
Letter #28: November 24, 25, 26, 27, 29, and 30, 1941

Alexander, Irvin to Lucile Alexander. Colonel Alexander wrote an ongoing letter to his wife during his imprisonment. This letter is postmarked February 23,1944, from Cabanatuan Prison Camp and includes notes written on the following dates:

November 5, 1942 (Alexander's 46th birthday)
December 20, 1942 (the couple's 13th wedding anniversary)
May 14, 1943 (two years since Lu and Sammy left the Philippines)
August 16, 1943 (Lu's 36th birthday)
December 20, 1943 (the couple's 14th wedding anniversary)
May 14, 1944 (three years since Lu and Sammy left the Philippines)
June 14, 1944 (Sammy's 12th birthday)
August 16, 1944 (Lu's 37th birthday)

October 15, 1944 (the day Alexander felt the prisoners were leaving Bataan for Japan)

Borneman, John K. to Mrs. Alexander. Lieutenant Colonel Borneman was with Colonel Alexander during the imprisonment and wrote Mrs. Alexander telling her of their friendship. Colonel Borneman was released earlier by the Japanese than Colonel Alexander and he is sending Alexander's wife his regards, dated April 2, 1945.

Cohen, Aaron, Director of the Johnson Space Center, Houston, Texas, to Mrs. Irvin S. Alexander offering condolences to her after her husband passed away, dated March 29, 1991.

Olson, John E. (Colonel, USA) to the editor dated November 18, 1995.

Spindle, Sara to the editor dated May 8, 1995. This letter includes information about the deaths of Lucile and Irvin, Jr.

Spindle, Sara to the editor dated June 8, 1995. Accompanying letters 1–13 and 17, Ms. Spindle provides much information on the relationships between Alexander and his family and the identification of many of the individuals cited in the manuscript. She deciphers each of these 14 letters explaining what may not be obvious to the casual reader.

Stearns, Mary. Letter to Ms. Sara Spindle dated June 3, 1942 concerning Alexander's disposition as a possible POW and what the family will do financially and emotionally with the possibility of Alexander's captivity. Mrs. Stearns is Lu's sister and was married to then-Captain Joseph E. Stearns who rose to the rank of Colonel and is a graduate of USMA (Class of 1932). Colonel Stearns spent most of the war in the European Theatre to include the Battle of the Bulge. After the war, Colonel Stearns was with the European Theater of Operations Military Government in 1945 where he was awarded a Bronze Star Medal.

INDEX